THE GREAT FASHION DESIGNERS

THE GREAT FASHION DESIGNERS

BRENDA POLAN AND ROGER TREDRE

BERG

Oxford • New York

English edition

First published in 2009 by
Berg

Editorial offices:
First Floor, Angel Court, 81 St Clements Street, Oxford OX4 1AW, UK
175 Fifth Avenue, New York, NY 10010, USA

Berg is the imprint of Oxford International Publishers Ltd.

Library of Congress Cataloging-in-Publication Data

A catalogue record for this book is available from the Library of Congress.

British Library Cataloguing-in-Publication Data

A catalogue record for this book is available from the British Library.

ISBN   978 1 84788 228 8 (Cloth)

        978 1 84788 227 1 (Paper)

Typeset by Apex CoVantage, LLC, Madison, WI, USA

Printed in Great Britain by the MPG Books Group, Bodmin and King's Lynn

www.bergpublishers.com

CONTENTS

Acknowledgements   *ix*

Foreword   *xi*

Introduction   *1*

PART 1   EARLY DAYS

Introduction   7

Charles Frederick Worth   9

Callot Soeurs   13

Jeanne Paquin   17

Paul Poiret   21

Mariano Fortuny   25

PART 2   1910s–1930s

Introduction   31

Jeanne Lanvin   35

Gabrielle Chanel   39

Jean Patou   43

Madeleine Vionnet   47

Elsa Schiaparelli   51

Mainbocher 55

Adrian 59

Salvatore Ferragamo 63

Madame Alix Grès 67

PART 3   1940–1950s

Introduction 73

Cristobal Balenciaga 77

Christian Dior 83

Charles James 87

Claire McCardell 91

Hubert de Givenchy 95

Pierre Cardin 99

Mary Quant 103

Rudi Gernreich 107

PART 4   1960s–1970s

Introduction 113

Norman Norell 115

Yves Saint Laurent 119

André Courrèges 123

Valentino 129

Karl Lagerfeld   133

Halston   137

Kenzo   141

Ralph Lauren   145

Issey Miyake   151

Geoffrey Beene   155

Calvin Klein   161

Giorgio Armani   167

PART 5   1980s

Introduction   173

Rei Kawakubo   175

Yohji Yamamoto   179

Vivienne Westwood   183

Paul Smith   187

Azzedine Alaia   191

Gianni Versace   195

Jean Paul Gaultier   201

Dolce & Gabbana   205

John Galliano   211

Donna Karan   215

PART 6   1990s–

Introduction   221

Miuccia Prada   225

Martin Margiela   229

Marc Jacobs   235

Tom Ford   239

Alexander McQueen   243

Nicolas Ghesquière   247

List of Illustrations   *251*

Bibliography   *253*

ACKNOWLEDGEMENTS

The authors wish gratefully to acknowledge the academics and fellow journalists who have been quoted and referenced in this book and the many who may not figure here but have, over the years, provided a basis of knowledge and insight upon which our own expertise is built. The history and culture of dress is becoming a well-explored field, but, in researching and writing this book, which is intended to inspire further study, we have concluded that, when it comes to fashion, among all the picture books, there are some lamentable gaps on the shelves, gaps that should be filled with real thought and analysis. There are many fascinating books, works of research and scholarship, on the great fashion designers and their often equally interesting peers just begging for an author. Both authors have worked closely with the photographer, Chris Moore, over several decades and would like to acknowledge both his invaluable help with this book and his long friendship.

Brenda Polan would like to thank the many editors who have employed her to write about fashion, particularly Dame Liz Forgan who, as the *Guardian*'s women's editor, glanced across a crowded features room and plucked her off the late subbing shift and on to the front row at Yves Saint Laurent. She dedicates this book to her siblings, Anthony and Sonia, and to her travelling companion, Colin.

Roger Tredre would like to thank his former colleagues at *The Independent*, in particular Sarah Mower, Lisa Armstrong and Marion Hume, and at *The Observer* and WGSN. Over 10 years, he has appreciated the support and encouragement of Louise Wilson at Central Saint Martins and of the 100 MA students he has been fortunate to teach. Thanks to Oriole Cullen at the Victoria & Albert Museum for suggesting the inclusion of Callot Soeurs and to Elizabeth Richardson for her efficient photo research. He dedicates this book to his parents and to his family—Jennifer, Olivia and Nicholas.

FOREWORD

There are 50 designers in this book. Are they really the greatest designers of all time? Your call! Our selection was achieved only through much debate, sometimes learned and courteous, sometimes outrageous and alcohol-fuelled. We acknowledge the impossibility of achieving consensus for such a list. Creating a list of fashion designer all-time greats is a wonderful parlour game that we hope all our readers can enjoy playing. Our choices reflect our careers and our personal interests, although not too much (we hope) our British nationality.

We began on this project modestly enough by simply planning to bring together in book form our collected interviews with designers over the years, published mostly in British newspapers and magazines. It was a comprehensive list, we thought, dating right back to Brenda Polan's interview with André Courrèges in August 1979 for *The Guardian*. They ranged from the detailed and in-depth (four interviews with John Galliano over a period of four months leading up to his spring/summer 1991 show in Paris) to the on the fly and brief (twenty minutes with Tom Ford backstage after a YSL menswear show in January 2001). In total, we have interviewed eighteen of the designers in this book (and many more who are not).

In his witty and insightful book, *The Glass of Fashion,* Cecil Beaton wrote: `Dressmakers … are apt to hate their *genus* and seldom meet one another, for jealousy, envy and rivalry consume them. With few exceptions they are a tiresome, unreliable brood. Almost all inarticulate, they have never invented their own vocabulary, and their abuse of the French words *chic* and *élégant* have almost robbed these adjectives of their significance.' Although we regretfully note that some designers do

indeed live down to Beaton's critique, we found the names we've spoken to over the years were often articulate—particularly if you caught them away from the frenzy of the show season. But our plan to turn our collected interviews into a book was abandoned after thoroughly rereading them. Although these interviews provide valuable insights into designers' thought processes and work methods, they are moments in time. Many of them read to us as outdated. The designers had moved on, and so had we. How much better, we thought, to write essays that summed up these designers' careers, drawing on our personal insights into their work and all those valuable transcripts gathered over the years. We also read widely, including the available books and academic literature and the wealth of interviews in newspapers and magazines (mostly in Britain and America) by our journalistic colleagues. We have endeavoured to cite all our sources accurately: if we have overlooked any reference, we will rectify it in future editions of this book.

The book evolved into a broader project as we discussed who were suitable subjects for inclusion. As we both segued in our respective careers during the early noughties from the arena of journalism to the world of teaching at University of the Arts London, our interests broadened and deepened. Exploring the career of Karl Lagerfeld naturally led us to revisit the career of Chanel; likewise Nicolas Ghesquière prompted a rediscovery of Balenciaga.

We have endeavoured to produce the book we wish we had in our hands when we were feeling our way into fashion: a comprehensive introduction to the most important designers, with guidance for further reading, written in an accessible but authoritative style. The personalities of the designers are as interesting to us as their designs—the two often intertwine, most notably in the career and life of Chanel. Our book complete, we marvel at the constant capacity of fashion to renew itself and stay fresh. And we hope that you, the reader, enjoy sharing this with us.

INTRODUCTION

In 2001 American fashion trade newspaper *Women's Wear Daily* (*WWD*) marked its ninetieth anniversary by asking fifty-three leading designers who were the three most important designers of the past ninety years. The results were fascinating, not perhaps for the runaway 'winners' (Coco Chanel with thirty-four votes and Yves Saint Laurent with twenty-nine), but for the other names cited and the explanations offered. Giorgio Armani cited Jean Paul Gaultier among his top three ('for his ability to make fashion ironic'). Nicolas Ghesquière included Issey Miyake ('he gave the Japanese concept of deconstruction a European femininity and sensibility'). More unpredictable names who are featured in this book included Adrian and Rudi Gernreich. The ever-prolific Karl Lagerfeld, who received three citations himself, sent a five-page fax dividing the twentieth century into three distinct periods: 1905–1939 (Poiret, Vionnet and Chanel); 1945–1960 (Dior, Balenciaga and Chanel); and 1960–1970 (Courrèges, Saint Laurent, Vionnet, Chanel and Balenciaga).

The very earliest couturiers received barely a look-in, perhaps reflecting the short-term memory of fashion (although Alexander McQueen voted for Charles Frederick Worth). The constant interaction between craft and commerce was highlighted, and designers were quick to applaud fellow designers who were skilled at business and marketing as much as creativity. Influence was paramount. 'Who has the biggest influence?' declared Karl Lagerfeld. 'It's unimportant who is the most gifted.'

One means of determining influence is to ask the question: who is the most copied? Designers have had an equivocal attitude towards this issue from the very early days of couture, on the one hand threatening legal action against copyists, and on the other hand happy to sell models to upmarket stores for copying. Few have been as relaxed about the issue as Coco Chanel—or American designer Norman Norell, who provided working sketches of his 1960 culotte suit to the trade free of charge to ensure that his design would be copied properly. These days, many designers work directly with their biggest copyists, the fast fashion chain stores, in effect copying themselves by creating low-priced collections in short- or long-term retail linkups.

For the *WWD* survey, the designers were also asked to decide who were the three most important designers since 1980: Karl Lagerfeld won the most votes, followed closely by Giorgio Armani, Rei Kawakubo, Jean Paul Gaultier and Tom Ford. Lagerfeld noted Chanel, Gucci and Prada but put fashion designers firmly in their place by referencing Nike, Levi's and Adidas. 'They are fashion for today, too, and worn by more people than the fashion of the fashion world we talk about.' Marc Jacobs brought the designers down to earth by recalling the celebrated comment from fellow American designer Bill Blass that the words 'dress' and 'important' should never be mentioned in the same sentence. 'I'm going to paraphrase,' said Jacobs. 'The words 'designer' and 'important' should never be mentioned in the same sentence.'

Over the past two decades, the meaning of the term 'designer' in relation to fashion has become a free-for-all, inviting a wide variety of interpretations. From business moguls to celebrities to genuine creative geniuses, everyone and anyone can claim designer status. The industry was dominated by couturiers until the 1960s when the ready-to-wear *styliste* and *créateur* came to the fore. In more recent years, the broader interpretation of designer has made it challenging to define true greatness—many designers are only as good as the team behind them. Is the product manager a designer? Can the famous personality behind a celebrity brand be considered a designer? For the purposes of this book, we have accepted an all-embracing interpretation of the word, covering skill sets ranging from pure design to brand management and marketing to pure business. In the final analysis, though, it is the *influence* of each individual designer that has driven our selection. Echoing Karl Lagerfeld's point to *WWD*, talent is not enough.

We have acknowledged the significance of commercial achievements in compiling our list. British designer Paul Smith may strike some readers as a surprise choice, but his success as an Englishman in creating an international fashion brand without the backing of a major luxury group gives him a unique status. Success is founded, he says, on being '90 per cent businessman and 10 per cent designer'.

Many great designers have also been great business people, and others have succeeded through long-lasting linkups with business-minded partners, such as Yves Saint Laurent with Pierre Bergé. We were inspired by the ground-breaking research of Nancy J. Troy, the American fashion historian, in *Couture Culture: A Study in Modern Art and Fashion* (2003). She explored the links between fashion and commerce, particularly through the work of early twentieth-century couturier Paul Poiret. Designers have always understood the importance of a creative image for driving forward their businesses. An observant reporter for *The New York Times,* writing back in 1913, said of Jeanne Paquin: 'She maintains the attitude of an artist, but we know she is the most commercial artist alive.'

Early fashion was dominated by men such as Charles Frederick Worth and Paul Poiret, who often overshadowed the achievements of women such as Jeanne Paquin and Marie Callot Gerber. This book tries to nudge back the balance a little more in these women's favour, although we acknowledge that the flamboyance of personalities such as Poiret was an integral part of the makeup that made him so influential.

Another important point to make is that the development of fashion—just as the development of history itself—is not a story of constant progress. Fashion (perhaps like history too) has an intrinsic cyclical nature. It looks backwards as much as forwards. Jeanne Lanvin, for example, made full-skirted evening dresses at a time when Chanel was championing short hemlines. The modernist wins out over the nostalgist every time. But Lanvin's very significant success, as noted by historian Nancy Troy, raises important questions about the conventional narrative of fashion history. Perhaps we should highlight more the retrospective and nostalgic characteristics of some of the greatest fashion.

It may become harder still in the future to identify the skill sets of a designer. New technology makes design by computer a doddle. In future, all of us can play the role of designer. Even the once time-consuming process of research can be shrunk in an instant to a few hours on the Internet.

Not all designers have been proficient in all aspects of design, as Dean L. Merceron points out in his biography of Jeanne Lanvin. For years, Paul Smith referred to himself as a 'getter-togetherer of fashion' rather than as a designer. Jean Patou once famously said: 'I wouldn't know how to design. I couldn't even if I wanted to, for I can't draw, and a pair of scissors in my hands becomes a dangerous weapon.'

The skills needed to be a fashion designer are certainly changing; there is less emphasis on technical prowess and more on an instinct for trends. In future, more consumers are likely to design their own clothing and order items directly from the manufacturer. In turn, the role of shops will change to become places where customers pick up pre-purchased clothing.

Designers are increasingly interpreters of other people's visions, playing a mercenary role, from Karl Lagerfeld at Chanel and Fendi to John Galliano at Dior and Nicolas Ghesquière at Balenciaga. But this book is not a lament for the lost world of couture. We share the view of Nicolas Ghesquière, the youngest name of our fifty. 'I don't think couture fits our world … Anyway, I have the luxury of using the couture techniques in my ready-to-wear.'

We have skewed our selection towards the second half of the twentieth century, reflecting our interests and the perceived interests of our readers. The fashion world has a notoriously short memory. As curator Harold Koda has written, 'The high fashion system with its seasonal advocacy of the new and an associated obsolescence of preceding styles, perhaps inevitably dismisses, if not obliterates, its own history.' How important is the fashion designer today? Harold Koda says designers rarely dictate. 'Now you can have so many designers that each one becomes a barometer of a different aspect of our consciousness of the world.' Fashion consultant Jean-Jacques Picart believes designer pronouncements on fashion are coming to an end. 'We have entered an era of fundamental change,' he says. 'Yesterday's recipes for success are no longer valid.'

The designer's job today remains challenging. Miuccia Prada reflected on changing times in an interview with Ingrid Sischy in 2006: 'In general, designers of past decades had to deal with a small community of rich bourgeois people in France, in Italy, in America, or in England … And so, to do clothes for these people in a way was much easier, because it was very simple. Now, in a way we have to dress people of different culture, different nationalities, different religions, different worlds.' Virtually all designers recoil at over-analysis of their work. Even a name such as Karl Lagerfeld, who has a deep understanding of the history of fashion, comments: 'I hate the idea of fashion being intellectualised.'

We acknowledge that the very title of this book has an old-fashioned ring about it. Academic research these days often prefers to play down the roles of individuals, exploring the broader socioeconomic context. There is an alternative history that explores the contribution of *les petites mains,* the women who toiled in the ateliers to bring the designers' creations to life. The word *atelier* should not be used to disguise the fact that the big couture businesses of the early decades of the twentieth century were essentially factories: in 1901, *Femima* magazine described the house of Redfern as 'a veritable factory of elegance'. Only a small handful of enlightened employers, most notably Madeleine Vionnet, showed compassion to their workforce. Chanel, by contrast, was monstrous.

That said, we believe the personal stories of the great names of fashion are an excellent starting point for more detailed reading and observation. Through the achievements of these designers, we see fashion at its most inspirational. The British journalist Claudia Croft, writing in *The Sunday Times* in February 2009, noted that 'one of fashion's great strengths is its ability to make us dream. As much as it reflects the times, it also provides respite from them.' We couldn't agree more. Fashion is a sociocultural indicator and it is a business, but it is also (to quote John Galliano) a journey into escapism, fun and fantasy. Join us on that journey.

PART 1

Early Days

Introduction

In the nineteenth century, fashion was a game of social status reserved for high-society women and theatre stars of independent means. Trends trickled down, but not very far and not very fast: the sheer cost of clothing ensured that. Women's fashion was spectacularly restrictive. The corset squeezed the rib cage while the crinoline and full-length hemlines restricted movement. Individuality was frowned upon: the role of a woman in genteel society was essentially conformist, focusing on children and social life.

Until the emergence of Englishman *Charles Frederick Worth* in Paris in the late 1850s, a customer would buy fabrics separately, and then take them to a dressmaker to be made up. Worth brought these activities together and created the model for the fashion house that dominated throughout the twentieth century and into the early twenty-first. Although his dresses reflected the restrictive ethos of their time, his achievement as the founder of the modern fashion system remains undiminished.

The late nineteenth century saw the first stirrings of women's emancipation. British tailors Charles Poynter at Redfern and Henry Creed, who both flourished with shops in Paris, had introduced tailoring to women's fashion. But Pre-Raphaelite artists and the Aesthetes promoted a new kind of dressing, drawing on ancient Greek models that followed the natural silhouette. Most of their ideas remained theoretical, but the guidelines were in place for change. Women were also beginning to find a place for themselves in the business of fashion. In the 1890s, *Jeanne Paquin* founded her own couture house, while Marie Callot Gerber and her sisters established the house of *Callot Soeurs.*

By 1900 and the dawn of the twentieth century, the core fashion message from Paris showed few signs of moving forward. The S silhouette, which thrust a woman's breasts forward and her derrière backward, was the fashionable look of the period. *Mariano Fortuny*'s loose Delphos Dress, created in 1907 and worn by the dancer Isadora Duncan, hinted at a radical shift in direction, but it was *Paul Poiret* who had the biggest impact, promoting a natural silhouette, loosening the constricted waist and doing away with the more severe versions of the corset. His emergence came as the brassiere received a mention in *Vogue* for the first time.

Both Worth and Poiret believed their expertise gave them the right—and duty—to dictate to their customers. A woman must be guided in her desire for a new fashion, they thought. But couturières such as Jeanne Paquin and Callot Soeurs were more inclined to listen to their customers. The first decade of the twentieth century concluded with Paul Poiret at his peak, inspired by orientalism, which drew influence from all points east.

1 CHARLES FREDERICK WORTH (1825–1895)

Charles Frederick Worth, an Englishman from the quiet county of Lincolnshire, was the first couturier of modern times. His one rival to that title, Rose Bertin, milliner and dressmaker to Marie Antoinette, was from a different era, the late eighteenth century. The story of how an Englishman rose from unpromising roots to international renown is one of the most extraordinary episodes in the history of fashion. Before Charles Frederick Worth, only women were dressmakers; men were tailors or haberdashers. Before Worth, a customer would purchase fabrics separately then take them to a dressmaker to be made up. Before Worth, clothes-makers were not society figures. Worth focused on fit and construction, the qualities that are at the core of haute couture. He was, said his biographer Diana de Marly, 'like an engineer or an architect for whom the soundness of the construction was the fundamental consideration.'

For four decades, Worth was the dominant force in Western fashion, developing many of the fundamental components of the modern fashion system. These ranged from the creation of a collection in advance of the season, to the development of styles that typically endured for around five years, and the creation of the fashion label (stamped, at the house of Worth, in gold on silk petersham ribbon). Charles Frederick Worth's apprenticeship in London and Paris was long and hard, but when the breakthrough came with a coveted order for a dress from Empress Eugénie of France, his career was made virtually overnight. To appreciate fully his achievements, it is helpful to understand the mind-set of high society in nineteenth-century Europe. The concept of a man fitting clothes to a woman's body was not merely unusual, it was considered immoral, indeed thoroughly shocking. The English, who did not have a word to match couturier, reported that Worth was a 'man-milliner' running a house that was, so the rumours ran, more of a bordello.

Worth also set the tone for the couturier as dictator, rapidly acquiring much of the arrogance of the French court he served, with prices to match. 'Those ladies are wisest who leave the choice to us,' he told an interviewer. According to his son, Jean-Philippe, 'in time he came to have no awe of anything . . . and to recognise only two higher in authority than himself—God and the Emperor.' He also had an innate appreciation of the insecurities and competitiveness of the ladies of high society. Speaking to the journalist F. Adolphus, Worth once said: 'Women dress, of course, for two reasons: for the pleasure of making themselves smart, and for the still greater joy of snuffing out the others.'

He was born in 1825 in Bourne, Lincolnshire, one of five children. Disaster hit the family eleven years later when his father, William, a solicitor, went bankrupt and left his family to fend for themselves. His impoverished mother was left with little choice but to find an apprenticeship for her son, who worked at a printer's shop. The young boy, however, hated the work and persuaded his mother to allow him to move to London to gain employment at Swan & Edgar, a haberdashers located in the recently constructed Regent Street. This was effectively Worth's home through his teenage years; legend has it that he even slept beneath the counter. The opportunity to work with textiles gave Worth an outstanding grounding for the future. Perhaps equally important were his frequent visits to the new National Gallery, within walking distance of both Swan & Edgar and Lewis & Allenby, the royal silk mercers, to which he moved in 1845. Society fashion drew heavily and freely on the costumes of past centuries, particularly for balls and masquerades. Thus, Worth's encyclopaedic knowledge of costume history, garnered from observation of portraits in the National Gallery, stood him in good stead.

At the age of just twenty, Worth arrived in Paris in 1845, determined to make his way in the capital of fashion. He lived on the breadline for more than a year, making money where he could and picking up French along the way. It took him two years to land a job at Gagelin in the rue de Richelieu selling fabrics and another eleven years before he was in position to set up his own business. Worth's breakthrough innovation went unnoticed at the time: he persuaded his employers at Gagelin to allow him to open a dressmaking department. Never before had textiles and dressmaking been brought together under the same roof—and never before had a man been a dressmaker. Gagelin entered dresses to the Great Exhibition in the Crystal Palace in 1851, the year Worth also married the Gagelin in-house model Marie. In 1855, Paris hosted its own international event, the Exposition Universelle, where Worth's court train, unusually suspended from the shoulders rather than the waist, won a first-class medal. Three years later, Worth joined forces with Otto Bobergh, a young Swede with similar skills to Worth, to open Worth et Bobergh at 7 rue de la Paix.

Paris had been in political and social upheaval during Worth's early years in the French capital. But the creation of the Second Napoleonic Empire in 1852 under Napoleon III, son of Napoleon I's brother Louis, unleashed a period of imperial extravagance that put Paris at the heart of the European social scene. Empress Eugénie required a new dress for every occasion, as did the guests at imperial balls, masquerades and country visits. A veritable gold mine awaited Worth, although breaking through the barriers of court convention to secure the first royal order required all Worth's skills of salesmanship, acquired on the shop floor over the years in London and Paris. The story goes that Empress

Eugénie did not like the first gown Worth made for her in 1860, rejecting the heavy brocade from Lyon as looking like 'curtain material'. Napoleon entered the room at that precise moment, whereupon Worth explained that support for the silkmakers of Lyon, a city with a republican tradition, might be very advantageous to the emperor. Remarkably, this Machiavellian switch of sales patter paid off—Worth was on his way.

Empress Eugénie's patronage opened the floodgates for Worth. If the empress wore Worth, then so did most of her ladies-in-waiting and guests. For one ball alone, Worth might be called on to make up to 1,000 dresses. The house's ability to respond to such a volume of orders was boosted by recent advances in technology, specifically the development of the Singer sewing machine for long seams. Worth also industrialised the process, creating standard patterns that could be used as the basis for apparently new designs. Countless variations were developed around similar dresses, often refreshed through trimmings alone. In colour terms, Worth was more restricted: white was the required colour for court dress, with silver playing the decorative role. For masquerades, the parties where the court collectively let its hair down, Worth was freer, often drawing inspiration from the eighteenth century and creating fantastical costumes that delighted his clients.

Worth's approach to design was to find simple solutions to the challenges thrown up by nineteenth-century propriety and society values. He was not afraid to innovate, using his wife Marie to test the market with some of his more daring designs. She was outstanding at presenting a dress to best effect, making her a forerunner of the modern fashion model. Princess von Metternich was another important ally for much of his career, not least because of her social connections. For Empress Eugénie's walk by the seaside, he created ankle-length skirts, a breakthrough after thirty years of ground-length hemlines. Likewise, he made the unwieldy crinoline more practical by pushing the volume round to the back rather than to the sides, enabling the wearer to walk through a doorway without having to turn sideways. Another innovation was the gored skirt with panels that are wide at the hemline and narrow at the top, a smoother option to gathering. Worth achieved such dominance as an arbiter of style that he could achieve remarkable changes in fashion in short order, such as replacing the bonnet with the hat as the favoured form of headwear or removing the crinoline altogether, a step he took finally in 1868.

By this date, Worth himself was a considerably wealthy man with a country house outside Paris at Suresnes, which he expanded and transformed into a chateau over the years. In Paris, he had more than 1,000 seamstresses working for his house. He created dresses for royal courts throughout Europe besides that of Napoleon III in Paris and also designed for the theatre and the opera. His clients would be expected to make an appointment at rue de la Paix and stride backward and forward in his creations while he observed from a sofa. Over the years, Worth came to consider himself as much more than a dressmaker—he was an artist and began to dress as such, wearing a velvet beret and a silk scarf round his throat and consorting and collaborating with artists such as Winterhalter. The adoption of aesthetic dress by Pre-Raphaelite artists in England struck a chord with him. Aesthetic style with its looser dresses and rejection of corsets was a reaction against the swift-changing whims of fashion in favour of more natural lines and less restrictive clothing. The glories of the 1860s ended abruptly for Worth in 1870 when Napoleon III was overthrown by the Prussians at the Battle of Sedan. By January of the following year the Prussians were in Paris, Napoleon III and Empress Eugénie were in exile in England, and even Princess von Metternich left shortly afterwards. Worth vowed to carry on the business, now without Bobergh. Such was his fame that business continued to pour in, although with a new clientele, including Americans and other international visitors to Paris. In 1874, Worth brought his sons into the business, with Jean-Philippe helping with design and his older brother Gaston focusing on business. In fashion terms, he continued to innovate, slimming down the skirt and creating the Princess line, a one-piece dress with a fitted waist but no waistseam. In the 1880s, he reintroduced the bustle with the launch of the crinolette. Even in the final years of his life, he was experimenting with seamless dresses and bias cuts.

After his death in 1895, his son Jean-Philippe followed confidently in the footsteps of his father, emerging as a couturier of assurance in his own right, creating the trousseau and wedding dress for Consuelo Vanderbilt's marriage to the Duke of Marlborough, the most feted society wedding of the 1890s. His brother Gaston ran the business and financial side of the house. Opulence, rather than innovation, was Jean-Philippe's key attribute. As Diana de Marly put it: 'He could not conceive of a dress that was without splendour.' Stepping down in 1910, Jean-Philippe was succeeded by Gaston's sons Jacques and Jean-Charles, the latter another couturier of note who responded confidently to the fashion trends of the 1920s. Jacques and Roger, a fourth generation of Worths, carried the Paris house into the 1940s, although it finally sold out to its London branch in 1946. As a fashion house, the business ground to a halt in 1954 when a perfume company bought the name.

Charles Frederick Worth created the modern couture system that remained dominant until the rise of ready-to-wear in the 1960s. Among his many innovations were the sale of toiles and patterns and the use of models. More importantly, he took dressmaking on to a higher plane through the rigorous focus on fit and construction, a tradition that was carried on by Worth's sons after his death. When he died of pneumonia in 1895, his funeral service drew 2,000 mourners and his widow, Marie, received telegrams of condolence from all the courts of Europe. But although the pioneer was dead, the new world of haute couture was only just beginning.

Further reading: Diana de Marly's biography, *Worth: Father of Haute Couture* (1980), is an outstanding introduction to the couturier's work and life.

2 CALLOT SOEURS (1895–1937)

Callot Soeurs, a Parisian fashion business run by three sisters, began as a specialist in lace, developing into a fully fledged house renowned for the quality of its work and precise details. Although the house closed its doors in 1937 and is little known today, in its prime it was one of the greatest of all couture businesses, rated by French novelist Marcel Proust as one of the four greatest in his novel, *A la Recherche du Temps perdu* (Remembrance of Things Past), alongside Paquin, Doucet and Chéruit.

A complete reappraisal of the house is long overdue, but even a brief exploration of its work suggests that Callot Soeurs deserves greater prominence in any consideration of early twentieth-century fashion. Making an important contribution to its rehabilitation, Camille Janbon researched Callot Soeurs for a Courtauld Institute of Art master's thesis in 1999. She highlighted the achievement of three sisters operating as couturières in an era when a business run by women for women was a novel concept treated with suspicion or open disapproval. It is clear the dominance of women at their couture house fed into the clothes that were created, typically combining comfort with elegance. The Callots were quick to abandon the corset in their designs. Putting a modern spin on their achievements, Janbon concludes the house was, in essence, 'a very feminist structure which promoted women and femininity but always in a discreet way.'

That said, as with all their competitors, they made clothes for a rich elite class of women, initially in Paris and increasingly in America. In their heyday,

a day dress was priced at around 2,500 French francs, compared with a ready-made dress price of less than 300 francs. They were supreme exponents of the orientalist style, producing dresses that drew inspiration from the Near East and Far East, spectacularly embroidered and coloured and dubbed *robes phéniciennes* for no very obvious reason. Dresses of embroidered satin featured panels with a cornucopia of motifs from all points east. During the 1920s, their cubist-influenced dresses continued to draw on oriental motifs and colours. Overshadowed historically by more extrovert personalities, such as Paul Poiret, the sisters were also considerable innovators. Callot Soeurs was the first couture house to show evening dresses made from gold and silver lamé, a fabric composed of metal threads. They also pioneered the combination of lace blouses with tailored suits and developed rubberised gabardine for sportswear.

In the beginning there were four sisters: Josephine, the youngest, committed suicide in 1897. Of the remaining three, Marie Callot Gerber was the design talent, a striking figure with red hennaed hair and a confident manner that impressed all who met her. The other sisters were Marthe, later Madame Bertrand, and Regine, later Madame Chantrell, who had a reputation for being domineering and conservative in attitude. Gerber was hugely admired by no less an authority than Vionnet, who worked as her toile maker for six years and rated her higher than Poiret. Madame Gerber, she recalled years later, 'was a great lady totally occupied with a profession that consists of adorning women . . . not constructing a costume.' In perhaps the most celebrated comment on the influence of Callot Soeurs,

Vionnet added: 'Without the example of the Callot Soeurs, I would have continued to make Fords. It is because of them that I have been able to make Rolls Royces.'

The Callot sisters were from a family steeped in textiles. Their father, Jean-Baptiste, was a painter and antiques dealer, and their mother, Eugenie, was a lacemaker from a lacemaking family. In 1879, Jean-Baptiste set up his daughters in a small shop in Place de la Trinité. Marie Gerber worked as première in the atelier of Raudnitz & Cie for most of the 1880s, learning her craft. The family shop became celebrated for its quality lingerie and above all for its lace, often antique lace from the eighteenth century reconstituted for modern tastes. The Callot sisters were fashion's supreme exponents of lace, even though the novelist Marcel Proust thought they used a little too much of it. Marie Gerber acknowledged the development of machine-made lace as 'a triumph of imitation and also an adieu to the past.'

In 1895, the couture house of Callot Soeurs was formally founded on the rue Taitbout and developed steadily. In the early days, the sisters played to their strengths, using antique laces and ribbons for lingerie and blouses, and then offering period gowns in the style of Louis XV in floral silks adorned with lace ruffles. Few couture houses had a better appreciation of the skills of the textile producers of Lyon, France's historic textiles centre. Business grew apace: by the time of the Exposition Universelle in 1900, they had 200 employees and sales of 2 million French francs. This event was a magnificent promotional event for all twenty couture houses involved, as 1 million visitors were exposed to their work. Few took as much advantage as the Callots, who doubled sales and tripled their workforce in the year after the exhibition. The S silhouette, created by a corset that propelled the bust forward and the hips backward, dominated the looks at the Exposition Universelle, but change was in the air. When Poiret abandoned the corset in 1903, the Callots were with him every step of the way. And when Poiret embraced orientalism, the Callots were once again singing the same tune. Gerber found inspiration through her friendship with Edmond de Goncourt, a renowned collector of Japanese art. Orientalism, particularly influenced

by Japan, had been bubbling under the surface in Paris since the late 1880s, although it was the Exhibition of 1900 that brought it to the fore. Gerber, who always focused closely on sleeve construction, developed a particular fascination for the kimono sleeve.

If Gerber had shared the ebullient personality, not to mention the gender, of Paul Poiret, perhaps her achievements would have been more widely recognised. Fashion historian Caroline Rennolds Milbank highlights Gerber's genius at turning the exotic into the new for her discerning customers. 'No one was more skilled at combing history and the far corners of the world and translating these foreign motifs into contemporary Parisian terms.' In her history of haute couture, fashion historian Diana de Marly preferred to highlight Gerber's heavily decorated gowns, overhung with networks of beads or tiers of lace. But many of the Callot dresses preserved in modern museum collections reveal a delightful lightness of touch and make it clear that Gerber was an innovative designer who reflected the trends of the period while making them her own. Richard Martin of the Metropolitan Museum of Art in New York revealed himself to be a fan in his catalogue for a haute couture exhibition in 1995: 'It is hard to describe Callot Soeurs as either conservative or radical, so thoroughly combined and compatible are the traits of each pole.'

The atelier was a hushed environment; work was carried out with rigour and precise attention to detail. Gerber herself was not a dressmaker in the conventional sense. She was interested in construction, developing her ideas by draping fabric on a line model in muslin, then leaving it to her toile maker (Vionnet from 1901 to 1906) to execute her designs. 'Carried by her creative genius she did not burden herself with the practical side of things,' said Vionnet. The Callots did, however, face up to the growing challenge of copying or, more seriously, counterfeiting. Fake designer labels were often sewn into garments in America, highlighted in an article written for *Ladies' Home Journal* in 1913 by Samuel Hopkins Adams and subtitled 'How American Women Are Being Fooled by a Country-Wide Swindle'. In response, Callot Soeurs published in *Women's Wear* a list of American companies that had made authorised purchases from them in Paris. By the following year Gerber, now fully aware of the originality of her designs, took to registering many of them at the Depot Legal—the records are now housed in the collection of the Musée de la Mode et du Textile in Paris.

By 1917, Callot Soeurs had added branches in London and Buenos Aires as business continued to flourish. The house's work had been popular since its early days with Parisian actresses, including Cécile Sorel, Jeanne Graiser and Eve Lavallière, but Callot Soeurs also built a substantial following in America, where their day dresses were well received at the Universal Exhibition in San Francisco in 1915. During the First World War, this support was critical: American buyers would descend on Paris in July and place orders for between 300 and 800 pieces. The house's greatest supporter in America was Rita de Acosta Lydig. This New York society lady of Spanish heritage had married an ageing millionaire from whom she was divorced within four years, leaving her with money and time aplenty. Camille Janbon points out that Callot Soeurs' relationship to this flamboyant character was similar to that of a nineteenth-century dressmaker, allowing the rich client to make the demands. This was good business sense because, as Janbon says, 'she never ordered one single dress but a dozen at a time with variations in the materials and forms.'

Rita de Acosta Lydig became renowned for her individualistic style, was painted in Callot dresses by the artist Giovanni Boldini, and remained an unwavering enthusiast for the house until her death in 1925. In 1919, Callot Soeurs moved location to 9–11 avenue Matignon, but even bigger change followed in 1920 with the sudden death of Marthe, Madame Bertrand, and the decision of Regine, Madame Chantrell, to retire (she had been widowed early and chose to devote her attention to her son's education). Gerber continued to run the house single-handedly for a further seven years, displaying a sureness of touch and ability to move with the times. A day suit in white ottoman silk and lace at the Musée de la Mode et du Textile is a striking statement in black and white, and a sumptuous but simple driving coat in soft leather trimmed with astrakhan was among the designs registered at the Depot Legal in 1925.

Despite the best efforts of Chanel, Orientalism continued to influence fashion well into the 1920s. The Paris Exposition des Arts Decoratifs in 1925 saw Callot Soeurs imbibing dark lacquer influences from the Far East. A beautiful piece from 1926 by Gerber features Chinese shawl motifs on a dress with an asymmetric hem, rising at the front to well above the knees. Callot Soeurs, as Camille Janbon notes, responded to Orientalism with a deftness of touch that might be contrasted favourably with Poiret's approach. The woman always came first for Gerber. 'The dress is everything which should be part of the woman,' she said. 'Not the woman part of the dress.' Callot Soeurs reflected other art movements of the 1920s, including Cubism, in a still preserved dress that mixes lace and embroidery in a collage effect. 'The dresses of Marie Gerber were true masterpieces,' reflected Vionnet, ever supportive of her former employer.

On the death of Gerber in 1927, an obituary in *Le Figaro* commented: 'One of the most beautiful figures of the Parisian luxury business has now disappeared.' Her sons Pierre and Jacques were left in charge. Jacques had focused more on the development of fragrance for Callot Soeurs, launching La Fille du Roi de Chine in 1923 (there was no king of China, but the continuing allure of orientalism made this name sound suitably seductive). Callot continued to sell to a loyal clientele who felt alienated by the unforgiving straight lines of much of 1920s style. As with many other businesses, the economic crash of 1929 had a heavy impact, and the business was finally absorbed by Calvet in 1937. Gerber's granddaughter published a memoir in 1978, but this did little to revive the reputation of Callot Soeurs until costume museums began to display their work in the 1990s.

Further reading: There is no full-length monograph on Callot Soeurs, although 'Callot Soeurs', an unpublished MA thesis by Camille Janbon at the Courtauld Institute of Art (1999), is informative. Diana de Marly's *The History of Haute Couture 1850–1950* (1980) sets the context authoritatively.

3 JEANNE PAQUIN (1869–1936)

Jeanne Paquin was the queen of haute couture for nearly thirty years. She was the first major female couturier, running one of the biggest couture houses of the early twentieth century, employing 2,700 employees at its height. She was also one of the pioneers of the modern fashion business, building her label as an international enterprise—and becoming the first Parisian name to open stores in cities such as London, New York, Madrid and Buenos Aires. Why, then, is so little known about Jeanne Paquin compared with Poiret or Worth? Fashion historian Jan Reeder speculated that she has been largely overlooked simply because she was a woman, lumped in with the myriad of other female Parisian dressmakers who emerged during the belle époque period, sandwiched between two men, Charles Frederick Worth and Paul Poiret, who have received much greater attention from historians.

Unlike Poiret, Paquin did not believe in dictating to her customers. Paquin's viewpoint was that designers should reflect and respond to the subtle changes in style initiated by 'women in the street', as she put it. Paquin modified the most adventurous of new trends to make them wearable to her customers. Poiret's controversial hobble skirts, for example, were also produced by Paquin, but, as historian Valerie Steele has highlighted, Paquin's versions had ingenious hidden pleats to make them more practical. 'This tendency towards moderation has probably made her seem less significant in the eyes of history,' suggests Steele. An unpublished paper by Laetitia Elting (Courtauld Institute 1999) makes a strong case for Paquin as a true innovator. In 1912, she produced a collection of coats and skirts for sports, travel and shopping, creating *tailleurs* (tailored suits) that were both practical and stylish. That same year she opened a sportswear department in her London shop for golf, motoring and shooting clothing. Paquin, it could be argued, predated many of Chanel's achievements in the 1920s. A report in *Health & Home* magazine in October 1912 praised Paquin's 'simple yet smart gowns, which are the very thing for golfing or motoring and yet will not disgrace their wearer should she elect to lunch at a fashionable restaurant in the meantime.'

As the fashion historian Diana de Marly has noted, when Paquin made an innovation, it was for very practical reasons. In 1913, she produced a dress that was a blend of tailoring and drapery, formal enough for daytime but soft enough for informal evening occasions. It was the first day-into-evening dress. Her tailoring tended to be less severe than that of English tailoring specialists, with a touch of softness and femininity. Paquin herself often wore dark blue serge suits decorated with black chiffon. Despite her moderation as a designer, Madame Paquin, as she was always known, was no shrinking violet. Interviews with her in the newspapers of the day built a picture of a passionate, highly articulate and confident woman. She could also write well and penned lyrical pieces on fashion and culture. She saw fashion as part of the broader cultural picture and encouraged collaboration and cross-fertilisation between designers and artists, theatre designers and architects (contrasting with couture houses such as Redfern, Worth and Doucet, which all rejected the collaborative approach).

Jeanne Marie Charlotte Beckers was born in 1869, the daughter of a physician. In the manner of the time, she was sent out to work while still a young teenager and learned her craft very rapidly, rising through the ranks at Maison Rouff to become première, in charge of the atelier. In 1891 she married Isidore Rene Jacob dit Paquin, an ebullient businessman who owned Paquin Lalanne, a couture house that had grown out of a menswear shop, Paquin Freres, back in the 1840s. They quickly renamed the business just Paquin and set about building the company with impressive energy and verve at 3 rue de la Paix. The success of Charles Frederick Worth, the first modern couturier, which had been continued by his son Jean-Philippe Worth, had overshadowed female dressmakers in Paris. With the arrival of Paquin, the dressmakers began to have their say. Paquin was the first woman to achieve the status of couturière. While the house of Worth bestowed dignity on its customers, the house of Paquin brought lashings of glamour.

As a confident and sociable woman, now with the inestimable advantage of a wealthy husband, Jeanne Paquin was well placed to make an impact. Designer Maggy Rouff later recalled: 'I can still hear the crystal voice of Madame Paquin [saying that fashion] must constantly renew itself, without weakness or fear, even with audacity.'

Paquin loved colour. She initially embraced the pastel tones that were popular in the early 1900s. Later, she developed her signature red—and often focused on colour as a starting point for her designs. She gave new life to black, associated with mourning and gravitas through most of the nineteenth century, but used by Paquin as a foil for her richer colours. Her dresses reflected the Orientalist fashions of the early 1900s, but there was superbly realised tailoring too, including wool decorated with inserts of crochet lace. She also had a strong eye for contrasting details, such as using fur trims on silk or chiffon rather than wool, raising the ordinary into something extraordinary.

Paquin focused on design while her husband nurtured the clients. They might range from royalty (the queens of Spain, Portugal and Belgium were all customers) to celebrated courtesans such as La Belle Otero and Liane de Pougy. Indeed, the house was happy to dress everyone who could afford the opulent dresses and fur-trimmed coats. The couple showed an astute touch to their marketing and kept their prices at a more modest level than their competitors. The main events of the social calendar were clearly communicated to the vendeuses at the beginning of every year. An in-house stage was created to serve as an aid for dresses for theatre customers. A Paris guidebook of 1906 praised their open-door policy: 'From the first this clever and ornamental young couple followed a new system. No haughty seclusion, no barred doors, at the Maison Paquin.'

By the standards of the time, they were also enlightened in their attitude towards their employees, purchasing a villa in Le Touquet that employees could use for relaxation. When the world of Paris couture was threatened by a strike in 1917, Paquin expressed sympathy for the strikers, a viewpoint that displeased many of her fellow couturiers. Isidore and Jeanne had shrewd business instincts, taking the bold decision to open a London store in 1896. It was here that the young Madeleine Vionnet worked. Stores followed in Madrid and Buenos Aires, plus a furrier on Fifth Avenue, New York, named Paquin-Joire, run with her half-brother Henri Joire. In 1900, she was appointed organiser of the fashion section of the Exposition Universelle, which raised more than a few eyebrows among her rivals. She confidently created a mannequin of herself for the display. By 1907, Paquin was a flourishing business, with customers delighted by the couturière's new Japanese kimono-sleeved coats. But then tragedy struck: Isidore Paquin fell sick and died at the age of 45. Some 2,000 people attended the funeral. Jeanne was a widow at 38.

After Isidore's death, the business became Jeanne's life more than ever. Henceforth, she dressed mostly in black and white, again predating Chanel. The Prix Isidore Paquin was created in her husband's memory to recognise gifted young artists. In 1908, she revived the Directoire look and introduced tailoring for the first time, a turning point that made Paquin into a full fashion house, including couture, lingerie, furs and accessories (Jeanne Lanvin went on to take this process further, turning Lanvin into arguably the first lifestyle brand). Between 1910 and 1915, Paquin participated in a number of international exhibitions that were important marketing platforms. The Paquin pavilion, decorated as a

Greek temple, was a huge hit at an exhibition in Turin in 1911, and Paquin introduced an entrance fee in an attempt to control the visitor numbers. The same year Paquin's love for art was given full flower with the creation of an album of designs for accessories, fans and clothes illustrated by artists Paul Iribe, Georges Lepape and Georges Barbier. Paquin was also swept up in the excitement over the arrival of the Ballets Russes in Paris and made up costumes designed by Leon Bakst and Paul Iribe. As historian Nancy Troy has made clear, beneath Paquin's genuine enthusiasm for the arts, she was well aware of the commercial advantages of such associations and was also aware of the complex balancing act that was required to appeal both to the avant-garde and to more traditionally minded customers. An astute reporter for *The New York Times,* writing in 1913, commented: 'She maintains the attitude of an artist, but we know she is the most commercial artist alive.'

Paquin was also tough-minded, proving just as ready to protect her designs as her rival Paul Poiret. In 1906, she took legal action against two magazines for publishing photographs of new models before they were displayed. She also won a long-running action against the Beer couture house for copying and was awarded 8,000 francs in damages. Yet another legal case, against a Paris-based tailoring house, launched in 1911, resulted in victory seven years later. Paquin was nothing if not dogged. The period leading up to the First World War was golden for Paquin, who became the first woman dressmaker to be awarded the Légion d'Honneur. That was in 1913, a year in which shareholders in the company received a 211 per cent return on their investment. 'I am glad that the government has acknowledged my work quite irrespective of sex,' she said. 'That is as far as my feminism goes. I only want justice, that work in any particular branch in which a woman excels shall be recognised.'

The tango dress of 1913 was one of her most celebrated designs, created for dancing the tango, a craze which was sweeping Paris. A typical Paquin design, it comprised a tunic and double skirt, including a chiffon underskirt, and made generous use of pleats and godets to ensure freedom of movement. In Paquin's hands, women did not need to fear ridicule—fashion was never allowed to triumph over function. The tango dresses featured in a tango fashion show at the Palace Theatre in London. The *Daily Express* newspaper, impressed by the public interest in the event, wrote that 'these new fashion shows were rivalling in popularity the ordinary theatre play.' The outbreak of war encouraged Paquin to develop new markets, including America, where the Paquin-Joire shop had thrived since opening in 1912. In 1914, four of Paquin's best mannequins toured America for three weeks with her sister-in-law, Madame Joire, to drum up publicity. The so-called *croisade de l'élégance* visited New York, Boston, Philadelphia, Pittsburgh, Chicago and New York, charging $3 a ticket, later raised to $5, and crowds were still turned away. This successful marketing ploy had been first initiated by Poiret, but Paquin appears to have been no less successful. The models' coloured wigs drew particular comment for their modern spirit.

Paquin's status was recognised in 1917 when she was appointed president of the Chambre Syndicale, which represented the couturiers of Paris, a post she held until 1919. By then, she had retired as house designer in favour of Madeleine Wallis, whose particular skill was in furs, which became the signature of Paquin. She finally retired altogether in the early 1930s and died in 1936. The house lasted twenty years after her death, continuing to make her celebrated fur-trimmed coats. In 1953, it acquired the French business of Worth, its old rival, before both were forced to recognise their time was past, closing in 1956.

Further reading: There is little on Paquin in English, but Dominique Sirop wrote her biography, *Paquin* (1989), in French. An unpublished paper by Laetitia Elting, *Revealing the Accomplishments of Madame Paquin, the Very Queen of Dressmakers* (1999), is at the Courtauld Institute in London.

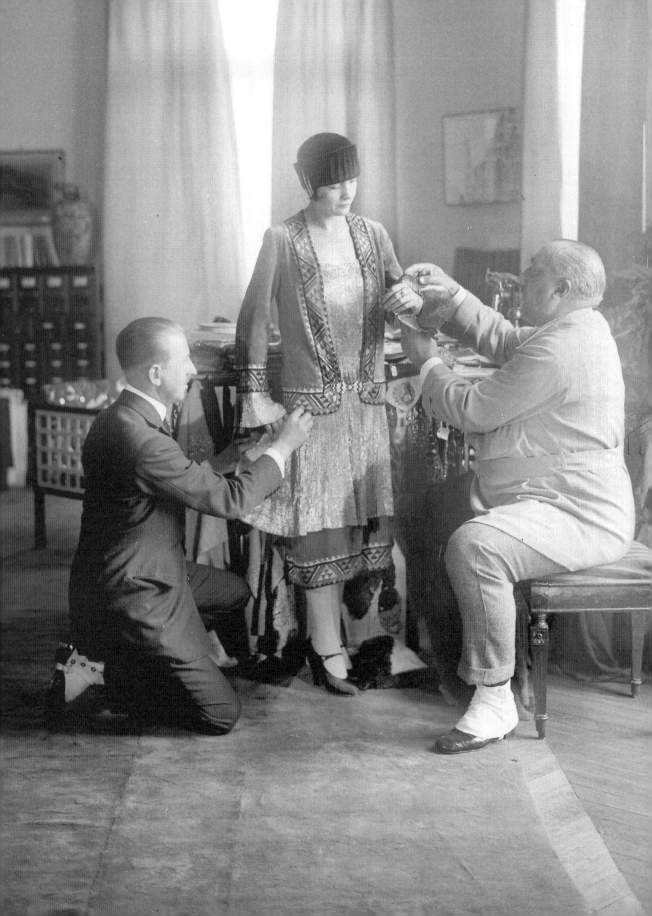

4 PAUL POIRET (1879–1944)

To describe Paul Poiret as a fashion designer may be to do him an injustice. Consider the achievements of the year 1911, his annus mirabilis, when he created the Rosine house of perfume, the Martine school of decorative arts (with accompanying shop), the Colin paper and packaging workshop, and a fabric printing factory in collaboration with the artist Raoul Dufy. That same year also saw his publication of *Les choses de Paul Poiret vues par Georges Lepape,* a book of exquisite fashion drawings that did much to fuel the revival of fashion illustration. All this, combined with his achievements as a couturier, made Paul Poiret a central figure in the artistic and creative development of Paris in the early twentieth century. In the 1910s, he was known in America as the King of Fashion, while in Paris he was Le Magnifique. To cap it all, he was also an outstanding cook.

As a couturier, his list of accomplishments was spectacular, led by his championing of a revival of the neoclassical style of 1790s France—high-waisted flowing clothes that followed the fluid, natural lines of the body. This revival swept away in a few short years most of the nineteenth-century styles that squeezed, exaggerated or disguised the body. Paradoxically, Poiret was also responsible for the hobble skirt, cut so tight that the wearer could barely walk, an innovation that aroused ridicule while fuelling the oxygen of publicity for the designer. More positively, his enthusiasm for Orientalism, drawing on influences from India to China and Japan, infused fashion and interior design with a burst of strong, dynamic colours, even before the Ballets Russes and Bakst had reached Paris. He paved the way for the style known as Art Deco, making a spectacular contribution both in terms of fashion and interior decoration to the Exposition des Arts Décoratifs in 1925, the event that gave the movement its name.

Poiret was a true Parisian, born in 1879 near Les Halles, to parents who owned a wool cloth shop. As a young child, he was an avid art gallery visitor, entranced by colours in particular. He was also a lover of the theatre, sketching the costumes of the actresses at the Comédie-Française. Forced by his father to become an apprentice to an umbrella maker, he preferred to spend every spare moment developing his sketching abilities. The breakthrough came in 1898 when the couturier Jacques Doucet offered him a job as a junior assistant. His first piece, a red wool cape, received orders from 400 customers. Poiret went on to design for two star actresses of the period, Gabrielle Réjane and Sarah Bernhardt, but was sacked by Doucet after a falling-out with Bernhardt. Following a brief and unhappy period of military service, he went to work at the house of Worth, where he created a coat cut like a kimono that famously upset its potential client, Russian Princess Bariatinsky, but was a precursor of his Orientalist style. Once again, however, he lost his job.

In 1903, with money from his mother, he opened his own house at 5 rue Auber. Encouraged by the magnanimous Jacques Doucet and championed by the actress Gabrielle Réjane, Poiret swiftly began to make waves. His muse was Denise, the daughter of a Normandy textile manufacturer. They were married in 1905. In those early days as a couturier, his enemy was the corset. As he put it himself, 'It was in the name of Liberty that I brought about my first revolution, by deliberately laying siege to the corset.'

Poiret always designed on live models, working from the shoulders, initially creating a series of surprisingly plain gowns that skimmed the outlines of the figure. By 1906, he had banished the corset, replaced by the girdle and the brassiere, which he can lay claim to have invented. Among the other designers of the period who also dropped the corset were Lucile and Madeleine Vionnet, but Poiret, a brilliant self-publicist, stole most of the credit. Unlike Vionnet, he tended to work on the straight grain rather than on the bias. As Metropolitan Museum of Art Costume Institute curators Harold Koda and Andrew Bolton point out, the new natural silhouette marked a fundamental shift of emphasis in fashion away from the skills of tailoring to those based on the skills of draping, inspired by a mixture of sources, including the Greek chiton, the Japanese kimono and the North African caftan. 'Poiret's process of design through draping is the source of fashion's modern forms,' conclude Koda and Bolton.

Between 1906 and 1911, Poiret revived a high-waisted line, referencing both the Directoire period of the 1790s and the ancient Greeks. He mischievously provoked outrage by appearing at the Longchamp racetrack, accompanied by three young women wearing dresses with the sides slit from the knees showing off coloured stockings. He received even more precious media coverage in London by showing his collection at a tea party organised by Margot Asquith, wife of the prime minister. Poiret was by then a considerable celebrity in his own right, with the élan of a theatre impresario and a swaggering, confident personality that swept all before him. In 1909, he moved his premises to an eighteenth-century mansion on avenue d'Antin and created a veritable fashion empire, kept in check financially only by the conscientiousness of book-keeper Emile Rousseau. Nor were his customers spared from his dominant, sometimes aggressive personality: Poiret, in his own eyes, could do no wrong. The cardboard sign outside his office read: 'Danger!!! Before knocking ask yourself three times—Is it absolutely necessary to disturb HIM?'

His glory years saw Poiret move far beyond fashion, developing links with a series of artists, most notably Paul Iribe (who produced a catalogue of illustrations for him in 1908) and Raoul Dufy, who became a lifelong friend. Poiret's catalogues prompted the creation by magazine editor Lucien Vogel of *Gazette du bon ton,* which was essential reading for the fashion set in Paris from 1912 to 1925. Poiret's love of the theatre was reflected in a series of extravagant parties, the most notable being his 'The Thousand and Second Night' or 'Persian Celebration' in June 1911, where his 300 guests dressed in oriental costume and his wife, Denise, was locked in a golden cage and released like a bird. Erté became an assistant designer for Poiret in 1913, working with him on his theatrical designs. Poiret's costumes for Mata Hari in a play, *Le Minaret,* were a sensation, featuring a tunic-crinoline shaped like a lampshade, which Erté said was 'inspired by the transparent veils of the Hindu miniatures and by the pleated kilts of Greek folk costumes.'

Poiret foreshadowed the magpie tendencies of designers in the latter decades of the twentieth century through his happy plundering of styles from all points east of Paris. From harem pantaloons to kimono coats to Indian turbans, the couturier found inspiration in everything. His colour explosion brought orange, green, red and purple to the fore as never before, marking a break with the understated pastels of the Art Nouveau period. For a while, Poiret was the most celebrated couturier of the age, particularly famed for his coats, capes and cloaks, notable for their sheer lavish use of fabric, often with fur trimmings. By 1913, his love of bold colours and extravagant prints reflected the work of the Wiener Werkstatte, an influential decorative arts company in Vienna. Poiret did much to popularise the design ideas coming out of Austria and Germany (which led to some criticism from French patriots during the First World War).

Poiret always had entrepreneurial instincts and was bursting with ideas for making money. In 1913, he was the first couturier to embark on the conquest of America, touring department stores. Poiret was also the first couturier to give lectures, attracting huge audiences in the United States and across Europe. Despite his overbearing personality, he always insisted that the couturier's role was not to be a dictator but to be a servant blessed with extreme sensitivity, able to detect the precise moment when a woman's enthusiasm for a fashion was beginning to wane. His American tour was a triumph, but Poiret returned in a state of shock at the widespread copying of his designs. This led him to push for the creation in 1914 of Le Syndicat de Défense de la Grande Couture Française, of which he was the first president. Two years later, he tried a different strategy, producing reduced-price copies of his own dresses, advertised in *Vogue* in 1916 and also promoted in America. In her groundbreaking research, American academic Nancy Troy (2003) has shown the contradictions in the way Poiret presented himself as an artist not only to sell to wealthy clients but also to promote the mass production of his designs. The First World War put a stop to grand plans for expansion in America, and any last pretence at financial discipline evaporated after the war. Likewise, after the horrors of four years of war, Poiret's love of theatrical extravagance struck a false note, contrasting with Chanel's functional style and the garçonne look. Although Poiret continued to produce many outstanding collections, his heyday had passed, and a period of slow, sometimes painful decline followed.

Behind the extravagant personality, Poiret was a devoted father to his three children (Rosine, Martine and Colin, who all gave their names to the spurt of initiatives in 1911; he was devastated by the early death of Rosine from otitis). He divorced from his wife and muse, Denise, in 1928, telling the governess, 'Make sure to tell Madame to take anything she wishes.' In the 1920s, Poiret continued to have no lack of admirers and opportunities. The sadness was that his creative energies were matched by a reckless attitude to money that resulted in years of penury and near ruin despite the constant efforts of friends and admirers to help him out. By 1929, his extravagance led to the closure of his house, and the final years of his life were a depressing downward spiral, exacerbated by the advent of Parkinson's disease. In 1937, a proposal raised at the Chambre Syndicale de la Haute Couture to grant Poiret a pension was vetoed by Jacques Worth.

However, the later years of his life were not empty and showed that Poiret was still a forward-thinking innovator. In 1927, he wrote a far-sighted article for *The Forum* magazine, predicting the future dominance of synthetics and plastics. In another groundbreaking move in the twilight years of his career, he designed for both Printemps and Liberty of London in the 1930s. Poiret's status was fully recognised

in 2007 through a lavish exhibition, *Poiret: King of Fashion,* at the Metropolitan Museum of Art in New York, prompted by a treasure trove of clothing from the collection of his wife, Denise, that came up for auction in Paris in 2005: the Met acquired more than twenty pieces. In particular, a pair of 1920s nightdresses, inspired by classical Greek style and worn by Denise, confirm the lightness of his touch and the importance of his influence. But his more extravagant costumes also struck a chord. By the late 1920s, as fashion historian Caroline Rennolds Milbank put it: 'Poiret's global exoticism would not seem modern again until the beginning of the twenty-first century, when the haute couture had found new resonance as one of the most dramatic of arts.'

Fashion historian Diana de Marly called Poiret 'a liberator' (hobble skirts aside): his lean line marking the death knell of the restricted waist, his narrow styles reducing the need for layers of petticoats. Thanks to Poiret, clothes for women began the shift from burdensome impediment to lightweight and more practical adornment. For Met curators Harold Koda and Andrew Bolton, Poiret 'effectively established the canon of modern dress and developed the blueprint of the modern fashion industry.' Poiret was indeed the precursor for much of the contemporary fashion world. Fashion historians are fortunate to have plenty of insights into his design philosophy from the couturier himself, thanks to his many lectures, magazine interviews and a late autobiography. Never mind that his message is sometimes as contradictory as those awkward hobble skirts. At his best, he stripped away the absurdities of late nineteenth-century European fashion and ushered in a new age for his customers, urging women to, in his own words, 'simply wear what becomes you.'

Further reading: Paul Poiret summarised his own career in *My First Fifty Years* (trans., 1931). Biographers include Yvonne Deslandres, *Poiret* (1987); Alice Mackrell, *Paul Poiret* (1990); and Palmer White, *Poiret* (1973). Nancy Troy's *Couture Culture: A Study in Modern Art and Culture* (2003) highlights the commercial acumen of the couturier. Harold Koda and Andrew Bolton's *Poiret* (2007), the catalogue to the *Poiret: King of Fashion* exhibition at the Metropolitan Museum of Art in 2007, includes an illuminating reappraisal of his achievements.

5 MARIANO FORTUNY (1871–1949)

Not without reason was Mariano Fortuny known as a latter-day Renaissance man. The Spaniard's span of interests was too broad for one-word descriptions. He was as much artist and inventor as designer: over three decades he registered more than twenty inventions in Paris. His great contribution to fashion, summed up in one dress, the Delphos, was to free the body from the restrictions of fashionable nineteenth-century dress. Created as early as 1907, the Delphos was a long, simply cut, pleated silk dress that hung loosely from the shoulders and could be scrunched up into ball for travelling. In an age when most women were tightly corseted and fitted, it represented a liberation, summed up best in photos from the period of the celebrated dancer Isadora Duncan in lithe, free-flowing garments. Fortuny recognised the importance of the Delphos, patenting one of the designs (with batwing sleeves) in Paris in 1909. Fortuny brought the worlds of art and fashion close together, as did his contemporary Sonia Delaunay. The interrelationship between art and fashion has been a theme in popular culture ever since, explored in the modern-day era by a host of designers, including Hussein Chalayan, Marc Jacobs and Viktor & Rolf.

Mariano Fortuny y Madrazo was born in Granada, Spain, in 1871 into a family full of artists and blessed with plenty of money. His father, Mariano, a distinguished painter, had married Cecilia de Madrazo, also from a family of artists. From 1872, they lived in Rome, where his father had a studio, and Paris. Mariano's father died of malaria in 1874 at the age of only 36, a loss that grieved the son throughout his life (he edited a book on his father as late as 1933). Besides the skills of a painter, Mariano

inherited from his father a taste for collecting antiques and objets d'art from exotic places, particularly the Arab world. The family collection included a treasure trove of textiles, often displayed as wall hangings.

After his father's death, the family moved to Paris, where Fortuny began painting at the age of seven. He absorbed the work of the Old Masters, such as Rubens, learning the importance of colour that stood him in good stead in the future. The young Fortuny was plagued with asthma and hay fever in Paris, brought on by an allergic reaction to horses. So, in 1889, his mother moved with him and his sister, Maria Luisa, to horse-free Venice and the Palazzo Martinengo on the Grand Canal. Venice remained his base for the rest of his life. He attended night classes at the Accademia in Venice to improve his drawing and continued to copy the Old Masters, including Tintoretto and other great Venetian artists. Further inspiration came from a visit in 1892 to Bayreuth, home of opera composer Richard Wagner. The grand all-embracing vision of Wagner inspired Fortuny, who immersed himself in the world of theatre for many years, developing new lighting systems. Fortuny was as much technician as artist. All art forms had merit in his vision, and everything could be harnessed by the artist.

In 1897, Fortuny met a young Frenchwoman, Henriette Negrin, in Paris. Despite his mother's lifelong disapproval (Henriette was a divorcee), Fortuny adored her for the rest of his life as wife, lover, companion and muse. She moved to Venice in 1902, by which time Fortuny had relocated to his own home, the Palazzo Pesaro Orfei. This splendid thirteenth-century palazzo, built on a truly Wagnerian scale, was the perfect stage for Fortuny to develop his ideas and inventions and display his antiques collection. A vast salon-studio was at the heart of the palazzo, though the private rooms were relatively small and simple. Here, Fortuny was able to play the host. A tall man with piercing blue eyes, he wore lightweight suits in dark blue serge with a white silk cravat and cut a dash in Venice, where a new generation of artists had been emerging since the 1880s. There was a sizeable foreign colony, attracted by this most romantic of cities. He got to know Italy's leading literary star, Gabriele D'Annunzio, whom he met for the first time in 1894.

However, any attempt to locate Fortuny within the context of artistic movements of the time is tricky because the man himself largely ignored the work of his contemporaries and rarely stepped outside Venice. His biographer, Guillermo de Osma, situated him most convincingly within the Aesthetic Movement, whose exponents thought clothing had become a prison. The Aesthete painters looked back for inspiration to classical Greece and the Middle Ages (the dress of that period was particularly admired by the Pre-Raphaelites). But these clothes were only featured in their paintings and never realised, with the single exception of some toga satin dresses produced by Liberty's of London, inspired by the work of Sir Lawrence Alma-Tadema.

Fortuny's move into the world of textiles and fashion is thought to have begun in 1906 by experimenting with the printing of textiles at his palazzo. Some sketches for a play, *Francesca da Rimini*, were turned into costumes, receiving a lukewarm response. More promising were costumes for a ballet in Paris in the same year featuring his distinctive silk veils printed with geometric designs inspired by Cycladic art. These became known as Knossos scarves, which was a touch misleading because they were rectangular pieces of silk that could be used in all sorts of ways, as much clothing as accessory. They remained a feature of his work for more than fifteen years. 'From these simple scarves, which showed him how to fuse form and fabric, Fortuny developed his entire production of dresses,' wrote his biographer Guillermo de Osma.

The Knossos scarf was most impressively worn over the celebrated Delphos dress. Fortuny's patent registration described it thus: 'Its design is so shaped and arranged that it can be worn and adjusted with ease and comfort.' To this day, there is some mystery over how Fortuny created the pleating on the dress. The folds are irregular and were probably developed by applying heat while the material was wet. With the exception of hand-blown glass beads from Murano, everything was made by hand at the Palazzo. To counter the stretchiness of the pleats, Fortuny sewed cords strung with beads along the sides of his dresses.

Fortuny began with silk, usually bought raw and in off-white and imported direct from China and Japan; later he added velvet, imported from Lyons. Both silk and velvet were used in countless variations. He experimented enthusiastically with printing, using wood blocks initially, then introducing hand-painting and developing his own high-quality stencils made of silk. He created his own colours, exploring ingredients from many sources and countries. Kennedy Fraser, writing in *The New Yorker* in 1981, commented: 'The colors that Fortuny created are still rare and luscious after the passage of decades: blushing peach and apricot, purple grape and candlelit claret, blue of fountains and of peacocks' tails.'

Fortuny was never recognised as a creator of fashion by the couturiers in Paris. In the early years, his dresses were worn only at home, considered far too louche for formal outdoors wear. He stood outside the rigidly controlled couture system and chose instead to develop his own sales and marketing operation. This included a ground-floor shop at the Palazzo and a small network of shops and sales agents across Europe. Two of the literary giants of the period did their best to create an aura around Fortuny's work. Marcel Proust refers to Fortuny no less than sixteen times in his novel *A la Recherche du Temps Perdu* (Remembrance of Things Past). Gabriele D'Annunzio referenced Fortuny beautifully for one of his fictional heroines, the Marchesa Casati Stampa: 'She was enveloped in one of those very long scarves of Oriental Gauze that the alchemist Mariano Fortuny plunges into the mysterious dyes of his vats and withdraws tinted with strange dreams, and with his thousand hand-printing blocks marks new generations for stars, planets, animals.'

In 1909, the arrival of Diaghilev's Ballets Russes in Paris marked the increasing dominance of Aesthete modes of dress; the costumes by Bakst were clearly inspired by Fortuny. Bakst had seen Isadora Duncan perform in a Fortuny dress on a tour of Russia back in 1906. Bakst reinterpreted her dress with loose, liberating costumes for at least three ballets in 1911 and 1912. This tribute turned out to be of great benefit to Fortuny, for it popularised his designs and boosted his order book to such an extent that he eventually opened a shop in Paris in 1920 at 67 rue Pierre Charron, not far from Paul Poiret. The ornate interior of the Palazzo was meticulously recreated. It seems likely that Poiret himself was influenced by the work of Fortuny; a green silk chiffon tunic made by Fortuny was sold in Poiret's shop as early as 1908. Other names who drew on the work of Fortuny included Maria Monaci Gallenga in Rome and Madame Babani in Paris.

By the early 1920s, fashion had moved on from the influence of the classical period, but Fortuny's emphasis on clothing the natural form chimed with the mood of the times. As Fraser Kennedy has noted, before the First World War, Fortuny's clothes essentially carried on the tradition of idealistic and artistic female dress begun with the Aesthetes and Pre-Raphaelites. 'After the war, they seemed liberated, even slightly naughty, and totally modern attire for wear to cocktail parties in the Jazz Age.' That said, Fortuny continued to stand aside from the fashion industry. At the celebrated Art Deco exhibition of 1925 in Paris, Fortuny did not even show in the fashion pavilion.

The decade proved a period of spectacular success for the designer, fuelled by the opening of a factory for cotton textile production on the island of Giudecca near Venice, using long-staple Egyptian cotton spun in England. More significant in the long term than the opening of the Paris shop was the addition of a stockist in New York from 1923. The Brick Shop ordered Fortuny's cotton fabrics, which became popular interior furnishings for the elite of Manhattan. The silk and velvet dresses, meanwhile, achieved a classic status that reflected their classical inspiration. Looking back on the decade, Lady Bonham-Carter commented: 'I think everyone I knew had a Fortuny dress . . . We all wore them, especially the "gels" with good figures. They clung a bit, you see, and they weren't quite so perfect on lumpy figures.'

The Great Depression of 1929 marked the beginning of hard times for Fortuny. He found crucial support from American interior decorator Elsie McNeill, later the Countess Elsie Lee Gozzi, who bought the rights to sell Fortuny in 1927 and opened a shop at 509 Madison Avenue. In quick succession, Fortuny endured the death of his mother in 1932 and the receivership of his Giudecca factory in 1933. Somehow he found the funds to buy the factory out of receivership himself. His sister Maria Luisa died in 1936, a troubled year in his homeland, with the Spanish Civil War under way. Elsie Lee continued to market Fortuny effectively in America, financing the rebuilding of the Giudecca factory. However, the advent of the Second World War forced its closure again. When it reopened after the war, it was on a much reduced scale. Fortuny's final years, until his death in 1949, saw his wealth significantly diminished.

During the 1950s, Fortuny's work was virtually forgotten, although from the 1960s and 1970s museums began to acquire his dresses and the word spread among costume collectors. The real explosion of interest in Fortuny dates from the 1980s. These days, Fortuny's status in the roll call of great designers is assured. His ability to thrive outside the fashion system of Paris makes him a very special case. Customers treasured their Fortuny dresses and returned time and time again, developing an emotional attachment to the clothes. Throughout his career, Fortuny worked with a handful of simple ideas and shapes developed in many different variations. It is famously hard to date his dresses because the themes did not evolve in a logical sequence, instead mutating according to his own interest. His biographer, Guillermo De Osma, wrote: 'Fortuny invented fashion outside fashion, fashion that does not change, fashion as art.'

Further reading: Guillermo De Osma's biography, *Fortuny* (1984, updated ed.), did much to remind the modern era of Fortuny's talents.

PART 2

1910s–1930s

Introduction

The First World War was a cataclysmic event. Fashion, like every other sphere of creativity, was turned upside down from 1914 to 1918. Couturiers were obliged to respond to years during which women had worn overalls and trousers as they worked to support the war effort. In the wake of the war, Paul Poiret, still believing in the allure of orientalism, never touched the heights of his pre-war career.

The new stars were *Gabrielle* ('Coco') *Chanel* and *Jean Patou,* fierce rivals in business although they shared similar outlooks on fashion in design terms. They both set up their houses in 1919 and responded to the post-war mood, reacting against ostentation and focusing on more practical style.

New freedoms for women were also reflected in the growing influence of America—everything from Hollywood movies to jazz and cocktails influenced Europe. Hollywood costume designer *Adrian* became an important name to watch for the clothing trade on New York's 7th Avenue. But American designers mostly followed the lead of Paris. Thus, the social freedoms of America were reflected in Parisian style and sold back to the Americans.

The belle époque social mores, which dictated that even a flash of leg was unseemly, were now but a distant memory. In the early 1920s, hemlines began to shorten and a boyish, almost androgynous, silhouette became fashionable. A novel, *La Garçonne,* gave its name to the garçonne look. Sports clothes for women now drew the attention of couturiers. In 1921, Jean Patou stirred up a sensation by dressing the tennis player Suzanne Lenglen at Wimbledon in a straight white sleeveless cardigan and a short white silk pleated skirt. Skirts (and hair) were at their shortest by 1926. A sweltering summer in Europe in 1928 was a boost for swimming costumes and the new fashion for a suntan. The art deco movement thrived, peaking at the Expo in Paris in 1925.

The twenties set in motion many of the trends that have continued to permeate fashion ever since. American designer Norman Norell commented in 1960: 'Women are still wearing, and throughout this century will continue to wear, the changes that came about in the twenties.'

Running counter to all this—and reminding us that fashion has often been nostalgic rather than aggressively progressive—*Jeanne Lanvin* produced robes de style, loved by the many women who would not dream of wearing flapper dresses. Fashion changed decisively with Jean Patou's collection for the winter of 1929. Dresses flowed from the waist rather than the hip, while hemlines dropped to mid-calf. It was the year of the Great Depression: American buyers and customers fell away from Paris, not returning in numbers until 1933. The couture houses trimmed their staff and struggled to stay afloat.

In the 1930s, Jean Patou faded from the scene, and Coco Chanel had a new rival, *Elsa Schiaparelli.* While Chanel developed her cardigan jackets and understated sense of chic, Schiaparelli enjoyed the grand gesture, the inspired joke, blending her love of art with her fashion sensibility.

In Paris, a number of individualistic names began to emerge in the period after the First World War. The perfectionist *Madeleine Vionnet* drew inspiration from classical influences and emerged as the great purist of Parisian fashion. *Mainbocher* proved that an American could also succeed in Paris. *Salvatore Ferragamo* returned from Hollywood to his native Italy in 1927, founding his legendary shoe business. Technology continued to drive fashion forward: in 1939, America began producing nylon. But then war intervened and fashion in Paris came to a near standstill.

6 JEANNE LANVIN (1867–1946)

The founder of the oldest surviving couture house in near-continuous existence, Jeanne Lanvin was established as one of the most commercially successful couturières in Paris by the 1920s. Until recently, she has been neglected by fashion historians: her romantic, nostalgic approach to design was considered backward looking, contrasting with the resolutely modern styles of Gabrielle Chanel or Jean Patou. Renewed interest in Lanvin has been boosted partly by the success of Central Saint Martins-trained designer Alber Elbaz, from Israel, at the helm of the design studio in the early twenty-first century but more fundamentally by the research of fashion historians such as Nancy Troy, who treats commercial achievements with the same seriousness as creative influence (and, indeed, explores the interlinkage between the two). And, although Jeanne Lanvin does not fall easily within the conventional narrative of the development of modern fashion design, her success raises important questions about the very nature of that narrative, highlighting the nostalgic and retrospective characteristics of much of the greatest fashion.

What is not in doubt is that Jeanne Lanvin made exquisitely beautiful clothes that celebrated traditional concepts of femininity. Her finest designs were her robes de style, full-skirted evening dresses typically in silk taffeta that looked back to the eighteenth century and were a reaction to the garçonne look of the 1920s. Renowned as a sensitive colourist, she created her own Lanvin blue and through her dyeworks developed a palette of harmony and exceptional delicacy. Lanvin was a pragmatic designer who responded to the varied needs of a woman's wardrobe and delivered time after time what her customers sought most. Furthermore, she created modern children's fashion, designing clothes specifically for her daughter, Marguerite. But her influence on fashion history has less to do with pure design and more to do with the evolution of the concept of a designer as it is known today. She ran her business like a modern designer: the Lanvin story is a case study in brand management and development that still has lessons for today's designer brands. She also researched like a modern designer, scanning museums, art galleries, history books and any resource that might provide inspiration.

Lanvin was also a lifestyle designer, creating a sophisticated fashion house that covered a broad array of products, invariably brilliantly marketed. The achievement is all the more remarkable because the couturière was a retiring, taciturn woman, reluctant to meet her clients. This reticence should not, however, be confused with lack of confidence. She had an iron will and a strong belief in her own abilities, based on a long apprenticeship and thorough immersion in her craft.

Born in 1867, Jeanne-Marie Lanvin was the eldest of ten children fathered by Constantin Bernard Lanvin, a staunchly middle-class journalist. In the manner of the times, she was in employment from the age of thirteen, initially as a dressmaker's errand girl. She was careful with her money from an early age: one story recounts how, when asked to deliver parcels and given her bus fares, she chose to run behind the bus and save the money. She worked for most of her teen years as an apprentice milliner at Madame Felix in the rue du Faubourg Saint-Honoré, followed by a spell at Talbot, a dressmaker, where she learned about fabrics, before setting up her own hat workshop at the age of just eighteen, initially in the rue du Marché Saint-Honoré. Saving money from a three-month stint working for a Barcelona-based dressmaker, Madame Maria-Berta Valenti, Lanvin opened her own millinery shop in 1890 at 16 rue Boissy d'Anglas.

In 1895, Lanvin married the Italian nobleman Henri Emile-Georges di Pietro, their initial encounter predictably occurring at the Longchamp racetrack, one of the primary locations for the fashion-aware to strut and court in late nineteenth-century Paris. Although the marriage lasted only eight years, it did result in the birth of a daughter, Marguerite Marie-Blanche, in 1897, who was dressed more beautifully than perhaps any child in history by her adoring mother. In 1907, four years after her divorce, Lanvin married again, this time to Xavier Melet, a journalist like her father, who later became French consul in Manchester, England. This marriage was business-like, rather than romantic, with Melet playing the role of loyal husband. It meant that Lanvin was no longer a single mother, which then had a status of some social shame.

Focusing initially on millinery, Lanvin's business grew organically, each achievement leading logically to the next. Clients' admiration for her dresses for Marguerite encouraged her to open a children's department by 1908. A year later, it made sense to extend this to women's clothing too, creating empire-waist chemise frocks in Fauvist colours and showing an assured use of black and white. She also emphasised her ambition by swiftly joining the Syndicat de la Couture. The First World War proved little more than an interlude in the development of the young fashion house; by the end of 1918 Lanvin had secured the entire building at 33 rue du Faubourg Saint-Honoré, comprising nine workshops, including two for embroidery—an innovation as this highly skilled work was usually passed on to outsiders, who had both motivation and opportunity to plagiarise. Keeping embroidery in-house did not solve the problem of copying, although it did prove over time to be a shrewd business move. Lanvin's exquisite beadwork was at the heart of the fashion house's reputation in the 1920s and beyond.

Lanvin visited America as early as 1915, so she was well aware of the opportunities across the Atlantic for her house to grow. Her instinct for business was finely tuned, developing steadily through the 1920s but always closely monitored with a strong personal touch that gave Lanvin the stamp of heartfelt authenticity. By the 1920s, Lanvin was a wealthy woman, commissioning Armand-Albert Rateau to design her shops at 15 and 22 rue du Faubourg Saint-Honoré as well as her town house at rue Barbet-de-Jouy and her villa at Vesinet. Rateau became a friend, designing the spherical bottle of Lanvin's celebrated Arpège fragrance in 1927 and managing her Lanvin-Sport business. With Rateau, she created Art Deco-inspired decorative objects for the home. Her bedroom, boudoir, and bathroom, commissioned from Rateau, are now installed at the Musée des Arts Decoratifs in Paris. Her daughter, Marguerite Marie-Blanche, was a true muse to her, always immaculately dressed in clothes that were both beautiful and practical. Previously, children from society families used to wear watered-down versions of adult clothing, but by 1921 Lanvin's influence on children's fashion was noted by Vogue—'loose and simple clothes . . . easy to put on and take off again.' Through the 1920s, Lanvin attracted many actresses, including Mary Pickford, the American silent screen star, and Yvonne Printemps, for whom she designed costumes. A stage set was created in her atelier for fittings for costumes. The year 1923 saw Lanvin create costumes for seventeen shows.

In 1924, Lanvin's daughter married the Comte Jean de Polignac, and she shortened her name to Marie-Blanche. This event was more than personal: it took Jeanne Lanvin and her family into a new social circle, elevating her status with knock-on benefits for the business. The Polignac family became important customers, adding social cachet to the company. A year later, Lanvin herself was made Chevalier de la Légion d'Honneur in recognition of her achievements. While Chanel and Patou stole the headlines, Lanvin simply went on expanding, with clothes that were beautiful and renowned for their exceptionally intricate seaming, beading and embroidery. Her career might, indeed, be hailed as the ultimate celebration of the work of *les petites mains;* the French name for the hard-working women who laboured in the couture workshops of Paris.

Lanvin had a number of signature touches, including a penchant for ribbons flowing at the hip, spiralling ruffles, taffeta applied to tulle for a floaty romantic effect. Flowers, ribbons and sunbursts were repetitive motifs that she adored. Over the years, she built up a memory bank of motifs, including the daisy (or marguerite) that was her daughter's keepsake, a series of three-part Japanese *mons* (family crests), and symbols that reflected her Catholic faith. 'A design inevitably reflects the artistic motifs stored in one's memory,' she said, 'drawing on those which are the most alive, new and fertile all at the same time.' Her robes de style were produced throughout the 1920s, in defiance of the rise of the flapper or garçonne, and right up to the late 1930s, when wartime austerity frowned on such lavish use of fabric. Artist Paul Iribe sketched Lanvin and her daughter in robes de styles (the sketch was actually based on a 1907 photograph), a sweet image that was refined by Armand-Albert Rateau to become the Lanvin signature, reproduced on labels.

Lanvin herself was already well into her fifties when the 1920s dawned. Thus, she was not strictly a contemporary of Chanel. Decades later, Karl Lagerfeld said: 'Her image was not as strong as that of Chanel because she was a nice old lady and not a fashion plate.' Looking at it from another perspective, it might also be instructive to compare Jeanne Lanvin's achievement in building a business founded on her own financial means and unrelenting hard work with Chanel's opportunism as mistress to a succession of wealthy lovers who certainly smoothed her path to fortune. As biographer Dean Merceron puts it, which of them is the greater exemplar for the modern woman? Although Chanel was the ultimate modernist, obsessed with function, Lanvin did not believe in creating clothes that were too practical. 'Modern clothes need a certain romantic feel,' she argued, reflecting her teenage years in belle époque Paris. Couturières, she said, 'should take care not to become too everyday and practical.' Speaking to *Vogue* in 1934, she said: 'I act on impulse and believe in instinct. My dresses aren't premeditated. I am carried away by feeling and technical knowledge helps me make my clothes become a reality.'

Her business strategy was, by contrast, thoroughly practical, exploring every opportunity that presented itself. Shops were created for home decor, menswear, furs and lingerie—a true retail empire. Thinking ahead, Lanvin invested in a company-owned dye factory in Nanterre as early as 1923, responding to the demand for her colours. Silver was often combined with black, or with an array of colours that included soft pinks, greens and blues. Above all, there was the Lanvin blue, a pretty lavender blue. These colours were researched intensively: Lanvin blue was most likely inspired by the blues in Fra Angelico frescoes, and other colours reflected her favourite artists, such as Édouard Vuillard, Pierre-Auguste Renoir and Odilon Redon (all of whom she collected). Lanvin was an avid collector throughout her life, assembling a remarkable array of paintings, sculptures, fabrics, exotic clothes and libraries, all catalogued and recorded with the meticulous precision that was her hallmark. Much of her collection was auctioned in Paris in September 2006, highlighting the diversity and richness of her interests, particularly her fascination with Japonism. Novelist Elizabeth Barille writes: 'She was like a bee, tasting everything in order to make her exceptionally delicious honey.'

The outbreak of the Second World War also marked the declining years of Lanvin herself, by then in her seventies. The continuity sustained at the house of Lanvin is one of its greatest achievements. After her death in 1946, the company was run by family members for several decades, going through a number of different owners (including L'Oréal) before turning private in 2001 under investment group Harmonie, headed by a Taiwanese media businesswoman. The appointment of the sensitive, intuitive designer Alber Elbaz, who has acknowledged the inspiration he has garnered from the Lanvin archive and works at a Jeanne Lanvin black lacquer Art Deco desk, marked a new phase in the history of the house, continuing a remarkable history well into the twenty-first century.

Further reading: Jeanne Lanvin's career is magnificently illustrated and documented in Dean L. Merceron's *Lanvin* (2007). An introduction by Harold Koda analyses in detail why Lanvin has been overlooked by fashion historians. Elizabeth Barille's *Lanvin* (1997) is a concise introduction to her work.

7 GABRIELLE CHANEL (1883–1971)

The most celebrated fashion designer in history, Gabrielle ('Coco') Chanel continues to be treated with reverence nearly forty years after her death. No designer can match her for influence on the modern women's wardrobe. No designer, with the exception of Karl Lagerfeld, inheritor of her mantle at the house of Chanel, has thrived for so long. Her Parisian fashion house was launched as early as 1915, reached remarkable heights in the 1920s and 1930s and blossomed once again in the 1950s and 1960s.

Mademoiselle, as she was always called by her employees, took concepts from sportswear and men's clothing and turned them into practical, effortlessly elegant clothes for women, launching her revolution at a time when women's fashion was so overwrought that many wealthy women could not dress themselves without assistance. Her early contemporaries recognised her achievements through gritted teeth. For Paul Poiret, Chanel's clothes were 'miserabilisme de luxe'. While he explored bright colours and great swathes of fabric, Chanel pared down her design message time and time again. Call it functional chic; she was synonymous with the concept that 'less is more'. She did not sketch, preferring to work directly on a model's body, with sessions often lasting many hours with no break. Photographer Cecil Beaton, lunching with her in the twilight of her career in 1965, recalls the way she moulded the napkins in the restaurant. He was captivated by this small woman with hard black eyes who spoke in a torrent of words. Publisher and journalist John Fairchild watched Chanel at the age of eighty cut an armhole on a live model, drawing blood.

To her artist connections, she was often extravagantly generous. In the atelier and with her employees, she was tough, demanding and ruthless—qualities that won her few friends and made her increasingly isolated in later life. Money, and the making of money, certainly transfixed her, giving her the independence she cherished so much. 'She possessed the wily foxiness of a country horse trader,' her lawyer Robert Chaillet said.

But there was something more to Chanel. She had an exceptional ability to scent change in the air, an attribute common to the handful of designers who were influential throughout their careers. 'Fashion is something in the air,' she said. 'You feel it coming, you smell it.'

Her life story is as remarkable as her talents as a designer. She was born Gabrielle Chasnel, the illegitimate daughter of market traders, in a poorhouse hospice in Saumur in 1883. Her mother died when she was only twelve, so the young Gabrielle spent much of her childhood in an orphanage near Brive-la-Gaillarde. At the age of eighteen she was accepted as a charity student at a convent boarding school in Moulins and attracted attention for her striking looks, particularly her elegant long neck and deep black eyes. Local trader Henri Desboutin hired her as a shop assistant in his lingerie and hosiery shop. Chanel sang for a while at a local music hall, La Rotonde, where she gained the name Coco, after a lost dog in a popular song of the time. She was boosted in her early career by the support of a succession of wealthy and well-connected lovers; these connections also permitted her to rise far beyond the social status usually associated with dressmakers or couturiers. Her first lover, Etienne Balsan, owned an estate in Royallieu, where she lived for several years: he subsidised her first solo business selling hats from his apartment on boulevard Malesherbes. There then followed a passionate liaison with Captain Arthur Capel, known as Boy, an English playboy and polo player. He financed her first project in the rue Cambon, the Paris street that has become synonymous with her name. A small hat shop opened in 1910, followed by a boutique in the seaside resort of Deauville in 1913, selling knit separates and dresses. Biographers agree that Boy was the big love of her life; his death in a car crash in 1919 was a devastating blow.

Her rise to fame was rapid and based on applying her own pared-down personal style to her business. That style was founded on knits and flannels, materials generally considered only appropriate for sports clothing. In later life, she liked to say her fortune was built on an old jersey jumper borrowed from Boy that she had customised by snipping through the front to create a cardigan. She borrowed ideas heavily from men's clothing, ransacking her lovers' wardrobes for inspiration, dressing her adolescent-boy physique in clothes that had been endlessly reworked to achieve the perfect fit. In her personal life, men brought her both great happiness and sadness. But in her professional life, there was no contest: magazine editor Alexander Liberman believed she learned all her sense of elegance from men.

By 1915, she had opened a fashion house in Biarritz, subsidised by Boy. A year later, she produced her first full collection, unveiled in Biarritz to immediate and widespread acclaim. It included her take on a men's sweater, with the neckline cut lower and a ribbon through the buttonholes, paired with a pleated skirt. Also included was a khaki jersey skirt suit with a jacket shape like a male army jacket. It should be remembered that this was wartime, when practical dressing was de rigueur. A year after the First World War ended, Chanel officially registered as a couturière and set up at 31 rue Cambon, where the house of Chanel is still located today. Together with Jean Patou, whose contribution has been underestimated, she brought simplicity and practicality to fashion in the 1920s. She blew away the ostentation of belle

époque fashion, producing accessible clothes that continued to borrow heavily from the working man's wardrobe. The youthful energy and vigour of Chanel's clothes chimed with the open-air sports-obsessed mood of the times.

In the early 1920s, she was the arch exponent of the garçonne or flapper look, the boyish style that dominated the decade. Her women wore sweaters, short pleated skirts with dropped waistlines and cloche hats. Boni de Castellane, a Parisian dandy, said: 'Women no longer exist. All that's left are the boys created by Chanel.' The little black dress, a reaction to Paul Poiret's orientalist colours and derived from the chemise dress, was a signature piece. Previously, black was for mourning clothes only; Chanel made it chic. Black and white, for her, created a 'perfect harmony'. In 1926, American *Vogue* made a celebrated comparison with the Ford motor car: 'Here is Ford signed Chanel—the frock that all the world will wear.' After the shock of Boy's death in 1919, Chanel dallied briefly with the Grand Duke Dmitri of Russia, picking up a penchant for all things Russian, including oversized pieces of jewellery, that fed into her collections. Perhaps more important was her friendship (and on-off romance) with Misia Sert, a well-connected society hostess with a fiery temperament to match Chanel's own mercurial personality and friends scattered throughout the art world, such as Cocteau, Picasso, Diaghilev and Stravinsky. The quick-witted Chanel adapted quickly to this milieu and the two women enjoyed a long-lasting love-hate friendship.

Her love life continued to flourish, culminating in an intense relationship with the Duke of Westminster, known to his friends as Bendor, the richest man in Britain. She admired his British tweeds, which she turned into coats for her customers, trimmed with fur for a luxurious and softer look. She even created flared trousers inspired by the sailors' bell-bottoms on Bendor's yacht. Meanwhile, he widened her social circle to include dignitaries on both sides of the channel, most notably Winston Churchill. All the riches of the world were now hers to enjoy; nothing and no one was beyond her orbit. The orphan girl had come a long way. But the Duke chose to marry elsewhere in 1930, leaving Chanel alone again. Her solution was to plough herself into her work. During the 1930s, the house of Chanel achieved new heights, with a team of some 4,000 employees and production of up to 28,000 dresses a year. A brief flirtation with Hollywood aside, Chanel was based in Paris, where she slept at her suite in the Ritz hotel and received guests in her apartment in the rue Cambon. A fierce rivalry with Elsa Schiaparelli, both personal and professional, gave a competitive edge to her work. Yet another lover, the illustrator and designer Paul Iribe, held out hope of marriage once again. However, after four years together, he died of a heart attack in 1935, collapsing right before her at their holiday home in Roquebrune in the south of France.

The advent of war with Germany in 1939 created hardship for all the Paris couturiers. Chanel's business solution was to close the couture house but to keep open the boutique, selling only her celebrated Chanel No. 5 scent and accessories. Her personal solution—finding a German lover, Hans Gunther von Dincklage, who was both a diplomat and a spy—proved an unmitigated disaster. When the war ended, Chanel was arrested, accused of treachery and forced into exile in Switzerland. For years, with her personal reputation in tatters, she mooched around Lausanne with occasional visits to Paris. Not until 1954, at the age of 70, did she astonish the Paris fashion world by announcing her comeback.

Dwindling sales of Chanel No.5 prompted the Wertheimers, the family that owned the rights to the scent, to make an extraordinary offer to Chanel. She would sell the house of Chanel to them, while they in return would pay all her bills for the rest of her life. With the deal sewn up, Chanel set about recapturing the magic of her pre-war house. The first show, staged on 5 February 1954 and attended by an adolescent Karl Lagerfeld, was not an instant success. The collection was like a 'time warp', recalled one junior American *Vogue* editor. But Bettina Ballard, then editor of French *Vogue,* felt differently. Her eye was caught by a navy blue wool-jersey suit that, she felt, summed up Chanel's style. The jacket had square shoulders and was lightly padded with patch pockets and sleeves that unbuttoned to reveal white cuffs. The Chanel suit remains one of the great creations of modern fashion. The armhole was crucial, always small and high, constantly reshaped by Chanel herself to create a close fit. This emphasised the slenderness and fragility of the wearer's shoulders and neck. Another internal detail, a gold chain sewn into the hems of the jacket, ensured that the jacket hung straight and did not ride up. The essential accessories included a hat, flesh-coloured stockings and two-toned sling-back shoes. As for jewellery, Chanel did not stint, from her trademark strings of pearls to her enjoyment in mixing both fake and real, which appears particularly modern from a twenty-first century perspective.

Within three collections, Chanel had made a spectacular comeback. The girl who came from nowhere now made the suit that every young high-society woman chose to wear. The suit was copied relentlessly in America and Europe, bringing Chanel style to a generation of women who could not afford couture prices. In her later years, Chanel became a French icon. She surrounded herself with her cabinet of young models and a close-knit circle of trusted friends and servants. Many of the celebrated Chanel maxims emerged from the 1960s, such as: 'A woman's education consists of two lessons: never to leave the house without stockings, never to go out without a hat.'

It is doubtful that the young Chanel, who broke through so many traditions back in the 1920s, would have had much time for such stipulations. But the old Chanel had come full circle, now locked in her own legend. Since her death in 1971, at the age of 88, that legend has remained intact, while the house of Chanel, driven forward by Karl Lagerfeld since 1983, has continued to flourish. Her status as an outsider may hold the key to her success. As Katell Le Bourhis, director of the Musée des Arts de la Mode et du Textile in Paris, put it: 'She had no references, no education, no upbringing, so she was free to invent her own rules of dress.'

Further reading: There is a wealth of writing on Chanel, from Edmonde Charles-Roux's early biography, *Chanel* (1976), to Alice Mackrell's *Coco Chanel* (1992) and Janet Wallach's *Chanel: Her Style and Her Life* (1998). Harold Koda and Andrew Bolton's *Chanel* (2005), the catalogue to the Chanel exhibition at the Metropolitan Museum of Art in New York, has some illuminating essays. *The Allure of Chanel,* by Paul Morand (translated by Euan Cameron in 2008), is also of interest.

8 JEAN PATOU (1880–1936)

Often overshadowed in his lifetime and beyond by his archrival Coco Chanel, French designer Jean Patou was equally influential during his heyday, which can be precisely traced from the end of the First World War in 1918 through to the Great Crash of 1929. Perhaps, like Chanel, he might have made a glorious comeback, but he died relatively young and impoverished by his great vice—gambling.

Of all his many achievements, his development of sportswear for women is perhaps the most significant. In 1921, he dressed the tennis player Suzanne Lenglen at Wimbledon in a straight white sleeveless cardigan and a short white silk pleated skirt, creating an instant sensation. This boyish, sporty look—known as the garçonne—dominated women's fashion for much of the decade, reflecting an era when women were enjoying freedom as never before, including the freedom to exercise, sunbathe and show off their legs. As with so much sportswear, many of the clothes were in reality bought by women who did not participate in sport and were more interested in showing off their Patou monogrammed cardigan sweaters to their envious friends. Patou knew this well enough, ensuring that his swimsuits, launched in the mid-1920s, included practical styles in shrink-resistant fabrics for real bathers and styles more suited for social display on the beach.

He never married but had, it appears, countless affairs and liaisons, living the life of a playboy. His perceptive biographer, Meredith Etherington-Smith, points out that Patou's boyish women contrasted curiously with his own voracious heterosexual appetites. 'Perhaps it was simply because Patou was not deeply involved with one woman that he was able to view women objectively, yet with a sympathy that enabled him, with an obvious sensitivity, to create clothes that combined the new spirit of freedom and yet appealed to men.' If there was a muse, it was his sister, Madeleine Patou, in the early post-war years, although Lenglen and other sportswomen and actresses also came to fulfill that role. Madeleine's husband, Raymond Barbas, played an equally important role on the business side, as did the socialite and publicist Elsa Maxwell in marketing the Patou name.

Patou had an unswerving eye, but he did not create his own models. As he told the photographer Baron Gayne de Meyer, 'I wouldn't know how to design. I couldn't even if I wanted to, for I can't draw, and a pair of scissors in my hands becomes a dangerous weapon.' Instead, he provided the raw materials for inspiration for his studio, edited the results ruthlessly and followed the process through every stage. Even at the final moment, when a model was ready to walk before an audience, Patou would frequently discard an outfit. This was notably the case for a *repetition generale*, technically a full dress rehearsal but in reality the name given to one of his seasonal gala fashion presentations that brought together an audience of fashion editors and the most prestigious buyers and clients. It was a foretaste of the modern fashion show, although Patou's version also included a champagne supper.

Jean Patou was born in 1880 in Normandy, the son of comfortably off parents, Charles and Jeanne Patou. Charles was a tanner, renowned for his bookbinding leathers in exquisite colours, passing on a sensibility for colour to his son. Quickly shunning the option of joining the family tanning business, Patou worked for an uncle in the fur trade before a series of stop-and-start ventures of his own culminated in the opening of Maison Parry in Paris in 1912. For two years, before the outbreak of war, he began to develop the neat sense of style that characterised his work, including the use of concealed pleating, inset godets and panels. Fashion historian Caroline Rennolds Milbank has pointed out that at this early stage he also created some of the first 'smokings'—tailor-mades with jackets fashioned after a man's dinner jacket. By the year 1914, Patou was ready to launch under his own name, encouraged by a big order from a New York retailer, but the outbreak of hostilities with Germany put an abrupt halt to his plans. The First World War saw Patou in action for five long years, fighting as far afield as Anatolia. The psychological impact of this period was immense, and Patou's brother-in-law, Raymond Barras, was convinced that it shortened Patou's life considerably. However, Patou also learned much from his wartime experience, most notably about leadership and the importance of delegation. Back in post-war Paris, ensconced at 7 rue St Florentin, he set about making up for lost time, finally founding the house that bore his name in 1919. The long-waisted shepherdess dresses of that year and equally long-waisted folkloric Russian peasant collections of 1920 and 1921 put him on the map. However, it was his step-by-step evolution of sportswear for women, borrowing extensively from men's sportswear, that was the most groundbreaking of his achievements.

By 1925, Patou had raised skirts to the knee, selling them at his new Coin des Sports shop in the rue St Florentin, managed by English society lady Phillis, Vicomtesse de Janze. At rue St Florentin, he had employed interior decorators Sue and Mare to create a total look that was sympathetic to the eighteenth-century style of the house. Design in the 1920s, the period of Art Deco, focused on the concept of a total look, with couturiers heavily influenced by artists: Patou's cubist sweaters, introduced in 1924, were only the most obvious manifestation of this trend. The total look was reflected in the Coin des Sports, where rooms were designed to present and reflect both the fashions

and the accoutrements of sports such as riding, hunting and fishing. Today, Patou's approach would be called 'lifestyle retailing'. His Jean Patou Bag of 1928 comprised a 14-piece coordinated wardrobe, with the monogram omnipresent. Careful attention was also paid to what Patou called 'les riens'—literally 'nothings'—including scarves, costume jewellery, hats and pocket books.

The sweaters of 1924 were sold with pleated skirts in matching prints and printed silk scarves, creating a style that dominated for years. Like his rival Chanel, Patou believed in clothes that were practical and straightforward, reacting to the extravagances of the late nineteenth century and of Poiret's orientalist period. In his reported comments to *Vogue* and *Harper's Bazaar,* he took the opportunity to snipe at Chanel and emphasise their differences. Edna Woolman Chase of *Vogue* recalled: 'Every time he saw her name in *Vogue,* he would compare the space given to her models with those from his own atelier.' From a modern-day perspective, however, Patou and Chanel had much in common.

Patou was slower than Chanel to make progress in America. In November 1924, all that changed when he advertised in American newspapers for three American mannequins to work in his Paris atelier for a year, sparking off a burst of media publicity. Sifting through some 500 applications, Patou rapidly decided to increase the number from three to six and went to New York to interview them in person along with senior editors from *Vogue.* One of the selected models, Lillian Farley, known as Dinarzade, recalled Patou paid closest attention to the models' ankles. 'Feet and ankles passing the test, he deigned to look at the hip or where the hips should have been. None were wanted.' The models headed across the Atlantic by ship, the *Savoie.* During the voyage, Patou became alarmed by the possibility of adverse publicity from the more patriotic elements of the French press and sent his assistant, Georges Bernard, to meet them in the pilot boat that guided the *Savoie* into harbour. They were warned to be on best behaviour and went out of their way to delight the French press. The first collection they showed, featuring 500 styles in total on twenty models, was a huge success, particularly with the American buyers.

In design terms, Patou chose the spring of 1925 to shift emphasis to the natural waistline with a hugely applauded collection of waisted dresses in rose-beige. Colour was a core component of Patou's work. Every collection had two new colours, with precise, evocative names such as dove's-neck grey or dark dahlia. The year 1927 saw the launch of his celebrated New Blue, a deep violet. But Patou's biggest moment came with his winter collection of 1929, when he abruptly altered course, lengthening skirts and creating a new silhouette. This was his princess line, with the dress flowing from a high waist rather than hip level, the hemline dropping to below the calf. Uncharacteristically nervous, he waited in his office during the presentation: his omnipresent *directeur*, Georges Bernard, soon placated him, reporting that women in the audience were already pulling at their skirts, as if they were trying to cover their knees. It was, said *Vogue,* 'the first dramatic change in dress that has occurred since the garçonne mode came in.' Also influential in this collection was his new evening look, introducing the bias-cut white satin evening dress as his riposte to the black dress ('I shall fight with all my influence to banish the much too simple little black frock from the ranks of the fashionable,' he said).

While the fashion world was enthusing over Patou's new ideas, the world was on the verge of worldwide economic catastrophe. The Great Crash of 1929 marked a shift in fashion as much as in the world's economic fortunes. Overnight, American buyers stopped travelling to Paris. Patou responded with characteristic bravado by staging an extravagant party at his home in the early 1930s with the trees in the garden lined with silver foil and three live lion cubs among the giveaways. But the mood of fashion was shifting fast and Patou (along with Chanel, Lanvin and other stars of the 1920s) abruptly found his preference for simplicity out of tune with the times. The ascendance of Schiaparelli was matched by the decline of Patou. His disastrous winter collection of 1932 was a desperate attempt to regain the initiative, creating a stodgy medieval look that focused on the hips and was roundly rejected by the market and the media. Patou was also suffering personally; he was ageing visibly and his obsession for gambling was spinning out of control. He never recovered his earlier influence and died in 1936, reportedly of an apoplectic fit. Raymond Barbas, his brother-in-law, commented, no doubt a touch simplistically: 'He died because he was worn-out. The First World War finally killed him.'

Jean Patou is better known today as a perfume house. In the 1920s, Patou developed a series of perfumes, including a trio conceived to match hair colours (Adieu, Sagesse was the scent for redheads). Sien, the first perfume for both men and women, was launched in 1929. The real breakthrough for him came a year later with the launch of Joy, conceived with Elsa Maxwell in Grasse and brilliantly marketed as 'the most expensive scent in the world'. Each bottle is reported to contain 336 roses and 10,600 jasmine flowers. After his death, the house continued under the guidance of Raymond Barbas. A series of young designers, including Marc Bohan, Karl Lagerfeld and Angelo Tarlazzi, kept the house alive for years. In the 1980s, Patou's couture operation enjoyed several years of flourishing fortunes under the inspired creative direction of Christian Lacroix, who brought a new gaiety and irreverence to the couture scene. Lacroix eventually left to set up his own label.

Has Jean Patou been properly appreciated by fashion historians? Biographer Meredith Etherington-Smith believes not, pointing out that museums tend to focus on special occasion clothes rather than the designer's everyday creations. A Patou design was so beautifully cut and fit for purpose 'that you lived in it until it wore out.'

Further reading: Meredith Etherington-Smith's biography, *Patou (*1983), is an outstanding read.

9 MADELEINE VIONNET (1876–1975)

In the fledgling years of the twentieth century, Madeleine Vionnet liberated women from the corset, inspired by the celebrated dancer Isadora Duncan, whom she never met but admired from afar. For that alone, Vionnet was an important force in the history of fashion, but there was much else besides. Her achievements overshadow her personality, for she was a reticent person compared with such contemporaries as the effusive Paul Poiret. Vionnet was reluctant to attend client fittings, locked herself away in quiet isolation in her rooms at 50 avenue Montaigne, and draped material for hours over three-foot-high rosewood dolls with articulated joints. Perhaps, if she had been less reticent, she might have made an even bigger splash. In 1973, two years before her death, a series of forty-one vintage dresses by Vionnet, displayed at the groundbreaking exhibition, Inventive Clothes: 1909–1939, stole the show at the Metropolitan Museum of Art in New York. Her inspiration was classical Greek dress, which she studied up close on ancient Greek vases in the Louvre. A plethora of modern designers continue to adore her work, applauding her ability to made fabric come alive. Japan's Issey Miyake commented: 'Vionnet's clothes are based on the dynamics of movement, and they never stray from this fundamental ideology.'

Contrary to legend, she did not invent the bias cut. This form-enhancing technique of cutting material across the grain was used before Vionnet for collars, cuffs and trimmings. Vionnet's achievement was to explore the full potential of the bias cut, creating entire dresses cut on the bias or using it for inserts or panels. Although the finished result was effortless to the eye, it was difficult to complete without the fabric puckering and bunching up. Fashion historians Caroline Evans and Minna Thornton point out that in order to meet the demands of cutting on the bias, fabrics were woven twice as wide as was then customary. The ideal fabric for her experiments was crêpe romaine or crêpe de Chine, although she also explored bias cut with velvet and even heavy tweed.

Although her skilful and original tailoring should not be overlooked, it was her talent with the draping of cloth for dresses that put her in a league of her own, much admired later in the century by designers such as Azzedine Alaia, who created a photo sequence to demonstrate exactly how he believed it was done. 'Dresses designed by Vionnet hang freely, and the technique of twisting the material gives us this unexpected draped effect,' he explained.

Born in 1876, Madeleine Vionnet was accustomed to working hard. From the age of twelve, she toiled for long days as a lacework apprentice to the wife of a neighbour in the village of Aubervilliers in the Loiret. Her family was from the Jura Mountains, but it was not much of a family, her parents separating when she was two, and her toll inspector father only too ready to put her to work at an early age. At eighteen, she was briefly and unhappily married to Emile Deyroutot, and bore one child who died in infancy. Then, at the age of just twenty, demonstrating exceptional courage and strength of character, she left both her husband and her country to move to England, where she landed a job in Dover Street, London, at the premises of Kate Reilly, who specialised in high-quality copies of Parisian designers.

These were the years of learning, although Vionnet was clearly quick at doing so, assuming responsibility for an atelier of twelve seamstresses.

By 1901 she was back in Paris, working as head seamstress at the house of Callot Soeurs, employed by the eldest sister, Madame Gerber. 'Thanks to her, I was able to produce Rolls-Royces,' Vionnet later remarked. 'Without her, I would only have made Fords.' However, it was at the house of Jacques Doucet, where Vionnet moved after five years, that she first enjoyed significant creative freedom. Doucet, who had an eye for new talent, hoped Vionnet would bring a young spirit to his house. He got more than he bargained for: a collection by Vionnet for Doucet in 1907, rippling with the spirit of Isadora Duncan (the models were both barefoot and corset-less), was not well received, either externally or internally. Vionnet did at least find an early champion in the radiantly beautiful actress Lantelme, who admired her '*deshabilles* that can be worn in public'.

Lantelme's early death robbed her of a possible muse and financial backer. Both Vionnet and Poiret claimed to have been first to ditch the corset, although Fortuny was producing his Delphos dresses in Venice in 1907 and Gustav Klimt was designing uncorseted dresses in Vienna as early as 1902 for the Flöge sisters' fashion house, as fashion historians Caroline Evans and Minna Thornton have highlighted.

By 1912, Vionnet had assiduously saved enough money to open her own house at 222 rue de Rivoli with backing from another client, Germaine Lillas. She achieved some progress until war intervened and forced her to close shop before the business was picked up again in 1918. Vionnet fast established a reputation for purity of vision and a series of immaculately conceived dresses, such as her exquisite four-pointed dress. Her core skill was in focusing intensely on a simple fabric shape such as a square, circle or triangle, building a dress with the shoulders and waistline as the natural anchoring points. In the 1970s, American conservator Betty Kirke exhaustively explored her technique and recreated many of the dresses, revealing many of Vionnet's tricks that had hitherto been somewhat of a mystery to modern designers. The dresses were also sometimes a mystery to the clients, some of whom were forced to call at the studio to be reminded as to the correct way to twist and drape the fabric.

By the early 1920s, Vionnet's work was attracting sufficient attention for her to become embroiled in a lawsuit over copyright, a perpetual issue for designers then—and now. In 1922, her business had achieved sufficient momentum for her to move to a spacious new location at 50 avenue Montaigne, where Georges de Feure was commissioned to decorate the walls with friezes that paid homage to both ancient Greece and Vionnet's own designs. Here, she had the resources to develop a fashion house that, at its peak in the 1930s, comprised twenty-six ateliers and 1,200 seamstresses. Vionnet rightly drew recognition for her responsible treatment of her seamstresses, which was well ahead of the standards of the time. The avenue Montaigne property was well lit, and the seamstresses were provided with chairs with backrests rather than stools. The young women also ate at a staff canteen and could make use of an in-house doctor's surgery. Madeleine Chapsal, her goddaughter, said: 'I never heard her use the word, yet indeed she was a feminist to the very depths of her soul.'

Through the 1920s, the house grew steadily. In 1924, Madeleine Vionnet, Inc. was founded in New York, with a boutique on Fifth Avenue and the sale of designs in one size with unfinished hems that could be altered to fit clients. Another boutique followed in 1925 back home in France in Biarritz. Besides bias-cut dresses, other innovations included the cowl collar that hung forward, sometimes known as 'the Vionnet drip', and her exploration of the scarf, considered by her to be an integral part of a look, whether draped round the neck or hips or knotted at the wrist. She also created a dress with different gradations of colour, achieved by soaking the material for varying lengths of time. On her behalf, Lesage even developed new embroidery techniques (such as the vermicelle straight grain, with each point worked to follow the warp or weft) to create embroideries that worked with bias-cut dresses. The rose was Vionnet's favoured motif, especially the American Beauty rose, which had caught her eye on a trip to the United States in 1924.

After the Great Crash of 1929, hemlines plummeted and the classical influences and sculpted forms of Vionnet's designs were appreciated more than ever. The essence of Vionnet is best summed up in the captivating black-and-white photos of Hoyningen-Huene, published in *Vogue* in November 1931, depicting house model Sonia as a dancing nymph in an ancient Greek bas-relief. The material floats as light as air, with body and dress flowing in effortless harmony. Vionnet responded to the romantic revival of the mid-1930s with a series of fuller skirts and period-style dresses, although these styles were perhaps more to the taste of Marcelle Chapsal, her closest collaborator throughout her career. Vionnet herself disliked the switches of direction that are so intrinsic to fashion. In a rare and comprehensive interview with *Marie Claire* in May 1937, she said: 'I proved myself to be an enemy of fashion. There is something fickle and superficial about the whims of each new season that offends my sense of beauty.' Instead, she said, her focus was consistent and rigorously concentrated on the four principles of 'proportion, movement, balance and precision.'

Although in later life she claimed to stand outside fashion (most interviews with her date from her retirement), detailed examination of her collections shows that she did seek to respond to the mood of the times. Madeleine Ginsburg reported that a collection in 1934 was scrapped two weeks before launch while Vionnet hurriedly responded to the more romantic mood sweeping through fashion.

Severely dressed and obsessively hard-working, Vionnet did find time for a private life. She married for the second time in 1923, although her choice of husband was ill-advised. Dimitri Netchvolodoff ('Netch'), a Russian, was extravagant and not possessed of Vionnet's own disciplined work ethic. She used to describe herself with a certain grim humour as his banker, although he did do some work, running a Vionnet-backed shoe shop at 8 rue Troyon. There were some happy times, not least at her

houses at Cely-en-Biere near Fontainebleau and 3 place Antonin Arnaud in Paris or her summer home (known as the Maison Blanche) in Bandol in the south of France where she holidayed with Netch and Marcelle Chapsal's family. But the marriage gradually disintegrated, ending in divorce in 1943.

By then, her fashion house had also closed. The final years were difficult for Vionnet after a traumatic falling-out with long-term company shareholder Theophile Bader, owner of the Galeries Lafayette. His proposal to create an in-store boutique selling copies of Vionnet and other couturiers incensed her, leading to a legal battle that Vionnet won in 1939. But Bader had simultaneously won control of the business, leading to Vionnet's decision to quit. The house went into liquidation in 1940. The donation of dresses, toiles and copyright albums to the Union Française des Arts du Costume (UFAC) in 1952 helped to ensure proper recognition of her contribution to design. Modern designers turn to Vionnet time and time again. As Betty Kirke pointed out, 'Whenever the silhouette is soft, people . . . look at Vionnet.' She lived for many decades beyond her retirement, becoming the grande dame of the couture world, always ready to dispense advice and occasionally presenting classes on sewing or bias cut. When she became bedridden, Balenciaga made for her a pink printed, silk quilted trouser-suit in which she received visitors. She died in 1975 at the age of 99. The Vionnet trademark was acquired in 1998 by the Lummen family, who sold it on to Matteo Marzotto and Gianni Castiglioni in February 2009. A retrospective at Les Arts Decoratifs museum in Paris in 2009 drew tremendous media interest.

Further reading: American Betty Kirke did much to keep the name of Vionnet in the spotlight, not least with her book *Madeleine Vionnet* (1998). Also worth reading is *Madeleine Vionnet* (1996), a biography by Jacqueline Demornex. *Women and Fashion: A New Look* (1989), by Caroline Evans and Minna Thornton, has some valuable observations.

10 ELSA SCHIAPARELLI (1890–1973)

Art met fashion head on in the form of Elsa Schiaparelli, an Italian designer who came to fashion late and proved a breath of fresh air in a world often caught up in its own high seriousness. She was a surrealist by instinct with a playful ability to change the predictable into the unpredictable. To the surrealists, one might also add the Italian futurists, whose verve, speed and joie de vivre excited the young Schiaparelli. All this energy was encapsulated in the intense pink—shocking pink—that became her hallmark. 'Bright, impossible, impudent, becoming, life-giving, like all the light and the birds and the fish in the world put together . . . a shocking colour,' she said with suitable hyperbole in an autobiography that shares some of the surreal characteristics of her design work.

Even now, her best work is startlingly, thrillingly modern. Choose from the crossword-puzzle sweaters and zippered dresses, the knitted hats and costume jewellery, the culottes and jumpsuits, the experimentation with new synthetic fabrics, and, above all, the bold way with colours. Her celebrated tear dress, made from a fabric designed by Salvador Dali, created the illusion of material that had been ripped: to modern eyes, it looks thoroughly Punk in spirit. Ignorance was bliss for this untrained fashion designer. Rules were there to break, and Schiaparelli enjoyed upsetting the bourgeoisie. 'Madame Schiaparelli trampled down everything that was commonplace,' said Yves Saint Laurent, who dressed her and adored her. She was, said her biographer Palmer White, 'a gifted bull in a china shop.' Meanwhile, her arch rival, Chanel, derided her as 'that Italian who's making clothes.'

Schiaparelli was from a conventional enough background, born in Rome in 1890, the daughter of Celestino, a Piedmontese intellectual who was in charge of Rome's historic Lincei Library. Her mother, Maria Luisa, was from an aristocratic family in Naples. She spent her childhood in Rome's Palazzo Corsini, surrounded by art and history, growing up with a surfeit of potential inspiration about her. A sensitive, shy young girl, she initially experimented with poetry and published her first book at the age of 20. The passionate subject matter shocked her father, who promptly dispatched his daughter to a convent. She in turn went on hunger strike and had to be withdrawn. In 1913, Schiaparelli visited Paris for the first time and was thrilled by the city's energy, attending a ball dressed in a hastily concocted pair of Poiret-style pantaloons. From Paris, she travelled on to England, where she had been invited to assist at an orphanage in Kent. While visiting London, she met the French-Swiss theologian Comte William de Wendt de Kerlor, to whom she was quickly married in 1914. The marriage was a disaster and did not survive a move to New York in 1919. But it was in New York that she met Gabrielle Picabia, wife of the artist Francis Picabia, and became part of an artistic circle that included Marcel Duchamp and Man Ray.

An impoverished Schiaparelli returned to Europe in 1922 with her baby daughter Yvonne (known as Gogo) and an American friend, Blanche Hays. She had no money but all the right contacts in the artistic and creative milieu of Paris. For her old friend Gabrielle Picabia, she made a gown, which drew compliments from the couturier Paul Poiret. Encouraged by this and despite her lack of expertise, she made more dresses and was further urged on by Poiret, who became both a friend and supporter. 'Display No. 1', produced in January 1927 and backed by French businessman M. Kahn, featured hand-knitted sweaters and matching crêpe de Chine skirts. The designs included sports, stripes and geometrical patterns, all clearly borrowed from the art movements of the time, including Art Deco, Cubism and Futurism. Her breakthrough was a butterfly bow trompe l'oeil sweater, knitted by an Armenian refugee using a technique that combined a white understitch on a black base. A Lord and Taylor Fifth Avenue buyer placed an order for forty copies; it was hailed by American *Vogue* as an 'artistic masterpiece'. By the following year, Schiaparelli was seriously in business and had an address to match at 4 rue de la Paix, although the premises amounted to a rambling and unprepossessing garret. The words 'Pour le Sport', inscribed below her name at the entrance, made clear where her initial focus was to be. 'Display No. 2' proved to be an inspired flow of ideas, ranging from beach costumes such as resort pyjamas (later to evolve into palazzo pyjamas) to tweed day suits. Besides the playful pieces that were already her trademark, Schiaparelli also put her energies into practical improvements, such as a swimsuit with a low back and transparent straps that allowed the shoulders to tan uniformly. The collection included beauty products and an innovative unisex perfume, named simply 'S'. Accessories, particularly scarves, caught the eye as much as clothes, with removable astrakhan and fox collars and detachable scarf collars. Her necklace scarves of 1931 were a big hit with American *Vogue,* and the tubular knitted Mad Cap of 1930 became a runaway best seller, so omnipresent that even the designer grew bored with it and withdrew it from sale.

Schiaparelli's progress was remarkably unaffected by the Great Crash of 1929 and ensuing depression. Partly, this was because she had moved away from the ultra-exclusive milieu of haute couture customers, creating clothes that were accessible to a broader market, including middle-class Americans. One by one, a series of influential women made their way to 4 rue de la Paix, including Marlene Dietrich, Greta Garbo, socialite Lady Diana Cooper, celebrated heiress Daisy Fellowes and Paris stage star Arletty. Simultaneously, the hype machine was on a roll. Although Schiaparelli described herself as shy in her autobiography, *Shocking Life*, she acknowledged that this did not extend to what she wore. In early 1930 she caused some consternation wearing a plain black crêpe de Chine evening dress that incorporated the low 'sunburn' back of 1928 and had a short jacket in contrast white crêpe de Chine with white cock's feathers. The concept of a short jacket for evening wear evolved into the Schiaparelli bolero, a long-running highlight of her collections through the 1930s. By evening, Schiaparelli's designs could be seductive, but by day she was on the defensive, borrowing freely from the male wardrobe to create daywear that came to be known as 'hard chic'. The year 1933 was important for her thanks to the success of her pagoda sleeve with its big epaulette, which led to a wide-shouldered look that dominated fashion through until Dior's New Look in 1947. At its most extreme, her Skyscraper Silhouette featured wide square shoulders and narrow hips. Toned down, the emphasis was on clean, precise lines based on rigorous cut: small wonder Balenciaga was among her greatest fans. Military uniform details ran through her collections in the immediate pre-war years.

In 1935, Schiaparelli moved to 21 place Vendôme, where she opened the pioneering Schiap Boutique and enjoyed the peak of her influence, creating fantastical collections that mixed clothing and art. Perhaps the most inspired was the Circus collection of February 1938, perversely presented at a time when Europe was lurching towards war. It was promoted with an elaborate and theatrical fashion show that set a new standard for the presentation of clothes not to be matched again until the 1960s. Her preference for creating collections around a theme also kick-started a modern trend. Her boutique was renowned for its curiosities as much as its products, including an enormous stuffed bear dyed shocking pink by Salvador Dali with drawers inserted in its stomach. By now, she had 600 employees producing 10,000 pieces a year, promoted through two major and two minor collections a year.

Her willingness to experiment with fabric is the less-appreciated story of her career. Schiaparelli worked with rayon and nylon, paper and Cellophane, even rubber and latex. In 1934, she created glass-look tunics that were fashioned from a synthetic called

Rhodophane. Even more conventional fabrics were used in unconventional ways. Tweeds were introduced to evening wear, a waterproof taffeta was explored for raincoats and cotton was passed off as linen. After her retirement, she was quick to appreciate the emerging influence of denim. Every detail required rethinking by Schiaparelli, who derided the mundane. Her buttons, for instance, were legendary. 'The most incredible things were used,' she recalled later in life. 'Animals and feathers, caricatures and paperweights, chains, locks, clips and lollipops. Some were of wood and others of plastic, but not one looked like what a button was supposed to look like.'

Although Schiaparelli breezed through the challenges of the Great Depression, the same could not be said of the Second World War. Deeply hostile to Nazi Germany and to Mussolini's fascists in her Italian homeland, she hung on in Paris for a while, producing a series of underrated but inspired collections that made the best of the shortage of materials and responded to the mood of the times for functional, practical clothes. In May 1941, on the advice of the American consul, she left Paris and spent most of the war in America, where she worked as a fund-raiser and nurse. With the end of the war, Schiaparelli hoped to pick up where she had left off, but Christian Dior's New Look swept most of the pre-war designers away. Schiaparelli's weaknesses—a tendency to overstate, a reliance on gimmicks—were exposed. A series of collections in the 1940s were politely but not enthusiastically received. The spirit of innovation was still there, such as her Constellation travel coat and bag for the new generation of air travelers, but her timing was off. Post-war women wanted escapism and a return to traditional femininity.

Only in America, a country that Schiaparelli had come to know well during prolonged residences in the early 1920s and early 1940s, did she appear to retain the same magical touch. In 1949 she opened a branch of her company at 530 Seventh Avenue, New York City, to mass-produce suits, dresses and coats. Her 'shortie' jackets, Pyramid line of coats and shocking pink lingerie were all well received. Back home in France, the business continued to bleed financially into the early 1950s. Despite this, she went on creating collections until 1954, with the continued success of her perfumes, most notably Shocking, carrying the financial burden. In retirement, she led an active peripatetic life, enjoying her home in Tunisia, until a series of strokes confined her to her home at 22 rue de Berri, Paris. Schiaparelli never married again after the disaster of her first marriage. Although she had affairs, she deliberately avoided serious attachments. Aged 83, she died in her sleep in 1973.

As an employer, Schiaparelli was demanding and sparing with compliments. That said, she paid well and inspired fierce loyalty among her staff. She also formed long-lasting professional liaisons that served her well, championing the embroidery house of Lesage and exploring new synthetic fabrics with Charles Colcombet. As for artists, there were few who did not know or collaborate with Schiaparelli, the results varying from a Salvador Dali lobster on an evening dress to a spirited Jean Cocteau sketch transformed into a Lesage embroidery. Such a symbiosis between art and fashion has never been equalled since. American curator Richard Martin called her 'a visionary [who] touched clothing with the capacity to be art.'

Schiaparelli was often frustrated by the transience of fashion. 'Dress designing . . . is to me not a profession but an art,' she wrote in her autobiography. 'I found it was a most difficult and unsatisfying art, because as soon as the dress is born it has already become a thing of the past.' Schiaparelli concluded her autobiography, published in 1954, with her 'Twelve Commandments for Women'. Commandment number five said: 'Ninety percent [of women] are afraid of being conspicuous, and of what people will say. So they buy a gray suit. They should dare to be different.' It was a philosophy that she followed herself with the utmost devotion.

Further reading: Palmer White produced a lively biography, *Elsa Schiaparelli: Empress of Paris Fashion* (1986). Schiaparelli's autobiography is entertaining, as the title, *Shocking Life* (1954), suggests. Richard Martin's *Fashion and Surrealism* (1987) is an authoritative overview with many Schiaparelli references.

11 MAINBOCHER (1890–1976)

The long life of American couturier Mainbocher spanned a remarkable period in the history of fashion, from the frothy confections of the belle époque to the ready-to-wear explosion of the 1960s and 1970s. In one sense, as a proud couturier who shunned the mass market companies of New York's Seventh Avenue, he looked backward to an era that became history during his lifetime. In another sense, the purity and refined severity of his finest creations suggest a designer who looked forward to the minimalism of the 1990s. Late in his career, when he was in his seventies, Mainbocher showed he could still lead the way with a series of pared-down dresses, including a bias-cut white crepe dinner dress, lauded and photographed by *Harper's Bazaar*. More broadly, as the first American couturier in Paris, he was an important symbol of the rising self-confidence of the American fashion industry.

If his achievement has been underappreciated, this may be connected to his reluctance to play the media game. He shunned interviews and was perceived as an aloof recluse in his later years—'the great loner,' according to *Time* magazine in 1963. The spectacular irony was that Mainbocher was himself a distinguished fashion journalist during the 1920s. Nostalgia for that period in his career did not extend to offering the hand of friendship to his former colleagues. *Vogue* editor Bettina Ballard speculated that this was all a ploy: 'He had a way of making *Vogue* feel guilty about something most of the time; so he could name his own terms when he let us take anything.' Always elegantly dressed and suave, he was a small and broad man with a serious manner and an old world sense of decorum.

'I am,' he said, 'the Rolls-Royce of the fashion trade.' The critic Dale McConathy called him 'one of the last of the great snobs—an eighteenth-century French cardinal who somehow got himself born on the West Side of Chicago.'

Countering this was his strong emotional connection with his Midwestern roots. Writer and friend Janet Flanner noted in 1940 that 'though Bocher takes pride in serving Lanson '21 champagne with dessert, he still thinks homemade banana ice cream is the ideal note on which to end a dinner party.' Mainbocher adored the women in the paintings of John Singer Sargent, admiring their individualism and sense of style. He saw a connection between the outer and the inner selves, telling *Vogue* in 1964, 'I have never known a really chic woman whose appearance was not, in large part, an outward reflection of her inner self.' Orientalist references were never part of his repertoire—he was no fan of Paul Poiret, describing his clothes as 'expensive expressions of clothing that is more of a costume than a dress.'

He was proud to be descended from French Huguenot pioneers who arrived in America in the 1640s. Main Rousseau Bocher (he contracted his name in 1929) was born in 1890 in Chicago, growing up on Monroe Street in a close-knit family with a sister, Lillian. Music was his great joy as a young man, particularly the opera, to which he remained addicted for the rest of his life. He was also skilled at drawing, which drew him to study art. The death of his father when he was in his first year at the University of Chicago forced Mainbocher to grow up quickly. In 1909, he attended the Art Students

League in New York and took his portfolio around magazines looking for illustration work. But his real goal was to go to Europe, which had an exalted status in the mind of the young man, as it did for many young Americans.

Persuading his mother to sell their house in Chicago, Mainbocher set off in 1911 for Europe, where, he said later, he was 'born again'. He studied art in Munich and travelled regularly to Paris, breathing in the music and culture of the Old World. The rococo period was a particular delight to him, a frothiness of style that as a couturier he chose to set against restrained shapes. The outbreak of war in 1914 sent him and his family heading back to America, where he made his first steps in the fashion industry, creating a dress for a friend for a charity fashion show and earning money from fashion drawings for a wholesale clothing manufacturer. By 1917, he was back in France, serving as a sergeant major in the American Expeditionary Force Intelligence Corps. In post-war Paris, Mainbocher determined to focus on music, studying voice and opera. But it was his sideline job as a sketcher for the Paris office of *Harper's Bazaar* that came to dominate, not least when Mainbocher lost his voice shortly before going on stage to sing (it took him three years to recover). His accomplished drawings and elegant writing, founded on a precise eye for detail and an innate sense of style, were highly prized attributes in the relatively new profession of fashion journalism. After three years at *Harper's Bazaar,* Mainbocher switched to *Vogue,* where he was both Paris editor and then editor of French *Vogue* over a seven-year period lasting until 1929. He was best known during these years for his discovery and encouragement of the photographer Baron Hoyningen-Huene and the illustrator Carl Erikson, known as Eric.

Many fashion journalists have attempted to make the switch to design. None has succeeded as triumphantly as Mainbocher. It was an abrupt decision, he later claimed. 'It was nothing that crept up on me . . . It was an immediate and very agreeable explosion. It came from the unconscious. The whole idea was born and in 24 hours became absolutely upright.' He bought some mannequins from the Galeries Lafayette and positioned them in the library of his Left Bank apartment. Through cutting, pinning and fitting, he taught himself the principles of couture. He also swiftly showed all the skills of the natural-born marketer, contracting his name, most likely in emulation of Augustabernard, a couturier he greatly admired. His sumptuous salon at 12 Avenue George V was filled with mirrored mantelpieces, Nymphenburg china and flowers. An aura of exclusivity was established from the beginning, although Mainbocher preferred to serve his guests iced water rather than champagne. He imposed a caution—a guarantee of purchase, priced at the cost of the cheapest dress—on all those clients who attended his show. Only a handful of magazines and newspapers, including *Vogue, Harper's Bazaar* and *The New York Times*, were allowed to cover his collections. If featured, Mainbocher dresses had to appear on facing pages, he insisted. Although he disparaged the power of the fashion magazines, their favourable coverage in the early days created a momentum that swiftly enabled him to build a successful business.

He was influenced by the refined and deceptively simple designs of Augustabernard, who was forced into retirement in 1934 by financial problems. A more celebrated influence was Madame Vionnet, whose use of the bias cut and skill with draping were closely studied by Mainbocher. Fabric, twisted and run through his hands, was the prompt for his designs, which were then sketched by an assistant. Less was more, superfluous details were ruthlessly eliminated. These frocks were so pared down they became known as 'don't dress frocks' by the press. Mainbocher's business grew rapidly on the back of four collections a year and a formidable client list including Elsie De Wolfe, Lady Mendl, considered the best-dressed woman in the world. Besides the social elite, Mainbocher was also favoured by the demi-mondaines, the mistresses who were openly flaunted in 1930s Paris. At its peak, the house employed 350 people and had sales of 100 million francs a year. His most celebrated client, the Duchess of Windsor, was, like him, an American living in Europe. For her wedding, Mainbocher designed a blue silk crepe dress with a wide inset corselet and fitted jacket—the most talked about and copied couture dress in European history, at least until the wedding of Diana, Princess of Wales. For the Duchess, he created a special blue, 'Wallis blue'— the colour of her eyes. The wedding dress, which is now in the Metropolitan Museum collection in New

York, has since faded to grey. One fashion writer, Ernestine Carter, writing in 1980, described it as 'one of the least happy of his inspirations and, unfortunately, one of the most copied.'

In 1939 the imminent threat of war spelt the end of Mainbocher's Paris period. His final collection, featuring nipped-in waists and corselets, was ill-timed but demonstrated his couturier's vision and anticipated Christian Dior's New Look by some eight years. Shortly afterwards, Mainbocher shut up shop in Paris and sailed for New York, together with his mother and sister. Profiled enthusiastically by *The New Yorker* in early 1940, Mainbocher quickly settled back into his native country. 'He has spent twenty years of his life in Europe with Europeans, but his Illinois identity has remained intact,' concluded *The New Yorker.* Thanks to a contract with the Warner Brothers Corset Company, he had the funds to reopen his house near Fifth Avenue at 6 East 57th Street, replicating the atmosphere of the salon in the Avenue George V and swiftly picking up where he had left off in Paris. The client list swelled again, including iconic society ladies such as Gloria Vanderbilt Cooper, Barbara Paley and Ceezee Guest.

Mainbocher's contribution to fashion design was precisely categorised by the couturier in later life. He loved the idea that his clients could reuse his designs time and time again. He admired clients who were individualists and perfectionists, prepared to endure his famously long fittings without complaint. Top of his list of achievements were his black evening dresses, typically short and versatile. He designed simple dresses with tie-ons, such as lace or brocade aprons or overskirts, creating a radical transformation. Belts were frequently used for simple effect. Also much admired and copied were his beaded cashmere sweaters, perfect for an evening look that mixed formal and informal in one. Furthermore, Mainbocher enjoyed experimenting with fabrics, such as batiste, voile, organdy, and pique, creating surprising juxtapositions, such as a lumber jacket in lamé or an evening dress in gingham. The versatility of his work chimed with the mood (and the regulations) of America during the early 1940s, when the country was at war. Repetition was a core theme of his repertoire. Drawing on his musical experience, Mainbocher described his design development as similar to classical musical development, where themes are restated and revisited. Critic Dale McConarthy wrote: 'For Mainbocher, there was nothing new in fashion. He possessed an extreme self-consciousness about his work that caused him to return again and again to his sources . . . He often repeated himself and glorified in the women who wore his dresses for twenty or thirty years and returned to have them copied.'

In America, Mainbocher maintained his status as a couturier and steered clear of Seventh Avenue and the ready-to-wear industry. He never licensed his name, although a fragrance called White Garden was released in 1948. While his costumes for Broadway brought his work to a larger audience, most notably for Mary Martin in *One Touch of Venus* in 1943, he showed no interest in reaching a broader market. Until her retirement in 1956, Carmel Snow, editor of *Harper's Bazaar,* was a champion of his work. In the early 1960s, Mainbocher was still a favourite of America's best-connected women, who adored his boxy suits worn with sleeveless blouses, his four-seam sheath dresses and, as always, his bias-cut evening wear that looked back to the 1930s and forward to the 1970s. He favoured simplicity over complication, decrying exaggeration in fashion (he had a particular loathing for Schiaparelli in the 1930s). 'I dislike fashions that go off in your hands like fire-crackers,' he said. Fashion editor Bettina Ballard described him as 'a sort of magic fashion mountain to climb for the woman who is sure enough of her money, her success, or her social position to wear his understated clothes.' But as the ready-to-wear sector developed through the 1960s, Mainbocher became increasingly irrelevant to the onwards march of fashion. By the time of his retirement in 1971, the years of his greatest triumphs were but distant memories.

Further reading: The definitive account of Mainbocher's life up to his return to America is 'Pioneer' (13 January 1940), an article by Janet Flanner published in *The New Yorker.* Mainbocher is also profiled by Dale McConathy in *American Fashion* (1975), edited by Sarah Tomerlin Lee, and features in Caroline Rennolds Milbank's *New York Fashion: The Evolution of American Style* (1989).

12 ADRIAN (1903–1959)

He was known simply as Adrian, enjoying a rise to success that was meteoric by any standards. He was the American costume designer who dressed Greta Garbo, Joan Crawford and a galaxy of Hollywood stars in the 1920s and 1930s, then switched to launch his own ready-to-wear fashion house in the 1940s. As chief costume designer at MGM during the golden years of Hollywood, he had a spectacular influence on a generation of American women and was copied relentlessly by the manufacturers of Seventh Avenue. Elsa Schiaparelli noted: 'What Hollywood designs today, you will be wearing tomorrow.'

Designing for films far ahead of their release put particular pressure on Adrian to think into the future. In 1938, he explained: 'With modern fashions, I get entirely away from current trends, for screen fashions must, of necessity, be designed so that they will be, dramatically, months ahead when they will be seen on the screen by the world at large.'

For all his talents, his inclusion in a roll-call of designer greats would probably have been questioned by contemporary American fashion editors. In her memoirs published in 1954, *Vogue* editor Edna Woolman Chase gave him merely one, somewhat patronising, reference: 'There was a time when, in all conscience, I had to be severe with him about his designing.' The failure to appreciate fully Adrian's important role in fashion history might be partly ascribed to a collective sneer at his origins in costume design and the vulgarity of his more fantastical designs for the Hollywood stars. Then there was the issue of his location on the West Coast, always second best for American fashion, which was (and is) driven by New York's Seventh Avenue. Finally, his greatest work was achieved during a period when the American fashion industry was still in thrall to the fashion houses

of Paris: the concept of an American designer was somewhat novel.

By the end of his life, the influence of Paris was less omnipotent, for which Adrian deserves some credit. This was the designer who faced up to Christian Dior in a much publicised public debate over Dior's New Look. That he would lose the debate was never in doubt, but he had struck a new defiant attitude for American fashion designers. Other design talents have emerged from Hollywood, including Bonnie Cashin and Irene of California. But Adrian, in the words of fashion historian Caroline Rennolds Milbank, proved that 'America could have its own style and that it didn't have to evolve from sportswear but could emanate from Hollywood, bypassing Paris altogether.'

Adrian arguably created no look or style that changed the course of fashion, but he was an influencer for millions of women, both in America and beyond. In 1930, 8 million Americans were going to the cinema each week. By 1938, *Vogue* acknowledged that Hollywood 'is certainly the most perfect visual medium of fashion propaganda that ever existed.' An outstanding example of Adrian's influence was the impact of a long dress in white organdy with extravagant ruffled sleeves, designed for the actress Joan Crawford in the film *Letty Lynton* (1932) and widely copied on Seventh Avenue. The film studio even encouraged copying by leaking details of the dress before the film had been released: Macy's was reported to have sold 50,000 copies, which was probably an exaggeration, but not by much. Adrian himself did not believe American women should try to dress in his more fanciful Hollywood creations. 'The average woman should limit herself to the costumes worn by the heroines of light comedies . . . in moderate-sized towns.' By switching from costume design to ready-to-wear in the 1940s, Adrian made explicit the connection between Hollywood and the American fashion industry that continues to this day. He was also a superb publicist and spokesman for his own brand, always immaculately dressed and ready with a quote.

His family background was ideal for a designer. He was born Adrian Adolph Greenburg in 1903 in Naugatuck, Connecticut, the son of milliners Gilbert and Helena Greenburg. Taught sewing by a Swedish nanny, he displayed exceptional early talent as a draughtsman, encouraged by his uncle Max Greenberg, a scenic designer. A place at Parsons School of Fine and Applied Art in New York beckoned by 1921, where teachers quickly agreed that his undoubted talents might be more challenged and developed in the Paris branch of Parsons. Changing his name to Adrian, he arrived in Paris in 1922 and stayed a mere four months—time enough to create a costume for a friend at the prestigious Bal Du Grand Prix and secure an invitation from Irving Berlin to design costumes for his New York revue.

That commission took Adrian back to America in double-quick time. Although Adrian's contribution in the revue turned out to be much smaller than he had hoped, it was not long before other theatre folk were taking notice of the confident young man. Natacha Rambova, the flamboyant wife of Rudolph Valentino, gave Adrian his first major break, inviting him to Hollywood to work on a Valentino film. He bought himself a white suit and a black cape lined in red satin and prepared to take the West Coast by storm. At the tender age of 24, he found himself designing costumes for Cecil B. De Mille's *The King of Kings,* a biblical epic on which no expense was spared. Adrian had arrived.

The popular new costume designer was blessed with exceptional confidence in his own abilities and a talent for charming people that made him a social hit in Hollywood. He was swiftly headhunted by Louis B. Mayer, the autocratic but perceptive boss of MGM. His first movie for Mayer was *A Woman of Affairs,* starring Greta Garbo. Right from the start, Adrian caught the eye of Seventh Avenue, too: Garbo's slouch hat and belted trench coat made the pages of American trade newspaper *Women's Wear Daily.* During Adrian's twelve-year stint working for

MGM, Hollywood emerged as an important influence on American women's style, arguably as influential as the fashion houses of Paris.

Adrian's output was extraordinary, regularly amounting to fifty or more sketches in a day. The work pace was relentless, particularly for the period epics, such as *Marie Antoinette,* which required some 4,000 costumes, including 34 for leading lady Norma Shearer. He designed virtually everything Joan Crawford wore both on and off the screen, including her signature square-shouldered suits, from 1929 until 1943. Rather like a method actor, Adrian spent time thinking his way into the period of each movie, determined to capture the essence of the era before creating his costumes. His way of working was punctilious and disciplined, aiming to fit his actresses early in the morning before they were tired out by shooting. No expense was spared, no director's fantasy left unfulfilled, from the spectacular coronation robe worn by his favourite actress, Greta Garbo, in *Queen Christina* to the bugle-beaded negligee with twenty-two inch ostrich-frond cuffs worn by Jean Harlow in *Dinner at Eight.* His futuristic costumes for Garbo in *Mata Hari* drew particular attention; perhaps only an actress of her stature could have carried them off. By contrast, he also designed Judy Garland's blue and white gingham pinafore and sequinned red shoes in *The Wizard of Oz.*

Hollywood studios worked directly with retailers for tie-in deals. At Macy's in New York, a Cinema Shop was opened where imitations of the clothes worn by actresses could be bought. For example, suits, coats and hostess gowns inspired by the film *Queen Christina* were offered for sale in 1933. Academic Anne Massey notes that sewing and knitting patterns were also created to imitate the fashions of the big screen. She points out that 'Hollywood cinema played a crucial role in creating and disseminating a streamlined *moderne* style that made a massive impact internationally.'

Adrian's lifestyle was comfortable and lavish, buoyed by a salary of $1,000 a week. He hosted lunch parties and oversaw an antiques shop on Sunset Strip. He also bought a ranch shack in the desert at Palm Springs, which he used as a retreat for painting and for visits by favoured friends who could handle the rudimentary facilities. Marriage to

Fox star Janet Gaynor completed the picture of a designer who lived life to the full. A colourful paisley print smock he designed for her pregnancy caught the attention of the media, and Seventh Avenue's copyists were not far behind.

The good times did not last. As MGM and other studios sought to impose cost controls in the late 1930s, the nothing-spared atmosphere was replaced by a more cautious attitude to film production. Garbo's last film, *Two-Faced Woman,* was also Adrian's last at MGM. Depressed by the new mood, one afternoon Adrian tore up his sketches and walked out. His next move, long nurtured and discussed with Woody Feurt, a friend with fashion industry experience, was to launch Adrian Ltd in Beverly Hills. The beginnings were not promising, with the rest of the world at war and America, after the Japanese attack on Pearl Harbour, poised to play its role, too. Struggling with the logistical and financial challenges of launching a fashion house, Adrian was obliged to show his first collection on the patio of his home. For a second collection, shown in August 1942, Adrian decided to pull out all the stops. The result was a storming success, with orders flooding in to the fledgling house. His broad-shouldered suits were applauded, and a black dress went on to become a long-term best-seller.

Adrian realised that the war, which had forced most Paris fashion houses to close their export operations, presented an opportunity for American designers. Together with the publicist Eleanor Lambert, he urged his fellow designers to take advantage. Material, particularly wool fabric, was in short supply, forcing designers to use all their ingenuity to keep the look fresh. Adrian responded to the L-85 regulations, introduced to restrict the use of materials for the fashion industry during wartime, by narrowing sleeves and introducing self-piping ties on jacket fronts to replace buttons. He mixed materials to conserve the finest for the key pieces. His broad-shouldered tailored silhouette was the wartime favourite, establishing Adrian as a household name—despite little support from the East Coast-edited fashion magazines. In 1944, he won a prestigious Coty award.

Adrian's skill with fabric was exceptional. Pola Stout's striped and geometric woven fabrics were a favourite for jackets, skirts and dresses. He enjoyed cutting the fabric into panels and resewing them in patches on jackets. He also combined similar fabrics in one look to dramatic effect. His suits often comprised long collarless jackets with a single closure at the waist worn with a straight skirt with a kick pleat. His evening dresses, perfectly draped, reflected his experience in creating show-stopping dresses for the MGM stars. His cocktail dresses and ball gowns sometimes tipped too far towards his roots in costume design, certainly way too far for the tastes of the arbiters of style at *Vogue* and *Harper's Bazaar.* Fashion historian Caroline Rennolds Milbank considered him at his best when working within the restrictions of a theme, such as for a Greek collection with columnar white dresses or for a Gothic collection with jersey dresses and trailing medieval themes. The link with the disciplines of his Hollywood career was self-evident.

After the war, Christian Dior's New Look, with its return to full skirts and restricted waists, caught a new mood. Adrian's response was to clash with Dior in a broadcast debate and to stick to his broad-shouldered look. 'I do not like padded hips,' he told *Life* magazine. 'To try and make women pad their hips in this day and age is a little like selling armour to a man.' Determined not to lose momentum, he showed his collection for the first time in New York in 1948 at the department store of Gunther-Jaeckel, prompting a buying frenzy from public and store buyers alike. What ultimately stopped Adrian was not the changing tides of fashion—uncomfortable though they were for the designer—but ill health. In early 1952, he suffered a heart attack and, after some soul-searching with his business partner Woody Feurt, decided to close the business. Thereafter, he spent much of his time with his wife and family in Brazil, where he designed a jungle hideaway. Tempted by friends back into designing costumes (for a stage musical, this time) in 1958, he was poised to re-enter the world of work again, only to suffer a second and fatal heart attack in September 1959.

Further reading: Christian Esquevin's *Adrian: Silver Screen to Custom Label* (2008) is a long overdue summary of the designer's career. In *American Fashion* (1975), edited by Sarah Tomerlin Lee, Robert Riley contributes a section on Adrian.

13 SALVATORE FERRAGAMO (1898–1960)

In the history of dress, shoes have never been accorded quite the consequence they deserve. In the drama that is fashion, shoes are quite literally accessories, supporting characters, there to facilitate the action and way down the cast list. True, in the first decade of the twenty-first century, they elbowed their way centre stage but that was probably more the result of marketing than a real shift in our perceptions. Yet, when it comes to defining gender, class and erotic intent, shoes have, through most of history, packed a bigger punch than mere clothes. It's safe to argue that nothing else people wear has been quite so thoroughly and repetitively fetishised—a factor exploited by designers and marketers at the beginning of the twenty-first century. Even so, fashion and its contemporary commentators have tended to overlook it, regarding shoemakers as artisans rather than artists or designers.

Many shoemakers have been great designers and innovators, but the first to break through those barriers of anonymity was Salvatore Ferragamo, the Italian born in respectable poverty in Bonito, near Naples, the eleventh of fourteen children, who left behind a dynasty that became a luxury goods empire. He wrote in his autobiography that he did not so much learn how to make shoes as 'remember', as if in an earlier life or many earlier lives he had already been a shoemaker. 'I was born to be a shoemaker,' he wrote. 'I know it; I have always known it. As I look back now on the long lesson of my life I can see quite clearly how strong, how remorseless, how unrelenting is the passion within me that has driven me on and on, along a path strewn with so many hardships. Many are the times when I wondered why I was not as other men . . . content with the things they possessed, hankering not after the fruits of tomorrow. Yet I could not swerve from my predestined path, no matter what the cost. It was against Nature, It was against God.'

His explanation of his unlearned skill was mystical.

> . . . but from whence does my knowledge come? It is not inherited. In later years I searched the records of my ancestors through 400 years. There was no shoemaker among them. I found many humble property owners, I found a poet, I even found an alchemist; but no shoemakers, not one. Nor have I had to learn in the accepted sense. From my first day with shoes—yes, even with the little white shoes I made for my sisters—I have remembered all about shoemaking. I have remembered: that is the only way to describe it. I have only to sit down and think, and the memory comes to me out of the days—it can only be this—when in some previous existence upon this earth, I was a shoemaker.

A lifelong experimenter with materials and structure, Ferragamo invented wedges, the rounded toe, Roman sandals, the invisible nylon shoe, the crystal-soled shoe, sculpted heels, the 'gloved' arch, shell soles and the stiletto heel (he called it the 'spike'). The political and economic exigencies of his century forced his ingenuity beyond even his fertile inclination, and he developed ways to use the unlikeliest materials in shoes of seductive beauty: crystal and cellophane, fish skin, feathers, crocheted silk, satin, embroidery and mosaics of gem-cut crystals and Venetian glass beads, mirror glass, pearls, diamonds and diamond dust, raffia and cork, wood and rubber, Bakelite and nylon thread, felt and all manner of animal skin, including antelope, kangaroo and lizard.

He was certainly a determined and driven individual, certain from his childhood what he was destined to do. His parents were poor farmers, and two of his brothers trained to be tailors but, in village society, the cobbler was 'the lowest of all the classes' and for their son to become apprenticed to him was beneath his family's dignity. 'It would bring the family into disrepute,' he recalled. It was only after he had played truant from several other apprenticeships and then, without training, sat up all night making his little sisters' First Communion shoes from canvas and cardboard (his parents were too poor to buy any for them) that they finally relented. Long before he was ten years old he had learned everything the village shoemaker could teach him. That year his father died and, in 1909 when he was eleven, Salvatore left home to go to Naples to attempt to learn more advanced skills. Moving from shoemaker to shoemaker, spending a day here, three there, he absorbed knowledge, before borrowing money from his mother's brother, a priest, and setting up as a shoemaker in his home village of Bonito. He was indeed a prodigy, not only in terms of skill and talent but also in his precocious business acumen. Rapidly he developed a good business making shoes for the local gentry. In 1912, he was persuaded to join his older brothers and sisters, all of whom had emigrated as they became old enough, in America. At fourteen he made the long sea journey alone, pausing only briefly on the East Coast to dismiss the shoe factory where his brother-in-law worked and head out West to join his brothers in Santa Barbara, where they opened a shoe-repair shop and Salvatore began his meteoric career as shoemaker to the stars—first on set and then in their private lives.

He was only twenty-four when he followed the fledgling movie business to Hollywood and took out an enormous $35,000 bank loan to open his Hollywood Boot Shop on the corner of Hollywood and Las Palmas Boulevards. Next to the shop was his workshop, and he developed a small manufacturing operation as well as employing ever increasing numbers of outworkers. Gradually he developed links with factories across the country, sold wholesale to stores throughout America and his own shop became focused on retail. He was commissioned by Cecil B. de Mille to put shoes on the feet of the actors and hordes of extras in *The Ten Commandments* and *The King of Kings* and also shod D. W. Griffith's *Way Down East* and *The White Rose* as well as James Cruze's *The Covered Wagon*.

He would research archaic costumes in the library, but there was little recorded so, once more, he 'remembered' it—very successfully. He also studied anatomy at the University of Southern California at Los Angeles. Although his creativity and inventiveness in terms of style and materials were boundless, his real quest was comfort, the secret of which he discovered through his study of anatomy. The weight of the body is borne by the arch of the foot, he learned; that is what needs supporting while the ball of the foot and the heel (the areas most shoemakers prefer to support) should float free so that the bones and muscles can move as nature intended. As a consequence, any dancer who had worn a pair of Ferragamo's shoes refused to wear any other. All Hollywood's leading ladies wore Ferragamo, from Mary Pickford to Ava Gardner, from Jean Harlow to Marilyn Monroe, from Katharine Hepburn to Audrey Hepburn.

When the machine production did not measure up to his high standards, Ferragamo decided to move back to Italy where he believed he could employ enough skilled artisans to make his shoes by hand. His return to his native land in 1927 was initially a disaster and, owing to greedy backers in America, deceitful debtors and perfidious creditors plus recalcitrant Italian shoemakers, ended in bankruptcy. Ferragamo paid all his debts, real and fictional, over the next few years, rebuilt his business and acquired the Palazzo Feroni-Spini in Florence and the Villa Il Palagio at Fiesole, on the hillside overlooking the city.

Then the larger world handed him another reversal of fortune. In 1935, Italy's fascist dictator, Benito Mussolini invaded Ethiopia, and in 1936, the League of Nations imposed sanctions on Italy, killing Ferragamo's export trade and cutting off his sources of raw materials. Ferragamo was forced to new heights of resourcefulness. Fiddling with the wrapper from a chocolate while seeking a substitute for the fine kid skins that could be painted silver or gold for evening shoes, he came up with a fine rolled transparent cellophane tube enclosing a gold or silver thread. It was strong and it was glamorous. The second invention forced upon him by necessity at this time was the 'wedgie'. He could obtain only low-grade steel at this time, and the shanks on his shoes were continuously snapping. After much thought he tried filling in the space between the heel and the ball of the foot, sculpting Sardinian cork. He then persuaded the most fashionable duchess in Florence to wear the wedge to church—and the queues formed on Monday morning.

By 1939, Ferragamo was shoemaker to most of the royalty of Europe as well as that of Hollywood. At one point, he recalled, four queens were being fitted simultaneously in his Rome salon—the queens of Yugoslavia, Greece, Spain and the Belgians. Queen Elena of Italy was a devoted customer, and he also made boots and shoes for Mussolini—thereby curing his corns and calluses—and for the dictator's wife and mistress as well as Hitler's mistress, Eva Braun. 'How was it possible,' he demanded in his autobiography, 'for a bankrupt in 1933 to own within five and a half years a great palace and a beautiful villa and, above all, to number among his clients the greatest names in the world?'

His answer was that his unique fitting system permitted 'Nature' to effect a cure of the 'crippled feet' of his clients. His theory was that many ills, from bad temper and obesity to insanity, could be traced to ill-fitting shoes. Throughout his career the style of the shoes, although an endless source of joy to him, was never as important as the structure and fit. He wrote:

> Normally I do not institute new fashions. There are a number of dress and shoe designers who struggle to be different for the sake of being different, meaning that they want to impose a startling new fashion line upon the woman but if designers must wait for their customers to become conscious of new styles who, then, determines fashion? The answer is: new fashion begins in the mind of the designer. He must not stifle all his ideas merely because the world is not yet ready for them. I have no season.

The war that broke out in 1939 meant the collapse of business as his workers were called up into the army and trade ceased. The 41-year-old Ferragamo took advantage of a period of relative inactivity to find a wife. Wanda Miletti, the daughter of the doctor and mayor of Bonito, was twenty-three years younger than he was, but it was love at first sight for both. Their six children were all to work in the family business. In 1947, on a trip to the United States to accept a Neiman-Marcus plaque for 'distinguished services to fashion' he shared the voyage with Christian Dior (of whom he had never heard). The two designers were astonished to discover that Ferragamo's shoes complemented Dior's clothes perfectly—both had instinctively been working in the same materials, colours and mood. 'I had for many years,' he reflected, 'believed that the fashion trend is not the exclusive prerogative of one designer but is "in the air"—a sort of manifestation of the world will, if I may put it like that—with the result that two men, working 400 miles apart, unknown to each other and with widely different means of inspiration (I draw my creations from my memory, while Dior prefers to find his inspiration from practical items like paintings and drawings) can arrive at similar conclusions at the same period in time.'

Further reading: Salvatore Ferragamo's autobiography (1957), *Shoemaker of Dreams,* is still an essential read. For a good historical perspective, see Stefania Ricci's *Salvatore Ferragamo: Evolving Legend 1928–2008* (2008) and for an understanding of the whole field, see Giorgio Riello and Peter McNeil's *Shoes: A History from Sandals to Sneakers* (2006).

14 MADAME ALIX GRÈS (1903–1993)

Revivals of classical dress have tended to be countercultural, a critique of a corrupt, oppressive or over-luxurious regime and an expression of a desire to return to the pure ideals of Hellenic Greece or the Rome of the Republic. Significantly, the style only became mainstream in the late eighteenth century, the time of revolutions and the setting up of new political orders, of the British regency and the French Directoire. The original clothes of antiquity were not really cut and stitched but made up of simple rectangles of fabric hung and draped around the body and secured with pins, brooches and belts. The Greek chiton or tunic was partially sewn together, but the *peplos* was folded, pinned and girdled. The *himation* was a loose wrap worn like a cloak or a poncho. Roman men dressed in a tunic and toga (the wrap-like garment), and Roman women wore a long tunic or *stola* with an overwrap called a *palla.* These were essentially simple clothes without much bulk, depending for richness on expensive dyes, embroidery and decoration. However, when the sculptors, the great (and very importantly, enduring) memorialisers of both cultures, got hold of them, they became something else. To generalise, in Greece they became ethereal, often erotic elements of the artist's composition, balancing, obscuring, revealing, emphasising human beauty; in Rome they became grandiose, plastic and imposing, insisting on their space—in short, what we have learned to call monumental (because in many eras no monument was complete without a togaed grave-faced statue).

Greece and Rome declined and died but the statues, idealised and elaborated, remained, an inspiration to artists, philosophers, politicians and dressmakers alike. Along with Paul Poiret, Mariano Fortuny and Madeleine Vionnet, Alix Grès, who had longed to train as a sculptor, loved the simplicity and purity of draped fabric softly clinging and floating around the body, unconstrained by the artificiality of corsets and padding. In 1981, Barbara Burman Baines wrote of her style, '. . . best summed up in a famous photograph taken in 1937 by Man Ray for *Harper's Bazaar:* a model in a long, white halter-neck dress, seemingly made of nothing but multifarious pleats, leans dreamily by an antique statue of winged victory attired in a long tunic of fluid folds.'

The year before, in 1936, the same magazine had written, 'Alix stands for the body Rampant, for the rounded, feminine sculptural form beneath the dress.' In Valerie Steele's judgement Grès was, along with Chanel, the most important post-war couturière. Their approaches were very different: Chanel was focused on dressing women for modern life, on 'sexual politics and social signals' as Anne Hollander put it; Grès simply wanted to create beauty using 'fabric as a fundamental artistic substance'. Grès's clothes, added Hollander, 'were solutions to abstract problems . . . beauty the overriding standard'. Like a sculptor, she worked directly with her material, leaving no sketches or pattern pieces to posterity. Patricia Mears wrote in her monograph on the couturière, 'Grès draped and manipulated fabric with great speed, dexterity and alacrity.' Sometime these dresses draped directly onto a mannequin used more than 20 metres of fabric. 'In her neoclassicism,' wrote Harold Koda, 'Grès conformed to the antique notion of uninterrupted lengths of cloth, stitched but not cut into shape. From her earliest work, Grès introduced windows on to the body with cut-outs that bared the back and midriff.'

Alix Grès was born Germaine Emilie Krebs in Paris in 1903. The secretive couturière hated her name and used two professional aliases during her career. The first, Alix Barton, was probably taken from an early employer, Julie or Juliette Barton, but Grès was content to let journalists assume it was her maiden name. However she did reveal that her family was bourgeois, her father an 'industrialist', and that one of her grandmothers was Italian and one of her grandfathers was German. She first wanted to be a dancer and then a sculptor, both of which ambitions were discouraged by her family.

Dressmaking was her default choice in that it would allow her to be creative while earning her independence. She entered her profession on the eve of an economic depression that adversely affected the business of all Paris's couturiers. The Wall Street Stock Market crash came in 1929 and Grès joined the couture house of Premet in 1930 for a three-month apprenticeship in sketching and cutting. As with much of Grès's life, the next stage is unclear. Mears quotes several conflicting versions, which include making toiles freelance, working for Julie Barton and opening a shop, adding that what seems clear is that she set up her own maison de couture, named Alix, in 1934. (One version told by Grès to Cathy Horyn of the *New York Times* was that Julie Barton renamed her own business after her more talented assistant.)

Alix Barton received much admiring press attention in the 1930s, her work featuring in magazines as often as that of Chanel, Schiaparelli, Mainbocher and Vionnet. One profile in *Harper's Bazaar* in 1938 commented, 'She is not yet 30 and she looks far more like a nun than a dressmaker.' It is noteworthy, perhaps, that Grès had already started to lie about her age. She was also a commercial success, especially in America, and attracted the attention of Paris's Bohemian elite. In 1935, Jean Cocteau and Jean Giraudoux commissioned her to design the costumes for their play, *La Guerre de Troie n'aura pas lieu* (The Trojan War Will Not Take Place). The costumes, 'whiffs of navy blue chiffon', received good press.

During the 1930s Grès did not restrict herself to Attic draperies. She also experimented with ethnic styles such as the sari or Chinese tunic, what Mears described as 'loose interpretations of "exotic" prototypes. Garments such as the "Serpent of the Nile" and the Dutch-inspired "Lowlands" ensembles were as fanciful as their names.' In the 1950s, however, she was more successful with her development of garment construction derived from traditional shapes such as the kaftan, poncho, serape and kimono.

In 1937, Alix married a Russian painter, Serge Anatolievitch Czerefkow, converting to the Russian Orthodox faith to do so. Czerefkow signed his paintings with a partial anagram of his first name, Grès, and his new wife appropriated it, becoming Alix Grès. Although their daughter, Anne, was born in 1939, Czerefkow chose to live a separate life, returning to his home in Tahiti and a string of affairs with Polynesian concubines. Alix brought up her daughter with the help of 'Muni', Anne's godmother, a former model and actress who shared Alix Grès's life for more than forty years and who has been the cause of much speculation about the couturière's true sexual orientation.

When the Nazis arrived in Paris in the spring of 1940, Grès fled, settling in a small village near the Spanish border. In exile she worked on cobbled-together mannequins made from hay, tin and wood and, because she could not visit a hairdresser, she took to covering her long hair with a turban. This was to become a signature look. Mears has pieced together what happened next. She returned to Paris in the same year to sell her 50 per cent of the business to her partner and former employer, Julie Barton, who seems to have denounced her to the Nazis as a Jew. In 1942 Lucien Lelong, head of the Chambre Syndicale de la Couture Parisienne, persuaded Grès to use the money to open a new house, Grès, on the rue de la Paix. The Nazi authorities closed the house in 1944 because of her infringement of fabric restrictions. 'I was,' she said later, 'doing the opposite of everything I was supposed to do.'

She was given permission to reopen in time to launch a legendary poke-in-the-eye collection in the *tricolore* of the French flag, red, white and blue just before the liberation of Paris. The two years that followed were tough: two harsh winters, rationing of essential goods and shortages of everything else.

The only thing that thrived was the black market. In October 1944, *Le Figaro* published a communiqué from the Chambre Syndicale: 'Prepared during a period of incredible material difficulties, these new fashion shows offering a reduced number of models, are the result of a tremendous collective effort, and demonstrate the desire of Parisian fashion houses to lead the way to a rapid recovery of the national economy.' The couturiers dressed miniature mannequins for an international touring exhibition entitled Le Théâtre de la Mode. The dolls were posed on stages designed by Christian Bérard, Jean Cocteau and Boris Kochno. For a secondary touring exhibition, the Gratitude Train, specifically created for America and concerned with historical outfits, 'Madame Grès created a gown with a high waist and draped bodice à la Grecque, from a design by Leroy, couturier to Empress Josephine, ca. 1808.' After the years of utilitarian clothes and fabric restrictions, Madame was back in business.

But it quite quickly became clear that the emphasis of Parisian couture had shifted. Although the private clients were still important, it was the sale of toiles to ready-to-wear manufacturers, especially those in America, and the granting of licences that would refuel the industry and boost France's economy. In the wake of Christian Dior's New Look, Grès adjusted her style, nipping waists, rounding shoulders, making longer, fuller skirts. She even introduced an interior corset made for her by Alice Cadolle, which allowed her to create strapless Grecian dresses which were a great success in the 1950s. Although the New Look was partially intended to promote the greater consumption of fabric, Grès's natural propensity to use it by the tens of metres was hardly appropriate for mass manufacture. She could not, however, compromise her artistic integrity.

Throughout the 1960s and 1970s Grès was to reinterpret the high-waisted neoclassical gown again and again, but she also developed more geometric shapes in stiffer, heavier fabrics which were less sensuously seductive but more imposing. What these had in common with the Grecian dresses was the way in which they proceeded from a three-dimensional sense of the body. Her fashion sense remained acute through the 1960s, when she designed op-art dresses and flower-power gowns for rich hippies, and the 1970s, when she was able to exploit fashion's nostalgia for the 1930s with updated versions of her own best pieces.

In 1979, she did relent on her refusal to create a ready-to-wear collection, but it lasted only two seasons. Two years earlier she had told Marian McEvoy of *Women's Wear Daily*, 'Couture always gives the ideas to prêt-à-porter. The prêt-à-porter designers are always influenced by the couturiers. I feel that prêt-à-porter has indeed given the woman in the street a better, neater appearance, but couture is the creative key. It is a grand work—it is truth—couture brings something to the world.'

Grès continued to design couture clothes of great beauty which kept pace with fashion and modern concerns (she developed less formal daywear and youthful leisurewear) but failing to make a go of her ready-to-wear line was only one of her mistakes. She was, says Mears, too influenced by Muni and by an employee named Mufthah, whose decisions embroiled her in legal actions that lasted years. Gradually, the press coverage grew less and less as the perception of her significance waned.

Grès did, however, become active in the politics of the industry, succeeding Lucien Lelong as president of the Chambre Syndicale in 1972. In 1983 she sold a controlling interest in her house, which eventually became wholly owned by the Japanese company Yagi Tsusho. Alix Grès retired after presenting her spring 1988 collection. She settled in her second home in Saint Paul de Vence with her daughter, Anne, who later moved her mother to an inexpensive nursing home in the Var, where she died in 1993, penniless. Anne hid her mother's death for more than a year. Mears concluded that the daughter, described as immature, simply wanted her famous mother all to herself at last.

In 1998 Hubert de Givenchy, who had befriended Grès in her declining years, acquired Alix Grès's personal collection, 300 dresses, he wrote in the introduction to *The Givenchy Style* in 1998, 'beautiful enough to go mad over.'

Further reading: Patricia Mears's *Madame Grès: Sphinx of Fashion* (2007) is the definitive read.

PART 3

1940s–1950s

Introduction

This period in fashion can be looked upon as elitism's last hurrah. At its start couture was dominant, spawning myriad watered-down copies; at its end mass-produced ready-to-wear, specifically designed for the young, was where innovation was happening, and a new breed of art-school trained designers was poised to make its mark. The Second World War naturally imposed stagnation; materials and labour were needed for other, more pressing purposes, clothing was rationed and fashion, for most people, became an irrelevant frivolity. In France, however, frivolity became an act of defiance, and Paris couture, so important not just in terms of exports but also as a symbol of French identity, fought hard to stay alive and functioning. Before the fall of France in 1940, the couturiers who had been called into the army were given two weeks' leave to design and make their collections before returning to the front. At the spring collections the Americans placed a huge number of orders. With the occupation of Paris its couturiers could no longer export to most of their usual markets: many moved to Vichy France; Charles Creed moved back to London, Mainbocher and *Charles James* abandoned Europe entirely to return to New York, and others, led by Lucien Lelong, chairman of the Chambre Syndicale de la Couture Parisienne, began the long struggle against the Nazis' efforts to relocate the industry to Berlin or Vienna.

The couturiers of London and New York now eclipsed those of Paris. The Incorporated Society of London Fashion Designers (ISLFD) was led by Molyneux and included Norman Hartnell, Elspeth Champcommunal at Worth, Digby Morton, Peter Russell, Bianca Mosca, Victor Stiebel and Hardy Amies—who doubled as a Secret Service agent. In compliance with the Utility Clothing Scheme introduced by the British government in 1942, the ISLFD created austerity couture—clothes that were functional, warm and skimpy. In America couture was led by the Hollywood designers Adrian and Omar Kiam, as well as *Charles James.* Norman Norell showed his first collection in 1940, and *Claire McCardell* seized her moment, removing shoulder pads and redirecting fashion towards comfort and ease of movement, becoming the most celebrated exponent of the first truly American style of dress, the mass-manufactured genre of designer sportswear. In her wake, *Rudi Gernreich* further developed the deconstructed, athletic, natural body shape that epitomised the relaxed, outdoors lifestyle of his adopted California.

At the end of the war the French government made it a priority to re-establish the country's pre-eminence in fashion. Coco Chanel, in disgrace because of her liaison with a German officer, was in exile in Switzerland but *Balenciaga,* Grès, Schiaparelli, Lelong, Fath and Balmain were back in Paris. However, it was *Christian Dior* who made modernity redundant when, in 1947, he introduced the New Look based on belle époque styles. Retrograde as it was, the New Look and its celebration of the hourglass-shaped female body captured the mood of men and women in the aftermath of a devastating war. The men returning from the battle front had witnessed things many could never bear to speak of. They needed the comfort of conventional relationships, they needed their jobs back from the women who had been enlisted to replace them—and they needed children to replace the depleted populations.

The resulting baby-boom generation fuelled economies in which there were jobs for all, particularly in a burgeoning media and a democratised fashion industry. The ultra-femininity of their mothers' clothes was replaced by an ethos based on the simplicity of children's and men's clothes. Couture, with its high-priced, labour-intensive clothes, was under threat from a ready-to-wear, factory-produced, throwaway culture that wanted something new and cheap every Saturday. The youthquake movement spawned the miniskirt, which sprang from the mods on the streets of London to the imaginations of *Mary Quant* in London and *Pierre Cardin* and *André Courrèges* in Paris. Couturiers such as Chanel, Schiaparelli and *Hubert de Givenchy* scurried to keep up, introducing boutique lines and moving into prêt-à-porter. The scene was set for a massive paradigm shift.

15 CRISTOBAL BALENCIAGA (1895–1972)

Balenciaga is without doubt the designer's designer, the most frequently credited by other designers as inspirational, the man even Chanel grudgingly admired (the only male couturier thus honoured) and Christian Dior graciously acknowledged as his master. This serious, shy and retiring Spaniard was a technical genius, the architect of cloth, conjuring flattering, dramatic shapes. He was also the most remarkable of far-sighted innovators, capable of sensing shifts in society's mood. His pre-war collections prefigured Dior's post-war New Look, and after the war he resisted Dior's retrospective fantasy and worked towards a crisp, pure-lined modernity. Cecil Beaton, who in 1954 casually referred to Balenciaga as 'the greatest dressmaker of today', also wrote: 'If Dior is the Watteau of dressmaking—full of nuances, chic, delicate and timely—then Balenciaga is fashion's Picasso. For like that painter, underneath all his experiments with the modern, Balenciaga has a deep respect for tradition and a pure classic line. All artists who, apart from their unique personal gift, are also mediums transmitting the message of the art of the past, inevitably are timely as well as timeless.'

Colin McDowell, in *McDowell's Directory,* asserts, 'He is unquestionably the greatest designer of the twentieth century', and Francois Boudot does not hesitate to write in awestruck hyperbole about Balenciaga as an artist. 'You may have thought you were looking at a Zurburan, a Velazquez or a Goya, but it was always Balenciaga. Discouraging imitators, he created his aloof garments in an atmosphere of secrecy and calm for a small and elite number of wealthy beauties who saw him as a cult figure.' As his self-appointed acolyte and life-long friend, Hubert de Givenchy was to say in 2006, 'Balenciaga was like his clothes, perfection. He is still my god.'

Cristobal Balenciaga Eisaguirre was born in 1895 in Guetaria, a small Basque fishing village. His father, the captain of a pleasure boat, died while Cristobal was still a child and his mother, Martina Eisaguirre, supported her three children by working as a seamstress, an activity for which her younger son developed a passion. The story goes that this untypical boy was forward enough to admire the Drecoll *tailleur* worn to church by an ageing local aristocrat, the Marquesa de Casa Torres. Her interest piqued, the Marquesa discovered that the thirteen-year-old's ambition was to be a couturier. She gave him a length of expensive fabric and the Drecoll suit to copy. Balenciaga described how petrified and yet how elated he was. He found the courage to cut into the cloth and, whatever the quality of the resulting outfit, the Marquesa was gracious enough to wear it. She became his first patron, arranging his apprenticeship with a tailor in San Sebastian.

In 1919, Balenciaga opened his own atelier, Eisa, in the town which was becoming the favoured resort of the Spanish royal family and its court. He established a Madrid branch in 1932 and one in Barcelona in 1938, employing members of his extended family to run them. His workroom staff were trained to high standards of traditional craftsmanship, and he visited Paris regularly as a buyer, attending shows and buying toiles, which he then translated for his own customers. Lesley Ellis Miller emphasises one other background factor that contributed to Balenciaga's unique and uniquely rigorous approach to fashion. 'His appreciation of art was similarly formed. In all parts of Spain, painting and sculpture are accessible to everyone in the churches and in the streets—as well as in art galleries and museums. Immense baroque churches dwarf the tiniest villages, and their interiors often contain elaborate chapels and overpowering altarpieces.'

Balenciaga was a devout man, and the church and its grandly modelled spaces, its monumental images, its sculpted draperies, and its lavishly painted, richly caparisoned saints would have lodged themselves securely in his receptive visual imagination—a semiotic language to be used in his search for an imposing beauty infused with dignity and meaning.

His colour sense, however, was simultaneously subtle (his range of greys, browns and blacks was a focus of press wonder) and bold, in their depth and richness often reminiscent of late Renaissance or baroque religious paintings. He would hazard unusual colour combinations that worked in a most spectacular way: ginger and bottle green, greige and granite, black and brown, honey beige on black.

Balenciaga moved to Paris in 1937 establishing a couture business on avenue George-V with two partners, one with Basque connections. Some commentators have suggested that he was escaping the dangers and uncertainties of the Spanish Civil War (both Madrid and Barcelona were under siege from 1935, and San Sebastian fell to Franco's forces in 1936), but it is likely that Balenciaga intuited the economic stagnation and isolation—and consequent poverty—that would follow a Franco victory. He tried London first but could not get a work permit and took the advice of Madge Garland, the fashion journalist and later educator, that he would be better received in Paris.

He was by no means in exile—he was able to run his business in Spain from 1940 on—but, as he told Prudence Glynn of the *Times* in an interview conducted in 1971 after his retirement, 'Paris used to have a special ambience for fashion because it contained hundreds of dedicated craftsmen making buttons and flowers and feathers and all the trimmings of luxe which could be found nowhere else.'

He stayed open through the war, supporting Lucien Lelong, head of the Chambre Syndicale de la Couture Parisienne, when the Nazis attempted to move the French couture industry to Berlin or Vienna, standing up to 'six enormous Germans' with the suggestion that '[Hitler] might just as well take all the bulls to Berlin and try to train bullfighters there.'

Although his circle of friends included the artists Braque, Chagall, Picasso, Miro and Palazuelo, he did not collect their work. Bettina Ballard, editor of *Vogue*, described his preferred decor as 'simple, almost austere', the atmosphere of the couture house as 'convent-like'. Photographs of his Spanish country home in Igueldo, however, show the dark carvings of traditional Spanish furnishings and religious antiquities.

After the war the French government concentrated on reviving the couture, levying a tax on all exports so that the Chambre Syndicale de la Couture Parisienne and its members could afford to mount the shows that would bring back the customers from around the world. Its reasons were only partially economic; Paris was couture and couture was Paris. The restoration of couture was essential for the restoration of a humiliated nation's self-respect. In the absence of Chanel, whose wartime collaboration with the enemy meant a necessary self-banishment to Switzerland, it soon became clear that two giants were to bestride fashion's next decade, Christian Dior and Cristobal Balenciaga. They were very different giants.

As Claire Wilcox wrote in 2007, 'Dior, an intuitive man, developed an extraordinary sensitivity to the climate of the day. Although shy and nervous of his own innovations, he moved quickly . . . The fanfare with which his first collection was met on February 12, 1947, set the designer on an upward spiralling path upon which innovation was vital in order to maintain media interest.' Part of that innovation was commercial—the necessity of ready-to-wear collections and licences. 'Balenciaga, in contrast,' wrote Wilcox, 'was resistant to the idea of producing luxury ready-to-wear on the grounds that only haute couture, to which he was totally dedicated, could meet his own exacting standards. He was a traditional man who built his work gradually, developing his ideas over two or three years.'

Gustav Zumsteg, the Swiss textile manufacturer, relates in the catalogue to the 1985 *Hommage à Balenciaga* exhibition in Lyon, that Balenciaga often repeated to him that a good couturier had to be an architect, a sculptor, a painter, a musician and a philosopher, all in one person. Otherwise he would be unable to deal with the different problems of planning, form, colour, harmony and proportion. In fact, Balenciaga, in his white coat and in the hushed, monastic atmosphere he preferred, must have been the ultimate nightmarish controlling boss. He involved himself in every stage of the process from first sketch and choosing, cutting and pinning the fabric through fitting, sewing, re-fitting, unpicking, remaking to meet his exacting standards of perfection, choosing accessories and supervising every last detail down to choosing and drilling the mannequins for the fashion show. Prue Glynn's interview reveals that his staff referred to him as 'the Master'.

His method, a subtle progression over his three decades of dominating couture, was a gradual refinement, paring away extraneous detail to achieve the impact of a pure line and a breathtakingly simple sculptural shape that cocooned the body as lightly as a whisper—however structured they might look. 'Balenciaga's clothes are the most extraordinary things,' reflected Hubert de Givenchy in 2006. 'He designed clothes that moved around a woman's body, caressing it . . . A dress of Balenciaga moves like the wind.'

Although his daywear always aimed for ease, his evening wear was the most glamorous, the most lavish and the most imposingly Spanish in Paris, often relying on some serious under-structure for its grand-entrance effect. But the battle for the headlines was then, as it is now, won in the trenches of chic daywear. Balenciaga did not name his collections for a new look as Dior did, but the fashion press identified new shapes and proportions as they evolved. In 1947, when the New Look was claiming column inches, Balenciaga's sac or

barrel-line jacket, slightly bloused to the hip, was preferred by many fashion editors to Dior's fitted jacket with its corseted nipped-in waist. Balenciaga gradually developed the cocoon jacket (1947), the box jacket (1949), the middy line (1951), the tunic line (1955), the sack or chemise (1957) and the empire line (1958).

However 1947 was difficult for him. His nephew, Agustin Medina Balenciaga, described Balenciaga's reaction when many of his clients deserted him for Dior.

> At the beginning of his career and during the war, he was not only designing but interacting with everyone socially as much as possible. He had a strict sense of what was right or wrong and felt betrayed if someone left him for another designer. He was dismayed when many long-time clients rushed to the house of Dior after the success of the New Look in 1947. From then on he became more selective as to whom he would trust. Ultimately he would concentrate on his work and not care about the opinions of a larger social group. However if one was fortunate enough to be included in the circle around him, one enjoyed a real intimacy with him, and his friends took pleasure in his sly sense of humour and irony.

And there are elements of his work that are undeniably playful. His architect's fondness for geometric forms, for apparently hard-edged curves and spheres, was reminiscent of an Eastern approach to dress where clothing does not cling to the body but rather cocoons it, frames it, floats around it. This was to inspire Cardin and Courrèges. In 1958, Balenciaga received the Légion d'Honneur, France's highest award, for his services to the fashion industry. In 1968, ready for a relaxed retirement, he closed his couture house, allegedly reflecting, 'It's a dog's life.' He died in Spain in 1972.

In a memoir for the Balenciaga retrospective exhibition in Texas in 2006, Hubert de Givenchy wrote: 'He would say, "Hubert, you must be honest with your customer. Do not try to do something that is only amusing. Be serious in your work. Be conscientious. If you use flowers, then place the flowers in an intellectual manner. Do not place flowers just to add to the drape or cut, if it does not make sense." A funny saying he had was, "Don't try to make *mouton* [sheep] with five legs! That is what another designer would do, just to surprise the press or the customer; not you. It is more important to be conscientious and always aware." '

Further reading: Lesley Ellis Miller's *Balenciaga* (2007) and *Balenciaga Paris*, edited by Pamela Golbin (2006), are the two most comprehensive and analytical books on the designer. Cecil Beaton, in *The Glass of Fashion* (1989), is an amusing read.

16 CHRISTIAN DIOR (1905–1957)

Christian Dior's Bar suit, the one with the white jacket nipped at the waist with a stiff peplum standing proud of the full, long black skirt with the archaically padded hips and worn with a white straw hat, is without doubt the most memorable image from all of twentieth-century fashion. Long after Dior's death, his was the name universally used as a short form for hugely desirable, hugely elitist couture fashion. Cecil Beaton named him 'King Pins and Needles' and 'the last of the great couturiers' and quoted him thus, 'Nothing is ever invented. You always start from something. It is certainly Molyneux's style that has most influenced me.'

Edward Molyneux (1894–1974) was a superb tailor whose refined style made him very successful between the wars. A cultivated man, he also designed for film, and it is generally acknowledged that his wonderfully romantic designs for 1933's *The Barretts of Wimpole Street* (the love story of the Victorian poets Elizabeth Barrett and Robert Browning), inspired by Winterhalter's sensuous contemporary portraits, remained in Dior's wistful imagination, a nostalgic dream awaiting its moment of realisation.

That moment came in 1947 in the dreary aftermath of the Second World War as Europe struggled to rebuild a civilisation that had been devastated economically, socially and morally. The New Look's extraordinary power was not derived from anything as simple as the fact that women were sick of short skirts made from rationed fabric and the square shoulders that went with wearing uniforms and endlessly recycling threadbare pre-war clothes. That was part of it. Nor was it just because the financial backer of Dior's house was Marcel Boussac, a fabric manufacturer who needed his factories back on full-time production. Nor even that France needed those factories producing, the workers working, the fashion industry back on its feet and exports beginning to grow again. All that mattered. Indeed, the French government was taxing all exports to subsidise the couture industry in its efforts to re-establish itself. But what was much more important was that everyone was so tired. Traumatised by six years of a terrible war, men and women alike succumbed to a general atavistic yearning to return to a safer time of economic security, social order and moral certainties.

Men were returning from the battlefields and re-entering civilian life only to find women doing their jobs and reluctant to relinquish them. Women had tasted independence, economic power, a degree of sexual freedom and the liberating camaraderie of the workplace, and they liked these things. Restoring the natural order required women out of the workplace and back in the kitchen, the bedroom and, as soon as ever possible, the nursery. Populations were drastically depleted, and the morale of nations depended on an investment in the future—in short, babies.

The exaggerated, Victorian-inspired New Look of 1947, with its crinoline skirts, corseted waists and softly sloped shoulders, was essentially the hourglass configuration of the fertility goddess who recurs throughout history. It was almost a caricature of femininity, but it was exactly what the moment required and Dior was the man who instinctively realised this. So can we blame the birth-rate bulge that produced the baby-boomer generation on Christian Dior? He certainly dressed the women who had the babies and, for a decade after, until his early death in 1957, continued to do so.

He wrote in his 1956 memoir, *Christian Dior et Moi,*

> In December 1946 . . . women still looked and dressed like Amazons. But I designed clothes for flower-like women, clothes with rounded shoulders, full feminine busts and willowy waists above enormous spreading skirts. Such a fragile air can be achieved only by solid construction. In order to satisfy my love of architecture and clear-cut design, I had to employ a technique quite different from the methods then in use. I wanted my dresses to be constructed like buildings, moulded to the curves of the female form, stylising its shape. I emphasised the width of the hips, and gave the bust its true prominence; and in order to give my models more 'presence', I revived the old tradition of cambric or taffeta linings.

He also used horsehair padding in his interlinings and directed his less curvaceous models to invest in a pair of 'falsies'.

Christian Dior was born in Granville, a fishing port and shipbuilding town on the Normandy coast that had turned itself into a smart resort. His father was wealthy, the owner of a flourishing business manufacturing agricultural fertilisers, which he and his partner expanded into other products, such as detergents. His mother was a talented gardener and that passion was to form an exceptional bond between her and her second son. When Christian was six his family moved to Paris, keeping the villa in Granville as a holiday home. It was here at carnival time that Christian learned to sew, helping the maids make up the costumes he designed for himself and his friends. His maternal grandmother, erudite, opinionated and fond of soothsayers and fortune-tellers, was also a strong influence on the boy.

This was the belle époque, a time of rococo furnishings and voluptuous women and, in Europe, a prolonged time of peace and prosperity which was to be terminated by the Great War in 1914. In his memoirs Dior described an idyllic childhood. 'I picture it now,' he wrote, 'as a happy, jaunty, peaceful time when all we thought about was enjoying life. We were carefree in the belief that no harm threatened the wealth and lifestyle of the rich or the simple, thrifty existence of the poor. To us the future would bring nothing but even greater benefits for all. Whatever life might have bestowed upon me since, nothing can rival my memories of those sweet years.' Doubtless those memories helped inform the New Look.

When he finished school, he wished to attend art school, but his father, a respectable bourgeois to his fingertips, demurred. Instead he sent his son to the École des Sciences Politiques in Paris in an attempt to satisfy his mother's desire to have a diplomat in the family. Nevertheless, Christian was drawn to the Left Bank haunts of the bohemian, arty crowd which included Christian Bérard, Jean Cocteau, Raoul Dufy, Giorgio de Chirico, Maurice Sachs—and failed his exams. After a painful scene his father agreed to fund an art gallery for Christian, but before it could come about he lost his fortune to a series of bad investments and the promise came to nothing. Christian lived in poverty, then, staying with friends, applying in a desultory manner to job advertisements, drifting rather aimlessly and developing tuberculosis. Convalescing in the South of France, he learned to weave and began to consider the possibility of a career in design. On his return to Paris he began to sell drawings to design houses and to *Le Figaro* until, in 1938, Robert Piguet employed him as a design assistant. In 1939, as Germany prepared to invade France, Dior was called up into the Army. After the collapse of France, he returned to Paris in 1941 and took a job at Lucien Lelong alongside the young Pierre Balmain.

In 1946, the textile magnate, Marcel Boussac, offered to back Dior in his own couture house. Dior dithered until his clairvoyant reassured him, and in February 1947, after an underground public relations campaign to build up anticipation, the 42-year-old showed his first collection. He called it the Corolle Line. The American press, headed by Carmel Snow of *Harper's Bazaar,* dubbed it 'The New Look'. Ernestine Carter, fashion writer for the *Sunday Times,* was there. 'The model girls entered the salon, their tiny hats by Maud et Nano tipped to one side, held on by veils caught under the chin, or else simply defying the laws of gravity. As Chanel had invented a stance, Dior invented a walk, perilously back-tilted, which added to the arrogance with which they pirouetted in their calf-grazing, voluminous skirts (one contained eighty yards of fabric). It was not only the length (a foot or more from the ground) that excited; it was the contrast of the discipline of the fitted bodices with their tiny wasp waists and the billowing grace of the full skirts, the softly curved shoulders and the nonchalant back-dipping, open collars.'

She described the consternation that broke out in the front row. 'To English journalists in their sharp-shouldered (a legacy from Schiaparelli frozen by the war), skimpy fabric-rationed suits, this softness and fullness was, as one journalist put it, "positively voluptuous". All round the salon the overseas press could be seen tugging at their skirts, trying vainly to inch them over their knees. The models, pushing, as Dior wrote," detachment to the point of insolence", swirled on contemptuously, their heavy skirts bowling over the standing ashtrays like ninepins.'

Alison Settle, covering the show for *The Observer,* was not seduced. 'What sort of clothes are these for today's active and restless life?' Edna Woolman Chase, editor-in-chief of *Vogue,* was restrained in her praise, 'His clothes,' she wrote, 'give women a feeling of being elegantly costumed.' The clue was in that last word. Christian Dior, finally his own master, had reverted to his first love, fancy dress costume. And by no means did everyone buy into the fantasy.

It was a time still of shortages and rationing and, famously, the first women brave enough to go out in the street with those dangerous skirts were beaten up by a furious crowd of impoverished working women queuing to buy food. For the Parisian couture industry, however, Dior's amazing coup was a magic potion. Cut off from Europe by the war, the American fashion industry had been forced to cultivate home-grown designers and not only had they done a good job but the American consumer had developed a loyalty to the new labels—based only partially on patriotism. However, thanks to Dior, February 1947 put Paris back in fashion's driving seat and back in the US market.

Over the next decade Dior was cannily to introduce a new 'look' every season, whetting his public's appetite and oiling the wheels of the international industry. Corolle was followed by Envol, Ailee, Verticale, Oblique and Muguet in a marketing masterstroke that accelerated the speed of fashion's imperative changes. In 1953, he shortened his skirts to 40 cm off

the ground. He called it the Vivante look; journalists preferred the 'Shock Look'. In 1954 he introduced his H Line, nicknamed 'The French Bean Line' or the 'Flat Look'. In 1949 he became the first couturier to licence his products. He took the collection on tour to America, playing to adoring audiences in major cities. Consequently, during the 1950s the house of Dior was responsible for 50 per cent of the couture exports to the United States. Thanks to licences and a shrewd understanding of how to exploit the brand through scent, accessories, stockings, furs, gifts and tableware, the house and Dior himself became immensely rich—and a grateful nation bestowed upon him every honour in its gift.

Writing about Dior at this time Cecil Beaton described him as looking like 'a bland country curate made out of pink marzipan . . . His egglike head may sway from side to side but it will never be turned by success.' Beaton and many other contemporaries have suggested that Dior's only true passions were for the good life in general and gardening and good food in particular. Writing in 1960, Phyllis Heathcote of *The Guardian,* who had also been there for that first presentation of the New Look, wrote:

> Christian Dior was a dear. In the world of high fashion (which is as tough as they come) you do not meet many personalities for whom you can imagine for a moment having any feeling of affection. Dior was the exception. He was kindly and simple and friendly and even after years and years of such spoiling and flattery as the world of fashion has rarely seen, utterly unspoiled. He stayed as sweet as he was.

Dior died of a heart attack in 1957, having made it clear that he intended his young assistant, Yves Saint Laurent, to succeed him. Diana Vreeland, in conversation with Colin McDowell many years later, reflected on Dior's gluttony, asserting, 'Poor Christian. He died for the table.' The black organza pall that covered his coffin was sewn with sprigs of lily-of-the-valley, his favourite flower.

Further reading: Nigel Cawthorne's *The New Look: The Dior Revolution* (1996), Colin McDowell's *Forties Fashion and the New Look* (1997) and Claire Wilcox's *The Golden Age of Couture: Paris and London 1947–57* (2007) all place the man in his context.

17 CHARLES JAMES (1906–1978)

Opinion is divided on Charles James. Balenciaga once called him the 'greatest designer of them all,' and Christian Dior described his designs for grand gowns, often draped directly on to the body, as 'poetry'. Later generations of designers, including Yves Saint Laurent, Thierry Mugler and Azzedine Alaia, have claimed him as muse and inspiration, the great 'lost' couturier who died friendless, penniless and forgotten in New York's Chelsea Hotel in 1978. And yet the fashion historian and distinguished head of the Costume Institute at the Metropolitan Museum of Art in New York, Richard Martin, remained not quite convinced. In his *Fashion Memoir* series book on Charles James he wrote,

> The term 'genius' is often used to describe James, and he certainly possessed the explosive temperament often associated with the word. But his achievement is, in truth, less than that of a genius. He compromised his 1930s elegance with his work in the 1940s and 1950s, and his pictorial imagination came to surpass his design innovation. So he was probably not a genius, but he was surely close enough to being one that we can still look at his dresses with a combination of awe and the more modest respect. TS Eliot has said that April mixes 'memory and desire'. In fashion no one mingles them more persuasively than Charles James.

Caroline Rennolds Milbank, in *Couture: the Great Designers*, brackets him with Balenciaga, Capucci, Cardin and Courrèges in one of her smallest and most interesting categories, 'the Architects', and concedes him the position of 'foremost among America's couturiers'. His reputation rests on the grand gowns he constructed from the 1930s onward, gowns which imposed an hourglass, fertility-goddess shape on the least curvaceous or pneumatic of figures and which prefigured Christian Dior's New Look by a decade at least. He seemed to take his inspiration from the last years of the nineteenth century and used similar methods, piling horsehair padding on top of layers of canvas, stiffened tulle and crinoline-style boning and anchoring bodice and waist with heavy-duty corsetry. The whole, however, was so brilliantly engineered, so well balanced that, although it might weigh between 15 and 30 pounds (half a kilo to more than a kilo), it felt light as a feather on the body and as comfortable. James enhanced the illusion of youthful lightness with ethereal layers of the finest, most fluttery chiffon, or satin or taffeta draped and sculpted into ruched effects, often making the bodice in a contrasting colour to the massive skirt so that the (artificial) slenderness of the tiny torso was emphasised and eroticised like a stamen offering itself from the heart of a rose or a concupiscent orchid. Milbank quotes him on what fashion meant to him: 'what is rare, correctly proportioned and, though utterly discreet, libidinous.'

Richard Martin connects this imperative to create garments that focus the observer's erotic interest to James's early career as a milliner. While a hat must frame or in some other way complement and draw attention to the face, it must also work with the proportion of the whole body, something which was often neglected in hat shops where women were waited on at dressing tables. In an obituary on the designer in the *Soho Weekly News* in 1978, photographer Bill Cunningham quoted James's belief in the dress as a sublime couture creation dependent upon the 'dialogue between the client and dressmaker' which, said James, 'no fashion world would exist without.' Martin doubted there was, in fact, very much dialogue between James and his clients. 'He was,' he wrote, 'chiefly the creator of his own vision of woman as muse, an image which differentiated little from one client to another.'

Charles Wilson Brega James was born in Camberley, Surrey, near London, in 1906 into an upper-class family. His father was an army officer and his mother, Louise Enders Brega, was from Chicago. Described as 'temperamental and artistic', Charles was sent to Harrow, one of Britain's top public schools, where his circle of friends included Evelyn Waugh and Cecil Beaton, who was to be a lifelong friend. James was expelled from school in 1922 for some heinous but undefined misdemeanour and sent by his sorely tried parents to Chicago to work in the architectural design department of a utilities company. Neither this job nor the one that followed on a Chicago newspaper, the *Herald Examiner*, lasted long, and in 1926, using the surname of a school friend, he opened a hat shop on north State Street. Two other small shops followed before, in 1928, he moved to New York where he opened another hat shop in a carriage house once rented by Noel Coward. At this point he began to design dresses as well.

In 1930 James returned to Britain and established a couture house on Bruton Street under the name E. Haweis James. Ernest and Haweis were, Milbank points out, his father's two middle names. She does not speculate but, given what is known of James's spiteful and pusillanimous nature, one has to wonder whether his intention was to provoke the military man who sired him. James identified himself not as a couturier but, in the kind of pretentiousness that marked his character, as a 'sartorial structural architect'. This establishment went bankrupt almost immediately, and James quickly started up again in premises down the street. Georgina Howell identified Charles James's first appearance in British *Vogue* in 1932. There's a photograph of a conservative-looking but softly contoured little suit and a caption that reads: 'A 12-guinea spring suit in marine blue facecloth. Raglan-sleeved top

gathered on to a belt and the neck twisted with a spotted scarf.' In 1934 there was another financial crisis, and his mother stepped in to underwrite a fashion show in the Wedgwood Room at Marshall Field & Co in Chicago. He showed his collection for the first time in Paris in 1937, and over the next few years he showed collections in London and Paris leading *Vogue* to refer to him as 'that itinerant designer'.

He was selling designs to several of America's most important stores, including Marshall Field, Bergdorf Goodman, Lord & Taylor and Best & Co, so the ground was prepared when, in 1940, he abandoned Europe (Paris was occupied by the Nazis and London was suffering the Blitz) and returned to New York and opened Charles James Inc. on East 57 Street. He was contracted to design couture for Elizabeth Arden's 'Fashion Floor', a relationship that ended in 1945 after he had shown twenty-five gowns at a Red Cross benefit evening for the opening of Arden's new store. He opened another house under his own name on Madison Avenue and, in 1947, made a brief, triumphant return to Paris to show his collection there, his lush gowns completely in step with Dior's New Look. 'His eye for colour,' wrote Annette Bissonette who curated an exhibition of James's work at Kent State University in 2007, 'resulted in unexpected combinations, in which pumpkin and mauve coexisted, linings added drama, and layers of tulle in many colours produced mysterious results. His ability to drape cloth, at times directly on a person, was at the heart of some of his most important work. Yet his legacy in the twenty-first century lies overwhelmingly in his ability to cut the cloth to produce abstract and complex shapes brought to life through experimentation and imagination.'

Despite the turmoil in his business life and despite the way he treated his clients, he retained some very important ones. Among them were Austine (Mrs William Randolph) Hearst, Mrs Harrison Whitney, Dominique de Menil, and Anne, Countess of Rosse as well as the wives of two rival designers, Mrs Lucien Lelong and Adrian's wife, Janet Gaynor, and powers in publishing such as Claire Booth Luce, Mrs Condé Nast, Elsa Peretti, Carmel Snow, Diana Vreeland and those two feuding couturières, Elsa Schiaparelli and Coco Chanel. You can almost hear the chuckle as Milbank points out that Schiaparelli got a bill but Chanel did not. Richard Martin wrote, 'He offended some of his most loyal clients, who longed for the designer's dresses and paid dearly for them, not only in money but in tolerating insults and abuse.' One of James's best customers was the beautiful, magenta-haired Standard Oil heiress, Millicent Rogers, whose extravagance, according to Cecil Beaton, outstripped that of all the other 'poor little rich girls'. He considered that her talents did too and in *The Glass of Fashion* pronounced them squandered. During one period in the 1930s, however, she patronised Charles James exclusively. Beaton wrote,

> Charles James is a superb tailor in satin and has affinities with the French in his master craftsmanship and attention to detail. He was naturally delighted that her orders should be so extensive, for it kept his business thriving. But after having put so much time and effort into the making of four dozen blouses which he felt were designated for the Manhattan Storage, he rebelled. When Mrs Rogers's maid telephoned for a further order, Charles James complained, 'Why, Mrs Rogers is nothing but a hoarder!'

> The maid replied, 'Not a hoarder, Mr James, a collector!' True to the maid's words, in 1949 Millicent Rogers presented to the Brooklyn Museum a collection of clothes created for her by Charles James.

In 1948 the Brooklyn Museum had mounted a retrospective exhibition entitled Decade of Design to display the dresses. It is upon these clothes that much of James's rescued reputation rests and why costume historians know so much about how he achieved the structure of his gowns. He named many of his designs—Petal, Swan, Tulip, Butterfly, Four-Leaf Clover, Tree—in a system that had more to do with an abstract shape, a curve or a plane, summoned at some remove by the object than anything representational. His most famous dress was probably the Sirene, where soft silk is wrapped, draped and gathered round a slender, rigid inner sheath. He, however, regarded the Four-Leaf Clover gown of 1953 as the culmination of his career.

The grand gowns James conjured were imagined in great rooms with high ceilings and classical decoration. In 1948, for a photograph entitled 'The James Encyclopaedia', Beaton, who shared his background, grouped nine of them in just such a salon, its decor pale cream carved panelling in the Second Empire style. The ladies, their bare shoulders and elegant, vulnerable necks glowing in the soft, pinkish light, their vast skirts jostling for space, are taking coffee while they wait for the gentlemen, still around the dining table passing the port and smoking, to join them. It is a pre-war world which the nostalgic yearned to return to and the socially upwardly mobile longed to enter. It may have appealed to Beaton, but Annette Bissonette wrote, 'Like those he inspired, such as Christian Dior . . . he generated garments that, although visually intoxicating, returned women to an era of discomfort and subjugation. His talents were nonetheless widely sought and his custom-work for clients and collaboration with manufacturers led to new silhouettes that had enormous impact on the fashion industry.'

In 1955, James, who was known to be homosexual and rumoured to go dancing in his own frocks, astonished everyone by marrying Nancy Lee Gregory, with whom he had two children. In 1956 he started to design children's wear, but in 1958 he found himself bankrupt once again. The marriage failed in 1961, and by 1964 James had moved into the Chelsea Hotel where he established a small studio. He attracted few clients; his reputation for falling out, failing to deliver and reneging on deals was, by now, poisonous. He did, however, make the acquaintance of the illustrator, Antonio Lopez, who, over the next few years made it his private project to draw the best of James's designs. In 1975 he held a solo exhibition at the Everson Museum of Art in Syracuse. New York. Three years later Charles James died of pneumonia in the Chelsea Hotel. He was alone. In 1980 the Brooklyn Museum mounted a second larger retrospective.

Further reading: Richard Martin's *Charles James*, part of the Fashion Memoir series, is a good analytical account of James's career and character, and Caroline Rennolds Milbank's account in *Couture: The Great Fashion Designers* (1985) places James in context.

18 CLAIRE MCCARDELL (1905–1958)

Impatient for a modern style of dress that reflected in both practical and conceptual ways the way women wanted to live and dress in the twentieth century, Claire McCardell invented it. Her ideas have so influenced and pervaded contemporary fashion that in 1990 *Life* magazine named her one of the 100 most important Americans of the twentieth century. Four years later, Bernadine Morris of the *New York Times* referred to her as 'this country's finest designer'. A quintessentially American designer often compared to Frank Lloyd Wright, Raymond Loewy and Martha Graham, Claire McCardell's democratic approach to fashion gave style to everyday clothing and led the way towards shaking off the long-distance, often vitiated, French dominance of American fashion—Richard Martin even characterised it as a 'thralldom to Parisian design'.

In her book, *What Shall I Wear,* published in 1956, McCardell looked back on her early days in the 1920s on Seventh Avenue. 'I did what everybody else did,' she wrote, 'copied Paris.' In particular she copied Molyneux, Maggy Rouff and Alix (not yet known as Madame Grès) and took apart the dresses of Alix and Vionnet to discover their structure—a structure she simplified for the mass-manufacturing techniques with which she worked. But her instincts could never be satisfied by second-hand inspiration. McCardell was a questioner of basic precepts, a revolutionary. 'Clothes,' she told one interviewer, 'ought to be useful and comfortable. I've always wondered why women's clothes had to be delicate—why they couldn't be practical and sturdy as well as feminine.' She co-opted easy styles and hard-wearing fabrics from all kinds of work wear and children's wear and made them smart: suits in denim, big-pocketed shirts in ticking or cotton calico, loose dresses and jumpsuits in gingham, madras check and flannel. Her guiding principles were clean-lined, utilitarian design that satisfied the modernist dictum that form should follow function, that a product should be fit for its purpose, and that one should have respect for the fabric. She produced instant classics which were to form the basis of the fashion genre known as American designer sportswear and within which she had many successors. Richard Martin wrote:

> Significantly, they re-thought fashion from its very roots, not simply paring away some of the accretions of traditional prettiness but founding a new standard for a practical, modern style more in accord with the lives of the women of their era. Furthermore the chief impetus came from women designers, not from men. The sportswear tradition in America includes male manufacturers and a few early-generation pioneers such as Sydney Wragge and later John Weitz, but the driving force of fashion's fresh invention resides with the women who answered women's needs.

It is a long roll-call; among these women were Elizabeth Hawes, Anne Fogarty, Muriel King, Emily Wilkens, Tina Leser, Frances Sider, Carolyn Schnurer, Jo Copeland, Bonnie Cashin, Ceil Chapman, Louella Ballerino, Vera Maxwell, Mollie Parnis, Clare Potter, Nettie Rosenstein, Pauline Trigere and Valentina. In the 1930s and 1940s, as American women made their way into the workplace in ever greater numbers, enjoyed an active social life often based on a sporting activity—golf, tennis, cycling, swimming—and demanded affordable, mass-produced clothes to look good in at all these times, these were the designers who, also living that life, answered their needs. Of them all, however, McCardell was the most creative, the leader in what was really a whole paradigm shift in fashion.

Claire McCardell was born in 1905 in Frederick, Maryland. She was the first child of Adrian Leroy McCardell, a state senator and president of the Frederick County National Bank, and Eleanore Clingan McCardell, daughter of a Confederate officer from Jackson, Mississippi. Three brothers followed, Adrian, Robert and John. Claire's first exposure to fashion was through her Southern belle mother who subscribed to all the American and European fashion periodicals. A school friend remembered five-year-old Claire cutting out pictures from the magazines and, with her scissors, remaking them, grafting a bodice from one on to the skirt of another, changing a neckline, editing out some sleeves. This was the point at which, McCardell remembered half a century later, 'my eyes began their training'. She would also, of course, dress up in her mother's clothes and reflected as an adult, 'It wasn't me in the clothes, or just wearing them that interested me—it was the clothes in relation to me—how *changed* I felt once in them.' Perhaps her most powerful influence was Annie Koogle, the family dressmaker who was a skilled adapter of Vogue patterns, often draping and fitting on the body. From her, McCardell learned to understand clothing's relationship to the body and its construction. A sporting girl, she was soon taking apart and remaking her clothing and that of her brothers in not always successful attempts to make herself more comfortable clothes for an active life. However, this intimate knowledge of men's clothing was to shape her approach to designing for women. She found men's wear infinitely more rational than contemporary women's clothing and was to filch for women generous side pockets in trousers, deeper armholes in jackets, sturdy topstitching borrowed from Levi's jeans, and practical, washable fabrics like cotton shirting.

In 1923, with graduation from Frederick High School approaching, McCardell announced her intention to study fashion illustration and costume design in New York. Her father would not hear of it and she spent the next two years studying home economics at Hood College, a liberal arts college conveniently close to the McCardell home. She dropped out towards the end of her second year and, with the support of her mother, convinced her father to let her go to New York to study at the School of Fine and Applied Arts which would, in time, become the Parsons School of Design. In her foundation year she shared a room with two other students at the Three Arts Club. To her delight the wealthy members would sell the students in residence their cast-off Paris originals—for a few dollars. She bought as many as she could afford and took them apart to discover their construction before remaking them. This was a practice she continued in her second year when she finally got to study fashion design and construction in Paris, arriving there in the autumn of 1926. Madeleine Vionnet, whose training as a lingerie designer gave her an intimate understanding of the sensuous possibilities of cloth on the female body, was a particularly strong influence on McCardell, who began at an early stage to explore several of her techniques including the bias cut and the sashes used for wrapping and tying. From Vionnet, McCardell said she learned 'the way clothes worked, the way they felt'.

Back in America McCardell graduated in the spring of 1928 and had a few false starts, including some modelling engagements and a short stint designing knitwear, which ended when she was fired after eight months for making clothes 'to please herself'. Yohannan and Nolf point out that this very tendency was to be the basis of her success and her status as a major fashion innovator. In 1965, *Time* magazine quoted her saying she had designed things she needed for herself, and 'it just turns out that other people need them too.'

She next went to work as design assistant to Robert Turk, an independent dressmaker, and, when his business was absorbed two years later into Townley Frocks, a mid-market Seventh Avenue dress and sportswear manufacturer owned by Henry Geiss, she went with him. In 1932 Turk drowned in a boating accident and Geiss allowed 27-year-old McCardell to complete the autumn collection—which she did successfully. Appointed chief designer, she adopted the habit of all contemporary American designers and travelled to Paris (and beyond) twice a year to copy current ideas. McCardell was not disposed to copy Paris couturiers but did find inspiration in Europe—sometimes from portraits in museums, sometimes from folkloric dress—as when she adapted the Austrian dirndl skirt for the American market. On a different trip she bought mounds of coloured glass beads in a Hungarian flea market and piled them on to both her own simple dresses and those in the showroom.

During the 1930s she began to develop the themes she would perfect in the 1940s. Valerie Steele listed some of these 'McCardellisms' or design innovations in her introduction to Yohannan and Nolf's monograph on the designer, '. . . her signature metal fastenings (such as brass hooks and eyes), double rows of top-stitching, spaghetti string ties, long sashes, wrap and tie separates and menswear details.' She also toyed with ideas for mix-and-match separates, the use of heavy tie silk for dresses and menswear tweeds and worsted suiting for women's coats, her deep 'wasp-waist' belts in elasticised leather and her buckle fastening borrowed from contemporary cold-weather sports gear.

In the autumn of 1938 McCardell designed her first successful original silhouette, the Monastic, a dartless, waistless, bias-cut, tent-style dress that could be worn with or without a belt. It sold out over and over again and was so widely copied that Geiss found his attention and fortune almost fully occupied suing copyists. Exhausted and impoverished, Geiss closed Townley Frocks in 1938. McCardell was immediately invited to work for Hattie Carnegie (already employing Norman Norell and Travis Banton) whose business was essentially copying and cannibalising Parisian styles. Although the job did not work out well, through it McCardell met Diana Vreeland (then at *Harper's Bazaar*) who was to become a lifelong friend and supporter. At this time she also met the man she was eventually to marry, Irving Drought Harris, a handsome Texan architect on the brink of divorce and not at all what McCardell's father would have had in mind for her.

In 1940 Townley Frocks reopened headed by Adolph Klein, a young imaginative manager who believed in McCardell's talent enough to invite her back, give her control over design and credit her on the label. This was the first marriage of cutting-edge design and mass production, and it birthed a new genre of clothing. It is possible that American designer sportswear would have taken a lot longer to establish itself without the Second World War which denied American manufacturers the opportunity to continue to plagiarise French designs. Thrown back on its own resources, however, Seventh Avenue eventually rallied and gave its designers their head. McCardell led the way, exploring the possibilities of the fine cottons produced in the Southern states and usually used for children's clothes, men's shirts and pyjamas and various household purposes. In 1942 she introduced the Popover, a wrap-around, unstructured, utilitarian denim dress to be worn over smarter clothes. This was a response to a request by *Harper's Bazaar* on behalf of women whose domestic help had left for wartime factory work. The Popover evolved in later collections into dresses, coats, beach wraps and hostess dresses.

In 1941 she showed her first Kitchen Dinner Dress, a cotton shirtwaist with a full skirt and matching apron for working women who liked to cook but did not want to look like a homebody housewife. Leather for shoes was heavily rationed, so McCardell promoted the ballet slipper as street wear, often covered in coordinating or matching fabrics to her clothes. A certain austerity in dress was appropriate for wartime, but as it drew to a close, McCardell understood the need for both femininity, prefiguring the New Look, and some lightheartedness, developing her sportswear and leisurewear and adding many new items to women's wardrobes, including braless halter styles, the hooded sweater, jersey leotards, shorts, bathing suits (including the famous Diaper) and playsuits.

In the late 1940s and through the 1950s McCardell's name, propagated by the doyenne of publicists, Eleanor Lambert, dominated American fashion. She died of cancer in 1958

Further reading: Claire McCardell; Redefining Modernism (1998), by Kohle Yohannan and Nancy Nolf, is comprehensive, and Richard Martin's *American Ingenuity: Sportswear 1930s–1970s*, the catalogue to the New York Metropolitan Museum of Art's 1998 exhibition, is excellent for context and detailed illustration.

19 HUBERT DE GIVENCHY (1927–)

The first 'Little Black Dress' (LBD) was probably Chanel's; when she introduced it in 1926, *Vogue* compared it to the Model T Ford (which you could famously get in any colour as long as it was black) and predicted that it would 'become the sort of uniform for women of taste'. Balenciaga focused on it, refined it, sculpted it to become the byword for chic and social comfort that it is. But the iconic LBD is, without a doubt, Givenchy's. It is the one Audrey Hepburn wore in *Breakfast at Tiffany's*. The conundrum for fashion writers is whether Hepburn recognised Givenchy's wonderfully well-bred, modern and unfussy style as a major force in fashion and wisely used it to cement her own image or whether the fact that a generation of women made her their role model precipitated her couturier and friend to an essentially unearned stardom. Certainly Hepburn's gamine look and breastless, hipless body was the one young women in the late 1950s and 1960s craved for their own. And certainly many critics of fashion have argued that Givenchy was no innovator. But, as Caroline Rennolds Milbank wrote in 1985,

> The originality is there, but always under complete control; never could one of his dresses or ensembles be termed loud, overbearing or offensive. For over 30 years, Givenchy, the perfect gentleman, has dressed a clientele ranging in age from debutante to dowager in a style that has been young and mock-elegant, pure and sculptural, refreshingly ladylike as well as addictive. His clients are women for whom elegance is not an end in itself, but merely the way they do everything. For them, Givenchy is a last bastion of quality.

The clue, in a way, lies in the word, clientele. Although he created a ready-to-wear line in 1968, Givenchy was essentially a couturier, truly focused on making couture clothes for real (rich) women. While sacrificing nothing of quality or refinement (he is a demanding perfectionist to his fingertips), he modernised their wardrobe, introducing separates in 1955 and, a little later, easy-care synthetics such as Orlon. He thought of it as a youthful update of a classic way of dressing. Unlike some other couturiers working at this time, he allowed for the modern woman's busy, multifaceted, working life; his easy dresses, suits and coats were adored by women such as the Duchess of Windsor, Jacqueline Kennedy Onassis, Maria Callas, Greta Garbo, Princess Grace of Monaco, Gloria Guinness, Bunny Mellon and Capucine. When the assassinated President John F. Kennedy was buried at Arlington National Cemetery in 1963, all the Kennedy women were wearing Givenchy, their mourning black flown in specially from Paris. It is said that at that time the Givenchy atelier possessed individual pattern sheets for every female member of the Kennedy family. In many ways Hubert de Givenchy, the discreet aristocrat, was nearer to the great events of a wider world than any other fashion designer before or since.

He is an immensely cultivated man, comfortable at the highest levels of any society, an expert on art, furniture, architecture and, perhaps his greatest passion, gardens, of which he has made many—including leading the restoration of the kitchen garden at Versailles. He is a man of great integrity, incapable of a self-aggrandising cheap trick of any sort. 'I persist,' he said, 'in not understanding flashy elaborations whose sole purpose, in my opinion, is to shock.' He has always been dismissive of mere notoriety, mere success, saying, 'For those concerned about quality, prestige is what counts.

Success is not prestige; prestige alone is what endures after you've gone.'

The relationship with Hepburn was at the centre of his professional life. Theirs was a stylistic partnership made in heaven. In 1953 she had been cast in her second major film, *Sabrina,* with William Holden and Humphrey Bogart, and the director, Billy Wilder, sent her to Paris to pick up some chic clothes appropriate for the transformed chauffeur's daughter. Hepburn's first choice had been Balenciaga, but he was too busy preparing his collection and could not see her. Givenchy was her second choice. He assumed the actress coming to choose clothes for a film was Katharine Hepburn. He hid his disappointment. He too was in the throes of creating a collection and unable to design anything specifically for her. Undeterred, Hepburn rummaged through previous collections hanging in the workroom and found the pieces she wanted. The Paramount costume designer Edith Head was credited with them on the film, and at the premiere an embarrassed Hepburn promised Givenchy she would make it up to him. She did—by wearing his clothes in her private life from then on and insisting that only he could design her wardrobe for *Funny Face* (1957), *Love in the Afternoon* (1957), *Breakfast at Tiffany's* (1961), *Charade* (1963), *Paris When It Sizzles* (1964) and *How to Steal a Million* (1966). 'His are the only clothes in which I am myself,' she said in 1956. 'He is far more than a couturier, he is a creator of personality.'

The two earliest films in which she wore Givenchy focus on the transformative power of clothes and were a gift to a couturier. 'In film after film,' wrote Givenchy in 1998, 'Audrey wore clothes with such talent and flair that she created a style, which in turn had a major impact on fashion. Her chic, her youth, her bearing and her silhouette grew ever more celebrated, enveloping me in a kind of aura or radiance that I could never have hoped for.'

Hubert James Taffin de Givenchy was born in 1927 in Beauvais, the younger son of the Marquis de Givenchy, who died of influenza in 1930. Hubert and his older brother, Jean-Claude, were brought up by their mother, Béatrice, and her mother, the widow of the artist, Jules Badin, who had studied with Corot and was artistic director of the historic Gobelin

and Beauvais tapestry factories. In fact, Hubert de Givenchy's maternal ancestors were a creative dynasty, involved in designing for the Beauvais factory and for the theatre. His grandmother cultivated his early taste for beautiful things. 'When I was a schoolboy,' Givenchy wrote in *The Givenchy Style* in 1998, 'my grandmother rewarded me for good grades by showing her treasures—whole cabinets filled with every kind of fabric, all of which left me utterly dazzled. Could I have sensed that one day fabrics in the hundreds and thousands of metres would pass through my hands?

'During those many years of couture collections, there were always fabrics which I liked more than others. The allure, the odour of silk, the feel of a velvet, the crackle of a "duchess" satin—what intoxication! How truly wonderful! The colours, the sheen of a faille, the iridescent side of a shot taffeta, the strength of a brocade, the caress of a velvet panel—what bliss! What extraordinary sensuality!' Throughout his career, Givenchy remained enchanted by fabric; he often worked closely with the textile factories to create unique textures, colours and effects.

At ten years old, he was taken to visit the Pavillon d'Elégance at the 1937 Paris Exposition, and he decided that he wanted to work in fashion. He attended college in Beauvais and moved to Paris to study at the École des Beaux Arts. He desperately wanted to train in the atelier of his great hero, Cristobal Balenciaga, but it was not to be. The seventeen-year-old's approaches were rebuffed, and it was to be many years before they met. In 1944, thanks to family contacts, Givenchy got a job with Jacques Fath, working at the couture house—a convivial place peopled by giggling mannequins and the generosity of spirit of Jacques and Genevieve Fath—in the mornings and going to class in the afternoons. On the recommendation of Christian Bérard he left Fath in 1946 to take a job with Robert Piguet, an altogether more sober establishment, leaving after a year to join Lucien Lelong. His stay at Lelong was even shorter, a mere six months before, on the recommendation of René Caron, he moved on to a covetable post as first assistant to Elsa Schiaparelli and director of her place Vendôme boutique. There he designed bright separates—often using up pre-war surrealist prints—that were much admired by Schiaparelli's urban sophisticates. By anyone's standards, it was a meteoric progress.

In 1952, at just twenty-five years old, Givenchy opened his own design house near the Parc Monceau in Paris. He named his well-received first collection, shown on plaster mannequins because live ones were too expensive, after Bettina Graziani, Paris's top model who was handling his publicity. The collection was made chiefly in inexpensive white cotton shirting fabric and featured the Bettina blouse with bell-like bishop sleeves ruffled in white and black broderie anglaise. It was very widely copied (and even had a twenty-first century reprise) and established his name in America as well as Europe. He teamed it with a narrow, nutmeg-coloured skirt or a wide, black dirndl and flat shoes, sometimes woven from straw. Dior still dominated Paris couture and Givenchy was seen as the young challenger, his style marked by the insouiance of the simple fabrics and a youthful cleanliness of line that was to become his signature. 'I've dreamt,' he said, 'of a liberated woman who will no longer be swathed in fabric, armour-plated. All my lines are styles for quick and fluid movement. My dresses are real dresses, ultra-light, free of padding and corseting, garments that will float on a body delivered from bondage.' The boutique that he quickly opened on the ground floor of his building was inspired by his time at Schiaparelli and allowed his clients to mix and match his easy separates in a truly innovative way.

In 1953, in New York at a party, he finally met Balenciaga, an encounter that was to lead to a long friendship and have a lasting effect on Givenchy's life and work. 'By then my house had already been established,' he wrote. 'Nevertheless, that first encounter with M. Balenciaga, a man I had admired since my youth, left me in a state of shock. His influence on my work was immense, and yet I realised I still had everything to learn. I had to acknowledge that, fundamentally, I knew very little about my profession.' He could not go back to apprentice himself, but Balenciaga did take on the role of teacher, allowing Givenchy to preview his own collections. 'He taught me it isn't necessary to put a button where it doesn't belong, or to add a flower to make a dress beautiful. It is beautiful of itself,' said Givenchy. The two most important principles imparted by Balenciaga and adhered to all of Givenchy's career were, 'Never cheat' and 'Never work against the fabric, which has a life of its own'.

Gradually, the acolyte and the mentor became linked in the minds of press and public. In 1956 they both banned the press from their shows until after the buyers had placed their orders unaffected by the opinion of any fashion editor. As a result their clothes would be reviewed, together, a month later. As Givenchy's style matured it fell into step with Balenciaga's, growing ever simpler and more sculptural. Both designers introduced the chemise or sack dress in 1955 and the sheath in 1957. Where Givenchy departed from Balenciaga was in his love of colour—buttercup yellow, electric blue, peppery red, singing purples and pinks. There is often, too, in his work, a sweet, flirtatious playfulness, something of which Balenciaga was never accused. Givenchy introduced the 'baby doll' look in 1958, collarless jackets, asymmetric dresses and, in 1967, light-hearted shorts ensembles, his riposte to the vulgarity of the micro-mini.

When Balenciaga retired in 1968 he sent most of his clients across the road to Givenchy. In that same year, as the youthquake eclipsed couture, the ready-to-wear line, Givenchy Nouvelle Boutique, was launched, perfectly catching the mood of the times with leopard-print trouser suits and denim pieces top-stitched in orange.

In 1981, while remaining in creative control, Givenchy sold his fashion house to the Louis Vuitton Moët Hennessey group. Showered with many awards at home and abroad, Givenchy was made a Chevalier de la Légion d'Honneur in 1983. In 1991 the Musée Galliera de la Mode et du Costume mounted a huge retrospective exhibition entitled Forty Years of Creation. He retired at the end of 1995 (but remained active as chairman of the World Monuments Fund for France and president of Christie's France) and a series of high-profile young designers has kept the house in the headlines.

Further reading: The Givenchy Style (1998) by Francoise Mohrt has a charming introduction by Hubert de Givenchy.

20 PIERRE CARDIN (1922–)

Asked in 2006 to define himself in one word, Pierre Cardin replied, 'as a sculptor.' Although coming from a fashion designer that might sound hubristic, there is justice in his claim. His style, which we call futuristic because so much of it seems inspired by 1950s modernism, by the romance of the space race and by images from sci-fi pulp magazines, was in fact the consequence of applying a bold abstractionism to the human body. Three-dimensional, plastic, his designs have always had a sculptural quality, a clean profile, occasionally a sense of monumentality and a hierarchical presence. He gave the world the bubble dress, the cocoon coat, the trapezoidal cut, enormous circular collars and sharp-edged asymmetric cuts that, along with materials like vinyl, Perspex and mouldable 'Cardine', proclaimed themselves the high-tech future. Long before he became the first designer to identify China as an emerging market, his design handwriting owed something to Chinese theatre and traditional dress in its love of geometry, illusion and drama.

The adjective most frequently applied to this designer, mega-entrepreneur and French academician, however, is egotistical. The clothes—witty, insouciant, very sexy—deceive you into expecting a sense of humour. The designer who, to celebrate his Chinese coup, gave his men's suits flicked-up 'pagoda' shoulders would surely be a giggle, but in person any levity is hard to find. In an interview he does not wait for the questions but leads with the assertion that his is the biggest fashion name of all time, circling back to that statement repeatedly to make sure one hasn't missed the point. Brenda Polan, who has interviewed him twice at length, is not the only journalist to be disappointed by his querulous demands for acknowledgement.

'I am a self-made man,' he told her in 1989. 'I was the youngest man in fashion in the world, the youngest to have a great, great success. In the beginning people thought I was eccentric. It was hard. From 1950 to 1958 I had to persevere. I needed great confidence. The difference between then and now is that success then came because you were creative, now it is because you are commercial. I was both. I was two personalities—something very unusual in fashion.'

'Cardin is hugely unreliable,' wrote Richard Morais in 1991. 'Cardin is a flake. A man who couldn't manage his way across a room let alone run a multinational corporation. And yet Cardin is a phenomenal success.' Allegedly, Cardin still does the company accounts himself in school exercise books and while guesstimates of what the business (composed of twenty-four separate companies, including Maxim's de Paris) is worth are in the billions of euros, no one knows for sure. And although he has talked of selling the business and encourages rumours of impending retirement, he is still working.

In the 1989 interview with Polan, he said, 'Fashion is my first love and last pleasure. In my theatre, in my restaurant, my hotel, I have a team but in fashion I do everything from A to Z. It is the reason I continue so strongly. I do not want to disappoint. I must get the headlines, project the name for the stores, the customers who buy my clothes. Remember, my first show was in 1950. It's very hard to stay so long on the front page. I am like a railway engine driver; all the wagons follow me.' He has been a great innovator and moderniser in so many ways and on so many levels, a powerful influence on the course of fashion and its global dissemination in the twentieth century.

In October 2008, at a sprightly eighty-six, he presented his dual-season 2009 collection at the Palais Bulles, his huge Cote d'Azur home and many-roomed homage to the curve, the circle, the bubble and the sphere—which is what the collection was all about, too. This was generously ignored by the fashion press; while still demonstrating some of his masterly skill with structure, it was nevertheless a debased and vitiated version of the vision that made him, in Francois Boudot's words, 'doyen of a new wave of fashion that straddled the world of the past and that of the future' and in Ernestine Carter's, 'less a couturier than an explosion of talent'.

And that talent is as much about commercial opportunities as it is about design creativity. Cardin was one of the epoch-defining designers of the 1960s. Together with Courrèges and Saint Laurent, he gave young women a wardrobe that was a generational chasm away from their mothers'. But it is as the king of the licensers (one estimate in 2005 was that he held 900 licences worldwide) that he has shaped contemporary fashion, fostering that first marriage of big-name designer and mass-market sales that is now a dominant force.

Pierre Cardin was born in 1922 into a once affluent farming family whose acres north of Venice were devastated by some of the bloodiest battles of the First World War. Pietro-Costante was the youngest of the eleven children of Alessandro and Maria Cardin who escaped economic disaster and Mussolini's blackshirts by moving to France in 1924, where workers for a slowly reviving industry were in short supply. Growing up in Saint-Etienne, a coal-mining town in central France, Cardin, the immigrant, was bullied and, he told his biographer, Richard Morais, dreamed of revenge. In 1930, when Cardin was eight, a school inspector asked his class what they wanted to become. Without hesitation, the young Pierre announced, 'A couturier.' He was already making clothes for a collection of dolls.

At fourteen he became apprenticed to the best tailor in Saint-Etienne, Chez Bompuis, and began to learn to cut and sew. From a sallow, shy adolescent he blossomed into a beautiful young man, joining a gym and an amateur dramatics company—the start of a lifelong love affair with the theatre. In 1940, as France was overrun by the Nazis and Saint-Etienne

became part of the client state of Vichy, Pierre Cardin seized his fate in his hands and decamped for Paris. His parents were alarmed but, recalled Cardin, 'They knew I was driven by an irresistible call.'

So he tied a cardboard case to his bicycle and set off to pedal the 480 kilometres along the Route Nationale 7, which was choked with refugees. Arrested and robbed by the German occupiers, Cardin diverted to the nearest town, Vichy, a glamorous, expensive spa and now bustling capital of unoccupied France. On the strength of his sewing skills he secured a job at Manby, the best store in town. In 1943, however, he was called up for compulsory labour in German factories. He initially went on the run, living rough, then evaded deportation by creating a wound in his leg that exempted him; he was nevertheless sent to do secretarial work at the French Red Cross in Vichy. At nights he studied accountancy and made clothes for his female co-workers and friends. As the war ended, Cardin finally headed for Paris, equipped with an introduction at the couture house of Paquin.

Jeanne Paquin had founded her couture house in 1891 on her husband's money and was the first couturière to achieve international fame. Her contribution to the death of the corset and rise of more supple clothes was considerable. By the time Cardin joined the house as first tailor she was widowed and retired, and Spaniard Antonio del Castillo was the head designer. Only six months later, Christian Bérard and Marcel Escoffier, working on the costumes for Jean Cocteau's film, *La Belle at la Bete* (Beauty and the Beast), erupted into Paquin's workshop to make up their designs and, in the absence of Jean Marais, the film's star, chose to fit his Beast costumes on Pierre Cardin. 'I was so overjoyed,' said the stage-struck Cardin, 'I used to dream about it at night.' His enthusiasm was such that the production team co-opted him for his cutting and stitching skills. His biographer has noted that in later years Cardin has rewritten history to claim he designed the costumes; he did not, but his small part in the making of Cocteau's cult film introduced him to the intellectual demi-monde and inspired an insatiable ambition to succeed in the arts as well as couture.

It also got him an introduction to Schiaparelli, whose place Vendome boutique he joined in 1946 as a cutter. He lasted two months before joining Escoffier as his assistant at the Comédie-Française, a post which quickly led to a meeting with Christian Dior, who was then engaged in putting together his own couture house. Cardin designed, cut and made a coat and suit for Dior and was offered the job of head of the coat and suit studio. He was one of the original team of forty-seven who created Dior's retrospectively feminine Carolle Line and with it, the New Look.

In 1948 there was evidence that Dior sketches were being leaked to an unprincipled mass manufacturer. The police were called and Cardin was questioned at length in front of colleagues. Eventually, someone from another studio was prosecuted, but Cardin was gravely offended. He resigned to start his own business making theatre costumes in partnership with Marcel Escoffier. Christian Dior, ever generous, would also send to him clients who needed extravagant outfits for costume balls. At about this time, Cardin met the young man, André Oliver, who was to become his life partner and design collaborator.

When Pierre Cardin finally launched his haute couture label in 1953 his work attracted respect but no fashion hysteria. The following year was different, however. He launched his 'bubble dress,' which was a worldwide success, and opened his two boutiques, Eve and Adam. The Eve boutique was in effect the first germ of designer ready-to-wear. Cardin realised quite quickly that there was more money to be made from manufacturing and distributing simpler, cheaper 'copies' of his own designs than there ever was from 'selling' a couture toile for a modest $250 to $500 to a manufacturer. There was, he then realised, even more money to be made from licensing the design and taking a cut on every copy made and sold. The godfather of logo-mania, Cardin was the first designer to license his name unashamedly, and the first to put clothes bearing his name in a department store—both of which are the standard practice today.

After the 1959 launch of a prêt-à-porter boutique in Au Printemps on the boulevard Haussmann, Cardin was expelled from the Chambre Syndicale de la Couture Parisienne, the strict governing body of Parisian couturiers. Unrepentant, he secured the first licence deal for men's shirts and ties, moving on to children's clothing and then in 1968 to his first non-fashion licence for porcelain, thus birthing the age of fashion designer–endorsed lifestyle goods. 'Recently,' he told Polan in 1989, 'The Chambre has invited me back as president. I turned them down because I am too busy.'

In the 1970s, Cardin fulfilled a dearly held dream, and on the avenue Gabriel, he opened L'Espace Cardin comprising a theatre, cinema, gallery, exhibition hall and restaurant, his 'cultural cosmos'. In 1977 he opened his Evolution Gallery and presented his first haute couture furniture collection, entitled Utilitarian Sculptures. He also opened a Maxim's boutique in his Faubourg Saint-Honoré building, an association which was to lead in 1981 to his acquiring the whole Maxim brand and business.

In 1979 he became the first Western fashion designer to show in China, knocking a chip in its long isolation and opening the door to today's powerhouse Asian market. Hard on the heels of the first whiff of perestroika, he was also the first designer to open a boutique in Russia. His vision of good design for the masses has proved inexorable. 'Why should I work only for rich people,' Cardin said when interviewed in 1983 for *The Guardian* by Brenda Polan. 'Why should only rich people have access to certain places, certain things? Everyone is entitled to have the best that they want to afford. I want to work for people in the street.'

Cardin's 900 or so licences—conservatively reckoned to be worth 1 million euros a week—encompass most product groups. If he uses something, he wants to put his name on it. 'Everything is Pierre Cardin, absolutely everything,' he said, referring to his home in Paris and the Palais Bulles. 'I can wake in the morning in my Pierre Cardin bed linen and shave with one of my razors, use my own aftershave and dress in Pierre Cardin from my tie to my pants to my shirt. Then I can go to my Pierre Cardin restaurant—Maxim's de Paris—or go to my Pierre Cardin theatre.'

Further reading: Pierre Cardin: The Man Who Became a Label (1991), by Richard Morais, is an excellent biography and cultural and character analysis. *Pierre Cardin: Past, Present, Future* (1990), by Valerie Mendes, is stronger on the fashion.

21 MARY QUANT (1934–)

Caught in the middle of the contest over who invented the miniskirt, Mary Quant has always been pretty phlegmatic in the face of competing cross-Channel claims from Pierre Cardin and André Courrèges, saying dismissively, 'It was the girls on the King's Road who invented the mini. I was making easy, youthful, simple clothes in which you could move, in which you could run and jump and we would make them the length the customer wanted. I wore them very short and the customers would say, "Shorter, shorter." '

Mary Quant did not train as a designer. She is the daughter of Welsh teachers who both came from mining families and who had, via scholarships to grammar school and Cardiff University (where they both got first-class degrees), travelled to London and into the middle class. Mary was born in Blackheath and in 1950, at age 16, won a scholarship at Goldsmith's College of Art to study for an art teacher's diploma. To please her parents, who would rather she had gone to university, she worked hard during the day and, with the fellow student who became her husband and partner, Alexander Plunket Greene, she would play hard at night. 'We were excited to be grown up and in London and at art school,' Greene told Brenda Polan in 1982, 'but it was a dreary city, really, for poor students. Restaurants were either expensive or they were unattractive places selling egg and chips or meat and two veg. The pubs sold warm booze and no food. There was nowhere for young people to go except the cinema or a jazz club.' The couple ricocheted between very expensive restaurants like Quaglino's when Greene's allowance arrived and seedy Chelsea pubs and smoky jazz cellars when it had run out.

But they were on the cusp of a historic social change. Quant failed her course (well, she never did want to be an art teacher) and, longing to leave home, got a job with Erik, the milliner in Brook Street, while Greene worked as 'a sort of photographer on the King's Road'. Quant made her own clothes because she had no money to buy any, and they were becoming 'rather odd . . . I was beginning to get more daring in the invention of my own clothes. People used to look at us wherever we went. They would laugh at us and sometimes shout after us, "God, this Modern Youth!" ' Their base was the King's Road, where they were founder members of what was to become known as the 'Chelsea Set', a loose circle of 'painters, photographers, architects, writers, socialites, actors, con-men and superior tarts. There were racing drivers, gamblers, TV producers and advertising men.' The creative and louche characters, in fact, who were to people the swinging sixties.

On the wings of an economic boom, the fully employed, salaried young were in a position to challenge what they called 'The Establishment'—its social stratification, values, morals and hypocrisies. That same boom created a new media, writers, photographers, publishers who took a more conceptual, contextual and political approach to fashion coverage and readily identified with a new generation of designers whose clothes were youthful, imaginative, challenging and modern. They celebrated, too, the egalitarian attitude of this new fashion generation, which valued availability over exclusivity. It is difficult to claim that the 1960s were not elitist; it was just a different elite—what those in it liked to call a meritocracy. Jocelyn Stevens, publisher of the iconoclastic *Queen* magazine and later rector of the Royal College of Art, wrote in 1966, 'All sort of completely accepted attitudes were proven wrong . . . we lashed out at everything with a vengeance. All the household gods were attacked . . . It was the most marvellous time to start everything.'

It was Clare Rendlesham, fashion editor of *Queen* magazine, who in 1965, on a black-bordered page, announced the demise of Parisian couture and ran a premature obituary of Balenciaga and his disciple, Givenchy. In the *Weekend Telegraph* magazine the story was followed up with a photo essay by William Klein entitled, 'Is Paris Dead?' and featuring clothes by Cardin, Dior, Lanvin and Ungaro. Klein answered his own question by declaring, 'No! Paris is jumping!' but, in fact, Paris was jumping to keep up. That year Emanuelle Khanh, a member of the new wave of young French designers working in upmarket ready-to-wear, insisted, 'Haute couture is dead.' She would, she said 'design for the street . . . a socialist kind of fashion for the grand mass.'

It was a pivotal moment in fashion, when it became obvious to all that the future could not really be resisted. But it was a change a decade in the making, its seeds sown when Mary Quant was finally able to indulge her long suppressed desire to work in fashion. In 1955, together with ex-solicitor and entrepreneur, Archie McNair, Mary and Alexander opened a boutique on the King's Road that, she wrote in her autobiography, 'was to be a bouillabaisse of clothes, accessories . . . sweaters, scarves, shifts, hats, jewellery and peculiar odds and ends. We would call it Bazaar. I was to be the buyer. Alexander inherited £5,000 on his twenty-first birthday and Archie was prepared to put up £5,000 too.' In the basement Alexander opened a restaurant.

It was something she 'desperately wanted to do,' but their inexperience nearly finished them off in the first weeks as they undercharged for the clothes and constantly ran out of stock. Mary only became serious about designing when an American manufacturer snapped up a pair of pyjamas she had made, telling her a mass-produced copy would make him a lot of money. Furious, she bought a sewing machine and some Butterick paper patterns which she altered and made up in fabric she bought retail at Harrods. 'No one had told me about buying cloth wholesale.' Her earliest designs were

inspired partially by the beatniks who paraded in the King's Road and partly by a memory from an early ballet class when she had glimpsed, through an open door, a girl dressed for tap-dancing in a tiny skirt over thick black tights worn with little white ankle socks and shiny black patent leather Mary Jane tap shoes.

In fact, as she was one of the first to acknowledge, a generation of women who did not wish to look like their mothers in the bourgeois uniforms dictated by couturiers in Paris opted instead to dress like breastless, hipless children, gauche and gangling, innocently big-eyed with blotted-out mouth and Bambi lashes. 'I wanted everyone to retain the grace of a child,' she said, 'and not to have to become stilted, confined, ugly beings. So I created clothes that allowed people to run, to jump, to leap, to retain their precious freedom.'

Gradually, Quant invested in more sewing machines and began to employ seamstresses to work in her tiny, crowded bedsit. Bazaar became a sensation, its stock snatched off the hangers as soon as it hit the rails. The clothes were unique, simple, neat, unfussy, in déclassé, hard-working fabrics which also smacked of the nursery and the schoolyard—the first embodiment of what was to become known as the 'youthquake'.

'It was about the moment,' Quant told Brenda Polan in an interview for *The Guardian* in 1982.

> We didn't realise at the time of course that we were in the middle of a social revolution. It took ten years for this country to start to recover from the war and suddenly the economy was booming and ours was the first generation which, when young, actually had the money and therefore the freedom to create a culture for itself.
>
> Before, the middle-aged had always tried to give the young what they thought the young needed; the youth revolution came as a terrible shock because the middle-aged hadn't noticed the new economic freedom and didn't know what had hit them. They were stuck deep in old attitudes; a woman was daddy's daughter until she became someone's wife. In the mid-1950s women started, without analysing it, to grab a

time when they were their own person by moving out from under daddy's roof and sharing a usually overcrowded, usually scruffy flat with other girls.

The mini was part of that. The mini said: 'Look at me.' It was very exuberant, pure glee. Looking back, it was the beginning of the women's movement. Clothes always say it first, you know, then comes the effect. All those retro fashions of the 1970s betrayed the nervousness that was to come.

In her autobiography Quant wrote:

Fashion is the product of a thousand and one different things. It is a whole host of elusive ideas, influences, cross-currents and economic factors captured into a shape and dominated by two things . . . impact on others, fun for oneself. It is unpredictable, indefinable. It is successful only when a woman gets a kick out of what she is wearing; when she feels marvellous and looks marvellous.

As Amy de la Haye wrote in 1996, 'Bazaar caused a fashion revolution. Its short production runs of youthful ready-to-wear clothes were a far cry from the established formula for formal, structures and highly accessorised styles. In comparison to haute couture pieces, Mary Quant's clothes were considered cheap. Rejecting the conventional categories of day and evening wear and seasonal collections, she produced new designs all year round.'

The short skirts of 1955 still covered the knee — as they still did in a photograph of Bazaar's window taken in 1961 (and it was not until 1966 that *Time* magazine noticed that something quite significant was happening and ran its cover story on Swinging London). 'Nevertheless,' said Quant in a radio interview with Colin McDowell in 2009, for his Radio 4 essay, *The Shock of the Knee*, 'from the beginning bowler-hatted types would knock on the window and shake their umbrellas at us to admonish us.' Asked if she was perhaps deliberately provoking that sort of person, she agreed that indeed she was. Felicity Green, fashion editor of *The Daily Mirror* in the 1960s, was challenged by her chairman, Hugh Cudlipp, for supporting Quant with regular exposure on her pages. She refused

to mend her ways and was told, 'I probably ought to fire you.'

The second Bazaar opened in Knightsbridge in 1957, and Quant accepted a contract to produce four collections a year for JC Penney, the American store group. She expanded the range of fabrics she used, including nylon, PVC, men's suiting and rugby-shirt jersey. In 1961 she launched her first wholesale collection with dancing models, and in 1963 she created Ginger Group, a lower-priced line. By the mid-1960s she was designing underwear, swimwear, night attire, stockings and tights, rainwear, furs, sewing patterns for Butterick and a hugely successful range of cosmetics beloved for its witty nomenclature (courtesy of Alexander). In 1965 she took her collection on a whistle-stop tour of the United States. With thirty outfits and her own models, she showed in twelve cities in fourteen days. Sporting miniskirts and Vidal Sassoon's five-point geometric haircuts, just like Quant's own, the models ran and danced down the catwalk. It was the epitome of swinging London, and it took America by storm. In 1966 she was awarded the OBE.

In the following decades Quant's name was also attached to stationery, spectacle frames and sunglasses, household furnishings, carpets, wine and toys. In 1981 she relaunched a fashion range and a shoe collection. Mary Quant remained a genuine fashion innovator well into the 1990s and into the 2000s. She adjusted to the great social and psychological changes of the century, becoming a designer for the lifestyle retailing boom in the 1980s and 1990s. Her market had grown up with her, and she was able to anticipate its demands. She wrote several books on beauty and cosmetics. Her husband died in 1990, and Quant stepped down as director of Mary Quant Ltd. in 2000 while remaining a consultant for the myriad products she had pioneered over her long career.

Further reading: Mary Quant's autobiography, *Quant by Quant* (1965), is a must-read. Amy De la Haye's *The Cutting Edge; 50 Years of British Fashion* (1996) and Christopher Breward, David Gilbert and Jenny Lister's *Swinging Sixties: Fashion in London and Beyond 1955–1970* (2006) are good background.

22 RUDI GERNREICH (1922–1985)

Rudi Gernreich was a blast of fresh air in the fashion world of the 1950s and summed up the youthful irreverent spirit of the 1960s. His flair for self-publicity was matched by an enthusiasm—bordering on obsession—with being ahead of his contemporaries. That mix makes him a controversial figure in the history of fashion, but the global media furore over the creation of a topless swimsuit in 1964 has obscured this Californian designer's more significant achievements. As his long-term muse and friend Peggy Moffit put it, 'I have always felt that Rudi's great talent was overlooked because of the headlines.'

In fact, Gernreich showed some reluctance to unveil his topless swimsuit, despite having predicted its emergence in 1962. He acknowledged that it was ahead of its time and had no plans to put it into production, until influential fashion editor Diana Vreeland urged him to do so. He was also haunted by the fear that Emilio Pucci, his rival on the other side of the Atlantic as torchbearer for youth-driven innovation, might beat him to it. Moffit, who modelled the suit in a celebrated photograph only published by trade newspaper *Women's Wear Daily* at the time, thought it was an unwise move in retrospect. 'Rudi did the suit as a social statement,' she said in 1985. The suit, she emphasised, was about freedom and was not intended to be judged too literally. Gernreich's much more significant contribution to the evolution of fashion was taking forward the pioneering spirit of Claire McCardell's sportswear for a new generation, producing clothes that were unconstructed, unrestricting and, he always felt, liberating. He believed the couturiers of Paris produced clothes that constricted and trussed up women. Gernreich's mission was to set them free. With the creation of the so-called no-bra bra in 1965, made from soft transparent nylon with neither padding nor boning, he did just that.

He was born in 1922 in Vienna, Austria, a world away from the California that became his home as an adult. His father, Siegmund Gernreich, a hosiery manufacturer, committed suicide in 1930 when Gernreich was just eight, so he grew up under the watchful eye of his mother and his aunt, who ran a dress shop that he later described as a 'sanctuary' from the austere world of interwar Vienna. Here, he could sketch to his heart's content and learn about clothes in a welcoming environment. Austrian influences popped up in his professional career years later in America: checkerboard trousers, memorably worn by Lauren Bacall in a shoot for *Life* in 1953, recall the geometrics of the Bauhaus movement. In 1938 the Austrian Anschluss with Adolf Hitler's Germany sparked a Jewish exodus from Vienna, and Gernreich and his mother were among those who chose California as their destination. Bizarrely, his first job in America was working in a mortuary. 'I do smile sometimes when people tell me my clothes are so body-conscious I must have studied anatomy,' recalled Gernreich. 'You bet I studied anatomy!'

More conventionally, he also studied art at Los Angeles City College. He then worked briefly in the publicity department at RKO Studios before becoming enthused about the world of dance and joining Lester Horton's West Coast troupe, inspired by the work of choreographer Martha Graham. His dance study was supplemented by freelance fabric design work for Hoffman California Fabrics in the mid-1940s. In 1950 he recognised that dance was not his future and left Lester Horton to move to New York for a job with George Carmel, a coat and suit company. Gernreich swiftly developed a profound dislike for the American garment trade's obsession with the word from Paris. 'Everyone with a degree of talent—designer, retailer, editor—was motivated by a level of high taste and unquestioned loyalty to

Paris . . . After about six months, I began to vomit every time I thought about the imperiousness of it all,' he recalled. 'I produced terrible versions of Dior. I was finally let go.' The early 1950s were a period of fits and starts for Gernreich, although a legendary meeting with Diana Vreeland at *Harper's Bazaar* in 1951 gave him some encouragement. 'Who are you, young man?' she said. 'You're very gifted.' Some degree of stability was established when he met Walter Bass, with whom Gernreich said he never got along. Nevertheless their business partnership lasted eight years, partly because Bass enticed Gernreich into signing a draconian seven-year contract. By the time it expired Gernreich was a star. His first gingham and cotton tweed dresses were snapped up by an influential shop in Los Angeles called Jax. In New York, buyers went into rhapsodies. Gernreich's flair for fresh, youthful, unconstricted sportswear struck a chord with buyers and fashion editors at a time when the influence of Paris was steadily diminishing.

Fashion magazines were emerging as ever-more important style arbiters, a phenomenon that Gernreich recognised earlier than many of his contemporaries and exploited to the full. In March 1952 he created the prototype for the first bra-free swimsuit in wool jersey with a tank top. His first magazine credit was in the February 1953 issue of *Glamour,* featuring a knitted tube dress which was a forerunner of the stretch minis of the late 1980s. Swimsuits really took off for him in 1955 through a deal with Westwood Knitting Mills, for whom he produced wool knitted and elasticated swimsuits. The late 1950s and 1960s were a golden period of creativity for Gernreich, who steadily expanded his business into a veritable empire. In 1956 he produced his first menswear designs, originally waiters' jackets for a Chinese restaurant, recreated as shirt jackets for the beach or home. A women's shoe collection for Ted Saval followed the next year, and stockings were added in 1959. Accessories were important to Gernreich, who believed in the concept of a total look.

The long-anticipated end of his contract with Walter Bass allowed Gernreich to launch his own company, G.R. Designs, in 1960. The youthful energy and bright colours of Gernreich's collections were a harbinger of the youthquake of the 1960s—Gernreich's hemlines were above the knee

as early as 1961. From his headquarters at 8460 Santa Monica Boulevard, Gernreich worked fanatically hard, producing thumbnail sketches as a starting point and working them up later with fabric samples and colour swatches. Often, ideas would come to him just before waking or falling asleep, moments that had a profound mystic significance for him. *The New York Times* picked up on Gernreich's soaring profile, dubbing him 'California's most successful export since the orange'.

But Gernreich's fellow designers, particularly on the east coast, were not so enthusiastic. When Gernreich won the Coty American Fashion Critics Award in June 1963, Norman Norell returned his own Hall of Fame Coty in protest. At the preparations for the Coty Award presentation, even critics who admired him thought a white lingerie satin trouser suit that he planned to include in the show was a little too louche for the times. The Coty jury asked him to withdraw it, a request in which he acquiesced in a rare moment of restraint.

In Europe, the designer who came closest to expressing Gernreich's spirit was Emilio Pucci, based in Italy. Both Pucci and Gernreich had predicted that breasts would be uncovered within a few years. Peggy Moffit believes competition with Pucci prompted Gernreich to move fast, but he was also encouraged by fashion editors sensing a scoop. Gernreich himself later described the topless swimsuit as the natural extension of his cutout designs. 'By 1964, I'd gone so far with swimwear cutouts that I decided the body itself—including breasts—could become an integral part of a suit's design.' Orders poured in for the controversial swimsuit, but across the United States store presidents stepped in to prevent the suits being delivered. One store was picketed, another had a bomb threat. Some 3,000 swimsuits were sold, although there is little evidence they were ever worn publicly, except by a club entertainer and a nineteen-year-old Chicago girl, Toni Lee Shelley, who was promptly arrested. The creation of the topless swimsuit made Gernreich a cause célèbre and media favourite for the rest of the career, alternately praised and mocked. All this tended to overshadow his more substantial achievements.

Although *Women's Wear Daily* had been quick to publish a photo of the swimsuit, publisher John

Fairchild dismissed Gernreich in his book *The Fashionable Savages* (1965), saying his clothes were badly constructed. By contrast, another critic, the designer Norman Norell, relented in 1966, acknowledging Gernreich's status as a major name in modern fashion design. It was a period of rich creativity for Gernreich with a series of firsts, both creative and commercial, ranging from the first fashion video (titled 'Basic Black') and the first chain-store link-up (with Montgomery Ward) to the creation of the chiffon T-shirt dress. In October 1966, Gernreich's collection showed two looks: short hemlines and thoroughly swinging sixties styles, contrasted with long and dressed up. The designer was turning social commentator: there were no rights or wrongs in fashion any more—nor in society. In a statement published for his resort collection in the following year, he declared: 'For the first time in the history of the world . . . the young are leading us. There is now a Power Elite of the young.' Once started on the social commentary path, Gernreich just could not stop. By 1968, he was pontificating on the film *Bonnie and Clyde,* castigating the period costume trend it inspired. 'History must be used,' he said. 'Not just restored.'

Gernreich's big theme by then was unisex dressing. 'Today our notions of masculine and feminine are being challenged as never before,' he said. 'The basic masculine-feminine appeal is in people, not clothes. When a garment becomes sufficiently basic, it can be worn unisexually.' Even the skirt was finished, he claimed, drawing a sharp rebuke from *Women's Wear Daily,* which said Gernreich had 'boxed himself into a corner.' The barrage of interest in Gernreich became overwhelming for the designer, who announced in October 1968 that he was taking a year off and disappeared to Morocco and Europe. But he returned from the sabbatical as effervescent as ever, producing a unisex stripped-down look for a special futuristic issue of *Life,* photographed on male and female models with shaved heads and bodies (it was brought to life for Expo

70 in Osaka). By this stage, there was a sense that Gernreich was relying on gimmickry rather than creativity to keep his name in the spotlight, although many of his ideas were forerunners of trends of the 1980s and 1990s. The 1971 spring collection featured models carrying guns and wearing dog tags and combat boots. Gernreich became ever-more obsessed with technology, including spray-on clothes and the concept of transmigration of fabrics to the body. In 1971, he forecast that 'the designer will become less artist, more technician . . . A knowledge of machinery such as computers will be essential.'

Home life for Gernreich was more measured. He lived in Laurel Canyon with his long-term partner, Oreste Pucciani, a professor of French. Interviewed in 1998, Pucciani commented that Gernreich 'lived in an eternal present'. The designer himself once said, 'I felt I had to be experimental at any cost, and that meant always being on the verge of a success or a flop.' His simplest and biggest innovation of the 1970s was probably the thong, a slim strip of fabric that became a best-selling piece of underwear for women by the end of the century. He also produced designs for furniture, rugs and kitchen accessories, plus a fragrance packaged in a chemist's beaker. In his final years, he became obsessed by the potential for gourmet soups and, in a parting gesture, produced the pubikini, photographed by Helmut Newton in 1985 shortly before his death from lung cancer. In the Newton photograph, this sliver of fabric left little to the imagination, revealing a triangle of the model's pubic hairs which Gernreich had dyed green. To the very end, Gernreich could not resist stirring up mischief.

Further reading: The best summary of Gernreich's career is Cathy Horyn's 'Naked Ambition' (May 1998), published in *Vanity Fair.* Former Gernreich model and muse Peggy Moffit collaborated with William Claxton on the well-illustrated *The Rudi Gernreich Book* (1991).

PART 4

1960s–1970s

Introduction

The two decades of the 1960s and 1970s were characterised by economic boom and bust. In the 1960s the post-war baby-boom generation provided both labour force and consumers for expanding old industries and vital new ones. Fashion was justifiably assertive, and many designers such as Pierre Cardin and André Courrèges adopted futuristic, sci-fi themes. The role model of the early years of the decade was Jacqueline Kennedy whose husband, President John F. Kennedy, committed America to the space race. The Council of Fashion Designers of America was founded in 1962 with *Norman Norell* as its first president. Swinging London fashion eclipsed Parisian couture and when Balenciaga closed his house in 1968, he declared its day was done. On the street gender distinctions were blurred as men became peacocks and women, leading more active, self-directed, so-called masculine lives, adopted trouser suits, jumpsuits, play suits and shorter and shorter miniskirts and shift dresses. The Pill generation felt free to flaunt its sexuality, to indulge in 'free love' without consequences. However, for the sake of decency, tights supplanted stockings and suspenders. Fashion became strongly identified with the music scene; both were at the heart of the oppositional counterculture.

The Vietnam War during the 1960s contributed to a growing revolutionary sensibility among disadvantaged minorities such as America's black population, homosexuals, women and the politicised young, resulting in riots in Paris (*les événements du mai* 1968), violent demonstrations in London's Grosvenor Square and on American university campuses, and leftist terrorist groups in Europe and the United States. Young designers, most of them coming from Britain's art schools rather than the Chambre Syndicale school in Paris, took inspiration from street styles and modern art movements primarily pop art and graphic op art. In 1965 *Yves Saint Laurent,* who was to dominate the two decades, presented his Mondrian collection. He was also to pay homage to Poliakoff, Braque, Matisse, van Gogh, Renoir, Lichtenstein and Warhol.

The early 1970s saw the downturn of the economic cycle, high unemployment, power cuts, strikes—and hippies. The highly politicised impetus of the 1960s gave way to a spiritual, often drug-fuelled altruism—turn on, tune in and drop out—and fashion became romantic, retro and eclectic, taking inspiration from other times and other places. In Paris *Yves Saint Laurent, Karl Lagerfeld, Issey Miyake* and *Kenzo* produced youthful collections culminating in the Big Look. In London Ossie Clark, Bill Gibb, Zandra Rhodes and Laura Ashley created romantic clothes just this side of fancy dress while Vivienne Westwood, equally historicist, was taking a more iconoclastic approach. The seeds of the Italian fashion industry were being laid at this time: Rosita and Tai Missoni, *Giorgio Armani,* Mariuccia Mandelli of Krizia and Walter Albini began to show in Milan while a small cadre of couturiers, including *Valentino,* survived beyond Rome of the dolce vita.

In America a design dynasty of minimalists was developing in McCardell's footsteps; *Roy Halston, Geoffrey Beene* and Bill Blass were followed by *Calvin Klein. Ralph Lauren* was getting his start with simple classics, and Donna Karan was doing her apprenticeship in designer sportswear at Anne Klein. A misty-eyed romanticism has never since quite disappeared from fashion; it is rarely done as beautifully as by John Galliano, but it was never again to be the dominant mode.

23 NORMAN NORELL (1900–1972)

When American designer Norman Norell died in 1972, shortly after a retrospective show of his life's work had opened at the Metropolitan Museum of Art in New York City, *The New York Times's* obituary headline ran, 'Made 7th Avenue the rival of Paris.' Such was the esteem in which Norell was held in America. Although the headline was stretching the truth in pure creative terms (the dominance of Paris continues to this day), it was certainly true that Norman Norell had turned the ready-to-wear industry of New York, focused on Seventh Avenue, into the heart of American fashion. He developed a wardrobe that suited the American lifestyle, with its emphasis on day-to-evening dressing and wearable, unpretentious clothes. For evening, he could also produce his own share of show-stoppers: sequin-covered sheath dresses were among his most celebrated creations.

By designer standards, Norell's life was uneventful, driven by the routines of his business. Most days, he worked from 10 a.m. to 6 p.m. out of his studio on the tenth floor of 550 Seventh Avenue and lunched at Schraft's on 43rd (always scrambled egg and crisp bacon). He researched his collection by leafing through fashion magazines in the New York Public Library. The design process began with the fabrics, usually ordered from Europe, and then his ideas were translated into rough sketches. Toiles were rarely used: Norell just got on with it in his no-nonsense style. He shunned the celebrity circuit, preferring to hang out with his friends and colleagues at Schraft's. Norell was equally embarrassed by overambitious claims for the significance of fashion. 'Arty talk about haute couture gives me a swift pain,' he said in 1962. In an interview towards the end of his life, he commented: 'I would rather see someone threadbare in something good than cheesy in the latest fashion.'

He was born Norman David Levinson in Noblesville, Indiana, to Harry and Nettie Levinson. Harry, who ran a men's clothing store, opened a men's hat store in Indianapolis where everything was priced at $2. This was such a success that the family moved to Indianapolis when Norman was five. He was a thin little boy with a hot temper, he later recalled. At the age of nineteen, fashion design was his chosen subject of study, but there was no such course so he studied illustration in New York at Parsons, a school with which he retained a lifelong connection. He also chose to contract his name, ditching the workaday Levinson in favour of Norell. He explained: 'Nor for Norman, L for Levinson, with another L added for looks.'

Norell took his first steps as a designer in 1922 in the field of costume design, working at the Astoria Studio of Paramount Pictures. The stars for whom he designed included Gloria Swanson in *Zaza* and Rudolph Valentino in *The Sainted Devil*. The studio closed shortly afterwards and Norell worked on some Broadway musicals before joining Charles Armour, a dress manufacturer, who sent him to Europe for the first time. The defining moment of his career came in 1928, when he joined Hattie Carnegie. A fierce perfectionist, Carnegie was brilliant in her own way, although the process was unoriginal—visiting the couturiers in Paris, buying pieces, pulling them apart back in New York to understand how they were designed, and turning them into more affordable clothes for their American clients. This was the way the American fashion industry worked, founded on the creative insecurity of the American industry and the dominance, often laced with arrogance, of the Paris-based couturiers. The regular visits to Paris were an extraordinary training ground for Norell, an opportunity to understand the secrets of the great European couturiers and develop a profound technical knowledge of the process of creating great fashion. Over twelve years, he developed his skills and his eye, benefiting from the formidable tutelage of Carnegie. He put it simply: 'I learned everything I knew from her.'

Carnegie never allowed Norell to take any credit. He worked for more than a decade in 'complete anonymity', as one Vogue editor put it. A shy and gentle man, this did not appear to put him out: the clash with Carnegie that led to his departure in 1940 was creative rather than ambition driven. They had a row over a dress worn by Gertrude Lawrence in *Lady in the Dark* on Broadway (he thought it perfect; she wanted it toned down). His decision to go solo came at a moment when the American fashion industry was poised to come of age—cut off from the influences of Paris during wartime and ready to make its own mark. Anthony Traina, a manufacturer best known for larger sizes, contacted him. 'He offered me a larger salary if my name were not used,' recalled Norell. 'A smaller amount if it were.' Thus Traina-Norell was created. From the beginning, it was conceived as a full collection rather than a series of pieces, which tended to be the way on Seventh Avenue. The principles of the Paris couture, founded on precision of fit, were now applied to ready-to-wear. Norell was therefore an important bridge between couture and ready-to-wear. Bettina Ballard, an influential editor at *Vogue* with a razor-sharp eye, recalled in her autobiography: 'I loved Norman's clothes. They had the same single-mindedness as Balenciaga's or Chanel's, and the same fanatical attention to quality . . . I bought as many as I could afford.'

He drew inspiration from the 1920s, a favourite decade for him, including silk jersey dresses and long wool evening dresses in his first collection. Norell had a sure sense of timing, a key ingredient of any designer's success. A full-length sweater dress, also shown in 1941, was another star piece. His friend, the fashion editor Bernadine Morris, wrote later: 'What Norman Norell had accomplished in that first collection was to give American

fashion—producers and wearers alike—a freedom from dependence on foreign sources of inspiration. The American industry felt it could set its own directions, its own styles.' Norell went on to play a dominant role in American fashion for three decades. As early as 1943, his achievement was recognized with the first Coty American Fashion Critics Award, recognising the quality of his chemise dresses, sequined cocktail dresses and fur-lined coats. An invitation to a Norell show was a prized ticket: the collection was shown at 9 p.m. (the dress code was black-tie) right through until 1969, when the time was shifted to 5 p.m.

No doubt drawing on his twelve years of visiting Paris, Norell had an instinctive feel for trends and very rarely got it wrong. In 1942, he introduced the no-waistline chemise or shirt dress, not seen since the 1920s, which became a staple of his collections. When he was once asked to sum up his major contribution to fashion, Norell chose to focus on a detail: simple, high round necklines. 'I hated necklines. I always thought they made women look older. So I started making simple Peter Pan collars or no collars at all. Just a plain round neckline, no crap on it . . . I do think it changed the look of clothes.' Another recurring theme was nautical, inspired by a childhood sailor suit he had worn and introduced as early as 1933 at Hattie Carnegie. Indeed, many of his ideas, according to Bernadine Morris, had their origin in the styles he bought in Paris for Carnegie in the 1930s. The influence of menswear, recalling his own father's roots in menswear retailing, also percolated through his work, such as in the creation of a sleeveless jacket over a bowed blouse and slim wool skirt.

Norell's own personal style was neat and precise. He believed day wear should be simple with the razzmatazz saved for evening, an attitude that is still at the heart of the New York way of dressing. During the 1950s, however, he adapted to changing tastes, creating shirtwaist dresses with full skirts in silk and lace and mixing tweed jackets with satin collars with satin ball gowns. Norell's sequined dresses were much admired, dubbed mermaid dresses for their slithery, sensual appeal. In 1960, Anthony Traina was obliged through ill health to step down, allowing Norell to take over the business entirely, with some financial backing. Traina-Norell became Norman Norell, and he created an imme-diate sensation with a culotte-skirted wool flannel day suit in his very first solo collection. Eventually, he bought out his backers too, buoyed by the suc-cess of a fragrance launched with Revlon. Norell was copied, naturally. But this time the flow was back across the Atlantic: Paris-based companies picked up many of his designs, such as his culotte suit and his gored ice-skating skirt. With great mag-nanimity, Norell produced working sketches of the culotte suit free of charge to the trade with the in-tention of ensuring that his design would be copied properly—an extraordinary gesture that won him huge goodwill on Seventh Avenue and beyond.

Through the 1960s, Norell remained a vibrant force in American fashion, often ahead of the pack. He designed the first evening jumpsuit in 1961, cre-ated trouser suits for 1963, and set the pace again by bringing back belts in 1966, heralding the return of emphasis on the waistline. He made news too, sending back his Coty Hall of Fame award in 1963 in protest at an award for the provocative Rudi Gernre-ich. There were mistakes: his culottes of 1960 were judged too early for the market. American trade newspaper *Women's Wear Daily,* then entering its golden age under the dynamic editorship of John Fairchild, also chose to give him the cold shoulder for a period. But by then Norell had attained the status of eminence grise. As the founder and first president of the Council of Fashion Designers of America, he can rightly be acclaimed as the father of the country's fashion industry. Sadly, the Metropoli-tan Museum's retrospective of 1972 was never seen by Norell. He suffered a stroke only a day before the opening and died ten days later. The house contin-ued for a further five years with designer Gustave Tassell. In 2004, Patrick Michael Hughes, a lecturer at Parsons, attempted to revive the label.

Norell always downplayed his approach to design. He could make it sound very easy, but this was founded on decades of study and reflection. 'I be-lieve in thinking out what the next logical and natu-ral trend in fashion will be,' he said in 1952. 'Once I have decided, the rest is easy. I simply take the most straightforward approach to it, without any extra, fancy trimmings. I don't like over-designed anything.'

Further reading: Bernadine Morris, who was fash-ion editor of *The New York Times* and a friend of Norell, summarised his career in *American Fash-ion: The Life and Lines of Adrian, Mainbocher, Mc-Cardell, Norell, and Trigére* (1975), edited by Sarah Tomerlin Lee. Norell also features in Caroline Ren-nolds Milbank's *New York Fashion: The Evolution of American Style* (1989).

24 YVES SAINT LAURENT (1936–2008)

Yves Saint Laurent was, in the words of the man closest to him, born with a nervous breakdown. Even so, he was also probably the most influential fashion designer of the second half of the twentieth century. He synthesised the ingenious modernity of Coco Chanel and the sensuous lyricism of Christian Dior, his mentor and first employer. The addition, as Francois Boudot noted in his account of twentieth-century fashion, of 'a breath of youth and his extrasensory perception of the needs and wants of his contemporaries . . . led to the YSL monogram leaving its stamp on a whole era.'

Saint Laurent reinvented Paris fashion for the young, giving the women of the baby-boomer generation a new wardrobe stocked with easy, youthful clothes which, in their energy, flirtatious assertiveness and borrowings from the active male wardrobe, prefigured the social and political emancipation women were just learning to crave. He was among the first couturiers to understand that, instead of standing by while his ideas were copied and disseminated to a wider market by others, he could produce his own ready-to-wear 'diffusion' or 'boutique' line (iconically named Rive Gauche), making those clothes more easily accessible to younger, less wealthy women. He was the first couturier truly to understand the importance of accessories in creating a look. Often the clothes were really quite simple; it was the accessory garnish that added the bravura and romance.

Hypersensitive, self-centred, narcissistic and emotionally fragile, Yves Saint Laurent was also highly cultivated, literate, diffident and charming and had a mischievous sense of humour. When he posed nude in the 1970s for the picture to advertise a YSL men's scent, he told the photographer, Jean-Loup Sieff:

'I want to create a scandal.' The resulting portrait is unforgettable. Backlit and shadowy, wearing only his spectacles, the designer looks directly into the lens, simultaneously confident in his slender, almost adolescent beauty yet projecting an eroticism that is wistful and tentative. In any other period a designer might very well have been ridiculed for such vanity, but this was the hippy moment of the Age of Aquarius, Flower Power, Woodstock, peace and love. He had his scandal and overnight became a gay icon. There were other scandals along the way: the trouser suit which rattled the composure of a thousand maitre d's, the first headline-grabbing transparent blouse, and the steamy mouth to mouth embrace with which he thanked Rudolf Nureyev for launching another fragrance, Kouros, onstage in the packed Opera Comique a decade later.

He attracted a gilded circle of protectors, defenders and friends upon whose loyalty he made great demands. In his latter years, however, there was scant amusement. Mischief turned to melancholy, and his shyness became reclusiveness. Rare sightings on the catwalk revealed an overweight, shambling figure with dyed auburn hair, a pasty complexion and a dazed expression. Even the coterie of rich, hedonistic friends and artistic collaborators fell away as he retreated into an introverted isolation. 'He is simply,' said his closest friend, former lover and business partner (and the man who made the natal nervous breakdown diagnosis), Pierre Bergé, 'not interested in other people'.

Rich, famous, multiply honoured by his country and the community of his peers, he succumbed to the despair and pain which had dogged him all his life. He was a man who wore his anguish on his sleeve.

He accepted it, indulged it even, as collateral to his genius. In his office he kept a framed quotation from Marcel Proust, whose *A La Recherche du Temps Perdu* (Remembrance of Things Past) he read and reread throughout his life: 'The magnificent and lamentable family of the nervous is the salt of the earth. It's they and no one else who founded religions and created masterpieces . . .'

Yves Saint Laurent's only real training was a brief period understudying Dior, the master of a formal and archaic ultra-feminine glamour, yet his only equal in innovation was Chanel who, in 1967 when she was eighty-four, declared him her 'only inheritor'. Like Chanel in the 1920s and 1930s, Saint Laurent perfectly answered the mood and needs of his time. Both responded intuitively to overwhelming impulses towards political and social emancipation for women, giving women the clothes in which to grasp equality. It became easy to forget, given the decades of Saint Laurent's decline into a threadbare and solipsistic reworking of his own best ideas, how dramatic and beautiful those epoch-defining collections were. The Mondrian (1965), with its bright blocks of colour; the Pop-Art (1966), inspired by Andy Warhol; the African (1967); the Safari (1968); the Marlene Dietrich inspired collection of 1969, when he introduced both the mini and the tuxedo; the Moroccan (1970); the Opera/Ballets Russes (1976) with its opulently clad peasants and gypsies ('My most beautiful collection,' said Saint Laurent); the Velasquez (1977); the Chinoiserie (1977); the Picasso (1979); the Collection Shakespeare (1980), dedicated to literature and poetry, Aragon, Cocteau and Apollinaire; the Matisse (1981); and the Cubist (1988) collections all stand out as milestones in fashion history.

Christian Lacroix, a designer of the generation which grew up in Saint Laurent's shadow, told Saint Laurent's biographer, Alice Rawsthorn: 'There have been other great designers this century but none with the same range. Chanel, Schiaparelli, Balenciaga and Dior all did extraordinary things. But they worked within a particular style. Yves Saint Laurent is much more versatile, like a combination of all of them. I sometimes think he's got the form of Chanel with the opulence of Dior and the wit of Schiaparelli.'

Yves Henri Donat Mathieu Saint Laurent was born in 1936 in Oran, Algeria, into a wealthy and prominent family. He grew up knowing himself a misfit in the close, conservative and Catholic *colon* community. 'No doubt,' he told *Le Figaro* in 1991, 'because I was homosexual.' It was a terrible secret, a preference to be expressed only in furtive encounters with Arab street boys. The gentle, fragile and timid youngster was doted upon by his mother and sisters—whose dolls he dressed. He excelled academically but was bullied and beaten by his classmates, who sensed that the puny, artistic and unathletic boy was unacceptably different. 'Maybe,' he said much later, 'I didn't have what it took to be a boy.' He had, however, all the vanity and arrogance of the outcast who knows himself to be better then his tormentors. He dreamed of escape, of Paris and, as he wrote in his introduction to the catalogue to the 1983–4 exhibition at the Metropolitan Museum of Art in New York, his 'name written in fiery letters on the Champs Elysées'.

Theatre and costume design were his first passion (and he was later to prove a brilliant designer for Roland Petit's ballets, for theatre and film) but at seventeen, he seized the first opportunity to present itself when he entered a competition for young fashion designers run by *Paris Match* magazine and the International Wool Secretariat. In Paris with his mother to receive third prize, he met Michel de Brunhoff, the influential editor of French *Vogue*, who advised him to finish school and then enrol on a design course at the Chambre Syndicale de la Couture Parisienne. The course, which he started in the autumn of 1954, quickly bored him and, having won that year's International Wool Secretariat competition, he was dispatched by de Brunhoff to show his sketch book to Christian Dior, who employed him immediately. When the originator of the New Look died of a heart attack in 1957, he had already made it clear that he considered Saint Laurent his natural successor.

In January 1958 Saint Laurent showed his first collection after Dior's unexpected death. The collection, which introduced the Trapeze Line, was a success; *The Sunday Times* fashion editor, Ernestine Carter, later noted that it was to become the classic and enduring maternity dress shape. So central was Dior's image to French couture and the lucrative concept of Paris fashion that the next day's newspaper placards announced: 'Saint Laurent has saved France.' He was just twenty-one years old. A quarter-century later he wrote, 'Luckily there is a destructive kind of suffering I've never known, the one that comes from lack of recognition.'

Perhaps that initial reaction caused the owner of Dior, the textile magnate, Marcel Boussac to give his stripling designer too much freedom. Instead of moving the collection forward by client-comforting increments each season, Saint Laurent went for a new look with every succeeding collection. When his second collection dropped skirts to calf length (ten years too soon, as Carter noted) the French press turned against him. When, in a hasty over-correction, he hobbled them above the knee for spring 1959, the response was vitriolic. Then in 1960, searching for a means of 'poetic expression', he elected to pay homage to the beat culture of the Left Bank with a collection that featured the biker's black leather blouson jackets (albeit trimmed with mink), black cashmere turtlenecks and short bubble skirts flattering only to the young and hipless. The predominantly mature couture clients showed their displeasure. So did Marcel Boussac, who had been protecting Saint Laurent from military conscription by pulling political strings. Boussac opted for patriotism and profits before poetry and lifted his protection.

Saint Laurent's brief induction into the army of France, then engaged in a savage struggle against Algerian nationalists, was a turning point in his life. It ensured that he was forced to start his own label because, as the barracks doors slammed behind the recruit, Boussac hurried to replace him at Dior with Marc Bohan. But it also precipitated his first breakdown—just nineteen days into his army career—and resulted in the treatment which wrecked his health and launched him on a lifetime of drug and alcohol abuse. At the Val-de-Grace mental hospital he was subjected to a primitive regimen of dangerously addictive heavy-duty sedatives. He could not eat and by the time his friend and lover, Pierre Bergé, secured his release two months later he was utterly debilitated. Bergé, supported by *Women's Wear Daily,* ever Saint Laurent's champion, set about suing the house of Dior and establishing Saint Laurent's own couture house. 'I had never, ever wanted to be a businessman,' said Bergé, whose interests lay in the arts and politics, 'but I agreed to do it for him.' He found an American backer, Jesse Mack Robinson, and in February 1962 the first YSL collection was shown in a small villa in Passy to a packed crowd of fashion cognoscenti. It nodded towards the sobriety of Balenciaga and the reviews were ecstatic; *Life* magazine announced, 'The best collection of suits since Chanel.'

It was the second collection, six months later, which established him as the man who was to dominate international fashion for two decades. It gave a glossy spin to youthful styles culled from the street, introducing the tunic over a pencil skirt, the Norman smock and the upmarket version of the working man's pea jacket. In this Saint Laurent's work paralleled that of the young Chanel who had plagiarised the clothes of French sailors and Scottish ghillies.

Twenty years later Saint Laurent reflected, 'The things I like best of all that I have done are the ones I borrowed from a man's wardrobe: the blazer, the trouser suit, the trench coat, knickerbockers, shorts, the safari jacket, the T-shirt, the suit, the whole suit idiom, the ambiguity of all that interests me.' The potent sexual content of androgynous dressing was a factor. Like most homosexual fashion designers, he adored women as long as they had boyish bodies yet, unlike some of the others, he created clean-lined, rational clothes which flattered the most womanly of figures. Breasts did not actually frighten him, but he liked them small, free and pert in a transparent chiffon shirt under a strict tuxedo rather than magnified into cushiony cleavage by archaic corsetry. His way was the way young women of the 1960s and 1970s perceived themselves—slender and lithe with an upfront, natural coquetry. Like them, he hated what he called 'transvestite' or 'Easter Parade' clothing, the elaborate, tortured confections which betray the essential misogyny of so many male designers.

Yves Saint Laurent retired in 2002, and died in June 2008.

Further reading: Alice Rawsthorn's biography, *Yves Saint Laurent* (1998), is excellent and Alicia Drake's *The Beautiful Fall: Fashion, Genius and Glorious Excess in 1970s Paris* (2006) is good background reading. For a critical appraisal, see Marguerite Duras in the 1988 catalogue *Yves Saint Laurent: Images of Design 1958–1988.*

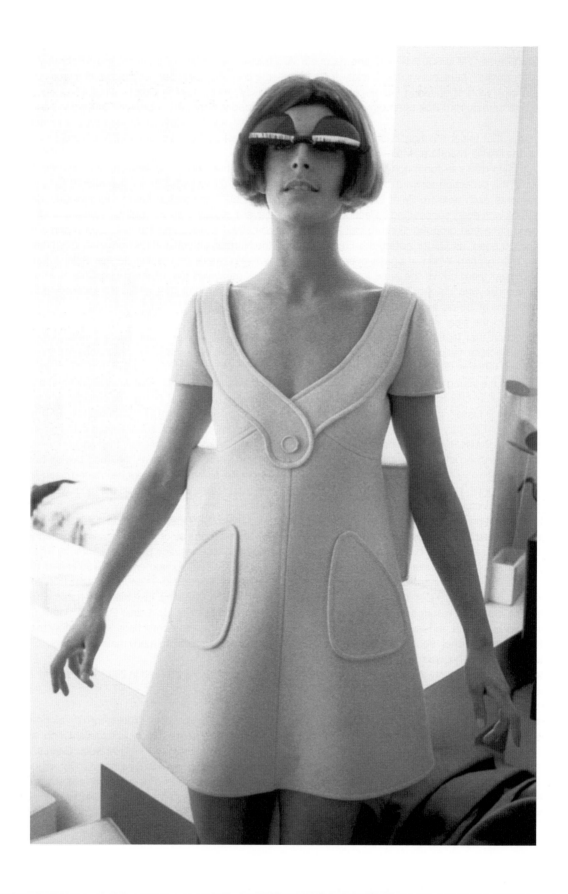

25 ANDRÉ COURRÈGES (1923–)

The debate about who exactly invented the miniskirt is best settled by quoting the designer credited with an earlier fashion sensation, Christian Dior. Speaking to Carmel Snow, editor of *Harper's Bazaar,* he said, 'No one person can change fashion—a big fashion change imposes itself.' Indeed, if all the theories of dress have any validity, it must be so. Designers essentially respond to the political, economic and social mood of their day. André Courrèges, Pierre Cardin. Mary Quant, John Bates, Yves Saint Laurent; they were all raising skirts to round about the knee at the same time. And they all exposed the knee and then the thigh at much the same time. As the 1950s, so much in the shadow of the war and so much about recovery of what had been lost, gave way to the 1960s, huge changes were in the air. The generation born during and immediately after the war had no memory of privation, no fear of risk. In Europe and America economies were booming, further education was more widely available and there were jobs and disposable incomes for everyone—including women.

The teenage market, invented in the 1950s, proved the most easily manipulable in advertising's history, and so the culture refocused on youth. Young people were drafted to fill jobs and professional positions they would once have laboured half a lifetime to attain. They invented new jobs, particularly in the burgeoning media, which they reshaped to meet their own agendas. And, sheltered and pampered as they were, they began to develop an altruistic approach to the world, embracing various strands of utopian politics and a romantic view of a perfectible world, one in which all the benefits of science could be bent to the advantages of the masses, where disease, ignorance and hunger could be vanquished and space conquered.

Women, in particular, wanted to distance themselves from the lives lived by their mothers, who had worn some variation on the New Look, which their daughters took, in its corseted hour-glass silhouette, to represent traditional womanhood and its traditional (at least in the middle classes) roles of motherhood and dependent wife. They needed a new way of looking that put fertility on the back burner while constructing a post-Pill please-myself sexuality that expressed independence, self-determination and a new sense of empowerment.

André Courrèges was not a member of this generation, but he largely understood it and identified with it. He told Brenda Polan in an interview for *The Guardian* in 1979, 'My revolution of 1965 was not a calculated volte-face; it was an instinctive thing, a reaction to a period which was both progressive and aggressive. A designer must be a sociologist; he must look at the lives people lead, the way their houses are built, what their needs and preoccupations are.'

On that occasion, just a decade and a half after the collection that set all Paris on its ears, Polan described Courrèges's salon in some detail:

> Today [it] still reflects his identification with the shiny, hard-surfaced clinical world of push-button machines and silicon chips. Like the offices and workrooms beyond it, it is all a startling high-gloss white . . . Here vast, untinted mirrors reflect shiny white walls, a gleaming white-tiled

floor, white leather and chrome furniture and rails of distinctively cut clothes in vibrant-coloured cottons, satins, silks, fine wools and fantasies of feathers and chiffon.

At that time it was easy to make the connection between the decor and the philosophy. The man who had delighted in an invitation to sit in at NASA Mission Control in Cape Canaveral was still locked into the sci-fi vision of a future where man (and woman) walked on the moon and lived in a then only vaguely imagined uncluttered and dust-free domestic world of technological miracles. But there was more to it than that. There was the Balenciaga connection.

André Courrèges was born in Pau, in southern France almost in the shadow of the Pyrenees, in 1923. His father was employed as the major domo in a private chateau and sent his son to a school that specialised in civil engineering—where he gained an understanding of three-dimensional structure that was to become the basis of his innovative garment construction. Growing up during the Second World War in Vichy France, young André trained in Aix-en-Provence as a pilot in the French Air Force but was certain that his interests lay in fashion. The great Cristobal Balenciaga had been born only miles away in the Basque country on the other side of the border with Spain and he, Courrèges decided, was the master from whom he would learn. So as soon as the war ended in 1945, André set out for Paris, aged twenty-two. He studied fashion design at the Chambre Syndicale school and attempted to get a job with his idol. Initially he could not obtain an appointment to plead his case, so he took a job at the Jeanne Lafaurie fashion design house. Eventually in 1950 he found a way. 'I went to a team of smugglers in Hendaye who carried Balenciaga's patterns and designs between Paris and his offices in Spain,' he told Valerie Guillaume. 'I had a letter passed on to him and I met him. I suggested I should work for him as a junior apprentice. He took me on in the tailoring atelier.'

Courrèges compared his entry into the House of Balenciaga to that of a novice monk preparing for holy orders. He told Georgina Howell in 1989, 'The atelier was pure white, unornamented, and intensely silent. People whispered and walked on tiptoe, and even the clients talked in hushed voices. Once or twice a day the door of Balenciaga's office would open, and you would hear him leave the building to go and pray in the church on the avenue Marceau.'

After five years, Balenciaga sent Courrèges to work in his Eisa couture house in Spain in order to give him 'more freedom and responsibility'. On his return, Courrèges told Valerie Guillaume that he had gone to Balenciaga and told him, 'Nothing grows under a tall tree. I am a little acorn and you are a great oak. I have to leave you to survive.' Balenciaga pretended not to hear. Three years passed and every time Courrèges brought up the subject, Balenciaga would feign deafness. Then came the day when he wandered into Courrèges's atelier and asked, 'Are you leaving? Do you need money? I'll give you some. Do you need help with administration? I'll send you my manager. Do you need clients? I'll send you clients.'

So in 1961, with some financial assistance from the great man, Courrèges set up his own house in partnership with Coqueline Barriere, with whom he had worked at Balenciaga and who was to become his wife in 1966. At first both were still very much under the influence of the master. 'In his atelier I had to think like him. That was no problem for me. Balenciaga taught me about the seventeenth century. The aesthetic simplicity of his clothes and mine was inspired by that period.'

Gradually, however, the couple began to develop their own style—from the feet up. Courrèges had always preferred flat shoes, and they were right for the times, for the mood of women—but they dictated an entirely new set of proportions. Coqueline Courrèges told Guillaume, 'Women needed to be able to walk and run again. And I was a dancer myself.' Flat heels, she said, forced the designer to recalculate the proportions of the female body. This created a delicate balance and a hat became essential 'to fill out the silhouette'. The garment had to fall from the shoulders and was accompanied by a mid-calf sock or boot. Courrèges continued, 'The clothes float. You don't feel them. I don't emphasise the waistline because the body is a whole. It is ridiculous to treat the top and bottom parts of the body separately.'

The Courrèges mini, first shown in January 1965, was the result of this thinking. Shown on unusually limber, active, athletic models, these designs included angular mini dresses cut four inches above the knee and trouser suits in heavyweight fabrics like gabardine. Many of the outfits had cut-out midriffs and bare backs and were worn without a bra. These were accessorised with flat white boots, goggles and helmets inspired by the equipment worn by astronauts. The stark shapes and white and silver colour scheme were immediately labelled 'Space Age'. Initially they met with a stunned silence. Backstage in the *cabine* with the models and dressers, the Courrègeses heard no applause. A shocked silence prevailed. As he tells it, tears welled in Courrèges's eyes. 'I received a note. "André," had written the editor of the magazine *L'Officiel de la Couture,* "you were crazy, your collection is too short, with boots in the summer. It won't work. What were you thinking?"

'I was thinking that I wanted to make women liberated, full of life, modern,' recalled Courrèges. 'I think I achieved all that.' Indeed, just three hours after the show, the fashion photographer Peter Knapp telephoned him to say, 'André, I hear your collection was fantastic; it was genius. The girls from *Vogue* are super-enthusiastic. They're saying you've revolutionised everything.'

In his interview with Polan in 1979, Courrèges said, 'I wanted to put women into a total-freedom suit, a ribbed-knit body stocking. In order to introduce an element of fluidity and because few women have perfect bottoms, I topped it with a gabardine hipster mini-skirt and a spaceman visor.' This was to become one of fashion's most enduring images and probably the most copied look in the history of fashion. Dismayed by how ruthlessly and universally his designs were plagiarised, Courrèges did not show to the press again until 1967, although he continued to produce collections shown only to clients. Through the next few seasons, he continued to develop this look, adding bright colours and fresh abstract motifs to the clothes.

In 1966 the Musée des Arts Décoratifs in Paris hosted one of the first exhibitions of early-century art movements that were to bring about a reassessment of their value. Les Années 25: Art Deco/

Bauhaus/Stijl/Art Nouveau marked a turning point, the beginning of a romantic revival which informed Barbara Hulanicki's Biba, the work of Ossie Clark and Zandra Rhodes and shaped much of the retro fashion of the 1970s. It certainly signalled the end of modernism's influence on fashion as perceived by Courrèges. 'An avalanche of folklore, hippie dressing, in short, everything you can get from a rag seller,' he lamented, surveying the Rich Peasant, Russian Steppes, Bedouin, Mongol, Mexican, Indian and general Gypsy looks that crowded each other for tent space on fashion's voyages of the imagination. In 1970 he renamed his couture collection Prototype, his ready-to-wear Hyperbole.

At the end of the decade of disguise, Courrèges's prescience did not desert him. Fashion was once more beginning to march in step with his vision. For some time he had been designing and selling worldwide some of the most desirable clothes for sport—skiwear, tennis, dance/exercise—and he understood that the coming jogging and aerobics trend among women would have a huge influence on the clothes they chose to wear for ordinary life. 'Now,' he told Polan in 1979, 'we have reached another turning point and I am starting again to develop the movement I started in 1965. Other designers want to give women the refined style of the 1940s. This does not correspond to their way of living.

'So the clothes made for sport must be ennobled and made into part of the rest of life. We must introduce a more relaxed, at-ease style to everyday clothes, even eveningwear. The ennoblement of sporting clothes is achieved not simply by making a tracksuit in silk or wool but by studying the tracksuit and incorporating the elements that make it so comfortably wearable in clothes which are stylish and flattering.' He was correct in this, predicting the upgrading of tracksuit, shell suit, sweatshirt fabric and hi-tech synthetics to daily wear and the importance of Lycra in everything from leotards to business suits. But his contempt for the fashion system was misplaced.

He declared, 'In 15 years women have freed themselves. The retro look is putting them back in prison. Women are no longer decorative coquettes or sheltered wives; they may be coquettes and they may be wives, but they are also workers with full and independent lives. What sort of service is it to them to change the style every year, one year dictating a frilly, layered peasant look, the next big, square shoulders and small waists? There is a decadent spirit of creativity.'

And yet, women still revel in fashion's wayward changeability. In 1983, the French daily *Libération* wrote, 'Courrèges evokes a modernism so dated one is almost amazed he still exists.' But he did. In 1990 he was still designing and marketing a boutique fashion collection (down to fourteen boutiques from fifty in 1979) worldwide and headed a licensing empire that reportedly grossed an annual $285 million with men's wear, fragrance, home products, champagne and gourmet foods. In the mid-1990s, after several adventures with investors, takeovers and buyouts, André and Coqueline Courrèges regained control of most of their enterprises, and in 1997 André stepped down to concentrate on painting and sculpture.

Further reading: Valerie Guillaume's *Courrèges* (1998), part of the *Fashion Memoir* series, is the most comprehensive account.

26 VALENTINO (1932–)

Although at the beginning of the twenty-first century Italy is a major producer of fashion, a dominant force in the luxury goods industry and second only to Paris in fashion creativity, it is a very new pre-eminence. Italy does not have a long fashion pedigree. Paris and couture have been indivisible for a century and a half, as have New York and industry, modernity and the thrill of the ever new. London has a long tradition of fashion, leading in menswear and tailoring, humbly following Paris's lead in womenswear until the 1960s and the explosion of youthful talent unleashed by the new art schools. But until the 1950s 'Italy' and 'fashion' rarely rubbed up against each other in a sentence. And it started in Rome.

Italy's history is as a handful of separate—and often warring—city-states, each with its own distinct identity; its own aristocracy, landed gentry, professional and merchant class; its university and developed culture; and its own fashionable elite. This was not, until Risorgimento in the nineteenth century, a single nation with a capital that could claim to be pre-eminent in politics, commerce, the arts and culture. Arguably, although it is certainly now a single nation, it still does not have that capital, but rather a series of beautiful, cultured, vital cities, each with a very different character. But after the Second World War Rome had the chance to become a city not just of priests, poets, painters and politicians but a real capital, symbolic of a resurgent nation, determined to put its world back together. The surviving members of the pre-war Roman establishment, the politicians, aristocrats and fledgling industrialists, were quickly joined by a new cast of characters. The Italian film industry and its studios at Ciné Citta began to attract an international cast of actresses, and,

hard on their Ferragamo heels, came all the players in la dolce vita and the louche, nouveau riche jet set. To cater to them, the old-fashioned dressmaking establishments that had survived the war were augmented by a new generation of modern-minded designers with a flair for easy, youthful clothes of impeccable quality; together they formed Roman haute couture.

From this start Italian fashion was to develop fast in the post-war years, brilliantly promoted as an industry from 1951 by Giovanni Battista Giorgini, an agent and entrepreneur, who invited the all-powerful American press to a series of shows and fashion exhibitions in and around the Pitti Palace in Florence 'immediately after the great Paris shows'. John Fairchild of *Women's Wear Daily,* who received the first invitation, remembered in 1992, 'The French at that point were struggling to get into the ready-to-wear business as they saw the demand for haute couture fashion melting away before their eyes. What Giorgini did was boldly leapfrog ahead of the French to bring the Italians into ready-to-wear before the French, always slow to move into new ways.'

When Valentino Clemente Ludovico Garavani, a 27-year-old Paris-trained couturier, returned to Italy in 1959 to set up his own studio, he instinctively located himself in Rome among the couturiers. He wanted the clientele that could afford his exacting perfectionism, the handmade craftsmanship, the clothes for a confident life lived publicly. He did of course develop many product lines, including ready-to-wear collections, but he remained at heart a dressmaker to the rich and famous. Their roll-call is interminable and includes Rita Hayworth,

Elizabeth Taylor, Jackie Kennedy (who married Aristotle Onassis in Valentino), Princess Grace, Audrey Hepburn, Sophia Loren, Monica Vitti, Claudia Cardinale, Ornella Muti, Gina Lollobrigida, Marisa Berenson, Elsa Peretti, Jessica Lange, Sharon Stone and Julia Roberts—who accepted her 2001 Oscar in Valentino. Long before the phrase 'red-carpet dress' was coined, Valentino was the master of the genre, producing flattering, impact-making gowns that looked good from every angle and were guaranteed not to be difficult to wear. His favourite colour, a lush Mediterranean summer poppy red, more orange than scarlet, became known among fashion cognoscenti as 'Valentino red,' and nothing was better qualified to make a grand entrance on the grandest of occasions. He discovered it when, as a student, he took a holiday in Barcelona and went to the opera. 'All the costumes on the stage were red,' he said later. 'All the women in the boxes were mostly dressed in red, and they leant forward like geraniums on balconies, and the seats and drapes were red too . . . I realised that after black and white, there was no finer colour.'

It is a colour that sizzles, that draws every eye in the room. 'I know [that],' Valentino told Susannah Frankel for *Dazed & Confused* in 2000, 'women often say, "Ah, if you want an evening gown, go to Valentino." What is the point of going out if nobody notices you? Stay home! Stay home and invite some friends and you can wear what you like. But if you want to go out and be, for one evening, beautiful, with lots of seduction, sexy and everything, you must do the big number, no?'

Valentino Garavani was born into an affluent family—his father owned electrical supplies stores—in 1932 in Voghera, a small town halfway between Turin and Milan in northern Italy, his country's industrial heartland. As a child he loved drawing and at school displayed an interest in fashion, going on to study at the Santa Marta Institute of Fashion Drawing in Milan while learning French at the Berlitz School. In 1950 his parents subsidised a move to Paris, where he enrolled at the school of the Chambre Syndicale de la Couture Parisienne. He won the International Wool Secretariat's design competition, earning a job at the couture house of Jean Dessès. He stayed for five years acquiring Dessès's taste for sweeping

drapery and exoticism—clothes inspired by classical Roman and Greek draperies and Egyptian decoration. For Valentino's 1991 retrospective, ten sketches from this period were made up to open the exhibition. They were, wrote Bernadine Morris of the *New York Times,* 'revealed to be the precursors of themes which he would elaborate on later in his career.'

They showed, she noted:

> the basic Valentino shape for day and evening as slender, except for a few bouffant dresses of calf or ankle length, as was the style of the early 1950s, before the mini. The surfaces of the slim, long evening dresses are encrusted with jewel embroidery and the narrow shapes are softened by back-flowing chiffon panels or capes. The day dresses are decorated with velvet bands or with a leopard-printed belt matched to an accompanying stole. They are accessorised with stiletto heels and small, forward-thrusting hats. We can see in this mini-collection the first appearance of Valentino's red, the prominence of graphic black-and-white embroidery suggesting Meissen china and the black-and-white dress in a shape suggesting a Greek vase . . . Far more important, however, than any of these details is the unmistakeable sense of elegance and authority.

In 1957 Guy Laroche, the chief illustrator at Dessès, left to set up his own couture house, and Valentino went with him. Two years later, with financial backing from his father, Valentino presented his first collection in his own salon in the Via Condotti in Rome. Elizabeth Taylor, in Rome filming *Cleopatra,* ordered a white dress to wear for the world premiere of *Spartacus*—and the beautiful women of the world began to beat a path to his door. In 1960, Giancarlo Giammetti, a student of architecture, joined the young company, becoming Valentino's partner and managing director; he was to run the business side until Valentino stepped down in 2007. In the same year, Valentino launched his ready-to-wear collection. He first showed with Giovanni Batista Giorgini's stars at the Pitti Palace in Florence in 1962. At just thirty, he was allocated the last slot on the calendar, one that meant the buyers would have to stay another night, delaying their flights home. But they had heard rumours and they stayed. They raced backstage afterwards, elbows out and chequebooks at the ready. International recognition was within his grasp.

In the mid-1960s Valentino abandoned Florence and the Pitti group and, as the closing couturier of the Rome shows, crowned the presentations of the Fontana sisters, Princess Irene Galitzine, Maria Antonelli, Roberto Capucci and Emilio Schuberth. Valentino's evening presentations became glittering social events in their own right, the audience composed of actresses and the wives of politicians, magnates and millionaires, all in evening wear and their best jewels. Perma-tanned and attended by a family of pugs, the couturier had become a member of the class he dressed, entertaining his clients socially in his many homes and on his yacht. His signature style was now established. Consistently elegant, it rarely changed direction suddenly but adhered to classic tenets of good taste while indulging in expensive detail and opulent decoration. These were clothes that looked rich but old-money rich, never vulgar, always glamorous, always grown-up. In 1968 he told *Women's Wear Daily,* 'I believe only in high fashion. I think a couturier must establish his style and stick to it. The mistake of many couturiers is that they try to change their line every collection. I change a little each time, but never too much, so as not to lose my identity.' His dominant themes—the floral and animal prints, the heavy encrustations of beading, the stark contrast of black and white, the fine pleating— were eagerly looked for in every collection.

In her 2008 monograph on the designer, Pamela Golbin wrote:

> As Valentino himself so rightly puts it, he is no innovator in the realm of fashion. Viewed within the broader history of haute couture, he is, however, the recognised champion of a unique silhouette, with a stylistic sensibility uniting supreme grace and timeless allure . . . Fluid silhouettes, subtle femininity, and refined sensuality are the hallmarks of Valentino's style . . . This sensibility— distinguished by a lean, graphic contour—is an integral part of his vocabulary, resulting in styles that are the epitome of understated luxury.

In January 1970, Valentino was the first couturier to put his name to the mini's death warrant when he dropped hems to mid-calf. He was making his influence felt commercially, too, opening ready-to-wear stores in New York, Geneva, Lausanne, London and Paris. In 1975 he began to show his ready-to-wear in Paris. Although no French couturier was likely to concede that Italian workmanship could rival that of the *petites mains,* on ready-to-wear Italian manufacturing was already superior to French, a phenomenon that was to lead eventually to Italy's pre-eminent position in high-quality fashion manufacturing. The 1980s was to be Valentino's decade. It was the decade of Reagan and Thatcher; Diana, Princess of Wales; and flaunt-it fashion, dress-for-success, wide-shouldered suits with tight skirts and gold buttons accessorised by aggressive quantities of gold jewellery and stiletto heels. In the late 1970s fashion had begun to turn Valentino's way as a new formality and grandeur made itself felt. He took inspiration for his big-skirted ball gowns from the romantic portraits of the eighteenth and nineteenth centuries, revelling in a fairy-tale prettiness not seen since Dior. As the 1980s progressed, the clothes acquired a harder edge, a more imposing, vampy feeling. He developed the body-sculpting complex pleating, the oriental-inspired embroideries and art deco appliqué work, his beloved animal prints (a tribute to his beloved animals) and his sophisticated colour combinations.

Italy acknowledged Valentino's contribution to its identity as a fashion force with many honours, including its highest decoration, the Cavaliere de Gran Croce (the equivalent of a British knighthood) in 1986. In 1982 the Metropolitan Museum of Art in New York City, then directed by Diana Vreeland, invited him to show his collection there. In June 1991 the city of Rome celebrated his thirtieth anniversary with a fashion show of 300 outfits and a black-tie dinner for 500. Valentino retired in 2007, having already sold his company some years previously. Alessandra Facchinetti took over as head designer until she was abruptly fired after her spring 2009 collection. Maria Grazia Chiuri and Pier Paolo Piccioli were named as the new creative directors. The duo had previously designed accessories for the label and, in the reports on the autumn/winter 2009 couture collection, were well received.

Further reading: Pamela Golbin's (2008) *Valentino: Themes and Variations* is an excellent book and touches on many aspects.

27 KARL LAGERFELD (1938–)

No designer has remained as influential for as long as Karl Lagerfeld, with the exception of Coco Chanel, whose mantle he inherited. Throughout the first decade of the twenty-first century, long after most of his contemporaries (including his long-time rival Yves Saint Laurent) had retired from the fray, Lagerfeld was still acknowledged as a vibrant, inspirational force and integral to the continuing allure of the house of Chanel.

That said, Lagerfeld the designer remains something of an enigma. His skill in updating other fashion houses' signature styles has tended to overshadow his own personal style. Lagerfeld, a line launched in the 1980s that bore his own name, never drew the plaudits of his work for Chanel, Chloé or Fendi. He is, perhaps, the ultimate, flexible, modern, mercenary designer, able to adapt, transform, modernise and amaze—a chameleon without equal who created the template for so much in contemporary fashion, inspired and prompted by a series of muses and alliances, such as his friendship with the Italian fashion editor Anna Piaggi. He has tended to eschew fashion theorising, making what he describes as 'just great clothes, no great theories behind it.' But behind the oft flippant and frivolous exterior is a designer who works fanatically hard and treats fashion with deep seriousness. In the twilight of his career, Lagerfeld has retained the capacity to surprise and delight, his designs for Chanel full of the *joie d'esprit* of a much younger man. His capacity for hard work is legendary, although even his most fervent supporters recognised that he had overreached himself in 1993, when he was simultaneously designing for Chanel, Fendi, Chloé and his own Karl Lagerfeld lines. His own signature lines

have had a chequered history; the core line, Karl Lagerfeld, folded in 1997, although it was subsequently bought by Tommy Hilfiger Corporation in 2006.

In 2007, Lagerfeld came charging back with a new signature collection, K Karl Lagerfeld, for young men and women. His determination to remain ever-relevant to a new young generation was palpable, reinforced by his dramatic weight loss three years earlier (forty-two kilograms in thirteen months), which made a statement to the world that he was an ageless designer with plenty yet to deliver. Likewise, when he auctioned off his collection of eighteenth-century art and furniture at Christies in 2000, he made it clear that he was resolutely looking to the future. Even a questionable decision to produce a signature capsule collection for mass-market fashion retailer Hennes & Mauritz in 2004 was a defiant statement of youthfulness. Despite his deep understanding of history, Karl Lagerfeld has shown little respect for it. His mantra is 'modern', a word repeated in countless interviews over six decades. Since his appointment as head of design at Chanel in 1982, he has simultaneously trashed and cherished the Chanel heritage. The appointment initially shocked the Paris fashion milieu—Lagerfeld was considered a *styliste* rather than a couturier, and he was a German outsider. But his skills, usually (although not always) applied with a lightness of touch and wit, have made him synonymous with the modern house of Chanel. 'Only the minute and the future are interesting in fashion—it exists to be destroyed,' he has said. 'If everybody did everything with respect, you'd go nowhere.' The

Wertheimer family, who control the label, have made it clear that he has a job for life.

Lagerfeld works at a feverish pace, producing a flood of detailed sketches, a veritable torrent of creativity. A Lagerfeld collection, for whichever label, is marked by clear ideas expressed with confidence and assurance, often with a high degree of wit. His debut for Chanel in 1983 was a triumph, the star piece a trompe l'oeil silk crepe dress featuring jewellery-effect embroidery by Lesage, a playful reference to Madame Chanel's delight in jewellery. For inspiration, his first Chanel collection looked back primarily to the 1920s and 1930s rather than to Chanel's post-war comeback. His extravagant use of Chanel's interlocking C motifs was there from the start. While there were always some ready to dismiss Lagerfeld's style as baroque showmanship sharing more in common with Chanel's arch-rival Elsa Schiaparelli, by the end of the 1980s few could seriously challenge Lagerfeld's position at the top of the fashion pyramid, particularly with Yves Saint Laurent close to retirement.

Over the years, Lagerfeld's designs for Chanel have drawn from all periods of the fashion house's history, often with unexpected juxtapositions, such as denim jeans mixed with a classic soft tweed jacket or a heavy leather biker jacket with a silk tulle ball gown. Lagerfeld's design aesthetic has always been brasher than the original Chanel—whether reflected in an intense colour palette for tweeds or in flashy luxury bags and other accessories or in a constant willingness to appropriate street style. But Lagerfeld's oft strident aesthetic has reflected a more strident age. 'I took her code, her language and mixed it all up,' he said in 2004. Humour is one of the most potent weapons in the Lagerfeld armoury. Anna Piaggi, a fashion eccentric of the first order, was drawn to Lagerfeld by his playful eclecticism: the first Lagerfeld-designed dress in her wardrobe was in silk embroidered with sequins with a motif of an art deco pop jukebox.

Lagerfeld grew up accustomed to money and luxury and never experienced the financial hardships of many of his contemporaries. He was born Karl Otto Lagerfeldt in Hamburg, Germany, the son of a Swedish business magnate who had made a substantial fortune in the condensed milk industry. He claims a birth date of 1938, although baptismal records suggest he was delivered five years earlier in 1933. His German mother, Elizabeth, was a formative influence on the young designer, a demanding personality who shaped her son to develop a similar iron will and continued to be an important force in his life until her death at the age of 81 in 1978. He moved with his mother to Paris in 1953, making his big breakthrough two years later when he won an International Wool Secretariat award for a coat. The young Yves Saint Laurent won the dress award, setting the stage for two careers that marched in parallel through the 1960s, 1970s and beyond. Lagerfeld's path to glory was, however, much slower than Saint Laurent's. The coat award in 1955 enabled Lagerfeld to land his first job at Pierre Balmain, from where he moved to Jean Patou after three years. But he was quickly bored and left within a year in a significant shift from the world of couture to ready-to-wear, freelancing for names ranging from Krizia, Charles Jourdan and Mario Valentino to supermarket chain Monoprix. He was avowedly a *styliste*—the French word for a designer who worked for ready-to-wear labels. That put him, in the eyes of the oft snobbish world of French fashion, at a considerably lower level than the couturier Yves Saint Laurent. Lagerfeld's response was to celebrate his role as *styliste*, deriding the craft of haute couture as old-fashioned and backward-looking. The fierce professional rivalry turned deeply personal in the 1970s when Saint Laurent had an affair with Jacques de Bascher, the long-term amour of Lagerfeld.

Ever restless, Lagerfeld was briefly disillusioned by the world of fashion design for a period in the early 1960s and moved to Italy in 1964 to study art. Within three years, however, he was back in fashion at the house of Fendi, forming a bond with the Fendi family that has lasted even longer than the Chanel connection. From 1964, he also worked fruitfully with the ready-to-wear house of Chloé under the guidance of founder Gaby Aghion, who taught him how to edit and simplify the flood of designs he was producing. In the 1970s, his work for Chloé established him as one of international fashion's leading designers. The 1972 Deco collection, featuring black-and-white prints and inspired bias-cut dresses, received universal acclaim. For ten years, as chief designer at Chloé, he produced a stream of collections that summed up the fashion spirit of the period, leading to his appointment at Chanel in 1982. He briefly returned to Chloé in 1993, although less successfully.

Lagerfeld's talents extend beyond fashion design into photography and illustration—and no doubt he would be his own best biographer. Speaking to Roger Tredre in 1994, though, he said he would never write his story for a simple reason—'I could not write the truth.' Author Alicia Drake was brave enough to exhaustively research Lagerfeld's rivalry with Yves Saint Laurent in the 1970s in her book, *The Beautiful Fall: Lagerfeld, Saint Laurent, and Glorious Excess in 1970s Paris* (2006). Lagerfeld felt wounded by the book, taking legal action which resulted in its withdrawal in France by publishers Bloomsbury.

Restless and easily bored, Lagerfeld is the German outsider who became the ultimate insider in the gossipy world of Parisian fashion. He is a media dream, accessible and obliging, enthusiastically ready with a pithy quote and a pleasure in stirring up mischief. His wide-ranging interests and exceptional gift for languages make him a one-man publicity machine for whichever label he is representing. He has a sense of theatre (indeed, he has designed costumes for theatre, opera and cinema), invariably arriving fashionably late for appointments, usually in a flurry of energy and impatience, borne with equanimity by his colleagues in the Chanel atelier. His showmanship and extraordinary speed of work were both depicted admirably in the French television documentary, *Signé Chanel,* first screened in 2005. He has been admired (and sometimes mocked) as a fashion spectacle in his own right. In the 1950s, Lagerfeld used to drive a cream open-top Mercedes, a present from his father, and wear high heels and carry clutch bags on holiday in Saint-Tropez. Fifty years on, his spectacular diet was partly linked to his desire to squeeze into the slim-line tailoring of Hedi Slimane, the young designer at Dior Homme whose work he has championed. He has often expressed a cultural affinity with the cultivated aristocrats of eighteenth-century

Europe, even half-jesting that in a previous life he was an eighteenth-century gentleman.

Much of Karl Lagerfeld has remained a mystery, the real man behind the fast-talking 'Kaiser' often obscured from view by the media persona. His predilection for dark glasses or the protective carapace of a fan suggests that this is the way he prefers it. Perhaps the truth is not so complicated—his life is his work. Certainly that has appeared to be the reality since the death of his long-time close friend Jacques de Bascher in 1989. On the subject of work, Lagerfeld has said: 'You have to remember that I do nothing else. That's how I manage. Twenty-four hours a day. I don't go on holiday.' Lagerfeld's offence at Alicia Drake's exploration of his rivalry with Saint Laurent in the 1970s was clearly deep. Drake sought to delve deep into the Lagerfeld psyche, soliciting comments from a wide variety of sources. She explored his many personal rivalries and his recurring tendency to fall out with even the closest of friends, ranging from Gaby Aghion at Chloé to the model Inès de la Fressange. On his obsession with youth, Drake quoted an anonymous former colleague: 'If you want to understand Karl, you have to understand his fear of death . . . He talks about the future non-stop because when he looks at the past he realises that life is behind him and there is only a small portion ahead. This is what makes him work so hard.'

As a designer, he has consistently set new standards for productivity and energy, driving fashion forward into the modern age. He also created a template that was followed by Tom Ford at Gucci and a host of modern designers, showing how fashion and fashion labels can be endlessly revived and made relevant for every new generation.

Further reading: Alicia Drake's *The Beautiful Fall: Lagerfeld, Saint Laurent and Glorious Excess in 1970s Paris* (2006), which was withdrawn from publication in France, provides many interesting insights into Lagerfeld in the 1970s. Lagerfeld has been interviewed innumerable times, including by Roger Tredre for *The Observer* newspaper ('Kaiser Karl', 7 August 1994).

28 HALSTON (1932–1990)

A fashion lover would say that fashion's minimalists have their moments and then become boring. If James Laver was right and 'clothes are the furniture of the mind made visible', then there is an excess of vacant space in the minds and the imaginations of minimalists. The pragmatists who just want a way to dress that looks elegant, sophisticated and as if they don't wish to make the effort to care much about keeping up with fashion's changes would say they are never boring. Roy Halston Frowick, known simply as Halston, was the minimalist's minimalist. He was granted high status by contemporary commentators, possibly because of his good looks and personal star quality, a phenomenon not really seen again in a fashion designer until Tom Ford; analysts reflecting on the period are more grudging. Patricia Mears, in *Halston* (2001) wrote, 'Halston was a groundbreaking figure. Best known as a modernist who fully advocated the minimalist aesthetic, Halston turned fashion on its ear in the over-accessorised sixties by blending simple, pared-down silhouettes with the most luxurious fabrics.'

Caroline Rennolds Milbank, who categorised Halston as a 'purist' in *Couture: The Great Fashion Designers,* wrote that he was the right designer for a certain moment:

> Halston began making clothes at a time when it was no longer fashionable to appear rich. The new social climate was one in which Park Avenue and Sutton Place matrons consigned their 'important' jewels to vaults rather than lose them to muggers; when cultural impresarios were throwing parties for Black Panthers and waging war on the stuffy, the traditional and the formal. Perhaps it is because his sensibility matured during this

period of 'radical chic' that Halston rejected most vestiges of formal dressmaking. Halston makes clothes without zippers or pockets, ruffles or notched lapels, practically without seams.

Roy Halston Frowick was born in 1932 in Des Moines, Iowa, the second son (of four children) of a Norwegian-American accountant with a passion for inventing. Roy developed an interest in sewing from his mother, and as an adolescent he began creating hats and embellishing outfits for his mother and sister. Owing to his father's alcoholism and the difficulties he had remaining in employment, the family moved often, first to Illinois then Indiana. Roy graduated from high school in 1950 and then attended Indiana University for one semester. After the family moved to Chicago in 1952, he enrolled in a night course at the Art Institute of Chicago and worked as a window dresser at the Carson Pirie Scott department store. At this time known as 'Fro', he began a relationship with André Basil, a celebrity hairdresser twenty-five years his senior whose salon was in Chicago's premier hotel, the Ambassador. Basil gave Fro a corner of the salon for a millinery atelier where he would attract the attention of Basil's clients who included the cream of Chicago's society as well as the celebrated guests who stayed at the hotel.

In 1956 Basil introduced Fro to Lilly Daché, the queen of New York milliners, and by 1958 he was working for her in her Park Avenue establishment. From this point on he used his middle name, Halston. His ambition quickly outstripped Daché's establishment, and he accepted a post as head milliner at Bergdorf Goodman, America's most exclusive store. When Jacqueline Kennedy attended her husband's presidential inauguration in January

1961, she was wearing a coat by Oleg Cassini and a pillbox hat by Halston. The hat was perfectly suited to Mrs Kennedy's rather large head. Unadorned, simple and overwhelmingly youthful, a fitting symbol for a new generation stepping up to power, the hat was one of the most copied items of clothing ever, bought and worn by women across the world.

Generally, Halston's style in millinery was more fanciful than that simple pillbox. Many of his designs bordered on the fantastic; he used mirrors, fringing, jewels and flowers to decorate hoods, bonnets, coifs and helmets. His innovative scarf hat, a silk square on a frame, was a much-copied design of the 1960s. He was an inventive and technically brilliant milliner with a sense of humour. Diana Vreeland said, 'He was probably the greatest hatmaker in the world. I'd say to him, "H, I had a dream about a hat last night" and I'd go about describing it, and then, by God, he'd give it to me, line by line.'

The chief advantage of working for Bergdorf Goodman, however, was that it opened his eyes to the wider international world of original fashion design. Since the beginning of the century Bergdorf Goodman had boasted a custom design salon where original French designs were copied for clients. As was the now dated way with many American fashion establishments Bergdorf's still sent its designers to Paris twice a year to the haute couture shows to glean ideas and buy toiles. This was to be Halston's equivalent of the Chambre Syndicale school; his 'sharp eye,' wrote Patricia Mears, 'greedily absorbed every detail, every cut of a seam in the creations he saw by Gabrielle "Coco" Chanel, Yves Saint Laurent, Hubert de Givenchy and, his favourite, Cristobal Balenciaga.'

At Bergdorf Goodman, Halston garnered a following of elegant society women, Broadway actresses, Hollywood stars and influential fashion editors who were to prove ready clients for his ready-to-wear clothing collection when, reluctantly, Bergdorf launched it for him in 1966. Both hats and haute couture were becoming less and less fashionable as the decade passed. Claire McCardell had led the way in marrying original design to mass production techniques. Halston did not aim to reach quite so wide a customer base, but he understood that a combination of luxury fabrics with cuts simple enough for mass

manufacture would be attractive to the kind of women used to couture and now beginning to buy the European boutique collections. Bergdorf Goodman gave him access to the Delman shoe salon to design a complementary range of shoes and a boutique for the collection on the second floor. The first collection, shown with music on dancing young models, consisted of eighteen interchangeable pieces. The presentation aroused media excitement, but sales were slow, and eighteen months later, Halston left Bergdorf's, setting up his own couture label three months later with modest backing from Mrs Estelle Marsh Watlington of Texas.

By now Halston was part of a glittering circle of clients and creative friends, including Jackie Kennedy Onassis, Elizabeth Taylor, Elsa Peretti, Rita Hayworth, Marlene Dietrich, Diana Vreeland, Martha Graham, Babe Paley, Barbara Walters, Lauren Bacall, Bianca Jagger, Anjelica Huston and Liza Minnelli. In 1972, *Newsweek* magazine designated him 'surely the premier fashion designer of all America'. The simplicity that was his trademark was perceived as clean-limbed, healthy and all-American in contrast to the over-decorated, decadent ethnic peasant looks that were being created by all the European designers. Halston hated fussiness and, in 1973, when invited to participate in a fashion show at Versailles where American designers showcased their work alongside top French designers, he stunned the fashion world by the strict purity of his dresses.

The Halston look spoke of understated wealth: cashmere sweaters, silk shirtwaist dresses, simple elegant wool pants. 'I didn't want to make clothes for kids,' he said. 'I wanted feminine clothes for women between 22 and 55.' Even his evening wear derived its glamour and sex appeal from the fabrics rather than any cleverness of cut. His colour palette was ivory, black, and red, but he understood the principle of accent and emphasis, using fuchsia, electric blue and deep burgundy. His best known garment was the Ultrasuede shirtwaist dress he introduced in 1972. It became a staple of his collections, re-run in many colours, and throughout the decade was one of the most popular dresses in America. Its success stemmed from its plainness and the fact that it did not wrinkle or crease and was machine washable. Halston became the Ultrasuede king, signing licensing agreements for a range of products in Ultrasuede, including hand-bags, shoes, boots, belts and bed spreads.

Although Halston showed his clothes on stick-thin models before it was fashionable among design-ers to do so, he boasted of dressing Miss Average America. In 1978 he told Bernadine Morris of *The New York Times,* 'You have to have something for the woman who is overweight—a loose tunic and pants is good because it elongates the body. You have to have something for the woman with hips—the princess line works for her. Caftans are fine for the woman whose figure isn't perfect.' That was the year he moved into the Olympic Tower skyscraper next door to St Patrick's cathedral and covered all the walls—including the washrooms—in mirror glass. He could sit at his red lacquer desk and look down on a Manhattan skyline multiply reflected.

In the early 1970s Halston's lover was a Colombian window dresser named Victor Hugo. Through Hugo Halston met Andy Warhol, who was to become a close friend. In the late 1970s and early 1980s, he enthusiastically embraced the celebrity lifestyle and was frequently featured in the gossip columns often as a walker for beautiful, sometimes troubled, women. He was one of the faces of the infamous New York nightclub Studio 54. One of the most famous evenings in the degenerate history of the club was Halston's birthday party for Bianca Jag-ger in 1977. During this period, he was also seen partying with his friend Liza Minnelli at the gay holi-day resort Fire Island. Patricia Mears reports that he took full advantage of the drugs and casual sex that were available at the nightclubs he frequented. Halston had been part of the pretty wild gay party scene since he moved to Chicago in the 1950s. When disco emerged in the 1970s he frequented the hottest clubs, socialised with celebrities, em-braced the most popular drugs, and designed clothes that the celebrities wore to 'make the scene'. His halter-neck dress of 1974 became a dance-floor staple as did his trademark strapless dresses, the one-shouldered sheaths and the asymmetri-cal necklines. All of his designs were simple and unconstructed, usually in solid colours and luxury fabrics. His narrow, elongated silhouettes skimmed over the body and flattered young and old figures alike. Halston's signature sunglasses, worn both day and night, completed the look.

In 1973 Norton Simon purchased all of Halston's companies, his trademark, and his exclusive de-sign services for approximately $12 million. In 1975 menswear and perfume were added to the empire. The perfume was known simply as Halston and came in a bean-shaped bottle designed by Elsa Peretti. In 1977 Halston was invited to redesign the uniforms and aircraft interiors and airport spaces for Braniff Airlines. His brief was to create a look that conveyed the urbane sophistication of the late 1970s and early 1980s. He was deemed at that stage in his career to be the designer who best understood a well-bred look. However, his part-nership with Norton Simon Industries did not bring the riches Halston had hoped it would. Refusing to allow his name to be put on anything he did not design himself, he found it difficult to meet the level of productivity expected of him. His signature was seen on everything from spectacles to the uniforms worn by Avis car-rental employees, but he increas-ingly felt under pressure to produce even more.

In 1982, amid proliferating licences, Norton Simon Industries asked Halston to design a range for the down-market store group, JC Penney. He agreed, but it was seen as a step too far down the market and Bergdorf's and Martha's dropped his collec-tions and formerly faithful friends and clients de-fected to other designers. Although the Halston III collection for JC Penney was successful, Halston's relationships with his bosses and colleagues de-teriorated until finally, in 1984, he was locked out of his offices after throwing yet another fero-cious temper tantrum. He was then fired, losing the rights to his own name. In 1988, after he was diagnosed with Aids, he sold his New York town house and moved to San Francisco, where he died in 1990. Of his glittering entourage, only Minnelli stayed true till the end. There have been three at-tempts to revive the label, the latest in 2008 by the president of Jimmy Choo, Tamara Mellon, and the movie mogul, Harvey Weinstein. They hired Marco Zanini, who had been head of couture at Versace for ten years, to design it. Reviews were mixed but the clothes, some of which went on sale online im-mediately, sold out. In 2009, Marios Schwab took over as desinger.

Further reading: Halston (2001), edited by Steven Bluttal with essays by Patricia Mears.

29   KENZO (1939–)

In 1970 Kenzo Takada was the first Japanese fashion designer to show his work in Paris. He was joined very quickly on the catwalks of fashion's capital by his compatriots, Issey Miyake and Kansai Yamamoto. They were three very different designers, and they were all well received. Initially, however, Kenzo, with his bright and cheerful, intensely youthful clothes, was the great success. The world of haute couture had only recently adjusted to the youthquake that was changing the world and shifting its spending power. The chasm that had existed between the couturiers and the manufacturers of ready-to-wear for the masses was narrowing. As London, Milan and New York began to challenge the pre-eminence of Paris as arbiter and producer of fashion, the couture houses, led by Cardin and Saint Laurent, were creating boutique lines, less expensive versions of their couture, and young designers such as Sonia Rykiel, Emmanuelle Khanh and Karl Lagerfeld at Chloé launched high-fashion lines that were firmly targeted at the ready-to-wear market.

In 1973 the Chambre Syndicale de la Couture Parisienne united with Didier Grumbach's Createurs et Industriels to form the Federation Française de la Couture, du Pret-a-Porter des Couturiers and des Createurs de Mode. This umbrella organisation established the Chambre Syndicale du Pret-a-Porter des Couturiers et des Createurs de Mode as a separate and parallel organisation to the Chambre Syndicale de la Couture Parisienne. Significantly, Kenzo was a member from the start, regarded then and always as a star of French fashion.

When Kenzo had launched his label three years earlier, the hedonistic 1960s were segueing into the more idealistic 1970s, when altruism and a global perspective would dominate youth culture. In the aftermath of 1968 and the Paris riots (which Kenzo witnessed) it was a time of making love, not war, of turning on, tuning in and dropping out. Some experimented with collective living, others took to the hippy trail to discover new, simpler cultures and hoped to find enlightenment there or at least some kind of spiritual experience. Kenzo's innate eclecticism, his sensuous appreciation of print and pattern, his historicism and understanding of the drama of mass and volume, lush layers piled on in sizzling contrast—all expressed the joy in colour and natural beauty of the zeitgeist and captured the attention of the world's press from his first showing.

It is arguable that history has already done Kenzo Takada an injustice. In the early 1970s his were the shows that attracted the hysterical crowds, his the name that defined youthful fashion. His innovations were hugely influential: he literally put the flowers into flower power and was part of a group which thoroughly democratised and rejuvenated high fashion. But he was eclipsed by the Japanese designers who came later and who did not integrate into the French system in the same way. Unlike Miyake, Kawakubo and Yamamoto, Kenzo always appointed French managers while recruiting Japanese creatives. But he was probably the hottest designer of the early 1970s.

The fifth of seven children, Kenzo Takada was born in the village of Himeji, in the shadow of a great castle. His elderly father ran a teahouse, and Kenzo grew up surrounded by the geishas who worked there. He has described his father as 'upright, taciturn, rigid'. His mother, he said, 'was active, attentive, courageous.' He did not enjoy the games the boys at school played and was usually to be found studying his sister's fashion magazines and using the free patterns in them to make clothes. He made dolls too, and dressed them. 'This,' he told Ginette Sainderichin, 'is how I edged my way into fashion and how, in my dreams, I sewed dresses for the round-eyed daughters of the far-off West.'

He dropped out of Kobe University in 1958 to join the Bunka Fashion College in Tokyo, which had just started accepting male applicants. He worked his way through college, winning prizes, including the coveted So-En award, and press attention. The lecturer who taught him draping, an alien technique to Japan where clothes were conceived on the flat, was Chie Koike, a graduate of L'Ecole de la Chambre Syndicale de la Couture Parisienne. She became Kenzo's mentor and encouraged him to think of further study in Paris. His first job on graduation was with Mikura, a designer of ready-to-wear; he later moved to Sanai, which specialised in fast fashion for the young. That was an important experience as he learned to produce forty models a month while keeping his vision fresh. In 1964 he used a windfall 350,000 yen to travel, with a classmate and friend, Hiromisu Matsuda, by sea to Europe. It was the proverbial slow boat. They visited Hong Kong, Saigon, Singapore, Colombo, Djibouti and Alexandria on the way to Marseilles. They diverted to see Milan, Venice, Rome, Florence, Munich, Madrid and London before settling in Paris in spring 1965. (This was only the beginning of a lifetime's travel, a lifetime's passion for new places and cultures.)

When Kenzo first arrived in Paris he spoke no French. Having no work and little money, except what his mother could afford to send him, he wandered the streets, observing, learning, studying shop windows and watching the people. Eventually he was offered a job at Pisanti and then moved on to Relations Textiles, where he specialised in knitting techniques. Of all the Japanese designers working in the West, Kenzo was the most assimilated, a process which began as soon as he began to try to find work. 'For the first four or five years in Paris,' he wrote in 1985:

I watched and observed what Parisian chic and elegance mean. Whether it is haute couture or

prêt-à-porter, French clothes are well fitted to the body. Well cut, fitted and finished impeccably, and they have curves. That is Parisian chic and elegance. Such clothes-making has its own rules for its shapes, fabric selections, colour combinations, and it seemed to me there are rules even for the way you wear these clothes. Those are all confined within a stubborn frame of mind. That was suffocating for me.

In 1970, with two fellow graduates of the Bunka, Atsuko Kondo and Atsuko Ansai, he launched the first Jungle Jap boutique in Galerie Vivienne near the Palais Royal. Its interior was inspired by the darkly threatening, exotically tropical dreamscape paintings of Le Douanier Rousseau and hinted mischievously at the nature of the clothes. He could not afford to buy the fabrics he wanted, so he bought some at flea markets and went back to Japan for some, buying printed cottons and silks, cutting them in fresh, simple, youthful styles and mixing new and old. This was the genesis of the Kenzo style which was to revitalise Paris fashion. In a first collection that was all about getting the attention of the press, he mixed plaids and florals, stripes and checks in a way that was reminiscent of how the geishas of his childhood layered their many brightly coloured, richly printed and embroidered kimonos, unafraid of colour clashes or the juxtaposition of patterns that refused to speak to each other.

Trained by his time at Sanai to the concept of fast-paced constantly renewed fashion, Kenzo produced five collections in his first year. He was an instant sensation, the darling of a fashion press that found what he had to offer exactly right for the times. From the kimono he also derived his cuts—all straight lines and simple squares. Reflecting on the birth of his signature style, he wrote in *Liberté: Kenzo* in 1987, 'No more darts, I like bold, straight lines. Use cotton for summer and no lining for winter. Combine bright colours together, combine flowers, stripes and checks freely. This was the beginning of my style.'

The American press called his style 'kicky', probably because the models used to love the clothes so much they would bounce and twirl, grinning broadly, down the catwalk. To Kenzo can be attributed many of the key looks of the 1970s: tunics;

Mao collars; layered looks; shawls and long, lushly patterned jacquard-woven scarves; Peruvian knits in vibrant colours; bobbles; big, big, square-cut jumpers; loose waistcoats; kimono-cut sleeves; baggy trousers; ingénue taffeta frocks bedecked with frills and flounces and folkloric and peasant looks inspired by traditional dress from all over the world. Mid-decade he was credited with introducing the unconstructed Big Look based on one-size-fits-all voluminous garments, a long, circular skirt worn with braces, topped with big shirts, big coats and capes that cut a dash as the wearer moved. 'Much too big is the right size,' Kenzo told *Vogue* in 1975, loosening his look even further with tent dresses, smocks and enormous striped dungarees with 'elephant' legs worn with thick-soled sandals.

The Big Look bombed in the United States but swept the rest of the fashionable world. However by the next year Kenzo was in a Tyrolean mood, cutting jackets closer to the body, starting a run on loden, boiled wool, braided trim and appliqué and introducing the hip-slung belt which, once again, the whole fashion world emulated. By 1978 he was playing with military looks based on Morocco's Zouave soldiers with their voluminous striped jodhpurs and romantically full-sleeved shirts crisscrossed by bandoliers. By this point international fashion had gone seriously fancy-dress and sentimentally retrospective. For winter that year Kenzo showed white Nehru suits and swaggering, ruffled pirate shirts over narrow breeches.

The 1980s brought recession and the dress-for-success phenomenon born of a competitive workplace and women's determination to shatter the glass ceiling that barred their route to the top of the professions and the business world. One strand of fashion became deadly serious and found many ways to ape the male business suit in an attempt to imply authority. This was the moment when minimalist designers like Calvin Klein, Armani and Zoran became dominant while iconoclastic designers in London, and then Antwerp and Japan began to challenge ideas of acceptable dressing and the fashion system itself. Another strand of establishment fashion became flirtatious, following the lead of Norma Kamali's ra-ra look and making skirts

shorter and flouncier and accessories cuter, girlier, almost infantilised. Kenzo found his place in the latter camp, doing easy, sporty collections that were still youthful, still pretty, still naive—possibly too naive for the decade—and consequently his importance began to wane.

In 1982 Rei Kawakubo of Comme des Garçons and Yohji Yamamoto showed in Paris for the first time. They, with Issey Miyake, became the definitive Japanese designers. 'Comme and Yohji were a big shock to the system,' Kenzo told Alicia Drake in 2006, 'but in a way I am closer to them. At least I understood their construction of the garment. But what really threw me were Mugler and Montana and then Azzedine. They were doing clothes that were beautiful, sublime, but they were clothes that I really *cannot* do, clothes that were so highly structured. For me someone like Montana was the polar opposite of what I was doing. Fashion had changed completely.'

Yuniya Kawamura, writing in 2004, summed up Kenzo's contribution succinctly, 'Kenzo was the first to bring to the West what was not considered to be fashionable in Japan, and he was able to turn it into fashion. He may not have been as radical or avant-garde as other designers who followed him, but he showed that making something unfashionable into fashionable depends on the context in which the clothes are placed and the process that the clothes have gone through.'

Throughout the 1980s and 1990s Kenzo's importance declined as he attempted to keep pace with fashion's moods while remaining true to his own vision. He retired in 1999, selling his company to LVMH and heading off to polish his painting and golfing skills. He said his goodbyes with characteristic exuberance, renting a Parisian theatre for the party, filling it with balloons and belly dancers and riding off into the sunset on the back of an elephant. The line is currently designed by Antonio Marras, an Italian.

Further reading: Ginette Sainderichin's *Kenzo* (1998), part of the Fashion Memoir series, for focus and Yuniya Kawamura's *The Japanese Revolution in Paris Fashion* (2004) for background.

30 RALPH LAUREN (1939–)

In September 2007 Ralph Lauren celebrated his fortieth anniversary as the king of American fashion by reprising his favourite fantasy worlds in New York's Central Park, taking over the historic Conservatory Garden for the presentation of his spring/summer 2008 fashion show and a black tie dinner under the stars. The guest list was as glittering as even Lauren could have desired. It included the actors Robert De Niro and Dustin Hoffman, the mayor of New York, Michael Bloomberg, Lauren Bush (then dating David Lauren), the talk show host Barbara Walters, the homemaker-tycoon Martha Stewart, Sarah Jessica Parker and her husband Matthew Broderick and fellow American designers, including Donna Karan, Vera Wang and Carolina Herrera. Designer Diane von Furstenberg declared, 'He's as American as Coca-Cola.'

Well, not quite. The man who started his business career by designing ties in the Bronx and now heads one of the world's most successful fashion and lifestyle companies, valued in excess of $4 billion, chose a thoroughly British theme for this career-crowning occasion. The fashion show was staged in a giant marquee against a painted backdrop which represented Royal Ascot Opening Day at the turn of the century and, in a reference to Cecil Beaton's famous black-and-white Ascot scene from the film, *My Fair Lady,* the show opened with a model wearing a black picture hat and a black and white, ruffled hourglass gown and carrying a silver-topped cane. Some of the supporting cast were dressed as turf club dandies in immaculately tailored jackets and jodhpurs, accessorised with monocles, watch chains draped over fitted waistcoats, top hats, cravats and spat-style boots. Then came the riders in

rose-pink jodhpurs encrusted with silver embroidery and a series of dazzling horse-print silks worn with tailored breeches and T-shirt dresses accessorised with riding hats.

Lauren then moved on to revisit some of the other major themes of his extraordinary career: the 1920s of both the Great Gatsby and jazz age Paris, the English country house scene of the 1930s, genteel garden parties and grand balls. It was not quite all the lost worlds Lauren has spent a lifetime persuading people they want to inhabit but some of the most evocative. He left out the prairies of the nineteenth century with its pioneer women in blanket coats, flounced skirts, ruffled blouses, silver and turquoise accessories and cowboy boots; the plains of Africa in the 1930s with its effete aristocrats, safari gear and cool white linens and the hints of Happy Valley set decadence; the New England hunting set with strictly tailored red redingotes; Hollywood's golden age with its glamour queens in their bias-cut slip dresses; the traditional American backwoods rough-wear of plaid jackets and time-honoured knitwear, cabled, Fair Isle, Navajo-patterned, over soft shirting, corduroy pants and denim jeans and skirts; and many more worlds that once existed but not quite as beautifully as Lauren imagines them.

Ralph Lauren is the great romantic of American fashion, a myth-maker whose own sensitivity to how clothes and artefacts define an era and its people have allowed him to recreate those eras—if not exactly those people—in his clothing collections, his complete-world home ranges, his elite theme-park stores and most powerfully in his advertising campaigns. He is a designer whose lyrical vision is capable of sweeping along the most minimalist of modernists in its technicoloured embrace. As Jane Mulvagh put it, 'He launched a look that endowed American and European utility and sports garments with nostalgic appeal. "I paint dreams. These clothes have a heritage, they're not frivolous but things to treasure even when they get old," he said.'

Colin McDowell, in his monograph on the designer, wrote:

> Refreshingly he has separated dress from the tyranny of fashion dictatorship. He has looked specifically at what makes American fashion not only different but unique: sportswear, casual elegance, the luxury of simplicity married to the highest level of workmanship and the very best of fabrics and materials—and he emphasised the timelessness inherent in it . . . But the skills of Ralph Lauren are not confined to clothes alone. He has taught us how to create our surroundings, he has educated our taste and he has revolutionised the way we shop.

He was the first to understand what has since been labelled 'experiential' shopping; we may take away a product in a bag but what we are really buying into is the experience offered to us by the constructed ambiance of the shop—whether it be a gentleman's club or a safari tent.

Lauren was born in 1939, in the Bronx, New York, the fourth and last child of recent immigrants from Russia, Frank and Frieda Lifshitz. Frank was a highly skilled decorator, a specialist in wood grain and marble effects. Ralph was an ordinary little boy who liked to play ball with his brothers and the neighbourhood guys. He did not, as so many other important designers did, make clothes for his sister's dolls. However, according to school friends Lauren's fashion sense was apparent at an early age when he would buy himself expensive suits with the money he earned working at his after-school job. Looking stylish was a priority.

McDowell establishes two patterns of behaviour in the boy which were to shape the man. He had a fertile fantasy life and totally immersed himself in the role of the moment, playing baseball as his hero, Mickey Mantle; sword-fighting his brothers as the Duke of York 'or some other duke'; and boxing, as Joe Louis, with his brother who was Sugar Ray Robinson. And, second, he began quite naturally to invest clothes with talismanic qualities, deriving a sense of identity and provenance from his brother's well-worn hand-me-downs. 'You don't need,' wrote McDowell, 'a crystal ball to see this as the beginning of a cultural approach that was to be the basis of the Polo Ralph Lauren empire, predicated as it is on the assumption that, while fashion is fickle, "real" clothes are better because they exemplify continuity. How many times has Ralph Lauren said that he responds to old, well-worn clothes and dislikes the concept of fashion because it presupposes newness?'

Ralph's brothers changed their name to Lauren while he was still a teenager, and he followed suit. By the time he finished high school, he realised that his dream of an athletic career was unlikely to be realised, so he enrolled at City College in Manhattan to study business management, dropping out before getting his degree. While waiting to be drafted into the military, he got a job at Brooks Brothers, a store whose merchandise—all the elements of the classic, upper-crust gentleman's wardrobe—was identified with a customer base that had gone to prep school and an East Coast Ivy League university. This was where the so-called preppie look of the early 1980s was spawned. It enchanted the young Ralph Lauren. 'I thought it was like Mecca,' he said. 'It was just, "Wow!"'

He was called up into the army reserve and on being discharged in 1964 took a series of jobs that led to the one with a tie manufacturer named Abe Rivetz, for whom he began designing wide 'kipper' ties that called for a 'big knot'; Rivetz told him: 'The world's not ready for you, Ralph.' So in 1967, he borrowed $50,000 and launched his own range of ties, which he sold to Bloomingdale's. 'They cost $20 in an era when men's ties were $5. I made the best stuff in America because I believed that beautiful things could be made here,' he said. He called his fledgling company Polo, because he wanted a sporty, classy name, and because he always saw himself as the dashing hero of the chukka. The movie of his own life was on a continuous loop in Lauren's imagination, the script endlessly tweaked, endlessly varied, its location shifting regularly. In 2008 he told Lesley White of the *Sunday Times,* 'When I started with clothes, it wasn't necessarily a fashion message. It was how would I like my kids to grow up? How do I spend my weekends?'

In 1964 Lauren married Ricky Low-Beer, the blonde 19-year-old only child of Viennese Jewish immigrants. A college girl with a classy, educated manner, she was his romantic ideal. They have three children, Andrew, David and Dylan. Despite strong and well-substantiated rumours (detailed at length in Michael Gross's book) of a run of long affairs with other women, Lauren has clearly never doubted that his marriage to Ricky would endure, the central relationship of his life.

Polo grew fast. In 1968 the full menswear range was launched, and in 1969, the first menswear shop-within-a-shop in Bloomingdale's in Manhattan. In 1971 he launched his first womenswear collection, a line of tailored shirts, and opened the first Polo store in Beverly Hills, California. In 1972 he introduced the short-sleeved cotton knit polo shirt with its polo-player logo. It was advertised with the slogan, 'Every team has its color—Polo has 24.' In 1974, Lauren provided the men's clothes for the film *The Great Gatsby*, starring Robert Redford, who was to become a lifelong friend. In 1977 he designed the clothes for Woody Allen and Diane Keaton in *Annie Hall,* starting a trend for androgyny in womenswear—baggy trousers, masculine shirts, waistcoats and ties worn at half-mast. In 1978, inspired by his ranch in Colorado, and, of course, by the mythic movies of the Old West, he launched Western wear for men and women, an enduring style within his canon and a riposte to those who accused him of being in thrall to an archaic and irrelevant Britishness.

In the same year Lauren launched his first perfumes, Lauren and Polo for Men, and his collection of boys' clothes. The following year he created the first of his multi-image advertising campaigns in which the pictures were styled as stills from a film. In 1981 his Santa Fe collection, based on traditional Navajo colours, patterns and details, was so beautiful fashion editors wept and so evocative it became the most copied collection of the decade. Simultaneously, the first Polo store in Europe—and the first American designer label store—opened on Bond Street. While women were scrambling to dress as hybrid Native American maidens and covered-wagon pioneer women, men were going 'preppy'. Polo's preppy look was considered the power suit of the early 1980s, the uniform of Tom Wolfe's 'Masters of the Universe' who peopled Wall Street. Lauren sourced many elements in his collections in Britain, especially knitwear and fabrics, and he went to London for his tailoring, commissioning classics like the blue blazer made leaner, younger for his customer. It was supplanted mid-decade by Armani's deconstructed, sleeves-rolled *American Gigolo* look.

In 1982 Lauren launched his home collection, each range within it a complete set dressing for one of his re-imagined worlds. Four years later he opened his flagship store in the Rhinelander mansion on Madison Avenue and the Polo store in Paris. In 1990 he introduced Safari, the fragrance, accessorised by a whole lifestyle package, and as the decade progressed, he developed the Polo Sport ranges for men and women and the Polo Jeans Co for the young. Expanding simultaneously up the market, he introduced the Purple Label men's tailoring collection, personally starring in the advertisements. In 1997, Lauren took his company public while retaining 90 per cent control, and in 1999, he opened the largest Polo store in the world in Chicago with an adjacent Ralph Lauren restaurant, launching the Ralph by Ralph Lauren collection for 16- to 25-year-old women and also acquiring Club Monaco. In the 2000s Lauren devoted much time to charities and film festivals but found time to launch ranges of fine jewellery and watches.

He is so immensely wealthy that he has said he couldn't possible spend it all. He has the ranch in Colorado, homes in Jamaica and on Long Island, an estate in Bedford, New York, as well as his Fifth Avenue Manhattan address. His collection of vintage cars ranges from a 1929 Bentley and a 1937 Alfa Romeo to a 1938 Bugatti and a 1962 Ferrari.

Polo generally preferred licensing to manufacturing, but in recent years it has been buying many back in order to reassert control over all aspects of the brand. The firm operates about 275 retail and outlet stores in the United States and licenses more than 100 others around the world.

Further reading: For Lauren's work, see Colin McDowell's monograph, *Ralph Lauren: The Man, the Vision, the Style* (2002), and for Lauren's life, see Michael Gross's *Genuine Authentic: The Real Life of Ralph Lauren* (2003).

31 ISSEY MIYAKE
(1935–)

In the introduction to the first book on the work of Issey Miyake, *East Meets West,* published in 1978, Diana Vreeland, then retired from US *Vogue* and heading the Costume Institute at the Metropolitan Museum of Art in New York, wrote, 'His clothes are totally his and his alone. I love you, Issey, and the way you carry on and on and on, from your centuries old traditions, down through the ages, utilising your total instinct and great integrity to present artistry and beautiful inspirations that are so well applied to the present tense of East and West.'

Miyake's vision is unique. He was the precursor, leader and mentor of a new school of Japanese design, which took the fashion world by storm in the early 1980s. He was not the first Japanese designer to find fame in the West, but he was the first to create something new and revolutionary. He drew deeply on both oriental and occidental traditions of dress to produce the hybrid style that was to change everyone's perceptions of what clothing could be.

Born in Hiroshima in 1938, he was cycling to school on 6 August 1945 when the Americans dropped the atom bomb. He lost most of his family, including his mother, who was severely burned and died four years later. She had carried on working as a teacher despite her injuries. Perhaps as a consequence, he has always surrounded himself with strong, clever women. At ten, Miyake developed a bone marrow disease which affects him to this day. 'The Japan I grew up in was a very poor country,' he told Brenda Polan. 'My generation dreamed of going to America. We believed the future lay there.' Post-war Japan was dominated culturally by the occupying American forces. Within that culture the most desirable clothing for men was the classic Ivy League leisure wear worn by off-duty American officers—club ties, button-down shirts, penny loafers and navy blazers. Japanese women of the time craved traditional Parisian chic of the kind featured in the copies of *Vogue* and *Harper's Bazaar* that his sister bought and he read curiously—a desire which Hanae Mori, the first Japanese fashion designer to make a name abroad, sought to satisfy.

Miyake never doubted, when he brought his clothes to New York in 1971 and to Paris in 1973, that they would have an international appeal. A lifelong experimenter and collaborator, seeking out the best, most creative minds to work with, he has probably always been confident in his vision of fashion, a vision which eschews voltes-face and looks instead to evolution. He is a clever, gentle, modest man, movie-star handsome and charismatic; consequently, he makes friends and lifelong fans wherever he goes. But a huge part of his magnetism derives from his passionate commitment to his ideas and his willingness to explain, to engage, to proselytise.

Miyake studied art at Tama University in Tokyo, graduating in 1965 with a degree in graphic design. He had begun designing clothing in 1962, and in 1963 he presented his first real collection, entitled A Poem of Cloth and Stone, at the Tokyo Chamber of Commerce and Industry. His stated—and possibly precocious—ambition was to show that clothes could be both utilitarian and visually creative. 'We want,' he said at the time, 'to stimulate the imagination through clothing. Though these designs draw their inspiration from contemporary style, it is not really a fashion show. I think the next step will be clothing that looks to the future. There are many long dresses in the show not meant as eveningwear, but simply because of the form. I would like this show to mark the birth of visual clothing in Japan.'

To develop his skills and his thinking, he enrolled on a course at the Chambre Syndicale de la Couture Parisienne and spent five years in Paris and New York working with established fashion designers. He was less impressed by his time at Laroche and Givenchy than by the youth-focused, mini-loving vitality he found in the weekends he spent in London, visiting the theatre and the galleries, wandering the King's Road, shopping and getting his hair cut.

While he was in Paris, the political revolt of May 1968 disturbed everyone, even the denizens of the bourgeois salons of couture. The workers occupied the Renault plant and the students took to the streets, manning the modern-day barricades of burnt-out trams and dustbins and digging up the cobblestones to throw through the clouds of tear gas at the armed and armoured police. London, too, was witness to student rebellion and violence on the streets as youngsters, some left wing, all indignant, marched in support of their American peers being drafted to wage war in Vietnam.

Miyake's friend, the architect Arata Isozaki, wrote in *East Meets West*:

I am not certain whether or not he had already formed his own critical opinion of haute couture, a staunchly regulated genre of international fashion. However, finding himself in Paris, a city full of suspicion and jealousy, faced by a language barrier which handicapped his liberty, he probably saw no reason to remain where he was, and thus, he took flight. One of the characteristics of the protest movement was impulsive body action; energy was burnt. After that, in the vacuum, the question loomed once again in front of him: 'As a designer, what are clothes?'

His flight from the world of couture took him to New York and the studio of Geoffrey Beene. There his attention was caught by the classless, genderless American uniform of jeans and T-shirt he saw worn by workers, weekending executives and militant students alike. Back in Tokyo in 1970, Miyake set up his design studio and looked back to his own cultural inheritance to examine the possibilities

of Japanese work wear, its cheap but laboriously worked textiles, the kimono and the costumes of the samurai of the Edo period, costumes that were elaborately constructed of many simple, rectilinear garments and swathes of fabric. 'I thought,' he told Brenda Polan in 1983, 'that the occidental clothing tradition was too tight. I wanted to make things that were free both mentally and physically. I had to free myself from the occidental tradition, of the occidental way, of occidental ideas. But there are still a lot of things to learn from them; it is important to respect that long tradition, the things that Paris couture was really about—even with all its elitism.'

For the Japanese tight clothing was traditionally not at all sexy. 'The Japanese body does not have sculptural beauty and expresses little sex appeal,' wrote the painter, Tadanori Yokoo. 'Sex appeal is a spiritual matter, not a physical one.' Sensuality is found in large volumes of fabric, luxuriously textured, cut in imposing, almost abstract shapes, layered and wrapped. The Japanese use the body as a template for a three-dimensional sculptural shape. At rest these costumes have a kind of grandeur; in movement they have a fluid grace. They tease the senses through the imagination. They are subtle, the product of a social system which is constructed to ease relationships on a few overcrowded islands and which, consequently, is heavily reliant on ritual, formality and restraint.

Miyake had developed a theory he called 'peeling away to the limit', throwing away all the inhibiting ideas about dress imposed by Western cultural imperialism and starting again from the beginning— the bolt of cloth, the hank of yarn. He began his great experiment with *sashiko*, the traditionally patterned, often striped, quilted cotton worn by Japanese peasants. He chose as his collaborator textile designer Makiko Minagawa, who was interested in mixing various yarns, natural and synthetic, to bring out the 'essence' of a fabric, exploring its potential for movement, texture and tactility as far as possible.

At first the resulting clothing consisted of pieces of irregularly shaped fabric almost suspended about the body—Miyake was interested in the 'space between' body and clothing—each piece of which could be stripped away. This he developed into layering and wrapping, and his unparalleled feeling for texture, mass and volume became apparent. He himself attributed much of his thinking to the influence of Madeleine Vionnet; she too preferred to suspend the fabric from the body and allow it to follow its own nature, assuming new shapes as the wearer moved. In his collections he would achieve magical effects, creating garments which arrived on the runway as one thing—a jacket, a kimono, a slender skirt—and which would, with the shrug of the shoulder, the swift movement of a wrist, become something else entirely—a skirt, a pair of shorts, a hooded poncho. His delight in all manner of materials led to experimentation with plastic, bamboo and various kinds of paper to produce masks, hierarchic headdresses, pseudo-armour reminiscent of samurai gear, and clothes that evoked thoughts of kites, heraldic banners, origami and modern abstract sculpture.

Speaking to Susannah Frankel of *The Guardian* in 1997, he described his first half-hour show in Tokyo thus: 'There was no music, just a sound system that picked up every little noise. The girl came out in many layers of clothing. She take off her shoes, throws them down. Bang! Bang! She take off garment. Ssh. She drop it on floor. Crash! She take off everything. She has no clothes. End of show. It become big Tokyo scandal. Sponsorship company beg me to stop.'

Miyake has a talent for the small scandals that get big headlines. In 1976 he showed his collection in Tokyo on 'Twelve Black Girls,' led out by Grace Jones. In the 1980s in Paris he showed his collection on dancers and volunteers of all ages and genders, culminating in the 1995 show starring a group of octogenarians. His collaborations with artists—such as Yasumasa Morimura, Nobuyoshi Araki, Tim Hawkinson and Cai Guo-Qiang among others—and the beauty of his exhibitions are legendary. Simply because they make such extraordinary pictures, the great photographer, Irving Penn, volunteered in 1986 to shoot all of Miyake's collections—something he did with no interference from the designer for a decade. Miyake has claimed that seeing what Penn made of his clothes enabled him to understand his own designs more acutely. He has been given major shows in the greatest museums and galleries in Japan, America, France and Britain but

making real clothes for everyone has always been at the heart of his work.

He created Pleats Please in 1993, the year he was made a member of the Legion d'Honneur, France's highest accolade. A-POC (a piece of cloth) was the similarly egalitarian 'cut-and-wear from a tube of fabric' system he developed and launched in 1999.

Miyake told Frankel:

My first dream, and why I decided to open my studio was that I thought to myself, 'If I could one day make clothes like T-shirts and jeans, I would be very excited.' But the more I worked the more I felt so far away from doing so. I was always doing such heavy things, far away from the people. And then I was thinking, you know, 'Are you stupid? Don't you remember why you started designing in the first place?' And then I thought, 'OK, Pleats Please.' So I started to think how to make it, how to wash it, how to coordinate it, even how to pack it. And I worked on how to keep the price down.

Pleats had long been a theme to which Miyake returned in his main collection, and now he developed a separate collection, chiefly in machine-washable feather-light, uncreasable viscose, of simple, useful, comfortable pieces pleated vertically, horizontally, diagonally, cross-hatched, straight and wriggly that made interesting shapes on the body and often could be worn several ways. As Richard Martin and Harold Koda wrote in their catalogue to the 1994 Orientalism exhibition at the Metropolitan Museum of Art in New York City, 'Hybrid styles by such designers as . . . Issey Miyake offer the paradigm of dress that cannot be located to a specific place but justly belong to the world.'

Though he handed over the design side of the main line to Naoki Takizawa in 1999, Miyake continues to work on Pleats Please, and his style and influence are apparent in the company's products. In 2007, a new creative director was appointed, Dai Fujiwara, after Takizawa left to form his own label.

Further reading: See Mark Holborn's *Issey Miyake* (1995) and, for background, Claire Wilcox's *Radical Fashion* (2001).

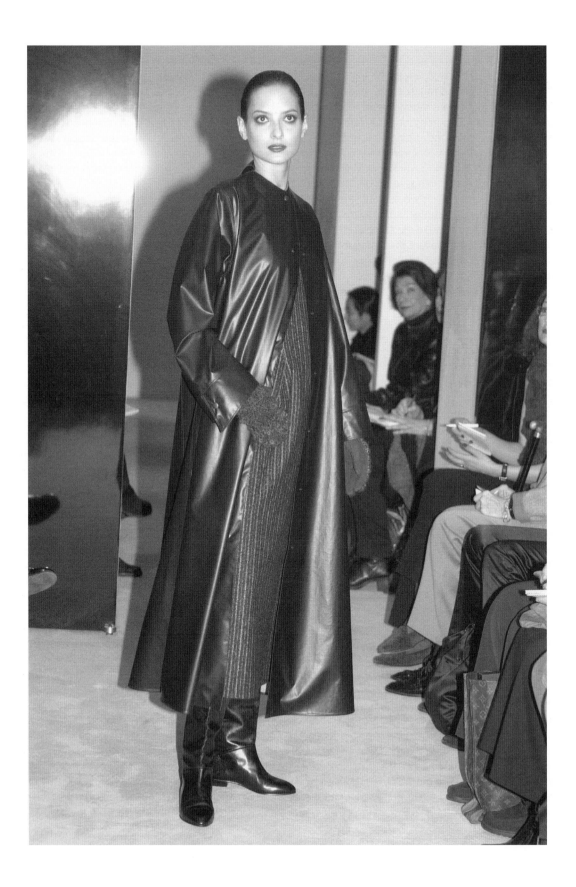

32 GEOFFREY BEENE (1927–2004)

Like all the great designers who helped to shift fashion on to a new track, Geoffrey Beene challenged accepted criteria. His area of greatest experimentation was fabric. He was an early champion of post-war synthetics, often in the pursuit of that holy grail of women who do not have ladies' maids or unlimited funds for dry-cleaning—uncreasable fabrics. A democrat both in terms of the modern lifestyle he assumed his customers led and in his refusal to accept ancien régime rules of dress or hierarchies of materials, Beene was a key exponent of the American sportswear style, a wearer-focused fashion concept which embraced the utilitarian and practical aspects of clothing and undermined all the conventions about what one could wear when and all the demarcation lines about appropriate fabrics.

Typically, American fashion rejects the distinctions between what should be worn by day and what by night, the kind of 'never wear diamonds before 6 p.m.' rigidity which permitted the dowagers who ran society to spot a parvenu at 100 paces. Beene instinctively pursued a youthful customer who cared as little as he did for all those shibboleths. He was, as Jane Mulvagh, has observed, a leg man. 'His clothes,' she wrote, 'were easy, flirty and showed legs, legs, legs.'

While never compromising on quality of cut, structure or couture-standard technique, Beene played with mischievous juxtapositions: metallic lamé teamed with grey flannel, cashmere knit and taffeta, blanket-plaid wool and lace. He was one of the earliest American designers to introduce baby-doll looks as well as gypsy styles and traditional ethnic fabrics, including simple cottons previously thought down-market. In the 1980s, when opulence was the order of the day, some of Beene's most enchanting evening designs were the result of taking a conventional daywear style—a shirtwaist dress, say—growing it to floor-length, and then outlining and encrusting the luscious print in sequins and beads.

Harold Koda, the celebrated curator of the Metropolitan Museum of Art's Costume Institute, told Brenda Cullerton, 'It's like someone who speaks the English language and through use becomes a poet. His affinity, his exploration of the abstraction of cloth, has allowed him to push its possibilities in ways that are unimaginable.'

Beene, who identified with the Pygmalion myth, said, in 1995:

> Clothes should look as if they haven't been born yet; as if a woman were born into them. It's a form of possession, this belonging of one to the other. You mould a woman into what you perceive her as being. What I do is the product of my admiration. I imagine women in an idyllic state. I create a vision of this woman, whether she exists or not. Doesn't every human aim for perfection? For the possibility of it?

At the heart of designer sportswear is the client, an active woman with a busy life and a need for comfortable, useful, easy clothes with pockets. The history of the style has two strands of antecedents: firstly, Parisian and American couture and conventional menswear for all occasions, formal tailoring to leisurewear, and secondly, Seventh Avenue, the commercial, factory-based heart of the American fashion industry which, like all of America's late nineteenth and twentieth century industries, was almost obsessively focused on modernism (the modern movement mantra, 'less is more' was to come to apply to Beene's work), on speed, practicality and the constant development and updating that fuelled consumerism. Industrial America has always been about hard-selling the latest thing, about whetting the consumers' appetites, about an egalitarian emphasis on mass availability. In terms of clothing, the early sportswear designers—Claire McCardell, Vera Maxwell, Tom Brigance, Anne Fogarty, Tina Lesser, Bonnie Cashin, Halston—embraced a kind of version of Italian Futurism, an art movement whose exponents liked to picture the world in constant motion. These were the first designers to envisage women striding out rather than remaining languidly at rest. Arguably, they saw it not in terms of feminism but in terms of modernity, liberty and the American way. Beene, talking to Brenda Cullerton in 1995, defined beauty as 'a measure of energy'.

'I have never much liked rigid clothes or anything constraining,' Geoffrey Beene told Brenda Polan in an interview in 1984. 'I like freedom. I am an American; I love freedom and the brilliant clothes that are the American working uniform. I love sweatshirts, skirts and loafers, denim, baggy chinos, and I have never in my work deviated from the premise of freedom and effortlessness.' Indeed in 1968 he famously designed full-length evening dresses based on the American football shirt and sequinned all over.

His experimental, almost transgressive, approach to fabric made him attractive to the manufacturers of the new synthetic fibres that became an important part of the development of fashion in the 1950s and 1960s. In the late 1960s he was one of ten international designers commissioned by DuPont to contribute to a promotional project for Qiana, a silky nylon yarn. He chose to have the yarn woven into a satin velour *decoupé* about which he said, 'Working with this material proved to me that synthetics could be perfected, for it was exactly like a pure silk velour, only it did not crease.' He was disappointed in the long run by the way these fabrics decayed in his archive.

Geoffrey Beene was born in 1927 in Haynesville, Louisiana, and he was never to lose that warm, melting molasses-over-ice-cream accent. There was also a formality to his diction that may have been dated but which was a joy to the ears of the literate. To call him a Southern gentleman is a cliché—and, anyway, he could be the most irascible and impatient of conversationalists, something of which even his biographer, Brenda Cullerton, complained. But he was cultivated, erudite and gently reared. The grandson of a plantation owner on one side and the town doctor on the other, one of his early sketches showed him attended by black manservant. He first demonstrated his interest in fashion as a boy by redecorating his room and getting his aunts to make up a fabric he bought—tiny orange flowers on a powder blue background—into beach pyjamas using a Simplicity paper pattern. A passion for the way cloth worked with the body was all he took away from three years in the medical school at Tulane University in New Orleans. 'Cadavers were the moment of truth,' he said. He wanted to cut for the body, not into it, and sketched movie star gowns on the margins of his copy of Gray's Anatomy.

He dropped out, spent three asthmatic, hospitalised weeks in the US Army, was discharged, moved to California to stay with an aunt in the movie business and took a temporary job in the display department of I Magnin in Los Angeles. 'I didn't leave the South,' he said in 1995. 'I fled. I'm still fleeing.' In 1947 he moved to New York to the Traphagen School of Fashion, to study the theory and practice of design, before taking a course at L'Académie Julien in Paris and apprenticing himself to a tailor who had worked for Molyneux. Tailoring is at the heart of his technique, and his love affair with geometry, especially triangles, probably had is origins here. 'My life began there,' he told Cullerton. 'It began the moment people understood what I wanted to do.' In 1951, he returned to the Seventh Avenue garment trade and worked anonymously for several houses before being fired by stylistically conservative Harmay Fashions for a collection considered dangerously avant-garde in that it featured a chemise dress. He joined Teal Traina in 1954, where he was given the freedom to do original designs rather than following Paris at a year's remove, staying until 1963 when, with backing from two partners, he launched his own label.

The company was successful from the start and Beene won his first three Coty Awards in his first five years in business. His first collection was already confidently Beene. The *Dallas Times Herald* reported, 'There was gingham, like a tablecloth, embroidered with the surprise of henna sequins. . .' And later in the same article, 'Here within the framework of a lean, supple streak of a dress, he has created real fashion excitement because, when he couldn't find a fabric he wanted, he invented it himself.' He became known for dresses that were lightly detailed but firmly structured— pretty body armour, such as the wedding dress for President Lyndon Johnson's daughter Lynda Bird in 1968. They sold well and were much copied (he resented imitation and worried about it endlessly). Some critics instinctively disliked what they saw as an archaic insistence on structure—a tailored formality just like the Paris-inspired crispness of the little suits and dresses worn by Jackie Kennedy. Beene's were criticised, notably by Kennedy Fraser, who described them in *The New Yorker* in 1972 as 'concrete'.

Beene himself was later to dismiss these pieces from his early period as 'uptight little dresses which hid all my misgivings'. In the catalogue to his retrospective *25 Years in Fashion* exhibition in 1988, he called them 'Superstructures', adding, 'They were so stiff they could stand up by themselves.' They were, he reckoned, a last sentimental tribute to all he had learned of French couture in Paris. He entered a period of experimentation, exploring techniques to enable cloth to move over and with the body—curved and industrial-weight zippers, spiral seams in none of the usual places, inserts of lace and chiffon, lingerie straps, and the use of synthetics, including the strangely popular faux suede. He protested, 'They work; they don't wrinkle; they take less care.'

The revised Beene style—'clean, clear and strong' as his late-1960s assistant, Issey Miyake, described it—was never a mass-market hit; his customers were women who had the sophisticated understanding to match his own—Paloma Picasso,

Jacqueline Kennedy. The daring work was subsidised by a cheaper line, Beene Bag, introduced in 1974, and by royalties from discreet licensing deals for men's shirts and colognes. He never aspired to be a big brand, admitting, 'I'm not a driven businessman, but a driven artist, I never think about money—beautiful things make money.'

In 1976 he showed his collection in Milan and in 1978 in Paris. It took every cent he had but he explained, 'I thought if they didn't understand me at home, maybe they would on another continent.' But possibly he was offended by the European press's assumptions that New York designers at that time showed a month after Paris so they would have time to copy the trends. Certainly no one in Paris was pre-empting Beene's inspired melanges of materials—sequins on mohair, diamonds on plastic jewellery, horsehair and gazar, rubies and hessian, mattress ticking and paillettes, silk tulle and straw, lace and leather, men's shirting and chiffon and industrial zips on diaphanous chiffon. No one yet was making evening frocks in denim or T-shirt jersey or formal outfits in sportswear styles. He had a skilled technician's pride in unique effects and a revolutionary's delight in overthrowing anything resembling a status quo. He called it, 'Alchemy. In elevating the humblest fabrics, in making them as luxurious and as desirable as the richest, I create a new context for both. I remove the stigmas attached to them.'

Kennedy Fraser of *The New Yorker* wrote in 1997, 'Other designers showed flashy furs and metallic fabrics that throbbed like Times Square neon with information about their cost. But when Beene showed a luxurious-looking coat with deep sable cuffs, the coat itself was made of a relatively humble chocolate-coloured corduroy.'

Beene claimed: 'I love standards but I don't mind breaking rules.' Through the late 1980s and 1990s, the clothes appeared ever simpler, the fabrics ever richer and, as he crowed happily, 'Uncopyable!' There was a delicious lightness to everything he made, whether a simple sequin-covered sheath dress, crew-necked, long-sleeved and bearing a neck-to-hem Matisse design or a satin embossed and appliquéd evening bolero made to stand away from the body to frame the simple black slip dress beneath. 'The more you learn about clothing,' he said, 'the more you realise what must be taken away. Simplification becomes a very complicated process.'

He won eight Coty Fashion Critics Awards and four awards from the Council of Fashion Designers of America. Louisiana has an annual Beene day. His retrospective exhibitions were at New York City's National Academy of Design (1988), and the Fashion Institute of Technology (1990).

Further reading: Brenda Cullerton's *Geoffrey Beene* (1995) is the most informative and thoughtful, although Kim Hastreiter's recent monograph, *Geoffrey Beene: Fashion Rebel* (2008), is full of interesting gleanings.

33 CALVIN KLEIN (1942–)

In the 1980s when Michael Douglas's febrile film character in *Wall Street,* Gordon Gekko, could declare, 'Greed is good' and have it become the mantra of a generation which was pleased to label itself 'yuppie', three American designers reached out from Seventh Avenue to become the world's biggest fashion brands. Ralph Lauren, Donna Karan and Calvin Klein have quite similar back stories, but they are very different designers. Although Lauren may have dressed Diane Keaton in menswear styles in *Annie Hall* in 1977, it is Klein who represents the lurch towards androgyny that occurred in the following decade. Nicholas Coleridge, writing in 1988, described a visit to Klein's office. The designer showed him photographs of the model José Borain in a man's white shirt, doeskin flannel trousers and a greatcoat. Klein asked him:

Do you like these pictures? I find these a very sexy way to look. It's like she has thrown on her boyfriend's shirt, man's pants, her friend's trenchcoat. It's a kind of sexiness quite different from hookers' clothes. If I mix tweed with a fabric like silk chamois so you can see the woman's body, and her blouse just rips, that for me is as sexy as anything. A woman in cavalry twill pants and no adornment.

As the monstrous shoulder pads of the time illustrate, the physical ideal for both men and women was gym-pumped, broad-shouldered, narrow-hipped, flat-stomached and flaunting boy-sized buttocks. This was the lean and athletic, cool and laid-back all-American achiever Calvin Klein chose to dress. In 1979–1980 Klein launched his designer jeans, the first of their ilk, with six television commercials directed by Richard Avedon and starring Brooke Shields, the fifteen-year-old who had played a child prostitute in Louis Malle's 1978 film, *Pretty Baby.* In the most provocative of the ads Shields asked, 'Want to know what comes between me and my Calvins? Nothing.' The response was predictable with television stations banning the ads amid welters of publicity. On a TV talk show, basking in the controversy, Klein asserted, 'The tighter they are, the better they sell.'

That goes some way towards defining the paradox at the heart of Calvin Klein's approach to design—and, probably, to life. Rather like that other icon of American style, that other Jewish boy raised in the Bronx, Ralph Lauren, Klein has an instinctive understanding of how to dress a woman or a man to make them look old-money rich, gently raised in a world of good taste and restrained luxury. He knows the associations of class that silk, glove-soft suede and leather, cashmere tweeds and gabardine bring with them. And he knows the look is a turn-on. He can take the credit for refining the American designer sportswear genre for the body-con generation. Yet at the same time he liked to strip down and get dirty with the most vulgar of transgressive imagery. As Michael Gross wrote, 'In Calvin's world, polymorphic perversity is par for the course. Quaint morality is banished.'

With the exception of Gianni Versace a decade later, no other up-market designer has used sex to sell in quite such an up-front (and up-front more than describes his ads for men's underpants) way. Until he finally eschewed drink, drugs, promiscuity and the whole Studio 54 lifestyle in favour of a second marriage to a classy younger woman and the all-American domestic dream in 1986, even his perfume ads had a pornographic, distinctly homoerotic edge to them. But as the first casualties to Aids in his circle began to die, Calvin Klein reinvented himself, becoming Calvin Clean, avatar of middle-class family values. He told *Women's Wear Daily*, 'Love . . . marriage . . . commitment. I think it is a feeling that is happening all over the country.' He sold his houses in the gay resorts of Fire Island and Key West and bought an East Side Georgian town house and a vast beach house on Long Island. On the shelf the 1988 scent, Eternity, supplanted 1985's Obsession, and in the ever-iconic ads a family picnic on a beach sidelined a sweaty naked threesome on a shadowy sofa. It's a rare brand that can survive quite such a radical volte-face.

In her 2003 biography of the business, Lisa Marsh wrote that the brand was arguably the most well-known fashion brand in the world. She added, 'It would be safe to say that every man, woman and child in America has owned something that bears the Calvin Klein label at one point or another. To most fashion watchers, professional and pedestrian, the company's brand can be summed up in a few words—modern, clean, sleek, and American.'

Born in the Bronx, New York, in 1942, the son of a Jewish grocer, young Calvin taught himself to sketch and sew. His mother was an elegant woman who played an important role in shaping her son's fashion sense by taking him with her when she visited her dressmakers, and his grandmother taught him to use a sewing machine. Klein graduated from New York's Fashion Institute of Technology in 1962 and worked for a series of middle- to down-market Seventh Avenue manufacturers whose product he loathed. 'Real hooker clothes,' he called them. On his marriage to Jayne Centre, a classmate from his Bronx elementary school, he began to moonlight, creating his own collection on his kitchen table in Queens and having it made up by a Jewish tailor on Coney Island. His current boss found out, threatened to sue him and confiscate the new designs. 'I just broke down and started crying,' he told Coleridge. 'He asked me to leave at that moment and I never worked for anyone again.'

In 1968 his childhood friend, Barry Schwartz, having inherited his father's supermarket business, invited Klein to go into business with him. Instead Schwartz became Klein's partner in his business, lending the designer $10,000 to open a small showroom in the York Hotel on Seventh Avenue, designing and selling youthful, simple coats for women. What happened next has become rag-trade legend. The merchandise manager of Bonwit Teller got out of the lift on the wrong floor, glimpsed Klein's coats, liked them and invited him to show them to Mildred Custin, the renowned president of the store. To ensure that the clothes did not get creased or soiled, the designer pushed his collection up Seventh Avenue on a clothes rail. Custin placed an order worth $50,000.

Klein has always focused on modernity and simplicity. 'I've always had a clear design philosophy and point of view about being modern, sophisticated, sexy, clean and minimal. They all apply to my design aesthetic,' he told *Women's Wear Daily*. He had no respect for the couture tradition, acknowledging Claire McCardell as a significant influence. Of her clothes he said, 'They are the only clothes from the late forties and fifties that could still be worn today beautifully.' Through the 1970s his classic and classy clean-cut look became a working uniform for large parts of a generation of women motivated by the women's movement to forge a path into many industries and professions. His spare sportswear style was most often executed in neutral shades and earth tones, the colours most associated with the semi-desert, bare-bones landscape of south-western America and the paintings of Andrew Wyeth—stone, sand, ochre, ubiquitous camel—and Georgia O'Keefe—azure, violet, white, oyster. His daywear classics were tailored in the most expensive flannels, worsteds and tweeds Europe could supply—he criticised American textile producers for poor quality and lack of innovation. Many jackets were cut like a loose shirt, which worked over both skirt and trousers. In 1971 he was a leading exponent of the Big Look, simple loose tops—his smock shape was wildly successful—loose skirts and baggy pants. In 1976 his T-shirt and chemise shaped evening dresses made headlines; in 1977 it was metallic effects and in 1978 slinky cotton jersey slip dresses and his all-year-round butter-soft, unstructured suede and leather pieces in pale, show-every-mark colours.

In 1974 Klein and his first wife, with whom he had a daughter, Marci, were divorced, and he adopted a hedonistic lifestyle. He was regularly seen at celebrity night spots, such as Studio 54, accompanied by a loose-knit circle of friends, including the designers Halston and Giorgio di Sant'Angelo, artist Andy Warhol and his Factory acolytes, and Bianca Jagger. Rumours of drug consumption and sexual excesses abounded, as did rumours that Klein had contracted Aids. In fact, an Italian radio station erroneously announced his death from the disease. In 1978, 12-year-old Marci was kidnapped and ransomed for $100,000; Klein paid the ransom and found her alive tied up in a New York tenement.

Both his lifestyle and the growing sexualisation of the image conveyed by his advertising fuelled wide speculation about Klein's own sexuality. In their 1994 unauthorized biography, *Obsession,* Steven Gaines and Sharon Churcher alleged that he is bisexual. They said that he has a preference for 'straight boys' and that he is a member of a so-called 'Velvet Mafia' of millionaires who swap lovers. The fact that, after their marriage in 1986, he and Kelly Rector continued to live in separate apartments appeared to confirm the stories. There were allegations about 'beards' and 'contracts' on the fashion scene, particularly among gay men eager to claim the glamorous Klein for their own.

In 1982 Klein achieved his second great coup with the introduction of Calvin Klein underpants. He launched the snug white briefs in an ad on an enormous billboard in New York's Times Square; the image was an overtly sexual one of a lithe and muscular man wearing nothing but white underwear. Questioned about the homoerotic appeal of their advertising by Karen Stabiner for *The New York Times Magazine,* a spokesperson for Calvin Klein deadpanned, 'We did not try to appeal to gays. We try to appeal, period. If there's an awareness in that community of health and grooming, then they'll respond to the ads.' Klein's billboard has been credited with heralding a new era in imagery of men in advertising. He went on to produce

many more of the same, working with iconic contemporary photographers such as Bruce Weber and Herb Ritts.

In 1983 he launched man-style cotton Calvins for women. Time magazine called them 'Calvin's New Gender Benders' and *Women's Wear Daily* deemed it 'the hottest look in women's lingerie since the bikini brief'. The boxer shorts had a fly opening. 'It's sexier with the fly,' said Klein. 'These things are carefully thought out.' Adapting to the ethos of the 1980s, he showed he could do classic glamour, opting for a more structured look to his tailoring and crisp details like ruffled lace. On the inauguration of President Ronald Reagan, Klein said, 'We all guessed on Seventh Avenue that glamour would be back and we'd be doing glam evening dresses to show it off because the Reagans are Californian and California is pretty showy. It was a great change from the Carter administration which was very much, you sewed your own dress!' He proved a masterly architect of dramatically streamlined evening wear which owed something to the Adrian and Banton gowns from 1930s movies—all lush satins cut on the bias.

Marsh wrote:

> Many in the industry like to believe the fashion business is all about the design, cut, colour and draping of garments—that it is an artistic endeavour—that the fashion industry is one based more on creativity than on commerce. However, the American designer houses that have reigned supreme . . . have proven that design is a small part of the business of fashion. These businesses draw breath from things like the marketing and positioning of the company's image, shrewd partnerships with retailers, regular support from the fashion press and, above all, astute business management who can see beyond the hype.

Certainly these things, done so consummately well in America, have resulted in some US brands gaining an undeserved dominance of world markets. But in the case of Calvin Klein, working so successfully to remould American designer sportswear for the 1970s and 1980s, the design input was more than a 'small part'.

In 2003 Klein and Schwartz sold the company to Phillips-Van Heusen for $739 million, and Francisco Costa took over as creative director, regenerating the brand and restoring its fashion profile.

Further reading: For Klein's life, see *Obsession* (1994) by Stephen Gaines and Sharon Churcher; for the story of a mega-brand, see Lisa Marsh's *The House of Klein: Fashion, Controversy and a Business Obsession* (2003).

34   GIORGIO ARMANI (1934–)

At the Milan menswear shows in February 2000, Bernard Arnault, the predatory head of the luxury goods conglomerate, Louis Vuitton Moët Hennessy (LVMH) was observed taking a front-row seat at the Armani show. Immediately, speculation was rife that Armani was about to join Dior, Givenchy and Lacroix in Arnault's stable of top fashion labels. The denial came promptly. The company was, according to a terse press release, considering taking preliminary steps to study the feasibility of various different proposals it had received. Such proposals, the statement implied, had become almost tediously frequent over recent years. That was hardly surprising. Giorgio Armani Spa is the most profitable company in Italy, a position it had then held for two years running. Giorgio Armani was the country's biggest taxpayer. 'Not because I am the richest,' he said. 'I am just the most honest.'

Fashion is, of course, big business in Italy, but business acumen, the kind that puts the flagship companies of other industries like car manufacturing and pasta production in the shade, is not that common. And Armani maintains its pre-eminence despite the fact that other fashion labels had pre-empted the big headlines. However, Giorgio Armani was sixty-five in 2000 and, while there's doubtless an ascetic side to his character, he did not, he told Brenda Polan a month later, want to work forever. Yet Armani passed his seventieth birthday still in the driving seat and as he approached the next milestone of seventy-five, he showed no sign of sliding out from behind the wheel. This is reassuring for the millions of women and men who have adopted Armani's cool, streamlined, modern-minded style as their own. Armani is committed to subtle change, to what he calls 'a soft evolution', at the heart of which is a consistent and rational view of the needs of a contemporary wardrobe. It is a utilitarian approach but far from bland; the Armani style is imbued with a refined sensuousness, expressed in the retrained luxury of the fabrics, in the sophisticated fluidity of the cut and in the perfection of details and accessories.

Although the late Gianni Versace, generally perceived as Armani's polar opposite in terms of taste, famously sniffed that a designer whose favourite colour was beige could hardly be expected to know much about sex appeal (this in response to a suggestion from Armani that Versace's own designs might be considered vulgar), Armani's clothes *are* sexy. It has to do not with direct display but with the way the soft, tactile fabrics and the easy, almost liquid cut make the wearer feel, feelings which are then reflected in the deportment: sensuous, relaxed, at ease.

The man himself appears to be anything but those things. John Fairchild of *Women's Wear Daily* called him 'the monk of fashion,' and he does have a reputation for a rather chilly reserve, but his biographer, Renata Molho, described the child and the man thus, 'He was an observer, timid, introverted, and keenly aware of everything going on around him. He was also restless, never contented, always looking for something, whether a rare checkered shirt or a special texture in his relationships with others. These qualities are . . . fundamental to his complex character; he is immensely adaptable, yet he seems incapable of real satisfaction with what he achieves. He always thinks there must be something more.'

And he does have a sharp sense of humour. He is, above all, intensely pragmatic. He told Brenda Polan, who interviewed him for the *Financial Times* in 2000:

I never had a desire as a young man to design fashion. A series of coincidences led me on to a fashion path. Perhaps this starting point is something which already makes me different; I considered this a job like any other. I was never spoilt by the fashion atmosphere, by its preciousness. I never had the attitude, 'I am a creative talent therefore this is what you have to wear.' It was a job, a profession. I came from a department store, not an atelier. When I realised—and it was very much as a result of my contact with customers—there was room for me to do something different, that I could devise a different way of dressing, I realised this was going to be my life.

His refusal to lay claim to any great creative destiny reminds you how very different the northern Italian temperament is to the southern. Historically, Lombardy is the home of bankers, merchant princes and industrialists. Armani was born in 1934 in Piacenza, to the south of Milan, one of three children of Maria and Ugo, an industrial manager who was imprisoned after the Second World War for his membership of the Fascist Party, a possibly disproportionate retribution that left its scars on his family. Giorgio enrolled to study medicine at the University of Milan but left in his third year to do his military service as a paramedic. However, on leaving the army he realised medicine was not for him. In 1957 he took a job in the advertising department of La Rinascente store and was soon promoted to assistant buyer. 'I was responsible for making sure,' he said, 'that the clothes they were buying for the stores were getting the right response from the public.'

In 1961 he was recruited by Nino Cerruti who had inherited the family textile company at age twenty and had expanded into clothing. Armani's job, after a month's training in the factory, was to design the menswear collection, Hitman. Instinctively he chose lighter fabrics than were common in tailoring and cooler colours. He discarded layers of internal structure, reduced shoulder pads, moved buttons

and pockets and took the stiff formality out of the man's suit, replacing it with something loose, relaxed, youthful. With the support of *L'Uomo Vogue,* launched in 1968, it was sensationally successful.

In 1966 Armani met Sergio Galeotti, the ebullient Tuscan who was to become his partner in life as well as business (he died tragically young in 1985). In 1970 the two set up an independent design consultancy working for important labels in Italy, France and Spain. In 1975, just as Gigi Monti of Basile orchestrated the move of the fledgling Italian high-fashion ready-to-wear shows from provincial, inaccessible Florence to Milan, the flourishing industrial hub, they launched the Armani label with a collection for men and women for spring/summer 1976. The womenswear show featured Armani's first menswear inspired jacket for women.

'It was the time when French and English designers were beginning to come to Italy for their production,' he told Polan in 2000. It was the beginning of fashion as a global industry, and Armani perceived that he could aspire to an international market:

To make a mark I would have to do something different. That would not be so easy. And it was a time when fashion was all about flower power, very baroque and decorated. So I made a choice. Women were beginning to be more emancipated and liberated in their way of thinking; I had been used to designing men's wear so I decided to bring into women's wear that sort of practical, rational way of dressing that really did not exist for women, although in America a lot of women embraced that style.

One thinks of Katharine Hepburn, of course. 'Obviously,' he continued with a humorous shrug of the shoulders, 'it was necessary to sacrifice any desire to be "creative" but that is what I saw was needed.'

But, of course, his whole approach was creatively fresh, a leap of imagination that was to capture the hearts of women seeking a way to look in the executive workplace. In 2007 he told his biographer, Renata Molho, that when he started out he 'aspired to emulate . . . Chanel and Yves Saint Laurent. "They modernised fashion, bringing it in line with the way people wanted to live nowadays. They allowed people to live differently through their clothing. They didn't create apparel, they created a different society."' Armani's great breakthrough in which he still takes pride (while making it clear that he resents being acknowledged for that alone) was his 'deconstruction' of the women's jacket. He stripped out the interfacing and the heavy-duty padding, eliminated the body-sculpting darts and co-opted worsteds and tweeds from menswear. And, although he cuts a great skirt, more often than not he teamed his easy youthful jacket with the best trousers women had ever had a chance to step into.

Armani and Galeotti built on their success to create a pyramid of labels which allow access to the Armani cachet at most levels of the market. 'No, no, there was no strategy,' he told Polan in 2000:

> I am not a creative genius and I am not a marketing genius. I am not a miracle on the fashion scene. It became clear to me, after the establishment of the Giorgio Armani label that there was another market out there interested in this style which was younger and had not as much money so, since I was not studying fashion creation on a yacht, I recognised this and created Armani Jeans. But where to sell it? That's how Emporio came about. Then I realised that the young wanted more than just a pair of jeans and a jacket—and that was because I would be in the shop in via Durini [in Milan] and they would come to me and give me advice. So it became a collection and the whole idea changed.

Armani labels are found at every level of the designer market, including a couture collection, Privé, which he shows in Paris, a Junior range, underwear, swimwear, ski wear, golf clothes, spectacles, scarves, ties, shoes, accessories, watches and fragrance. The brand has stores at every level all over the world. Said Armani:

> I could have become much richer much quicker if I had decided to take advantage of my name by licensing. The decision not to has meant that every line is successful and there is no confusion, no overlapping. The identity is clear and controlled. We financed ourselves every step

of the way; I have never had half a lira debt in my life. I don't think this Cinderella story could happen now; I am happy it happened to me but the system has changed. Nowadays there are the big groups which decide who is going to be successful; the press, the industry, finance, it all works together to promote a certain designer. That is the limit of fashion today and the embarrassment.

He deplored the triumph of manufactured image over honest product.

> For someone my age, it is an embarrassment; anyone starting out does not know any different. But I have always liked to fight; I have always fought against the system in a certain sense. If a certain system exists, even if it is in my interest to belong, I have never wanted to be part of it. Yes, I have always been a loner. Obviously, I have had a lot of support from the press but I have never really been part of an explosion of a huge celebration of my fashion and my style. If I have had problems it has been with the media. Perhaps these subtle changes in my style are not shocking enough. The press like to be shocked; they like to find something which gives them a shock every season. They like revolution, big explosions, not evolution. They just say: Armani is Armani and [he mimed spitting on his hands and swiping them together in a gesture of dismissiveness] wipe their hands. That's not good for me.

What, he said, he dislikes about the fashion media's hunger for abrupt change is the way it ignores the customer. 'What they all forget,' he said, 'is that we really only have one purpose: to make women and men look better. And anyway, after an explosion, there's nothing left, only ashes. But then there's another explosion, and more ashes.'

This view overlooks the prolonged explosion of the late seventies and most of the eighties which was all about Armani, when everyone, from sleekly ambitious executives of both sexes to brand-obsessed football fans, aspired to the label. In the 1980s the grown-up Armani look was what women finally making their way in the workplace needed. Interviewed by Brenda Polan in 1983 for *The Guardian,* Armani said:

My clothes are for women who have money. They are not for a teenager who expects novelty; she could not afford them and the quality would be wasted on her since she does not wish to keep anything long. Too much of fashion is aimed at her so that mature women start to think that, since that is all there is, they must wear that too. I hate most of all the idea of women trying to look like children, trying to be a baby doll. So women like to look younger, that is natural but the general trend is for women to try to look like children and that is unnatural.

Armani felt unfairly ignored in the 1990s and 2000s, although the major retrospective of his work mounted by the Guggenheim in New York in 2000 and shown in Bilbao, Spain, and Berlin, London and Rome reminded people of his importance. He remained, in 2009, in control of his many companies.

Further reading: The biography by Renata Molho and Antony Shugaar *Being Armani: A Biography* (2007) is up to date; the catalogue *Giorgio Armani,* from the Guggenheim exhibition of 2000, is brilliantly illustrated and the text is good.

PART 5

1980s

Introduction

If the 1980s is the decade of excess, when greed was good and glamour was very much the order of the day—in Ronald Reagan's White House and the London of Diana, Princess of Wales—then fashion had the designers to dress it. This was the time of high-glam Dynasty dressing, Joan Collins in Bruce Oldfield, Nancy Reagan in Oscar de la Renta, Princess Diana in the Emanuels. It was also the decade of the first of the great reinventions; Karl Lagerfeld took Coco Chanel's legacy, shook it up hard and put it back together mischievously exaggerated and in slightly the wrong order.

By the start of the 1980s Paris had regained much of the initiative in world fashion but it was no longer possible for one national industry to be dominant. The women's movement was gaining momentum, and high-earning women in all kinds of professions were becoming consumers of fashion. They did not, however, all want to consume the same kind of fashion. The decade's archetype is doubtless the high-flying executive 'dressed for success'. Derogatively known as the 'executive tart' or 'boardroom bitch', she was suited and stilettoed, broad-shouldered, tight-skirted, plunge-necklined, decked in gold buttons, buckles, bangles and chains and cast as the predatory villain in several contemporary movies. In Paris, Thierry Mugler, Claude Montana, *Azzedine Alaia* and, when in the mood, *Jean Paul Gaultier* did the parody version. In Italy, Giorgio Armani and the young *Gianni Versace* and in America, Halston, Geoffrey Beene, Calvin Klein, *Donna Karan* and, when in the mood, Ralph Lauren did the well-bred, seriously grown-up version. In Britain, minimalist designers like *Paul Smith*

and Margaret Howell kept pace with classics featuring, as Smith always puts it, 'a twist'.

But there were many alternative ways to dress. At the beginning of the decade London was experiencing a creative renaissance with a large number of exciting young designers including *Vivienne Westwood,* Jean Muir, Zandra Rhodes, Katharine Hamnett, Body Map, Betty Jackson, Sheridan Barnett, Sheilagh Brown, Wendy Dagworthy, Jasper Conran and *John Galliano*. They had varied styles ranging from Big Look to body-con, androgynous to lyrical. The Antwerp Six—Dirk Bikkembergs, Walter van Beirendonck, Dries van Noten, Dirk van Saene. Ann Demeulemeester and Marina Yee—presented their collections in London in 1985, adding to the prevailing atmosphere of innovation. In Italy *Gianni Versace* found his signature style, an upfront eroticism that offended feminists and delighted many others. The new kids on the block were *Domenico Dolce* and *Stefano Gabbana* who also purveyed a corseted and clichéd sex appeal.

Almost as a counterbalance to all the exhibitionistic sensuality heating up the catwalks, the most remarkable moment of the 1980s came at the beginning when the Japanese designers, *Rei Kawakubo* of Comme des Garçons and *Yohji Yamamoto,* first showed in Paris. In 1981 both separately sent out an army of grim-faced models, hair shorn, faces painted white or with smeared make-up, wearing clothes that were to change fashion forever. It made high heels, cartoon glamour and impeccable make-up look dated. Both designers eschewed occidental ideas of female beauty in favour of a more cerebral approach which used the body as an armature for extraordinary shapes sculpted in fabric. It provoked all fashion's observers and many of its practitioners to reassess their subject.

35 REI KAWAKUBO (1942–)

Of the Japanese designers who made a worldwide impact in the 1970s and 1980s, Rei Kawakubo has perhaps strayed furthest from the pure, strict vision of the first collections she brought to Paris in 1981. It is possible that nothing so sensational had happened in fashion in Paris since Christian Dior had unveiled his New Look and the press, in shock, did running mental readjustments on their senses of proportion, propriety and aesthetics. In 1947 they re-embraced their inner fertility goddess; in 1981 they were forced to reassess the provenance of female sensuality and sexual attraction. Traditional Western fashion has generally (but not exclusively) situated them in the body. Rei Kawakubo insisted that they were, in fact, located in the brain. She told Nicholas Coleridge in 1988, 'The goal for all women should be to make her own living and to support herself, to be self-sufficient. That is the philosophy of her clothes. They are working for modern women, women who do not need to assure their happiness by looking sexy to men, by emphasising their figures, but who attract them with their minds.' This dream of anonymous self-sufficiency had, said Kawakubo, been her beacon since childhood.

Small and self-effacingly modest, Kawakubo is intensely work-focused, perhaps even slightly masochistic in her passion for doing things the hard way. 'It's boring if things are accomplished too easily, right?' she insisted to Leonard Koren in 1984. 'When I work I think about the excitement of achievement after hard effort and pain.' In terms of her approach, Deyan Sudjic identifies her as a modernist (she admires Le Corbusier) but Harold Koda pointed out in his text for the 1987 Fashion Institute of Technology (FIT) exhibition, Three Women, that Japan's 1,000-year-old philosophy of aesthetics encompasses irregularity, imperfection and asymmetry as reminders of the fragility and transience of beauty. And Kawakubo was a student of philosophy. It is possible to identify postmodernism in her approach, too, in that she frequently deconstructs—literally and conceptually—and questions the clichés and familiar elements of Western and oriental clothing and makes us think. Not that she has any didactic purpose; she is on an exploration of her own which is to do with the relationship of clothes to the body and the body to clothes, of how sexuality is expressed or not in clothes and how something entirely new may be made within the challenging limits of what it is possible to make and wear.

Unlike the other designers who changed both fashion in Japan and the world's perception of Japanese fashion, Rei Kawakubo had no formal training. Born in Tokyo in 1942, the daughter of a professor at Keio University, a respected private institution, she started school in a defeated, occupied country and was part of the flowering of talent prompted by the post-war economic boom and the gradually widened horizons that came with it. She studied both Japanese and Western art at her father's university and, on graduating in 1964, went to work in the advertising department of Asahi Kasei, a major chemical company which was Japan's biggest producer of acrylic fibres. In producing promotional material for print and television advertising intended to give acrylic a fashionable image, Kawakubo became a stylist, one of Japan's first. Three years later, alienated by the paternalism traditional within Japanese companies, she became the first freelance stylist. However, gradually she became aware that styling would not satisfy her urge to stretch her imagination for very long. She had invented the Comme des Garçons label (because she liked the way it sounded) for the clothes she designed and made for the advertisements she styled and by 1973 she had established a company and began to make clothes for sale. 'It wasn't a major decision,' she said. 'Working as a stylist my responsibility was very small compared with that of the art director and the photographer. I became frustrated with what I was doing and wanted to do more.' She does not regret her lack of formal training. 'If you can afford to take the time to train your eye and develop a sense of aesthetics in a natural way, it has a lot to recommend it.'

If Comme des Garçons had a certain ring to it, it also seemed appropriate for the simplicity of the clothes she was making, clothes which took a masculine wardrobe as a distant starting point. Interviewed by Geraldine Ranson of the *Sunday Telegraph* in 1983, she said, 'Most men don't like women who are capable of working hard. They do not like strong independent women with their feet on the ground.' She did not expect men outside the fashion industry to understand her clothes. 'It's not cute or soft and it doesn't fit a man's image of a woman.' But then, as she had told Mary Russell of *Vogue* in 1982, 'I do not find clothes that reveal the body sexy.'

In 1975 Kawakubo showed her first womenswear collection in Tokyo and began her collaboration with the architect Takao Kawasaki to develop a very particular identity for her shops. She also produced the first of a series of catalogues which enabled her to disseminate images of her clothes styled as she wished them to be seen. 'I try to reflect my approach not just in the clothes, but in the accessories, the shows, the shops, even in my office. You have to see it as a total impression and not just look at the exposed seams and black.'

In 1978 she launched Homme, her menswear collection; it was followed by Tricot and Robe de Chambre in 1981 and Noir in 1987. The biggest step, however, was in 1981 when, in order to gain recognition internationally, she took her collection to show at the Intercontinental Hotel Paris—to mixed reviews, some bewildered, some dismissive. However, both she and Yohji Yamamoto (the pair had been lovers) were invited to present a catwalk show

the following season, the first time the Chambre Syndicale had ever extended such an invitation to foreign designers. Kawakubo showed an asymmetric monochrome collection which included trousers with sweater cuffs at the ankles topped with hybrid tunic/shawls, voluminous overcoats buttoned left to right *comme des garçons* and boiled-wool knits with the neck hole cut into the chest or the shoulder so that, on the body, the garments made gauche but intriguingly eccentric, abstract shapes. There was no music, just a noise like a train clanging over points, and the models, their make-up dark, hungry-looking and out-of-synch with the features of their impassive faces, moved sedately, joylessly.

These clothes were at first sight puritanically austere and intellectual. Fashion was going through a stale patch, repeating itself, and the only hope for rejuvenation appeared to be young London. However, those who were there on that evening will never forget the shock and the delight. Shock because no one had made clothes like this before; and delight because although they appeared to espouse a deliberately ugly anti-aesthetic, they were strangely compelling and demanded that one did more than react with the senses; they insisted that you think about them. In 1984 Leonard Koren described Kawakubo as having the purest, most uncompromising and strongest avant-garde vision of all the designers to come to prominence in the 1970s. From the 1990s onwards, you are much more likely to find hand-painted crinoline ball gowns than dark, torn shrouds in her collections. In 1983, however, she gravely told Geraldine Ranson that her taste for working exclusively in black and white had remained unchanged for ten years or so.

In the early days of a palette of various shades of black, she wryly acknowledged the inherent weakness of her method. 'I realised clothes have to be worn and sold to a certain number of people. That's the difference between being a painter or sculptor and a clothing designer. It is, in a sense, a very commercial field. Unfortunately my collections tend to be very concentrated and focused on very few ideas and this is a commercial problem. I try to get more variety. But I can't; it's not my way.'

Fortunately it has become her way. Each collection is indeed focused but Kawakubo is an instinctive innovator, constantly challenging her own ingenuity. Having worked through her initial preoccupation with the structure of clothes, she turned her attention to surface and colour. The creation of her collections depends very much on a series of collaborations with key creatives. She has famously said that with every collection, 'I start from zero.' Hiroshi Matsushita of the Orimono Kenkyu Sha textile company was an early contributor, developing fabrics in response to Kawakubo's questions, suggestions, thoughts and moods. Deyan Sudjic wrote in 1990, 'It was Matsushita, for example, who devised the rayon criss-crossed with elastic that allowed Kawakubo to make the garments in the women's collection of 1984 bubble and boil as though they were melting. And it was Matsushita who formulated the bonded cotton rayon and polyurethane fabric Kawakubo used for her asymmetric dresses of 1986.'

Her method of work is often more about whim and mischief than any straining after pre-imagined effects. She told Leonard Koren, 'The machines that make fabric are more and more making uniform, flawless textures. I like it when something is off, not perfect. Hand weaving is the best way to achieve this. Since this isn't always possible, we loosen a screw of the machines here and there so they can't do exactly what they're supposed to do.'

The fabric is a continuous journey of experiment because, as Matsushita told Sudjic, 'She never likes to do anything twice, so to meet her requirements the mills have had to come up with techniques that have not been tried before; they have had to invent new fabrics. Lately the words she uses [as her starting point] have been softer, a little sweeter. Maybe she has mellowed; it's reflected in the language and in the fabrics.'

With the fabric in place, Kawakubo then works with her large team of pattern-cutters. 'Some designers,' she told Sudjic. 'produce detailed sketches and have a pattern made that is based directly on them. I begin with a much more abstract drawing and the pattern-makers need to be able to interpret what I am trying to do. They help me to design.'

In 1996 she showed for spring/summer 1997 a collection which perplexed even her most die-hard admirers. Known to Kawakubo as 'Dress Becomes Body Becomes Dress,' and to everyone else as the collection of the humps, it distorted skinny, body-hugging clothes in bright spring colours with a series of protuberances that appeared to be attached like some alien limpet-like succubus to random spots around the body, occasionally growing elongated and tyre-like to embrace the waist or hips. There were also waxed brown-paper puffball skirts and fantastically rosette-pleated tops and jackets in Prince-of-Wales check and pretty, girlish gingham. An uncomfortable crowd shuffled out muttering about the Quasimodo Collection and what do you call the particular political incorrectness that mocks deformity? The collection sold, the clothes were great talking pieces and then great collector's pieces and Kawakubo continued to experiment, her reputation undamaged.

In 1995 she said, 'I don't think my clothes have changed enormously over the years, though I hope I always change in the sense of making progress. In the past perhaps I was more obvious about exposing construction techniques. I used patterns that were very complex; I found that a passion. Now I am more interested in the general mood of a collection.' Observers and collaborators do keep reflecting that they think she has 'mellowed' over the years and her marriage to Adrian Joffé, a South African–born architect who is managing director of her company, may have something to do with that.

If the mood of those earlier collections was sombre and aggressive in its confrontation of the fashion world's expectations, the mood of her mature years is much more light-hearted with a strong bias towards Western shapes. But they are shapes transformed by Kawakubo's unique sense of architecture, her intellectual distancing from her medium and, the factor it was so easy to miss at the beginning, a playful sensuality which lies in tactility and abstract form, a garment's movement on the body whether it flows or, stiff and static, merely changes in silhouette as the wearer turns and moves.

Further reading: Deyan Sudjic's monograph, *Rei Kawakubo and Comme des Garçons* (1990), is a must-read.

36 YOHJI YAMAMOTO (1943–)

Yohji Yamamoto's aim is to synthesise the traditional understated Japanese aesthetic—with its emphasis on simplicity and purity of response—and what he perceives as the more 'human', body-oriented Western tradition. Less disciplined than Miyake, he casts his net wider in his search for a vocabulary of shapes and textures to express that strange amalgam of intellectualism and sensuality that is uniquely his. Those witnessing a Yamamoto show are uneasily aware that a mental adjustment is required, is in fact irresistible. These clothes are not there to display the body; the body is there to display the structure, the harmonies and the sometimes harshly discordant unorthodoxies of the clothes. 'For me,' said Yamamoto, 'the body is nothing. The body is change. Every moment it gets older so you cannot count on it. You cannot control time. I can't believe in the human body. I do not think the human body is beautiful.'

The traditional Japanese approach to dress, as demonstrated in the many layered kimonos that make up a formal ceremonial outfit, is not about the body; it is about the shape the clothes assume on the body—hierarchic, imposing in the case of men and dignified, modest, adorned in the case of women—and the colour and surface texture. The latter is historically a matter of weave, pattern and embroidery. The body is treated like a sculptor's armature, the metal skeleton the artist will clothe in clay. In fact, the sculpture analogy is a good one; not only does Yamamoto tend to think of himself functioning within the ranks of artists, but his design handwriting is sculptural, plastic, his clothes very much things of curves, planes and tactile volume, of fragments of geometric shapes. Like

Miyake, who had been showing successfully in Paris for a decade when Yamamoto and Kawakubo first showed there, Yamamoto is preoccupied with the texture of fabrics and the potential of large, abstract, asymmetric shapes to display it. With Kawakubo, Yamamoto started a look which was consistent to a large degree with the work being produced at that time by the avant-garde designers of Britain and which became known, just as derogatively, as 'bag lady chic'. His method is a more intellectually purposeful postmodern than the methods of Vivienne Westwood and John Galliano, but there is a connection.

Although Yamamoto is drawn again and again to the strict tailored curves of the fin de siècle—often topping his ingeniously cut and gathered up long skirts and long narrow jackets with the vast lampshade-like tulle and organza hats of the period—they are more of an insistent backbeat than the melody. He is, as François Boudot points out in his book in the Fashion Memoir series, 'exceptionally responsive to contemporary trends—in the same way that couturiers of preceding generations responded to Cubism, say, or the Ballets Russes or Pop Art.' Boudot identifies Arte Povera, work pulled together from detritus—rags, wood shavings, mud, coal—as a major influence on Yamamoto's approach. He, says, Boudot, '. . . tried to break away from a fossilised conception of what clothes were. He did this by disrupting the codes by which clothes made their appeal; by rethinking the glamorous signals sent out by their external appearance; by redefining their relationship with the male or female body; and, ultimately—to near universal incomprehension—by radically reinterpreting the respective contributions of beauty and ugliness, past and future, memory and modernity.'

When Geraldine Ranson of the *Sunday Telegraph* visited Tokyo in 1982, she remarked that on Yamamoto's labels was printed the statement, 'There is nothing so boring as a neat and tidy look.' In 2002, in *Talking to Myself* with Carla Sozzani, Yamamoto wrote, 'I think perfection is ugly. Somewhere in the things humans make I want to see scars, failure, disorder, distortion.' Indeed, although they may be evocatively beautiful, there is often something uneasily disjointed about his sombrely dramatic clothes, something reminiscent of some moody forgotten dream one once woke from, vaguely disturbed, and, for that reason, they are loved by adherents of the Goth subcultural style.

Born in Tokyo in 1943, Yohji Yamamoto was brought up by his mother, Fumi, who was widowed by the Second World War and worked for sixteen hours a day as a dressmaker to pay for her son's education. He initially took a law degree at Keio University (where Rei Kawakubo was studying at the same time) but decided he wanted to work with his mother in her dressmaking business. She—who had dreamed of an important career in the law for him—agreed on the condition he train for the job at the famous Bunka School. He still remembers his discomfort at being the only boy in his class and the oldest student by far. He graduated in 1969, winning a competition for a trip to Paris—where he managed to survive for eight months on no money, observing, learning and haunting the Left Bank boutiques. He returned to Tokyo, and, in 1971, he started his own business, the Y's Company Ltd. He did not show on a catwalk until 1977, when he already had a strong following. In Japan the women who wore his black clothes were already known as 'crows'. 'The samurai spirit is black,' said Yamamoto. 'The samurai must be able to throw his body into nothingness, the colour and image of which is black.'

In 1981 he and his colleague and former lover, Rei Kawakubo of Comme des Garçons, set the fashion world on its ears when they showed in Paris. Many commentators loathed what they called 'Holocaust Chic' or 'Post-Hiroshima Style', but many others loved the challenge it offered to conventional ways of thinking about fashion. In *Libération*, under the

headline, 'French fashion has found its masters: the Japanese,' Michel Cresson wrote, 'The outfits he offers us in 1982 for us to wear in the next 20 years are infinitely more feasible than those proposed by Courrèges and Cardin in around 1960 for the year 2000, which today look as old-hat as a Soviet sci-fi film.'

In 1984 Yamamoto told Nicholas Coleridge:

There was a moment when the Paris Prêt-a-Porter looked set to die. It had run out of ideas. Thierry Mugler and Claude Montana, what they were doing was almost couture; it was so restricted. Then we went to Paris and it happened, the spirit of our clothes was free. *Marie-Claire* were the first to understand, yes, they had the first understanding . . . In fashion I think there is always a feeling of anti-something. In magazines they think anti, anti, anti. They like a certain look for a time, then they are anti it; not indifferent but anti. In 1981 they were anti western clothes, so they needed and accepted us, and tried to understand my concept of sexuality. I don't feel sexuality at all in the normal meaning. A fantasy of mine is a woman, 40 or 50 years old. She is very skinny with grey hair and smoking a cigarette. She is neither a woman nor a man but she is very attractive. She is sexy for me. She is walking away from me and as I walk after her she calls out, 'No, Yohji, do not follow.'

In 1984, in the first of the many new collections he has developed over the years, Yamamoto deconstructed and reconstructed men's clothing, creating a new classicism—severe white shirts, puny-shouldered dark suits with three-button jackets with narrow lapels and slender trousers. Embraced rapidly by the artistic intelligentsia, the look powerfully influenced menswear for a decade. More than most designers, Yamamoto is interested in the contribution the wearer makes. 'Whether a season's fashion is interesting or not does not depend on the designers who created it, but on those who see it and buy it.' His men's clothes as much as his women's have always attracted a particularly interesting wearer, one that responds to the boldness of his intention and the subtlety of its execution, to the seriousness of his approach to design—which many of them share—and to the lightness, mischief and wit that can always be found at the heart of the collection. He told Boudot in 1997:

> Making a garment means thinking about people. I am always eager to meet people and talk to them. It's what I like more than anything else. What are they doing? What are they thinking? How do they lead their lives? And then I can set to work. I start with the fabric, the actual material, the 'feel' of it, I then move on to the form. Possibly what counts most for me is the feel. And then when I start working on the material, I think my way into the form it ought to assume.

His collaboration with Adidas was one of the first and most successful between a cutting-edge designer and a mass-market brand. It was carefully chosen of course. The trainer was modern, fit for its purpose from a purist's point of view and, above all, an iconic item of clothing in the mainstream and across a range of subcultures. Best of all, its origins lie in Western campus sports, making it something Yamamoto, an outsider to all those things, could have a lot of fun with. Of all the Japanese designers he is perhaps the most in denial about the influence his own culture has had on his work—even though some of his most beautiful clothes are largely sourced from what appear to be cannibalised kimonos. 'I happen to have been born in Japan. But I've never labelled myself in that way,' he has said. He was always rather impatient with the fashion press's somewhat bewildered initial tendency to lump Japanese designers together into a school or movement and its assumption that this must be the way all Japanese women were dressing. He said, 'People talk about the Japanese as if they're all together in some kind of designers' mafia. In Japan, maybe they're popular somewhere at the edge of things. But it's got nothing to do with ordinary people.'

If it sounds elitist, it was meant to. Yamamoto started off more the fine artist than the fashion designer. His clothes were difficult to understand, loaded, like a difficult poem or painting, with references and symbols—often disguised or distorted— and layers of meanings. His collections still include garments of great strangeness and a sort of theatrical ugliness which makes unusual demands on the understanding of the observer. His attitude has inevitably undergone some changes. In 1984 he told Leonard Koren:

> Since I began this fashion-making job, I have been thinking, 'What is fashion for me?' For about ten years I couldn't believe in it because fashion is always changing. The people who follow it are superficial. The most important thing is, 'What's new?' But in the last two or three years I've found something in it. In fashion one can find new kinds of expression about human beings—things that pure art like painting, sculpture and cinema can't express. Only fashion can. I can't explain exactly why it is, but the problem of what people are wearing and the influence over people of fashion is awesome. I think there's a new way to create so I think there's a future for me.

So it has proved. In shedding some of his seriousness, Yamamoto learned to love fashion and over the years a new joyfulness has been evident in his work. He enjoys the way women enjoy his clothes, recognising that the spirit of self-conscious playfulness they bring to them is that extra human element that makes them work, that extra element that neither a picture not a sculpture nor even a movie contains.

Further reading: See Francois Boudot's *Yohji Yamamoto: Fashion Memoir* (1997), for a quick overview, supplemented by Yuniya Kawamura's *The Japanese Revolution in Paris Fashion* (2004) and *The Cutting Edge: Fashion from Japan* (2005) by Louise Mitchell, Bonnie English and Akiko Fukai.

37 VIVIENNE WESTWOOD (1941–)

In terms of creativity and the ability to place fashion at the heart of a vital popular culture, Vivienne Westwood may be the greatest designer of the twentieth century. Her method is not so very different from that of many designers, particularly other British designers trained in an art-school tradition and, interestingly, a generation of Japanese designers who used this occidental approach to invent an original oriental fashion, but the conscious, didactic way she demonstrates it is unique. In 1991 when she was working through ideas related to both Christian Dior's New Look and early eighteenth-century clothing, she told Brenda Polan, writing for *The Independent on Sunday*:

> Clothing has always reconstructed and modified the structure of the body and it still does today. What seems to surprise and upset people is reconstructions that don't accord with what they consider to be the norm, the present accepted idea of beauty. If you design a dress with a *sellier,* the padding that gives it a rounded form has become a subversive act. Perhaps I mean it to be a subversive act. Perhaps I want to question people's prejudices about what is beautiful, what makes a lady beautiful. Through fashion I try to re-evoke the past and reflect on it.

Westwood trained as a teacher, and there is still a good deal of the pedagogue about her; ideas and analysis excite her. Clothes are a language she uses to deconstruct cliché and convention. She confronts prejudices and questions them — not always totally coherently but with courage and purpose. The subjects of her explorations of dress and its emotional and rational subtext have always

been clearly signposted in the names and themes of her collections, which, when watched on a catwalk, stimulate the intellect as well as the senses — including the sense of humour. While she revels in the joy, the sheer fun of the fashion she makes, she is serious and very political in the way she uses it as an investigative tool. She is much preoccupied with the culture and its decline, believing the French are the inheritors and keepers of a true intellectual tradition. In 2007, in a conversation with Brenda Polan at the ICA in London as part of a conference on *The Death of Taste,* she answered a question on her response to current culture and its relationship to her concept of civilisation thus:

> The best thing about my job, and the worst thing is that it is non-stop and you never, never can stop. Some of my best thoughts occur at night, just because I am reading and I am hatching ideas. Everybody must have that experience where the ideas are sort of there and then you develop them and you think you mustn't forget that, and sometimes you even get up and write it down. And then I must just say, because it's an incredible, fantastic tip to give to people, I always write 30 quotations, a few of them in French when I can, because it's so brilliant, the body of literature in France, it's amazing. I'll write 30 quotations, poetry and all kinds of things. For example, Rousseau — if you read some it's so concentrated, you can just go over that quotation and you can find answers for all sorts of things that are in your mind at that particular time . . . And culture is connected with human rights. If you want to be able to lock people in jail and never tell them why, then you can't have

civilisation. I mean you have to have *habeas corpus;* you have to have justice before the law. And I've recently incorporated this into my fashion. And it interests me much more to be able to do that because I am very literal and I really like to work out my ideas.

As Susannah Frankel remarked in *The Guardian* in 1997, 'At any given time Westwood has at least two, maybe three ideas, or even sentences on the go concurrently, uttered in hushed Derbyshire tones, that career and collide until they either explode into meaning, often minutes and even hours later, or at times peter out entirely, leaving anyone who's interested to fill in the gaps.' Among fashion journalists and academics, there are very many who, out of admiration for the woman and her spirit as well as her work, are happy to do that.

Vivienne Isabel Swire was born in Glossop, Derbyshire, in 1941, the first of three children. Her father came from a long line of shoemakers, and her mother worked as a weaver in one of the town's cotton mills. She always liked fashion and remembers her mother pointing out a neighbour's New Look outfit in 1947. It was a look she would emulate in her teenage years when she made her own clothes. She remembers customising her grammar school uniform into a pencil skirt. 'It was a new thing, putting that on was such a symbol of sexuality,' she told Claire Wilcox in 2003. In the late 1950s, the family moved to Harrow on the outskirts of London and at sixteen, Vivienne started a foundation course at Harrow School of Art but left after one term and began to support herself selling jewellery from a stall in the Portobello Road market. She abandoned this for work in a factory that would enable her to save up for teacher-training college. In 1962 she was working as a primary-school teacher when she met her first husband, Derek Westwood, at a dance, but the marriage failed some time after the birth of their son, Ben. In 1965 she met Malcolm McLaren, the father of Joe, her second son, born in 1967. Malcolm was to change the course of her life.

McLaren, a typically rebellious child of the sex, drugs, and rock and roll 1960s, was influenced by the situationists and Guy Debord's book, *Societé du Spectacle,* a collection of perverse aphorisms

that was later to give a language to Punk. He loved clothes but thought there was nothing for him in the current boutique culture of London. He would style Vivienne with traditional garments juxtaposed in subversive ways and encouraged her to razor-cut and bleach her hair. They opened their first shop, Let It Rock, which launched Punk, on the King's Road in 1971. By 1975, however, the shop had been renamed Sex, the interior sprayed with pornographic graffiti, hung with rubber curtains and stocked with sex and fetish wear. Westwood thrilled to the sense of trespass the clothes aroused. 'All the clothes I wore people would regard as shocking, I wore them because I just thought that I looked like a princess from another planet.'

In 1976 McLaren, now manager of the Sex Pistols, renamed the Kings Road shop Seditionaries— Clothes for Heroes and redesigned its interior to feature shots of an upside-down Piccadilly Circus and a ruined Dresden, spotlights poking through roughly hacked holes in the ceiling, and a live, caged rat. The Seditionaries collection summed up Westwood and McLaren's work so far, encompassing the ripped garments of 1950s pin-up pictures; the leather, chains and badges of the bikers; and the straps, safety pins and buckles of the fetishists. As Westwood said, 'You couldn't imagine the Punk Rock thing without the clothing.' Deliberately confrontational, of course, the look was first excoriated then absorbed into mainstream fashion as a style element with a frisson of danger.

By the early 1980s McLaren was focused on music and Westwood began to see herself as a fashion designer. In need of change, they chose to examine history. The shop was renamed World's End, and the interior was transformed into a pirate galleon complete with a sloping deck, a low ceiling and small windows. The fascia featured a large clock displaying thirteen hours and hands that travelled backwards. The new collection, shown at Olympia in spring 1981, was accompanied by cannon fire and McLaren's rap music and was reminiscent of the age of pirates, highwaymen and dandies. It was immediately acclaimed and copied all around the world. That autumn, they showed Savage, which combined Native American patterns with leather frock coats, Foreign Legion hats worn back-to-front, 'petti-drawers' and shorts. Nostalgia of Mud (autumn/winter 1982) followed and featured large tattered skirts topped by raw-edged sheepskin jackets in muddy colours. Punkature (spring/summer 1983) maintained a rough, slightly distressed feeling but, melding 'punk' and 'couture', also referenced Ridley Scott's film *Blade Runner.*

Witches, the collection for autumn/winter 1983, was the final collaboration between Westwood and McLaren. Borrowing motifs from Keith Haring, a New York graffiti artist, it featured oversized, double-breasted jackets and coats, huge cream cotton mackintoshes worn with knitted jacquard bodies, tube skirts and pointed hats. In 1984 Westwood moved her production to Italy (she had found her current business partner, Carlo d'Amario). Her spring/summer 1984 collection was called Hypnos and was heavily indebted to synthetic sportswear fabrics in fluorescent colours. The Clint Eastwood collection was a development, much inspired by Tokyo's neon nights and Italian company logos.

In 1985 Westwood deliberately broke with the wide-shouldered, executive-tart/Dynasty look that was dominating fashion. Taking the ballet *Petrushka* as her inspiration, she created a 'mini-crini,' which combined the tutu with a shortened Victorian crinoline. The mini-crini was pure Westwood, its blending of ingénue's party frock with hints of a Dior-derived mature sexuality decidedly titillating. She herself was interested, too, in the fact that although a crinoline has become a modern symbol of women's oppression, the sheer space it claimed, the presence it imposed signified something very different. The result of similarly mixed motives, the Harris Tweed collection that followed celebrated Westwood's delight in traditional English clothing and her growing obsession with a royalty that was simultaneously frumpy and glamorous—the princess of her youth grown into deep-bosomed country housewife. Many of the garments—the knitted twin sets, the 'Stature of Liberty' corsets and the tailored 'Savile' jackets—became Westwood classics

The collections that followed became known collectively as 'Britain Must Go Pagan' and promiscuously juxtaposed traditional British themes with classical and pagan elements, the latter often derived from the pornography of ancient Greece. In Time Machine she made prim Miss Marple tweed

suits, the jackets articulated like medieval armour. Voyage to Cythera, named after a painting by Watteau, represented a renewed interest in archaic construction methods, this time of eighteenth-century France, and was developed in Pagan V in which Sèvres patterns were printed on classical togas. It was at this time (1989) that John Fairchild of *Women's Wear Daily* named Westwood one of the six best designers in the world.

From 1990, with the Cut and Slash collection inspired by Elizabethan men's clothing, Westwood's hours spent in museums, art galleries and libraries provide the dominant themes in her work. In a period of minimalism, she preferred decoration, romance and aristocratic grandeur—never, of course, played totally straight. She cited the refinement she found in French design and the 'easy charm' and impeccable tailoring of English dress. 'Fashion as we know it,' she claimed, 'is the result of the exchange of ideas between France and England.'

As Claire Wilcox wrote in the catalogue to the Westwood Retrospective Exhibition at the Victoria and Albert Museum in 2003, Westwood 'sees fashion as personal propaganda, as an agent of arousal both physical and mental. The way clothes feel is as important as the way they look. To this end, she distorts, exaggerates and pares away the natural shape of the body, often using the constructions that she found in historical costume. She also gives each ensemble an agenda, laden with historical references that she says, "have a certain type of nostalgia which is how I would define glamour. They are part of the story of human culture."'

Vivienne Westwood was made a Dame of the British Empire in 2006 at a ceremony presided over by the Prince of Wales. She confided that she was not wearing knickers.

Further reading: Jane Mulvagh's *Vivienne Westwood: An Unfashionable Life* (1998) and Fred Vermorel's *Fashion and Perversity: A Life of Vivienne Westwood and the Sixties Laid Bare* (1996) tell differing tales. Barbara Baines's *Revivals in Fashion: From the Elizabethan Age to the Present* (1981) provides context and food for thought. Amy De la Haye's *The Cutting Edge: 50 Years of British Fashion* (1996) is excellent background.

38   PAUL SMITH (1946–)

Since the 1980s, Paul Smith has been an outstanding force in British fashion, best known for a quirky, humorous design sensibility applied to classic British tailoring. For years he played down his abilities as a designer, but by the early 1990s Smith emerged as the complete package—a designer, retailer and businessman all rolled into one. A pioneering Western designer in Japan, Smith outsold Armani and Chanel there in the late 1980s.

In creative terms, Sir Paul Smith (he was knighted in 2001) has been overlooked, perhaps because of his lack of formal fashion training. His consistent challenge to notions of good taste has made him an important postmodern influence in men's fashion, spilling over into womenswear too (he launched a women's collection in 1994). Smith loves the traditions of Savile Row–style tailoring, but he also loves kitsch and off-the-wall eccentricity. 'What is good taste? What is bad taste?' he said in 1990. 'They are both so near. It's just lovely to shove these in a food-mixer and throw them around.' In a later comment, he said: 'The wrong thing with the wrong thing is the speciality of the house.' American novelist William Gibson, taking as his point of reference a nineteenth-century London clothes market, summed up his style neatly: 'It is as though he possesses some inner equivalent of the Houndsditch Clothes Exchange—not a museum, but a vast, endlessly recombinant jumble sale in which all the artefacts of his nation and culture constantly engage in a mutual exchange of code.'

Gibson highlights Smith's fascination with the found object. Whether in London or Tokyo (undoubtedly his favourite city outside Britain), Smith is perpetually looking out for things that might be reinterpreted in the arena of fashion or simply sold in one of his shops for fun. Countless products, ranging from postage stamps to piles of fruit, are turned into T-shirt photo prints, reflecting a love of photography and the surreal inherited from his father. A childlike imagination is at work: a pair of fake eyeballs, for example, is turned into cufflinks and buttons. In the 1980s, veteran British designer Sir Hardy Amies was one of many who found his shops a treasure trove of ideas and entertainment.

Smith was, and is, a unique figure in British fashion. Although British designers since the 1980s have proved among the most thrillingly imaginative in the world, filling the design studios of major fashion houses in Italy, France and America, they have shown little ability to build and sustain their own businesses. Before Smith, it was left to an American, Ralph Lauren, to translate classic British style for a modern international market. In the menswear market, some British names, such as Sir Hardy Amies, remained traditional in outlook, while others, including Aquascutum, Daks-Simpson, Jaeger and Gieves & Hawkes, made half-hearted efforts to move forward, rarely causing more than a ripple on the international scene. Only Burberry, through the services of a farsighted American chief executive, Rosemarie Bravo, made progress in the late 1990s and the early noughties. Paul Smith might be compared to Vivienne Westwood, another great British designer who has played around with classic style. But where Westwood was an aggressively subversive force, Smith's approach was playful and more accessible. He turned a quirky idea of Britishness into a global language of fashion. 'My thing has always been about maximising Britishness,' he has said. As he put it himself in an interview in 1981, he produces 'classics with a twist'—a term that has since been used so often it has become a cliché.

Smith has no time for conceptual fashion, saying 'I don't like . . . stupid ideas that can't be worn.' He is also proudly anti–big business, challenging the corporate style of the modern designer fashion business and the sameness of designer stores the world over. A portrait of the designer by James Lloyd in London's National Portrait Gallery sums up his character well: energetic, irreverent, level-headed and perhaps a good deal tougher than his easy-going public persona might suggest. Interviewed by Roger Tredre in 1990, Smith was modest about his design skills: 'A few years ago, I would have said that I was just a getter-togetherer of fashion. But more recently I would say that I am a designer because I do have ideas that start with a blank sheet of paper.'

Paul Brierley Smith was born in Beeston, Nottingham, in 1946. He left school without qualifications at the age of fifteen, whereupon his father, Harold, instructed him to work in a clothing warehouse, where he was little more than a gofer. It was the early 1960s, when fashion was on the verge of a youth-led explosion. Smith began putting together displays in the warehouse and creating his own fashion shoots. His ambition at this point was to become a professional cyclist, but a major accident at the age of seventeen changed all that. Smith spent six months in hospital and emerged with a different outlook on life. He started hanging out with art students in pubs and ingesting the art and fashion of the time. For a few years, he energetically embraced the late 1960s counterculture, dressing the part to the disgust of one elderly man who stopped him in the street to admonish him: 'I fought in the war for you and you dress like a bloody girl.' He joined forces with a student womenswear designer named Janet, taking charge of the menswear department of her shop in 1966 and learning the rudiments of retail. Smith opened his first shop, Vetement, in 1970, selling such designers as Kenzo and Margaret Howell and initially a few locally made shirts and jackets. The shop evolved at a slow pace, developing steadily, if unspectacularly, throughout the decade. Smith's personal style had shifted towards a more dressed-up look, including bespoke suits, cashmere sweaters and made-to-measure boots with Cuban heels.

The Paul Smith label was not formally launched until 1976 in Paris. New lightweight fabrics were expanding the options for men's tailoring. Giorgio Armani was making softer suits in Italy. Smith took some of these lessons but did not push them nearly as far, preferring to make his impact by playing with suits in different ways. A pinstripe suit was paired with a navy blue spot shirt and white plimsolls. A Prince of Wales check or a chalkstripe might turn up in unconventional colourways, with brightly coloured linings. From the beginning, he had support in his experiments from his lifelong partner Pauline Denyer (they married in 2001), who studied at the Royal College of Art and therefore had a technical training that Smith had never enjoyed. She designed the early collections, he later admitted. In their early twenties, they visited the couture shows in Paris, attending Chanel, Cardin, Balmain and Yves Saint Laurent. Smith's approach to design was more in line with this tradition than the unconstructed shapes that swept through fashion in the early 1980s, inspired by Japanese designers such as Rei Kawakubo and Yohji Yamamoto. 'At that time, a lot of our art colleges lost the ability to create clothes in a traditional way,' recalled Smith. 'A lot of exciting things were happening, of course . . . but I really wish that this foundation had continued. Unconstructed suits hurt my eyes.'

Smith's influence extended far beyond his own label. For many years, he was discreetly working as a menswear consultant for Marks & Spencer, Britain's biggest clothing retailer, ploughing the money he earned back into his own business. Likewise, a thriving wholesale business enabled him to maintain momentum whenever his own shops were quiet. A key move was the freehold purchase and opening of a shop at 44 Floral Street in London's Covent Garden in 1979. It was the first fashion store to open on the street. He bought the unit next door shortly afterwards and resolved to keep its old wooden-panelled fittings, developing the Paul Smith retail style, an eccentric mix of old and new. The shop evolved to become one of the most important stores in modern British fashion history, a place of pilgrimage for modern menswear enthusiasts, not least for its artistic and witty shop windows. Smith's retail experience, learned the hard way, was invaluable as he developed his business. 'You have to be 90 per cent businessman and 10 per cent designer,' he said.

The 1980s were a golden decade for Smith. While the made-to-measure tailors of Savile Row struggled to survive, British tailoring was assured of a place on the modern map of fashion thanks to Smith, with a number of smaller designers, such as Richard James, also developing in his wake. The Paul Smith label caught the wave of a newly prosperous Britain. Every go-ahead young creative type in 1980s London had a Paul Smith suit, along with a pair of boxer shorts and a Filofax personal organiser, which were both sold and promoted by Smith. Well ahead of many European designers, Smith spotted the golden potential of Japan, signing a license with C. Itoh in 1984 and travelling back and forth twice a year ever since. This commitment reaped rewards and prompted other designers to follow his lead. Regular *tenjikai* (exhibitions of new collections) are staged in Tokyo, where Smith has a celebrity status of extraordinary dimensions. He was more cautious about the emergence of China as an important new market in the early years of the twenty-first century, opening a first store in Shanghai in 2004.

Elsewhere, the retail development of Paul Smith continued apace, with a first store opened in New York on Fifth Avenue in 1987, a store in Paris in 1993, and a new London shop on Sloane Avenue in 1997. Perhaps his most unusual shop was Westbourne House, a large Victorian residence in Notting Hill, redesigned by Sophie Hicks. In six rooms over three floors, the complete Paul Smith collection was sold, together with a bespoke tailoring service. Smith's womenswear, launched in 1994 and produced in Italy, has had a lesser impact than his menswear, drawing on his menswear collection for much of its inspiration and look. Smith has often stood aside from the mainstream of the designer industry in Britain, avoiding the British Fashion Awards, which he once criticised as 'self-congratulatory'. He became frustrated with the failure of British industry to produce the management to nurture new designers although he worked hard behind the scenes in an advisory capacity to try and drum up some momentum. The designer also spoke out regularly against the uniformity of modern fashion designers. In speeches around the world, he argued the case for a new spirit of individuality in fashion—a viewpoint that had became widely accepted by the late noughties. A great shop, he said, should be like an Aladdin's cave 'where you'll see something hideous next to something wonderful, something low-priced next to something high-priced.'

Smith also ardently believes everyone can have a go at design. In that sense, he may point the way forward for the future of design, with a do-it-yourself mood sweeping through modern popular culture, supported by new technological advances. Perhaps the twenty-first century will see the end of the concept of an omnipotent designer, replaced by a more collaborative process in which the end consumer has a significant say. As an outspoken individualist, Smith also represents a note of hope for fashion during a period of globalisation. Now in his sixties, Smith continues to work at a ferocious pace. His design philosophy is best summed up in the title of a book he authored in 2001: *You Can Find Inspiration in Everything (and If You Can't, Look Again)*. Smith himself is reluctant to over-philosophise about his contribution to fashion. 'I ended up designing clothes that I wanted to wear myself and felt good in,' he said. 'Well made, good quality, simple cut, interesting fabrics, easy-to-wear. No-bullshit clothing.'

Further reading: Paul Smith effectively explored his approach to design in *You Can Find Inspiration in Everything (and If You Can't, Look Again)* (2001).

39 AZZEDINE ALAIA (c. 1940–)

Life for fashion editors trying to pin down a handful of consistent trends to guide their readers got pretty tough in the early 1980s. The round of catwalk shows felt like chaos, but it was possible to identify three main strands. In the first and most exciting category were the experimental/intellectual designers, the Japanese in Paris; the young Britons, such as Vivienne Westwood, Bodymap, Katharine Hamnett and Betty Jackson; and the Antwerp group, which included Anne Demeulemeester, Martin Margiela and Dries van Noten. Then there were the modernist/minimalists headed by Giorgio Armani, Calvin Klein and Zoran.

Holding the centre ground were what one might call the fantasists or romantics represented by the restrained, soft romanticism of Yves Saint Laurent, Karl Lagerfeld and the early Gianni Versace and more aggressively by the comic-strip boys whose vision of womanhood was a bit like Barbie takes a trip and gets a corset and a bit like the heroine from an erotic pulp sci-fi or horror comic. In this set the most eclectic imagination belonged to Jean Paul Gaultier but Thierry Mugler and Claude Montana were both capable of giving their movie-inspired, pop-culture sirens large wardrobes which sometimes included moulded plastic breastplates with tip-tilted 1950s breasts, cinched torsos, bondage details and the highest of stilettos. However, the dress-me-as-a-vamp hero of the time was Azzedine Alaia, the diminutive Tunisian dubbed the 'King of Cling' by *Women's Wear Daily* and 'the Titan of Tight' by Georgina Howell.

In 1982 Brenda Polan was taken to meet Alaia in his cramped and crowded studio in the Latin Quarter of Paris. Introductions were performed by London-based retailer Joseph Ettedgui, who had introduced Kenzo to Britain and was about to do the same for Alaia. It was the only interview Polan had ever conducted sitting on a (closed) lavatory while the interviewee stood in the doorway. At that point the small man dressed all in black—black Nehru jacket, black cotton trousers, black velvet slippers—was suddenly and to his own surprise, the hottest name in Paris. There were no press clippings for some basic research so the bread-and-butter questions had to be asked. In response to one of the first Alaia was evasive but charming. 'How old? Does it matter? I am as old as the pharaohs.'

Chastened, Polan moved on. 'Success? It is not important to me, not something I ever really cared about or desired. For me the work, the clothes, the customers, the women are the pleasure. I have never had possessions but I have always had people; they are what matters to me. The beautiful women, they matter to me. I am a sculptor and I can maybe make them more beautiful.'

Alaia was born round about 1940 in Tunis and was raised by his grandmother, who enrolled him on a sculpture course at the École des Beaux-Arts. As Francois Boudot relates in his book in the Fashion Memoir series, 'the history of art would have claimed another sculptor' had not Alaia chosen to moonlight as an assistant for a local midwife, Madame Pineau. She kept fashion magazines in the waiting room of her clinic and, when his water-heating, towel-tidying duties permitted, the young Azzedine, already immersed in the world of women and the physical realities of their bodies, cultivated an addiction to fashion images. He was later to develop strong working relationships with many photographers, particularly Jean-Paul Goude.

Alaia said his epiphany was the realisation that his future lay not in chiselling the female form in stone or modelling it in clay but in shaping it in cloth and leather. And, he knew, there was only one place to do that—Paris. His grandparents were initially alarmed at the idea but eventually, after the boy had taken a job with a dressmaker in Tunis to prove his commitment, his grandfather gave his permission. In 1957, Alaia arrived in Paris a prearranged job at Christian Dior. He lasted five days. Baudot writes that the Algerian war had broken out and a young Arab boy was not welcome. Alaia shrugs and says, no, he knew the clientele was too establishment for him. Beautiful women have always taken care of Azzedine, and in this case Simone Zehrfuss introduced him to Guy Laroche, for whom he worked for two seasons. Alaia learned but was not content.

Alaia left Laroche and went to stay with the Comtesse de Blegiers in the sixteenth arrondissement. He looked after her children, helped with the cooking, worked on his first designs and, courtesy of the Comtesse, expanded his circle of friends and clients to include Louise de Vilmorin, Greta Garbo, Cecile de Rothschild and the actress Arletty, to whom he was particularly close. Eventually he moved out of the Comtesse's kitchen and into the four rooms in the rue de Bellechasse that were to witness his ascendancy in the early 1980s. For a very long time, however, he functioned as a couturier or private dressmaker, a very well kept secret with a large and faithful clientele.

Alaia became what he set out to be, a sculptor of female flesh. The couture tradition is, among other things, very much about imposing an ideal shape, the currently fashionable ideal shape, upon bodies that are not ideal. Because the great majority of couture customers are beyond the first flush of willowy youth, the bodies are often very far from ideal. So couture structures and techniques are calculated to lift and support, tighten and flatten, create curves where there are none and expunge bulges where there are many. Azzedine Alaia began to acquire these techniques at Laroche, but, during the 1960s and 1970s, he refined his skills by buying

and dissecting a vast collection of vintage couture garments.

Alaia applied these skills in a way that was uniquely his own, however. Using fabrics that could stretch and cling, he developed a cut that tenderly emphasised and enhanced all the female erogenous zones. Although he used jersey, knitwear and bias-cut woven fabrics, it was with Lycra-rich or Lycra-bonded fabrics that he made his unmistakable mark. He could also make leather—not always soft kid leather either and sometimes suggestively metal-studded—do things just the proper side of fetishism. Francois Baudot wrote, 'The mischievous tailor, of course, took risks with his more daring customers. To show off their figures, he particularly emphasised the small of the back and the buttocks.'

He would probably have continued as a private couturier if in-the-know fashion editors had not started pushing him, suggesting that he design some ready-to-wear. In 1979 he designed a raincoat and a suit for Madeleine Furs, and the two garments were photographed by *Elle* magazine. Encouraged by this and ensuing successes, Alaia began to think of a ready-to-wear line. It was launched in 1980, in the tiny apartment. There were no invitations. As ever, he relied on word of mouth. As ever, his faith in the fact that his inner circle would tell the right insiders where to be was absolute. After all, his women always looked after him.

The collection was all black, big shouldered, caricature curvy and loaded with punk references— diagonal zips, pins and needles. The Parisian press adored it, and after the American photographer Bill Cunningham photographed it for *Women's Wear Daily* (which coined one of its succinctly apposite labels and called it 'second-skin dressing'), all America wanted it and beat a path to Alaia's modest door. Perhaps most notably in that first collection Alaia invented a new garment, the body. The streamlined silhouette was central to his look, so he adapted the dancer's leotard for everyday wear with skirt or trousers. The fashion body, unlike the dancer's version, closed at the crotch, secured by poppers or small buttons. In 1985 Donna Karan was to popularise the body, basing her first collection of her own label around it.

Reflecting in 1983, the journalist Marina Sturdza of the *Toronto Star*, explained that long before Alaia became the hottest story in Paris:

> his address has been a loosely kept secret of the Paris cognoscenti (such as internationally acclaimed interior designer, Andrée Putman, or the super-avant-garde editors of *Elle* magazine) for at least a decade. That's why it's a giggle to see the beau monde of fashion, press and buyers alike, rank and position regardless, protocol be damned, crammed by the dozen into a meagre space intended to accommodate a very few at best; craning and jostling to catch even a glimpse of Alaia's models as they sporadically flash by. In fact, it's not a showroom at all, it's Alaia's apartment, long since transformed into workroom/office/dressing room and feeding station. The bed lies under the drawing board, the drawing board is buried under an ocean of paper, the models dress in an antechamber, the international buyers are stacked in the vestibule, and life during the prêt-a-porter collections has become a round-the-clock state of siege.

What they had all come to see were some of the sexiest clothes ever to grace an inadequate excuse for a catwalk. Apart from the zips, Alaia always chooses a clean and simple line with little in the way of decorative detail or fuss and prefers dark or neutral colours—the expensive palette of the very rich: black, navy, brown, beige, greige, taupe and soft pastels. His genius lies in the intricate cut and the way it displays the body—without vulgarity—revelling in pneumatic womanly curves. He works directly on the body, repeatedly draping, fitting and cutting. One inspiration was Madeleine Vionnet's multi-seaming techniques and bias cuts; another was Charles James's engineer's obsession with a carapace-like structure.

What was new was the freedom of movement that came with Alaia's alliance of stretch fabric and intricate structure. Feather light and unconstraining, these clothes permitted a woman to move in a way that was both modern and stride-out easy and, because she felt so sexy in them, terribly seductive. The husbands and lovers of Alaia's customers are among his biggest fans and good friends.

Alaia dominated Parisian ready-to-wear for a few seasons, opening boutiques in Paris, New York and Los Angeles, and influencing the mass market everywhere. But there were worse problems for the press and buyers than the discomfort of his shows. His fame could not help but attract many more private clients—including Tina Turner and Madonna—and as a consequence his attention was brutally divided. In addition his perfectionism meant an endless reworking of the clothes for his ready-to-wear collections, which became later and later. Initially one would have to stay on a couple of extra days in Paris to see his show, then it was a week, so one would fly back, but when it became a month, press and buyers became exasperated. In October 1986, *Women's Wear Daily* chose to interpret Alaia's dilatoriness and lack of professionalism as disdain for the hand that fed him—the major store groups in the United States—and ran an editorial saying his day was done.

He riposted, 'I'll rub them out in a second—even the biggest customers. I'm not afraid of anyone, even the President of the United States.' But *WWD* had not just power on its side; it had the right of it. Azzedine Alaia, influential as he was, did not move on when fashion moved on and, at the heart of the problem, he could not deliver the clothes into the stores when he said he would.

In 1992 Alaia stopped producing ready-to-wear collections but when, in 2000, a 1980s revival resulted in Alaia tribute outfits on several catwalks, Patrizio Bertelli of Prada SpA bought Alaia's company to add to its portfolio, which already included Helmut Lang and Jil Sander. The revival was not a success. In 2007 Prada sold the company back to Alaia, and he refinanced it with backing from the Companie Financiere Richemont, the luxury group that owns Cartier, Chloé and Dunhill. Richemont, Alaia told the *International Herald Tribune,* plans to set up an Alaia Foundation in the building next to his headquarters in the Marais. It will hold some 15,000 samples and patterns created over his thirty years in fashion.

Further reading: Francois Boudot's *Alaia* (1996), part of the Fashion Memoir series, is a good overview, and Francesca Alfano Miglietti's *Fashion Statements: Interviews with Fashion Designers* (2006) gets a little closer.

40 GIANNI VERSACE (1946–1997)

From the 1950s onward, Italian fashion, wherever it was made, was primarily showcased in two cities, Rome and Florence. But as the 1960s gave way to the 1970s a group of ready-to-wear designers grew dissatisfied with the shows based at and around the Palazzo Pitti in Florence. Many of them were based in the industrial north and considered the edgy commercial city of Milan, with its international airport, more appropriate than provincial, inaccessible, tourist trap Florence. In the initial breakaway group, organised by Gigi Monti and Beppe Modenese, were Mariuccia Mandelli of Krizia and her husband, Aldo Pinto, Rosita and Tai Missoni and Walter Albini. Newcomers Nino Cerruti, Giorgio Armani, Gianfranco Ferré and Gianni Versace quickly joined them.

Born in 1946 into an impoverished, devout and hard-working family in Mafia-dominated Reggio di Calabria, Gianni Versace learned dressmaking at his mother's knee. He studied architecture but in 1972 opted for fashion, moving to Milan to work for various design houses, including Complice, Genny and Callaghan. In 1978 he showed his first womenswear collection under his own name at the Palazzo della Permanente art museum of Milan, following it, that autumn, with his first menswear collection. His work was acclaimed from the first showing and, from the earliest days, in the Italian way, his company was his family. His older brother, Santo, ran the business side and his sister, Donatella, ten years his junior, learned from him as he had learned from their mother and became his assistant and eventually his successor. In 1982 Versace met his partner, Antonio D'Amico, a model who also worked as a designer for the company,

and the relationship endured until the Versace's death.

Known as the couturier to courtesans, the king of high-class hooker style, 'the first post-Freudian designer', Versace designed as effectively for theatre and opera as for rock stage, club scene and grand, grand occasion. He almost single-handedly created the supermodels—who would walk down his runway five abreast, arm in arm, and whose legendary status reflected back to enhance the glamour of their creator—and changed the direction of fashion, pushing it towards a high-octane eroticism that earned him a fervent following among the demi-monds of rock stars and expensive groupies and the equally fervent disapproval of many fashion commentators. Judy Rumbold, writing in *The Guardian* in 1993 and describing the collection Versace showed in March 1991, sounded weary:

> It was the usual benign smutfest, featuring trademark vertiginous heels, high hair and prohibitively priced tartwear for the rich and famous. The finale, however, was a little bit different. Accompanied by something loud and earnest by George Michael, Versace sent several thousand pounds' worth of liberally oiled Euroflesh—Naomi Campbell, Cindy Crawford, Christy Turlington and Linda Evangelista—down the catwalk wearing babydoll mini-dresses in pink, orange and lime. But they weren't just showing off the clothes; here was modelling way beyond the call of duty. Amid much rock-chick posturing and ostentatious miming, there were frenzied whoops and catcalls from a front row boasting the sort of celebrity turn-out that would

have done Harvey Goldsmith proud. Clearly this wasn't just about frocks. This was showmanship, theatre, but most importantly for Versace, the oldest swinger in Milan, it was near as damn it rock n' roll.

While other designers had dressed the stars of Hollywood, Ciné Citta and the music industry, Versace actively sought the connection, not only importing references to the rock scene and its flamboyant, excess-driven, decadent lifestyle but also doing hard-nosed contra deals whereby the celebrities wore the clothes he gave them and turned up to his parties and shop openings in return for the clothes and, in many cases, a generous fee. Rebecca Arnold wrote in 2001:

> For his customers, flaunted wealth snubbed its nose at good taste. His advertising was equally extravagant, parading an array of supermodels in various stages of undress, caught in a sundrenched world of Italian villas, furnished with the designer's home-style range of silk cushions, throws and fine china, all embellished with the splendours of classical and Renaissance motifs. His gilt Medusa head logo had gained status during the 1980s, made famous by the rock stars and celebrities who wore the clothes, blurring the lines between the fashion and entertainment industries still further, as each gained credibility from the association. His work provided a fantasy version of decadent excess, which spread from his hugely successful (and widely pirated) designer denim line, to the couture range he developed.

Rumbold's 1993 article was pegged to the opening of the most expensively shopfitted (£11 million) store in the history of London, Versace's many-floored Old Bond Street emporium, which housed all the collections from denim to couture. The shop itself, for which Siena marble in ten different colours, gold leaf by the kilo, craftsmen by the score and a team of fresco painters from La Scala were all flown in and specially accommodated, was breathtakingly expressive of Versace baroque. The morning after the opening party (which Versace attended clad in one of his swimming-pool blue scarf-print silk shirts and tight black jeans), Brenda Polan reported in *The Daily Mail*,

'While the rock stars and well-kept girlfriends fingered the clothes, the commercial establishment and society rent-a-guest crew as well as the press, gawped uneasily at the rococo décor. Behind me, a voice redolent of Eton and the City murmured, "It's the prettiest laundrette in London."'

Given Versace's origins in Reggio Calabria, the extraordinary speed with which his label was established, his enormous wealth and opulent lifestyle and some of the characters he was seen to hang out with, it is not surprising that rumours of Mafia connections dogged him. After he was assassinated on the steps of his Miami Beach mansion in 1997, the rumour circulated that a dead pigeon had been left beside the body, a well-known symbol, insisted the conspiracy theorists, for a Mafia execution of someone believed to have betrayed the organisation. In the end the police decided the murder was the work of a lone psychotic obsessive, Andrew Cunanan.

Reflecting a decade after his death, Cathy Horyn wrote in *The New York Times* in July 2007, 'A lot has been lost in the decade since Versace's death in Miami beach—a great talent, most visibly. Try to imagine your wardrobe without the jolt of a print, the vitality of a stiletto, the glamorous bric-a-brac of chains and doodads. This was Versace's doing. His influence melted and spread far beyond the sexual heat of his runway.'

The origin of that sexual heat is not hard to find. He was happy to tell any interviewer. He told Brenda Polan interviewing him for *The Guardian* in 1981, 'When I was a small boy and my mother would take us to church we had to pass the street of the prostitutes and my mother would say, "Cover your eyes. Do not look at these women. Never look at them." But, of course, I would look and to me they were so beautiful, so glamorous. They were forbidden. They were attractive. So, of course, they stay in mind. Until now.'

Gianni Versace was one of the most skilled designers in the history of fashion, because he learned the intricacies of structure before he learned to sketch. Even more than Azzedine Alaia, Versace could cut and stitch garments from many pieces so they would reshape the body while remaining light and comfortable. He could construct skimpy dresses that blatantly revealed more than they concealed yet stayed in place—like the safety-pin dress Elizabeth Hurley wore to the premiere of *Four Weddings and a Funeral* in 1994. His work with glove-soft leather has never really been equalled, and his development of gilded fabrics and a unique patented metal 'chain-mail', Oroton, allowed him to sculpt garments that satisfied both a fetishist's fantasy and an art lover's pleasure in the most beautiful of baroque decoration. The cerulean blue satin sheath decorated with glass beads and gold studs in curlicues that Diana, Princess of Wales wore to be photographed by Patrick Demarchelier cleverly expressed her latter-day personality: part lady, part saint, part vamp. Garments that embodied within them such conflicting references came easily to him. He was steeped in art history, borrowing motifs from Minoan ceramics, Graeco-Roman imagery (his private collection was museum quality), from statues and coins and the lush and florid decorative style of the seventeenth and eighteenth centuries and the gilded Art Deco. He understood equally well street style and popular culture—particularly rock culture—and the subcultures of sexual deviance with their props of leather and metal, rubber and shiny PVC, straps and studs, buckles and shackles, corsetry, cross-lacing and safety pins.

Richard Martin, who curated the Metropolitan Museum of Art's 1997 exhibition just after the designer's death, situated him within a history of fashion which, before it adopted bourgeois values of property and propriety, focused on sensuality. He was the epoch-defining designer of the late 1980s and early 1990s because he restored to high fashion its erotic purpose. Martin wrote, 'Gianni Versace reorganised the etiquette of apparel. He did not aspire to decorum. Rather, he accorded fashion with desire, substituting the lust of fashion and body concupiscence for the cause of correct behaviour and social calibration.'

Many twentieth-century designers—from Yves Saint Laurent to Jean Paul Gaultier, from Vivienne Westwood to John Galliano—have found vibrant references from street culture and oppositional or marginalised subcultures, but Gianni Versace fixated on and celebrated characters only sketchily referenced by the others, the prostitute and the rent boy. What so many female fashion writers found tedious in Versace's oeuvre was not only his relentless drive to make women look like whores, but the all-pervading and far from subtle homoeroticism which particularly dominated most of the publicity photographs (taken by the premier photographers of the day) and the glossy picture books that issued regularly from the house of Versace.

Yet Versace was not alone in his preoccupation with the sex worker, the fallen woman, the magdalen. She was a heroine of Federico Fellini and Luchino Visconti, great Italian film directors of Versace's formative years, the years during which an impoverished Italy reconstructed itself. 'No one,' wrote Martin, 'had taken the prostitute into fashion as Versace did. In a feat worthy of literature, Versace seized the streetwalker's bravado and conspicuous wardrobe, along with her blatant, brandished sexuality, and introduced them into high fashion. But Versace did not . . . simply convey the prostitute to the salon and the runway. He did what fashion can do when it finds inspiration on the street. He represented her as glamour, accepting the extreme flirtatiousness of her short skirts, the seduction of shiny cloth and cognate materials, and understanding the motive of sex, but rendering each hyperbolic and expressive, not merely a portrayal of what had existed in the wardrobe of the street . . . In making his deliberate choice to exalt the streetwalker, Versace risked the opprobrium of the bourgeoisie. As a designer and as a human being, Versace never sought the middle road or the middle class. Rather, he forged a unity between the independent of spirit and will, the rich, the young and the intrepid.'

Although some of the homoerotic images to issue from Versace's private darkroom were often discomfortingly parodic and vulgar, his insistence on showcasing the male as sexual commodity has been seen by some commentators as liberating for both genders. The supermodels on Versace's catwalk so often referenced drag queens 'doing' Marilyn Monroe, Brigitte Bardot, Tina Turner or Madonna and posed interesting questions about femininity and identity. A generation of young women claimed to be 'post-feminists' and 'in control' of their provocative and sluttish sexuality. Rebecca Arnold wrote, 'Fashion had been growing more playful in its appropriation of references to gay culture since the 1980s. As fashion shows became more grandiose, more theatrical, they drew upon the tenets of camp, revelling in the freedom to exaggerate and dramatise femininity in a manner that was self-conscious in its postmodernity. The role of fashion as entertainment, reinforced by Versace with his flamboyant shows . . . had brought overstatement and parody to the industry.' And to the culture.

After Versace's death, his sister Donatella took over as creative director. He bequeathed his share of the company to her daughter, Allegra.

Further reading: The best, most analytical book is Richard Martin's *Gianni Versace* (1997), which accompanied the exhibition at the Metropolitan Museum of Art in New York City.

41 JEAN PAUL GAULTIER (1952–)

The long-lasting image of Jean Paul Gaultier as a perpetual enfant terrible of French fashion took many years to lay to rest. But now the great iconoclast of modern French fashion has become part of the establishment he once shunned. Who would have guessed back in the 1980s that the eclectic mould-breaker of Parisian fashion would become creative director of the house of Hermès, a byword in understated luxury?

This is not to disparage Gaultier's achievements, for many great arch provocateurs before him have, over time, become accepted by the mainstream—a sign of their influence. Gaultier's openness about sex and homosexuality was considered shocking to many in the 1980s but was part of mainstream popular culture by the noughties. And Hermès recognised that behind the many playful and provocative designs, such as the celebrated corsets for the pop star Madonna, was a rigorous technician with great tailoring skills. At heart, Gaultier has also remained indisputably French and Parisian, despite his love of London street style and international travels. He was a dominant force in designer fashion through the 1980s; the tickets for his shows were the most coveted in Paris. But his critics said he was a designer for fashion victims, who pinched most of his ideas by wandering round Camden Market in London. His clothes made all the headlines but were considered unwearable—skirts for men, conical bras for women. Pastiche fashion, the critics said.

But by the early 1990s, his status as a pioneering designer who mixed up styles and embraced cross-cultural diversity was being recognised. Likewise, his experiments with sportswear, stretch fabrics and underwear used as outerwear were influencing all levels of the fashion market. To Gaultier's delight, there was also a new appreciation of the talents he had picked up in his early days in the design studios of Paris: his exquisite tailored jackets, the delicacy of his colour sense and the immaculate finish of his clothes. Gaultier has mellowed in his later years, although his collection of autumn/winter 2008, which attracted much negative comment for its surfeit of exotic animal skins, showed that he has not lost the ability to be controversial. He has probably taken more risks, both creatively and personally, than any other designer in history—and sometimes paid the price. Arguably his greatest career mistake was to become a television presenter on the British TV show *Eurotrash,* a satirical romp through the wilder extremes of contemporary European popular culture. Although the show was an undoubted hit and authentically reflected Gaultier's eclectic creative inspirations, it almost certainly deprived him of the opportunity to take up the reins at Christian Dior. LVMH boss Bernard Arnault was not amused.

The greatest Gaultier shows have been cavalcades, carnivals of the imagination, inspired by an extraordinary host of references, blending couture and street fashion with gay abandon, often presented on models who defy conventional interpretations of beauty. Inspiration has ranged from Jewish rabbis, the Dadaists and Mongolian Inuits to tattoos, sadomasochism and flea markets. At the heart of so many of his shows, however, is an enduring affection for Paris, particularly the Paris of the interwar years. Popping up at the end of the show is the man himself, one of the most instantly recognisable figures in world fashion, usually in his trademark striped sailor T-shirt, always with an impish grin.

Jean Paul Gaultier was born in 1952 in the suburbs of Paris to hard-working parents, Paul, a book-keeper, and Solange, a secretary. Marie Garrabe, his grandmother, was the biggest influence on his childhood, allowing the young Gaultier consider-able freedom on his weekly visits. In modern-day terminology, she might be described as an alterna-tive therapist, operating from her own home, which was decorated with old-style furnishings. His other childhood influence was television, particularly a documentary about the Folies-Bergère, where the feathers and glitz excited him and were the be-ginning of his creative and sexual awakening as a gay man. Feigning sickness, he bunked off school to pursue his interest in fashion, looking at news-papers and magazines and drawing obsessively. In his formative years in the 1960s, his interest was in the world of haute couture rather than the new gen-eration of ready-to-wear *créateurs,* although any-thing the teenage Gaultier learned was self-taught, gleaned from magazines. Gaultier's first dresses were for his mother, an achievement that encour-aged him to compile sheaves of drawings to send to would-be employers. At Christian Dior, Marc Bohan showed no interest, but Pierre Cardin offered the eighteen-year-old Gaultier work in 1970. Although he only lasted eight months before becoming a victim of a redundancy round, it was an important period. Cardin served as the perfect mentor for Gaultier for he had an open mind and was develop-ing his innovative L'Espace Pierre Cardin, a theatre and exhibition venue. 'He told me that everything is possible,' Gaultier recalled years later.

Gaultier then worked briefly at Jacques Esterel and at the Cincept style agency before landing a job at the house of Patou under design director Michel Goma and, later, Angelo Tarlazzi. At Patou, though, he became disillusioned by the straitjacketed for-malities of the world of haute couture, which he had previously held in such high esteem. Much of the rest of his career was spent reacting against the restrictions of couture, inspired by visits to Lon-don, where he felt energised by the city's creative (and sexual) energy, particularly in the post-Punk period. By 1974, Gaultier was back at Pierre Car-din in a curious position at Cardin-Philippines, part

of the designer's fast-growing international em-pire. Such an experience opened Gaultier's eyes to new cultures and influences, encouraging him to look widely for inspiration in the years that fol-lowed. Back in Paris within a year, he made con-tact with an old school friend, Donald Potard, who introduced him to the fledgling jeweller Francis Menuge, who became his lover. Another important influence was the exotic model Anna Pawlowski. Scraping together funds, the friends produced the first Jean Paul Gaultier collection in October 1976, including a studded leather jacket paired with a tutu—a sign that Gaultier was an unconventional kind of designer.

The early Gaultier collections were characterised by a flood of contrasting designs and ideas, cre-ated in circumstances of financial desperation. An initial two-year contract in 1979 with Japan's Kashi-yama, thanks to the support of Kashiyama creative director Dominique Emschweiller, set Gaultier on a more professional footing. Simultaneously (and not coincidentally), the press began to take fulsome notice of Gaultier, even if much of the interest was founded on his ability to entertain—he was an odd-ity, a cult, a cause célèbre. He was 'Paris's Court Jester', according to *WWD* in 1984. In a prolonged interview with biographer Colin McDowell, Gaultier denied that his intention was to destroy the past. 'I use and respect tradition, but try to find new ele-ments which will make it younger.' His goal was to question notions of good taste, but founded on the solid base of the tailoring skills he had acquired in the milieu of haute couture.

Gaultier was also keen to break down what he saw as artificial barriers between menswear and wo-menswear. Why shouldn't men wear skirts? His introduction of men's skirts in 1985 and constant repetition of the theme was no gimmick but was based on a fundamental belief that clothes should not be gender specific. 'Masculinity is not con-nected to the clothes you're wearing—it's in the mind,' he said.

The late 1980s saw Gaultier's business expand rap-idly, backed by Gibo in Italy and Kashiyama in Japan. The Gaultier aesthetic was well represented in his Paris store in rue Vivienne, blending ancient-look mosaics with his innovative clothes, and in stores in Milan, London and Brussels. Gaultier's openness about his sexuality and mix-it-up approach to design brought him into the heart of rapidly evolving popular culture, working with photographer Jean-Baptiste Mondino on advertising campaigns and videos, choreographer Régine Chopinot, film directors Peter Greenaway and Pedro Almodovar. The early 1990s were even better for Gaultier, who forged on with growing confidence, despite the personal loss of his partner, Francis Menuge, from Aids in 1990. A commission to design a wardrobe for Madonna's Blonde Ambition tour in 1990 led to the creation of a corset including a conical bra, which Gaultier later chose as the bottle shape for his fragrance, launched in 1993 and packaged in a tin can.

Gaultier has continuously challenged mainstream thinking and stirred up controversy, ranging from nuns as strippers in 1991 to a collection shown on black models in 1997 at a time when the French government was clamping down on immigration. His fashion shows have often been spectacles, lavishly mounted in a variety of different locations, paving the way for the imaginative shows staged by designers such as Alexander McQueen and Viktor & Rolf in the noughties. Gaultier's arrival under his own name in the haute couture arena was a long time in coming, despite the infusion of new talent that gave haute couture renewed vigour in the 1990s. His first collection, in January 1996, was shown to no music in a pastiche of the old couture style, but the collection, called the Couture Man, was entirely for men. A women's collection followed a year later.

Gaultier was treated with reverence in French fashion circles into the noughties, although by then many of the barriers he had broken through were no longer considered barriers. His work, it could be argued, was done. Hermès bought a 35 per cent stake in his business in 1999, providing him with a solid foundation for the years ahead. But the pressures of maintaining a couture operation, always a loss-making part of the business, forced Gaultier to make job cuts in 2004. 'We've run up the stairs two at a time,' said Donald Potard, his long-term business partner and president of the house. 'Now we need to catch our breath to continue operating all of our activities.' At Hermès, where he was appointed

creative director of womenswear in May 2003, he showed that he could adapt to another house's style. Pascale Mussard, artistic director, said: 'People ask what Gaultier has brought to Hermès but it's not arrogant to consider what Hermès brought to Gaultier. You could say we help each other see with each other's eyes.'

For Gaultier, the distance between himself and Hermès was not so great. When he worked at the couture house of Patou, he used to wear riding boots and was teased by the vendeuses ('they asked me where was my "orse"'). In interviews he recalled the comment of the photographer Helmut Newton that Hermès is 'the most important sex shop in the world,' highlighting the leather, whips and stirrups. His biographer, Colin McDowell, points out that Jean Paul Gaultier 'hides his seriousness behind a facetious facade.' In so doing, he sums up the playful postmodern spirit of contemporary popular culture and has inspired young designers and other artists in the 1990s and beyond (including Martin Margiela and Nicolas Ghesquière) to dispense with convention and pursue their inner dreams. Academic Barbara Vinken sees him as inheriting the mantle of Elsa Schiaparelli—'a kind of surrealism against the grain, which consciously makes a fool of itself.' But another, more straightforward Vinken observation may be more appropriate: 'Gaultier has plundered the attic of fashion, and offers his customers his most daring and cheeky finds.'

What shines through in all of Gaultier's work and career is his lifelong love of fashion. 'I am not interested in business,' he said in a newspaper interview in the early 1990s. 'I didn't do fashion to be rich and famous. Of course, I like the rewards. They are a luxury for me, but my first luxury is to do what I want. I don't want to hand everything over to assistants and become a businessman.'

Further reading: Farid Chenoune's *Jean Paul Gaultier* (1996) is a short introduction to the designer, but the biography *Jean Paul Gaultier* (2000), by Colin McDowell, is a more detailed read. Gaultier himself had fun with a comic book–style autobiography, *A Nous Deux La Mode* (1990), which is only available in French. The designer was also interviewed by Roger Tredre for *The Independent* ('A One-man Revolt Against the Cliché', 2 August 1990).

42 DOLCE & GABBANA (DOMENICO DOLCE 1958–, STEFANO GABBANA 1962–)

The most successful design partnership in fashion history, Domenico Dolce and Stefano Gabbana, burst onto the fashion scene in the mid-1980s through a mixture of talent, perspiration, inspired marketing and luck. They were the last Italian designers of the twentieth century to make a real mark, creating extravagant fashion collections that played with themes and periods with happy abandon. Their success was founded on sharp tailoring combined with street style and a flair for bringing to life the Italy of their and their customers' dreams.

The fashion press called them fashion's mix masters, making the comparison with DJs who mix music to create a kaleidoscope of sounds. Domenico Dolce and Stefano Gabbana were rarely hesitant in their creative vision, churning out ideas in abundance and ransacking the decades (in particular the 1930s to the 1980s). In their magpie approach to fashion design, they summed up the free spirit of modern fashion. Among their hits: pinstripe mannish tailoring for women, underwear worn as outerwear, curvaceous dresses, spectacularly colourful coats and, invariably, lashings of leopard print. Despite an occasional misstep, they have a talent for tuning in to the mood of the times. As Gabbana put it, 'Fashion has to be in step with the times. Today more than ever, conceptual just doesn't pay back and is destined to fail.'

Although in later years their collections displayed a taste that teetered into kitsch, the Dolce & Gabbana signature often encapsulates the best of Italian fashion. Journalist Sarah Mower, who edited their celebratory twentieth anniversary book, said they represented 'a kind of psychic map of Italy.' The success of their partnership rested on the attraction of opposites, as they acknowledged in interview after interview; Dolce is the craftsman while Gabbana has his finger on the pulse of popular culture. As Gabbana put it: 'We start from two really different points. He starts from the left, I start from the right. And we meet in the middle.'

Domenico Dolce, the older of the two, was born in Sicily in the village of Polizzi Generosa in 1958. His father was a tailor specialising in suits for local gentry's weddings, while his mother owned a general haberdashery store. Legend has it that Dolce's crib was set up in his father's workroom. Dolce grew up playing with fabrics; at seven he made a pair of trousers. At an exceptionally early age, the pattern was set for his life. Stefano Gabbana was born four years later in 1962 in Milan. There was no fashion in his family background: his father was a printer from Venice. An exceptionally good-looking young man, Gabbana moved to Milan to study graphic design in the early 1980s, a period when the city's fashion industry was flourishing as never before. The designer that caught the eye of Gabbana most strongly was Elio Fiorucci, Italy's ebullient king of kitsch style.

Gabbana met Dolce on the phone initially when the latter answered a job enquiry call in the office where he was working. Dolce had moved to Milan from Sicily to study design and quickly landed a job as an assistant at a local fashion house. Taking Gabbana under his wing, he taught him to sketch and understand the design process before Gabbana was obliged to spend eighteen months on military service. By late 1982, Gabbana was back in town and the two were sharing an apartment. Their focus on work was relentless (Gabbana thinks he was probably thirty before they took their first holiday). But they also partied hard, out until the early hours at Amnesia and other hot clubs of the time, enjoying the sheer decadence of the fashion industry.

Dolce & Gabbana staged their first show in October 1985 as part of a group showing for three young designer labels at the back end of the Milan show season. Despite avoiding the power dressing that was dominant in fashion at the time, their complicated geometric cuts received encouraging press coverage. But their manufacturer took fright and promptly pulled out. The duo appeared to be out of business before they had even started. Dolce's family came to the rescue, producing a second collection for the two young designers. It was named Real Women, not least because they could not afford models and had to enlist friends to model the clothes. The collection was full of fabrics used in unconventional ways, including a coat made out of sweatshirting and a dress in a rubberised wool. The beginnings of a buzz began to ripple through the Milanese fashion scene. By the third collection, for spring/summer 1987, store buyers were showing interest, even if the versatile clothes, which could be worn in two or more different ways, were not easy to explain to customers. Was it a skirt or a dress? In fact, it was both. Dolce & Gabbana were also drawing on the innovative brilliance of Italy's textile manufacturers, working with such new fabrics as stretch silk and a transparent organza jersey.

Up until their fourth collection, Dolce had resisted drawing on his Sicilian roots for inspiration. 'I'd come to Milan because I wanted to break from the past,' he explained. 'I dreamed modern! I resisted going back there.' Gabbana, by contrast, had no such qualms. For a photo shoot, he persuaded a non-fashion photographer, Fernando Scianna, to join them in Sicily with the model Marpesa to produce moody black-and-white images that had an authentic aura of Sicily. Black and white paid homage to the Italian cinema of the 1940s, when neorealist directors such as Roberto Rossellini produced gritty movies set in the Deep South. Another key influence was Visconti, whose film The Leopard was the inspiration behind the designers' spring/summer 1988 collection. All this was laced with erotic elements, as academic Barbara Vinken has noted: 'There is a touch of Sicilian passion, in the manner of Sophia Loren: an affirmative, even aggressive feminine eroticism, adult and dominant.'

Curiously, British and American store buyers were quicker to appreciate Dolce & Gabbana than the Italians. From Rossellini to Sophia Loren to Anna Magnani, all the great icons of twentieth-century Italian popular culture were referenced by the two designers. Their models, ranging from Isabella Rossellini (daughter of Roberto) to Linda Evangelista (of Canadian Italian parentage), were chosen for their Italian spirit. Rossellini recalled: 'The first piece of theirs that I wore was a white shirt, cut in such a way that my breasts appeared to be exploding.' It was, perhaps, all too much for their countrymen and women. As Dolce acknowledged, 'At first, Dolce & Gabbana were too Italian for the Italians.' In truth, Dolce & Gabbana have looked as much to Britain as to Italy for creative ideas. 'Italy has too much culture, too much history about clothes, and sometimes this is negative because they care too much,' said Gabbana in 2000. 'They have no humour about it. The English have humour. We take inspiration from London all the time.'

The early 1990s—the era of the supermodels—saw any doubts about the talents of the duo swept aside worldwide. Reacting against the constraints of feminism, powerful, successful women were more prepared to celebrate their sexuality. Dolce & Gabbana delivered the fashion to match, creating lavish beaded and embroidered corsets and bras festooned with Swarovski stones. The pop star Madonna became a fan, customer and friend. Photographer Steven Meisel and supermodel

Linda Evangelista produced memorable images for the Dolce & Gabbana advertising campaigns that somehow pulled off the difficult trick of being romantic, nostalgic, modern and relevant all at once.

From meagre beginnings, the business flourished. While many other designers of the 1980s and 1990s soared only to crash and burn within double-quick time, Dolce & Gabbana sustained momentum. They were blessed with reliable production, signing an agreement in 1988 with Dolce Saverio, the clothing firm based in Legnano, near Milan, and owned by Dolce's family. Two years later, a menswear line was launched to instant acclaim, drawing unapologetically on the comfortable shapes and easy style of Sicilian men's tailoring. For four years in the early 1990s, the designers also worked as consultants on Complice, a collection produced by Genny, a deal that gave them further financial strength. A series of licensing deals followed, including a women's fragrance in 1991, a men's underwear collection in 1993 and the D&G younger line in 1994.

The Dolce & Gabbana homage to Italy was rarely subtle: the spring collection of 1993 featured trouser suits with photo prints of *The Birth of Venus*, the Renaissance masterpiece by Sandro Botticelli. Season after season, the styling was brash, exuberant and celebratory. At a time when many designers were opting for minimalism and an austere vision, Dolce & Gabbana were like a breath of fresh air. In 1997, the designers decided to show their collections in their palazzo rather than on a conventional runway. As the craftsmanship in their collections became more pronounced, drawing on Italy's craft traditions that still flourished (in contrast to elsewhere in Europe), they decided to bring the collection closer to the audience: they wanted people to see the clothes. When the minimalist wave in fashion finally burned out, Dolce & Gabbana were well positioned to welcome back maximalism. The collections of the turn of the century saw them go 'totally crazy', to quote the designers themselves. Brazilian Gisele Bündchen was their favourite new model, dressed in patchwork jeans or lace miniskirts for the autumn/winter 1999/2000 collection.

That the two designers, working and living in tandem, remained lovers as well as partners for around

nineteen years of their label's existence was some achievement. The full story of their relationship is unlikely to be told, although they acknowledged the pressures, admitting in their twentieth anniversary book that their collection for spring/summer 1999, focusing on fabric innovation, was an explosive period in their partnership. Their personal relationship was under profound strain, although the final announcement of their separation did not come until 2005. 'We have a different type of pillow-talk now,' Gabbana said in typically direct fashion, while emphasising that the business was unaffected. 'While we are not in love any more, we are very much in love with our business.' It is true that their comments about each other over the years are based on an extraordinary degree of mutual professional and personal admiration (although when Gabbana once bought a YSL coat, Dolce refused to speak to him for days).

The two designers marked a strong shift in direction with their collection for spring/summer 2008, sending out a series of tulle gowns hand-painted with beautiful floral designs. The designers announced they were moving away from their overtly sexual signature style towards a more sensual approach. The dimensions of the mannequin form on which they designed were changed, Dolce said in an interview with *The New York Times:* the bust size reduced, the waist elongated and the hips enlarged. Indeed, just at the point when the pair were in danger of becoming a pastiche of themselves, they found a new lease of life. For autumn/winter 2008, they explored masculine English tailoring; for the following spring/summer, baroque brocades came to the fore. Once again, fashion editors, buyers and high street copyists paid close attention.

Their advertising campaigns still retain a provocative streak: one advertisement was withdrawn from Spain in 2007 after government representatives claimed it encouraged violence against women. The designers expressed bemusement. 'We play sometimes and we love sexuality,' said Gabbana, possibly with a twinkle in his eye. 'We take a risk. People say it is too much, but it depends on the eye.' Dolce & Gabbana have played the modern fashion game better than most: sales totalling $1.4 billion in 2007 make that clear. Although their relentless plundering of the styles of the past can sometimes create a sensation of ennui even for their most loyal enthusiasts, their energetic ability to reinvent themselves is likely to keep them in the front line of fashion for some time to come.

Further reading: Dolce & Gabbana published books to mark both their tenth and twentieth anniversaries. The latter, *20 Years Dolce & Gabbana* (2005), includes a well-written text by Sarah Mower that exhaustively documents their collections.

43 JOHN GALLIANO (1960–)

British designer John Galliano is arguably the greatest of a steady stream of talents who have emerged from London's Central Saint Martins School of Art & Design since the 1980s. He was the first British designer of the modern era to head a Parisian haute couture house. He has consistently taken fashion shows to new heights of theatricality, most notably for the house of Christian Dior, where his shows are of unequalled extravagance, displaying fantastical imagination. Galliano brought back romance to fashion in 1997 when he became chief designer at Christian Dior, fifty years on from the launch of Dior's New Look.

To his critics, his clothes can veer close to costume, bearing little relation to the modern-day world (and often with no connection to the showroom range sold to buyers). But the fashion show is, for him, a theatre, where the imagination should roam. His meticulously themed collections, often inspired by complex fictional tales with a heroine at the centre, have unashamedly pursued flights of fancy. Over the years, he has produced many complex, difficult-to-wear, unforgiving clothes that have delighted fashion editors although less so store buyers and customers. But, thanks to his romantic spirit and personal charm, he has ridden a surf of goodwill—and in the process created some of the most beautiful clothes of the late twentieth and early twenty-first centuries. His willingness to experiment has inspired a generation of young designers. Even as a college student, he had an obsessive curiosity, a desire to push ideas to their limits. Early in his career, for example, he devised his own form of cutting in the round so that sleeves followed the shapes of the arm and jackets turned into curvy sculptures. Invariably he cuts fabric on the bias, so that it clings to the body. 'It's a sensuous way of cutting, very fast and fluid, with a great respect for women's bodies,' he told Roger Tredre in 1990. 'It's like oily water running through your fingers.'

Juan Carlos Antonio Galliano was born in Gibraltar in 1960 to a Spanish mother and Gibraltarian father, moving to London as a child. He joined Saint Martins before its merger with Central when it was still known as St Martin's School of Art. Among the lecturers was the fashion writer Colin McDowell, who later became his biographer. Galliano researched his collections intensively, spending hours in the library of the Victoria & Albert Museum building up a meticulous picture of an imaginary heroine who would be the true muse of each collection. Multilayered stories were created that fed directly into the design process. The theatricality of Galliano's approach to fashion might be traced to his student days: he worked as a dresser at London's National Theatre and frequented a nightclub called Taboo where his friends included Leigh Bowery, the flamboyant Australian costume designer and living artwork, and Stephen Jones, the milliner and a long-term collaborator.

Galliano's initial rise was meteoric. The 1984 graduation collection, Les Incroyables, inspired by the costumes of the French Revolution period, was famously bought by London designer store Browns, and the young designer was inundated with interview requests by fashion editors. Commenting on that first collection, a college contemporary of Galliano said: 'It was streets ahead of everyone else.

I felt physically sick. It was so good I felt I might as well give up designing because I would never get anywhere near that.' Galliano immediately launched his own label and became the darling of London Fashion Week: within three years, he was British Designer of the Year. However, the bare facts of this rapid rise conceal a story of struggle, partly financial to secure backing and resources for each new collection, and partly personal as the strains of the fashion world's expectations wore down the designer. He was always a highly strung and intense individual, sometimes literally trembling with nerves before a new collection was shown.

In the mid-1980s, Galliano became one of a group of young designers, including Alistair Blair and Richard James, backed by the Danish businessman Peder Bertelsen. He staged his first show in Paris in 1990, albeit without the support of Bertelsen, who had withdrawn from the fashion fray. Next, he found backing from Fayçal Amor, the businessman behind the Plein Sud label, although this partnership again faltered as the orders failed to materialise and the costs of Galliano's extravagant shows soared. Despite an exalted media profile, Galliano was dropped by Amor and was at a low point in a promising career, apparently doomed to follow the path of many young British designers before and since: lauded too early, pressurised to the limit and obliged to drop the dreams of a signature collection and join the backroom design studio of a major foreign label. However, he had a powerful fairy godmother in the form of Anna Wintour, editor of American *Vogue,* who lobbied on his behalf in early 1994. 'She flew me to America and introduced me to the right people,' recalled Galliano. A backer was identified in the form of John Bult of American investment house PaineWebber. Within three weeks of Bult's stepping in, Galliano had produced a small but perfectly formed collection of seventeen high-glamour outfits shown in the Parisian townhouse of Portuguese millionairess Sao Schlumberger. 'The marketing director said, "Look John, you need to edit your collection, produce it in so many colours and so many fabrics, and you need to be really choosy about who you sell to,"' recalled Galliano. 'I really learnt a lot from that little collection.'

Friends and long-term collaborators rallied around, including the British designer, Steven Robinson, who was by Galliano's side continuously until his tragically early death in 2007. Another key supporter was Lady Harlech, born Amanda Grieve, who acted as both stylist and muse for Galliano for many years before being lured away to work with Karl Lagerfeld at Chanel. They sensed that women were tired of dressing down, of the grungy looks that had dominated fashion through the early 1990s. Working day and night, they came up with a sharply focused collection inspired by the fitted tailoring of the 1950s and with a preponderance of outfits for the evening and cocktail hours. The fashion world went into a collective swoon. Back in Paris, he produced a second collection of fit-and-curve daywear and oriental-inspired evening wear, which had journalists and buyers grasping for superlatives. In just two collections, he had killed off deconstruction and encouraged women to dress up and dream again.

In 1995, Galliano landed a major breakthrough when he was appointed head designer at Givenchy by Bernard Arnault, chairman of LVMH (Louis Vuitton Moët Hennessy), the luxury goods conglomerate. Not since the days of Charles Frederick Worth had a British name pulled off such a coup in the capital of fashion. He completed one couture and two ready-to-wear collections before moving on to the ultimate prize—artistic director at Christian Dior, a fashion house also owned by LVMH. Simultaneously, he continued to develop his own signature label with a spectacular show in October 1996 staged as a circus in an empty wine warehouse. His first couture collection for Dior was presented in January 1997, an auspicious year for the house of Dior, marking the fiftieth anniversary of the New Look. Galliano had immersed himself in the Dior archive in rue Jean Goujon, much as he had done in the Victoria & Albert Museum as a student in the early 1980s. For once, he fell in love with a real personality from the past, Mitzah Bricard, a muse to British couturier Edward Molyneux in the 1930s and later to Dior himself. Part homage to Dior, part assertion of Galliano's own romantic spirit, the collection was staged at the Opera Salon of the Grand Hotel in Paris and was hailed as a dazzling triumph. Among a plethora of ecstatic press comment, *The International Herald Tribune* summed it up: 'Surely Galliano's 16-year career has been a dress rehearsal for this sublime moment?' Galliano's finest homage to Dior himself, however, came eight years later in 2005 (autumn/winter) with a series of ten tableaux inspired by the couturier's work, including the Bar suit, which has been frequently reinterpreted by Galliano.

The backing and security of LVMH also gave Galliano the platform to sort out his personal life, where all-night partying and hedonism were the order of the day. Galliano stepped back from the brink to focus on his work. He believes strongly in the capacity for self-improvement. In 1995, still relatively fresh in Paris, he was eager to take lessons from the work of the great couturiers of the past, notably Vionnet, and contemporaries he admired, such as Azzedine Alaia. 'I'm still learning,' he said. 'I'm only just beginning.' Others of his generation, including John Flett, a former boyfriend and Central Saint Martins fellow graduate, who died in 1991, were not so fortunate. Galliano's new sense of self-discipline was best exemplified by a new enthusiasm for aerobics and working out, including a regular six-mile jog along the river Seine in Paris. In January 2000, he said that he had found inspiration for a controversial 'homeless chic' couture collection during his jogging sessions, when running past the homeless people lining the river. He added that he hoped to expose the pure decadence of couture by 'turning it inside out'.

In his 1997 biography, Colin McDowell highlighted Galliano's love of historicism and the exotic allure of Orientalism. Those elements have continued to run through Galliano's work ever since. He is a true Postmodern designer, drawing on a rich resource of references (although always decontextualised, as historian Farid Chenoune has pointed out). While as a student, he used the library as his source of inspiration, as a designer, he has travelled regularly ('the most powerful source of ideas,' he says). He loves the process of researching a collection, saying research feeds his mind—wherever it might take him. 'Creativity has no nationality, so I don't want to leave any stone unturned. I love understanding and seeing different cultures.' Galliano is a fierce defender of the role of fashion. 'Fashion is escapist, not elitist, and I think now more than ever it has a role to play,' he said in 2008. 'Dior dared women to dream, to bring back romance, femininity, and seduction. He brought joy back onto the streets. I think this is my role.'

Galliano's work is often laced with unsettling elements and references (although rarely pushed as far as Alexander McQueen, who graduated from Saint Martins after Galliano). Referencing his student days at the club Taboo, he has explored sexual fantasy, most notably through his autumn/winter 2001 couture collection for Dior, which was unofficially dubbed 'Freud or Fetish'. In a thought-provoking comment, he argued that Dior was 'the first true fetishist designer. He had an Oedipus complex, he was in awe of his mother and his New Look was full of fetish symbolism.' The shock of the arrival of a British designer at the head of a French fashion house has long since dissipated. Always well-mannered and appreciative of the glories of French cultural heritage, Galliano has adapted to Parisian style without losing his British sense of irreverence, displaying continuity in his creative evolution from his French Revolution college graduation collection. In recent years, he has shown himself to possess shrewd commercial instincts too: the autumn/winter 2008 ready-to-wear collection for Dior, full of classic luxury dressing, was skilfully pitched at the emerging luxury markets of Asia. Galliano's story is far from over.

Further reading: John Galliano's impact at Dior is eulogised and explored in *Dior: 60 Years of Style* (2007) by Farid Chenoune. A decade earlier, Colin McDowell wrote an insightful monograph on the designer, *Galliano* (1997), published in the year of his arrival at Dior. Galliano has been profiled exhaustively in the media since the very beginning of his career and was interviewed on several occasions by Roger Tredre in the early 1990s. See in particular 'The Grind Behind the Glamour' (1990) and 'Galliano Meets His Maker' (1992).

44 DONNA KARAN (1948–)

In 1996 when Donna Karan took her company to the stock market, *New York* magazine put her on its cover. The picture showed a youthful, doe-eyed woman with glossy long dark hair looking straight to camera, her hands before her mouth in a praying posture. The selling copy beneath read, 'Donna Karan, Corporate Goddess. The most successful woman on Seventh Avenue has gone New Age, and now she's going public. Will Wall Street love Donna as much as her customers do?' Inside, journalist Rebecca Mead concluded, rightly, that Wall Street doubtless would. Donna Karan is the third and youngest of what fashion observers came to think of as the great triumvirate dominating American fashion in the 1980s and 1990s, the threesome—Lauren, Klein, Karan—who made the rest of the world take American fashion seriously for the first time.

Backed by the marketing, advertising and public relations techniques at which Americans excel, these three designers became global brands at an astonishing speed, each quickly establishing an identity which not only set them apart in terms of all-American modernity but neatly set them apart from each other. If Lauren appealed to the romantically aspirational, the dreamer and the fantasist, and Klein to a classic, understated, minimalist, country-mansion moneyed chic, Karan was sharply focused on young, ambitious working women, those moving up the corporate and professional ladders, paying their own bills and making their own rules. She put them in clothes— mostly black—that were easy, chic, carefree. While Lauren's twenty-page runs of movie-still style advertisements recorded re-imagined mythic times

and communities, Karan's best-known multi-page advertisement from 1992 shows the inauguration of a woman president (played by model Rosemary McGrotha), all pinstripe suit and pearls. The ad's slogan, 'In Women We Trust,' was Karan's mantra and one reason the women of the press loved her. However hard they tried, she implied and women believed, male designers could never get inside women's skins in the way she could. 'I am a woman,' Karan told Brenda Polan for *The Mail on Sunday* in 1994. 'I'm a female designer, a working wife and mother. I understand the lives of other women and the last thing any one of us wants to do is worry about our clothes. We want a simple system whereby we get dressed fast and go.'

An article in *Vogue* in 1989 put it this way: 'A kid from Queens is now Queen of Seventh Avenue. Karan's professional rise has a lot to do with the current rise of "fortysomething" female executives, like herself, who want to look pulled together but not prim.' Valerie Steele gives context to the relief with which women embraced Karan's capsule-wardrobe dressing in the mid-1980s. 'At a time when the strict man-tailored Dress for Success look was getting tired, and when executive women no longer felt so much pressure to look like men, Karan developed a sophisticated, sensual alternative to the business suit. Based on her own experience, Karan suspected that women would appreciate a system of dressing that was as easy as men's wear, while also retaining the comfort and sensuality of clothes to fit a woman's body.'

In fact, John T. Molloy's *Women: Dress for Success* was one of the most proscriptive and pernicious little tomes ever written. It droned at tedious length and in tendentiously enervating prose about the imperative necessity for women to adopt the 'skirted' suit if they wanted to be respected in the workplace and advocated wearing it in background-blending tones and softened by only a pussy-cat bowed blouse tied right up under the chin. In response to the surrogate man theory of how to smash the glass ceiling American designer sportswear at all levels of the market had got harder-edged, bulkier and bigger-shouldered season by season. Karan's collaboration with Louis dell'Olio at Anne Klein was in this vein—which made her new vision all the more sensational when she launched her own label in 1984. 'Yes,' Karan said at the time, 'women's clothes should be almost like men's but they should be more comfortable, sensual, womanly.'

The designer was born Donna Faske in Queens, New York, in 1948. Her father, Gabriel, ran a haberdashery and tailoring shop called Gabby Faske and her mother, Helen, was a model and then a saleswoman on Seventh Avenue. Her father died when she was young and she was, she has said, bitter because the mothers of her friends did not go out to work as hers did. Nevertheless, she was, she said, obsessed with fashion from a very early age and, at fourteen, she began working part-time as a sales assistant in a boutique. She was a baby boomer growing up in the 1960s when youth fashion became a dominant force and girls were being encouraged to envisage careers in their future rather than simply marriage and motherhood. Karan was completely focused on design as her future career; she began designing clothes as a teenager, fitting patterns on her own body. After high school she attended Parsons School of Design but never graduated because, in 1969, a summer job at Anne Klein secured for her by her mother led to a permanent post as designer. Anne Klein was a major sportswear designer who pioneered the concept of tailored separates. 'She was,' said Karan, 'a woman who understood women. I was in awe of her, she was such an innovator.'

After nine months she was fired because her concentration was not on the job but on Mark Karan, the boutique owner who was to become her first husband and the father of her daughter, Gabby. Anne Klein rehired her and by 1971 she held the post of associate designer. Anne Klein died in 1974 just five days after Karan had given birth to Gabby. Although Karan admitted to feeling 'terribly guilty', she went back to work immediately, working with a classmate from Parsons, Louis dell'Olio. Together they polished up the Anne Klein style, giving it some urban sophistication which precipitated it into the Fashion Week limelight. Suddenly, the international fashion press recognised it as a brand worth watching.

Ten years after taking over, the restless Karan decided it was time to move on, time to do something of her own. 'It was time to start something from nothing,' she told Ingrid Sischy. 'That's what I love to do the most. I wanted to start a new project which was going to be oriented around a system of dressing—my seven easy pieces. But my bosses at Anne Klein didn't go for it so I decided to leave and do it for myself. I found leaving Anne Klein very hard to do.' Since that epochal first Donna Karan collection and the press frenzy with which it was greeted, the growth of Karan's company brand has been exponential. One of the selling points she loved to reiterate was that her body as well as her lifestyle more closely resembled that of most women—unlike most of her competitors. 'I'm a woman with a rounded figure,' she said. 'I'm not a model size 8. I won't design clothes that cannot be worn by a woman of size 12 or 14.' She would use size and what she calls 'the fallibility of a woman's body' as a bonding device with other women, especially the press, passing on tips like her trick of tying a sweater around the waist so that it draped concealingly around the hips, creating an illusion that all the perceived bulk in that area was knitwear.

The collection with which Karan launched her own label—'a little niche business for me and my friends'—in 1985 was based around the body, a leotard with poppers closing it at the crotch, and various wrap pieces that were layered on top of it. The body stayed put and did not wrinkle or ruck up or come untucked as ordinary shirts and jumpers did. It looked trim and tidy all day. In the 1940s Claire McCardell had been one of the first to incorporate the leotard into everyday fashion. Later Azzedine Alaia would use the leotard as an integral part of his mega-streamlined, second-skin approach to dressing. However, no one has ever had quite the impact as Karan did when she made the leotard, revamped and renamed as the body, the central theme of her first collection under her own label. Her rationale was closer to McCardell's than Alaia's—not eroticism but convenience—although the wrap skirt showed a lot of leg.

The clothes were photographed in ads showing various working-woman scenarios—disembarking from a plane, catching up on office work at home. In 1978 Karan told Caterine Milinaire and Carol Troy for their book, *Cheap Chic*:

> I believe that a woman's professional clothes have to come from the inside out. The clothes are never going to make the woman . . . But I guarantee you that if a woman's together, she's going to know enough about herself to look outta sight . . . And when you have an assurance about yourself, honey, you can walk into any room and command anything. But you've got to work at it. It doesn't come easily.

In 1982 Karan had married for the second time. Stephan Weiss, who died in 2003, was a sculptor who joined Karan in her company. The Donna Karan collection is pure luxury using the most expensive of materials and perfectionist of manufacturing techniques so in 1989 they launched DKNY (Donna Karan New York), a younger, less expensive line. For this, she said, she

> wanted a name bigger than me, one that expressed my passion for the world. New York, to me, is the visualisation of the entire universe. Paris is Paris, it's not the world. Italy is Italy. New York is the world. It is the bridge. It's the spot that expresses the world. I wanted to say that I was a conscious designer of the people of the world, inspired by Chinatown, uptown, downtown, all the aspects, Central Park, people living in the street, all or it, the beauty, the electricity, the sickness, music, dance, theatre, art; it's all here. Both companies, Donna Karan and DKNY, which evolved later—and which came out of my

need for a pair of jeans, jeans that would fit a woman's body—are about everyone, all of us, the larger family.

The hugely successful DKNY collection was followed by a jeans collection, menswear, children's clothes and scent—Weiss sculpted the sensuous templates for the perfume bottles. 'Stephan was a genius,' Karan told Ingrid Sischy in 2004. 'I couldn't have done it without Stephan . . . He understood the art of doing business.'

Her fan base is wide and impressive, including as it does Isabella Rossellini, Anouk Aimée, Demi Moore, Jeremy Irons, Bruce Willis, Hillary Clinton, Barbra Streisand, Liza Minnelli and Candice Bergen, the last four of whom all wore her 1993 cold-shoulder gown on the red carpet. 'The ball of the shoulder,' said Karan, 'is the only part of a woman's body that does not age. A woman never gains weight at her shoulder point.'

In 2002, Karan sold her company to Louis Vuitton Moët Hennessey (LVMH), the luxury stable that also includes Christian Dior and Givenchy. But its heart remains in America, a country where women aspire to look neither hard-edged and threatening in the boardroom nor vulgarly seductive in the bedroom. The urban American woman, an achiever in her chosen field, wants to look grown-up, intelligent, confident and in control of her own sensuality. It is a balance that Karan is uniquely skilled at maintaining. In 2004 she said, 'Twenty years ago I set out to design modern clothes for modern people. Today that is still my mission. I'm inspired by the artist that lies in all of us, a sense of character, individuality, creativity, the soul that learns from the past, the spirit that anticipates the future, the body that is alive with sensuality, and the heart that knows no bounds.'

Further reading: Ingrid Sischy's *The Journey of a Woman: 20 Years of Donna Karan* (2004) contains all the major advertising imagery and an extended interview with the designer. For context, however, Valerie Steele's *Women of Fashion* (1991) is excellent.

PART 6
1990s–

Introduction

The 1990s saw a decisive rejection of the power dressing of the previous decade. Fashion became minimal and decidedly low key in the early years of the 1990s. Grey was the preferred colour, and slimline silhouettes with narrow shoulders dominated the fashion catwalks. Names such as Germany's Jil Sander and Austria's Helmut Lang focused on evolution rather than revolution, advancing step by step.

For a while, this led to a new emphasis on casual style (American retailer Gap was a hip choice in the early years of the decade) and a deviation into grunge, a dress-down look inspired by rock bands and teenagers from Seattle, picked up by young designer *Marc Jacobs.* A more conceptual response was the deconstructionism of Belgium's *Martin Margiela,* creating new shapes by rethinking garments in their component parts.

The sense of moderation could not last. Dolce & Gabbana, in their very irreverent way, Gianni Versace (until his death in 1997) and *Tom Ford* at Gucci led a return to glamour. Ford's success encouraged the business trend for hot young designers to be parachuted in to revive venerable old fashion houses. The globalisation of fashion advanced apace through the decade, creating untold wealth for luxury brands but also prompting fears about the homogenisation of world culture.

The boundaries between high and low culture were decisively rejected during the 1990s. Designers stole from the street as much as the street stole from designers. Cross-cultural references were piled high. Whereas designers working in previous decades of the twentieth century had tended to reference one earlier decade, the 1990s saw *every* decade of the century plundered and remixed. Retro fever swept through fashion, worn best by the supermodels (replaced as cover girls by Hollywood celebrities by the end of the decade). Always ready to challenge the status quo was the intellectual *Miuccia Prad*a, who became influential for her deliberate championing of 'bad taste', including 1970s furnishings prints.

Two British designers, John Galliano and *Alexander McQueen,* led the way for a revival of haute couture in a modern idiom, with Galliano at Dior proving particularly influential. British designers, including conceptualist Hussein Chalayan, created the most buzz in the final years of the twentieth century, often emerging from the hothouse of London's Central Saint Martins School of Art & Design.

A new century opened with the dot.com crash, but in truth this was no more than a blip. The Internet transformed communication around the world, also influencing the process of design and the pace of cultural development. The 9/11 terrorist attacks on America in 2001 prompted insecurity in Western society. Fashion's response was a further retreat into the past, turning chic and ladylike in homage to the 1950s.

But the mood changed again—and fast. Speed, driven by technological progress, was the new mantra. Fast fashion, with rapid changes of style and colour, swept through chain stores in Europe, led by names such as Zara and Hennes & Mauritz (H&M). Responding to this, designers swelled their bank balances by working directly with the chain stores. At the luxury end, they championed the limited edition and the made to measure, seeking to create a point of difference with the mainstream market.

After a long period of minimalism, fashion emerged more colourful and maximalist. Handbags and accessories became as important as clothing, driving profits in luxury goods companies. The environmental threat of global warming, which was widely accepted by 2007, raised questions about the very existence of fashion, with its reliance on built-in obsolescence. Vintage and second-hand clothing enjoyed a surge in popularity.

In the late noughties, the world became a darker place, and the global economic slowdown hit designers hard. Ostentation was firmly out of fashion; the rich avoided flaunting their wealth. Emerging economies, such as mainland China and Russia, became more important to designers, although these countries were not immune to the worldwide downturn. The fashion world looked to *Nicolas Ghesquière* at Balenciaga for direction.

45 MIUCCIA PRADA (1949–)

When Miuccia Prada, who had a PhD in political science but no fashion or design experience, took over the family business in 1978, she did so through gritted teeth. But this Italian intellectual went on to become the most consistently influential international designer through both the 1990s and noughties. Perhaps her status as an outsider gave her a broader vision of fashion design, understanding how it fits into the wider creative firmament and beyond to the world of politics and current events. Even today, she stays relatively aloof from the fashion game, with a much-cited penchant for walking in the mountains in her spare time, wearing the dirndl skirts of her youth.

As the journalist Alessandra Galloni pointed out in 2007, Miuccia Prada has spent most of her career apologising for what she does, her collections expressing her own ambivalence towards her involvement in fashion. By the time she had reached her mid-fifties, she had formulated a strong case for fashion, convincing herself (as much as anyone else) of its importance and relevance in society. 'It's true women often don't want to admit it. And yet fashion enthralls everyone . . . Some say it's about seduction, but I think that's limiting. What you wear is how you present yourself to the world, especially today, when human contacts are so quick. Fashion is instant language.' She is a risk-taker, constantly pushing the boundaries of taste, including her own, excited by the challenge of moving fashion forward. Each of her collections, said Ingrid Sischy, editor of *Interview* magazine, is 'some kind of throwing down the gauntlet to established ways of thinking.' An outstanding example of this was her autumn/winter 2008 collection in which she explored lace,

treating its reinvention as an intellectual challenge. Her starting point was to avoid the colour white. Lace, for her, was an opportunity to explore ambiguity, to posit a series of interpretations, although in the final analysis she expressed herself still uncertain. 'I still don't understand why I like lace,' she said. 'But it is such an accompaniment of women, through childhood, marriage and being a widow.'

The very speed of change in fashion both frightens and enthralls Prada. 'In the end, I like the changes,' she said in an interview in 2004. 'In fashion, once you've got something, you're already thinking about what's next . . . Every day I'm thinking about change, it's a constant anxiety and probably a reflection of society's anxiety in general. The big deal about fashion is really very recent, this hysterical pursuit of newness. It may be a good thing, or a bad thing, but it's really defining this moment.'

Suzy Menkes, fashion editor of *The International Herald Tribune,* made the contrast with many of Prada's contemporaries in fashion: 'While designers mostly live in a fashion bubble, she has an urgent connection to what is happening in the world . . . No other creator has the same ability to distill the essence of what is modern, sampling the cultural heritage, anchoring shifting society and making it all seem relevant.' Paradoxically, Miuccia the intellectual has recently sought to theorise less about fashion, voicing a plea in interviews that the clothes should simply be allowed to speak for themselves. While enjoying the pressures of the modern fashion system and its commercial imperatives, she has also gone through periods of depression over its constant demands. 'Now the world is so complicated and loud, unless you scream no one listens,' she said in 2006 with a hint of resignation. Her youthful enthusiasm for communism has clearly influenced her approach to design: challenging bourgeois notions of good taste, opting for the unconventional time after time, creating seemingly ugly colour combinations and looks that both bemuse and enchant. Ironically, the price tags on her accessories and clothes put them out of reach of all but the wealthy—a paradox that has certainly not escaped her attention.

Like many great designers, she was a double act from the beginning, having met her husband Patrizio Bertelli shortly after she took over at Prada. A passionate, combative personality, Bertelli was a supplier to Prada through his company, I Pellettieri d'Italia, based in Arezzo. He is generally considered the business brains behind the growth of Prada, although his wife has emphasised his creative contribution, too. 'If I hadn't met him, I probably would have given up—or at least not been able to do what I have done,' she said. In the late 1990s, Prada developed into a group of designer labels, overextending itself through ambitious acquisitions that delivered poor returns. The financial fallout, which took many years to sort through, hampered the growth of Prada but did not stop Miuccia from producing a stream of outstanding collections that delighted and baffled fashion buyers and editors in equal measure.

Grandfather Mario Prada founded Fratelli Prada, an Italian leather goods business, in 1913. Miuccia was born Maria Bianchi in 1949 to Luigi Bianchi and Luisa Prada and had an isolated childhood for reasons that are still unclear but which culminated in her being adopted by her mother's sister in adulthood. By the time she reached university in the late 1960s, the student wave of political activism was at its height. Miuccia, with a PhD in political science in her sights, was captivated by the energy of the period, signing up to the Communist Party and becoming fully engaged in the fight against capitalism. She has played down this period in interviews: 'I was young in the Sixties, when Italian society was first becoming obsessed with consumerism, but my big dreams were of justice, equality and moral regeneration. I was a Communist but being

left wing was fashionable then. I was no different from thousands of middle-class kids.'

However, she had another side to her intense personality—that of the bohemian with a creative streak, dressing in Yves Saint Laurent for a student march, studying mime at Milan's Teatro Piccolo. All this changed in 1978 when she took over Prada, which had been run by her mother following her grandfather's decision to step aside after World War II. Progressing to the family business was a tough move, she recalled. 'You know, I had to have a lot of courage to do fashion,' Prada recalled, 'because in theory it was the least feminist work possible. And at that time, in the late Seventies, that was very complicated for me. Of course, I liked it a lot but I also wanted to do something more useful.'

Miuccia Prada's impact was not immediate. For seven years, she learned the nuts and bolts of her new trade, developing experience and confidence with the support of Patrizio. She did not sketch, preferring to work at a conceptual level, and then building a collection from there. The breakthrough came in 1985, when Prada sidestepped the family heritage in leather and produced a collection of heavy-duty nylon bags that became must-haves for fashion editors the world over—with their readers in hot pursuit just a step behind. The handbag was reborn as a key fashion accessory, while nylon was rediscovered as a fashionable material. The nylon bags rapidly turned the Prada label into a fashion powerhouse, although it was another four years before Miuccia launched ready-to-wear in 1988. Her first collections received a mixed response, but by the end of the decade were setting the tone for a new spirit of minimalism, following on from a decade characterised by excess and extravagance. 'The reason Prada works is because it whispers, it doesn't shout,' she has said. 'If you want to be recognised wearing my clothes, you can be. And if you don't, you don't have to be.'

But sometimes Prada could shout—regularly, her collections oozed a sense of a designer challenging her own instincts, attempting to work against her own notions of good taste, as if embarked on an intellectual exercise for personal stimulus. 'It's very easy to know what I like and it's very easy to do what I like. But I tend to have, let's say, good taste,' she said. 'This is very boring for me. So, basically, I have to work with what I think is bad and wrong. In my company they're always worried about that, everyone is always complaining.' Prada says she is rarely interested in a look. She works on a concept, often referencing the past, but resolute about making it contemporary. For her spring/summer 2009 collection, she drew criticism for sending the models down the runway in python-skin platform heels (some of them fell over). The clothes themselves—'cave-woman couture', she called them—were still more provocative, deconstructed, mixed up, crinkled and rumpled. It was an exercise in sophisticated seduction that puzzled and excited her audience in equal measure.

With her interest in other creative forms, Miuccia set up the Prada Foundation in 1993 to showcase leading contemporary artists. Outside her office window, she installed a playground slide that descended three levels; this playful touch was in fact an art work by Carsten Höller. She also worked with leading architects on her stores, including Rem Koolhaas for New York and Herzog & de Meuron for Tokyo. An installation, titled *Waist Down*, which toured Asia, America and Europe in 2005 and 2006, highlighted both her seriousness and playfulness with its focus on skirts designed by Miuccia, including her popular circle skirts. In 2008, she commissioned a short animation, *Trembled Blossoms*, to mark the spring collection, a lush landscape of flowers and nymphs with suggestions of Art Nouveau, Liberty and Aubrey Beardsley. Other projects have included temporary architecture-specific wallpapers, environments and interactive media for the Prada Epicenters in New York, Beverly Hills and Tokyo in a series of collaborations.

The fashion business grew simultaneously. A second label, Miu Miu (her nickname), was launched in 1992, bringing the Prada vision to a wider audience. Prada Sport followed in 1994. In the late 1990s, Prada Group joined in the enthusiasm of the time for acquisition, snapping up an extraordinary portfolio of labels, including three of the most admired designers of the era—Austria's Helmut Lang, Germany's Jil Sander and France's Azzedine Alaïa. This marriage of talents proved disastrous: Sander resigned twice as the business that bore her name struggled to break even, while investment was unsuccessfully lavished on turning Helmut Lang into a superstar. Prada Group hinted at a stock market flotation on a number of occasions in an effort to put its finances back in order, only to cancel time and time again. When the global economic crisis erupted in late 2008, Miuccia Prada was left lamely musing that maybe her business was not the kind of business that was best suited to the financial markets. The more high-profile scrutiny of the markets would certainly not be to her tastes. Prada herself avoids the celebrity circuit. 'I am a very private person and don't like the high-profile nature of the fashion business. It's dangerous to have such a large public image and I'm not as interested as some designers in becoming famous because it would take away the realities of my life.'

She has adapted more enthusiastically than many of her contemporaries to the speeding up of the fashion system in the early twenty-first century. This trend was driven by the fast fashion of mass-market companies such as Spanish retail brand Zara. As a young woman, Miuccia Prada was content to develop an idea that could be relevant for six months. By 2008, however, she commented that an idea might satisfy her for two days. The turnover of ideas has become ferocious, she acknowledged. 'My goal now is to change our stores every two months—that's what I would like.' An eloquent interviewee, Miuccia Prada has made comments over the years that reflect the insecurities that many people working within the fashion industry share as to the true status of their chosen profession. Her brilliance has been to turn this insecurity to powerful use through a series of inspirational collections, driving forward fashion to its current status as a key component of modern popular culture.

Further reading: Miuccia Prada speaks eloquently about her own work, so interviews with her are frequently illuminating. Vanessa Friedman's interview for *Ten* (autumn 2000) was particularly incisive. Susannah Frankel spoke to her in 'The Feeling Is Miuccia' (21 February 2004) for *The Independent*. Alessandra Galloni wrote 'The Designer Defends Prada' (25 January 2007) for *The Wall Street Journal*.

46 MARTIN MARGIELA (1959–)

The emergence of the Belgian designers in the late 1980s was one of the more unexpected twists in fashion history. A country with no great reputation for creativity produced not simply one but a veritable profusion of design talent, spawning a movement that continues to throw up surprises into the twenty-first century. Top of the list from the original wave was Martin Margiela, who showed new ways of wearing familiar clothes, drawing on inspiration from flea markets and introducing a new kind of fashion that was swiftly labelled deconstructionist, with a stripped-down functionalist aesthetic.

Although not one of the so-called Antwerp Six, who first showed their work collectively at London Fashion Week in the mid-1980s, Margiela is regularly categorised together with his fellow Belgian near-contemporaries (the most influential of the other six was Ann Demeulemeester, and the most commercially successful was Dries Van Noten). The Belgians all imbibed the earnest hard-working fashion aesthetic of their college, Antwerp's Royal Academy of Fine Art, developing outstanding technical skills coupled with a high seriousness in their approach to fashion design. Antwerp, at the heart of Flanders, was also the centre of a broader cultural boom, reflecting the rising confidence and dominance of the Dutch-speaking north of Belgium.

Margiela's high seriousness was approved in France, where the conceptual approach to fashion design has always been respected. An exhibition staged in Rotterdam in 1997 featured a collaboration between the designer and a microbiologist. Margiela chose one outfit from the eighteen collections he had made to date, recreated in white, then sprayed with mould and yeast and allowed to grow. Another snapshot of Margiela's approach: in spring 1998, he produced a collection full of flat garments inspired by the shape of plastic supermarket shopping bags. The seams were cut so that the clothes could lie flat, demonstrated in the show by men in white coats carrying around the clothes on hangers. A season later, he showed T-shirt dresses on ten life-size wooden puppets, with the folds heat-bonded to polythene vinyl. All this was a fashion conceptualist's heaven. Likewise, the stores, usually in backstreet locations with no name above the door, have become cult locations. A recurring feature of the shops is a line of thrift store sofas and chairs, covered by one continuous white slipcover. Footprints on the white carpeting are stamped with one of Margiela's signature Tabi boots dipped in black ink. The previous life of the store location is respected; thus, in Taipei, where Margiela opened in a former fast-food restaurant, the burger bar's original fixtures were retained and simply painted white.

Martin Margiela was born in 1959 and grew up in Genk in the Limburg region of Flanders. After studying in Antwerp in the late 1970s (some years before Demeulemeester, Van Noten and Dirk Bikkembergs), he initially found work designing raincoats for a Belgian firm and then briefly worked in Italy. But Margiela's heart was set on the higher planes of creativity and for him there was only one place to learn—Jean Paul Gaultier, the great iconoclast of Parisian fashion, who was at the peak of his influence in the mid-1980s. Margiela applied several times for work at Gaultier's studio; sheer persistence eventually got him through the door. Margiela left Gaultier after three years to set up his own business with friend Jenny Meirens, who had run a boutique in Antwerp. The business was financed on a shoestring through well-paid commercial work for Italian manufacturers. For all the uncompromising aesthetic of his own label, Margiela was from the beginning a highly versatile designer, as was made clear a decade later in 1998 with his appointment as womenswear designer at the house of Hermès.

Margiela's early collections instantly intrigued buyers from Europe's more avant-garde stores, although few placed orders. His first collection featured the exceptionally narrow shoulder—Margiela called it the 'cigarette shoulder'—which was a statement of defiance at a time when 1980s power dressing ruled. In October 1989, he caused a sensation by showing his collection on a rubble-strewn wasteland in the 20th arrondissement of Paris. The models stumbled down a makeshift catwalk with eyes painted white, wearing plastic dresses, papier mâché tops, jackets with the sleeves ripped off, skirts apparently made from lining materials and oversized men's trousers. It was an experimental tour de force, making the mainstream shows of the Paris season seem blandly conventional. Geert Bruloot, owner of Louis, an Antwerp store, was an early supporter and friend: 'It was a shock, but it was also a revelation. Margiela smelt what was coming, what was in the air. He was looking seasons ahead, taking the most everyday kind of clothes and showing new ways of wearing them.' Other designers, such as Helmut Lang and Jean Colonna, were also presenting a challenge to the major fashion houses, following the challenge that Japanese designers such as Rei Kawakubo and Yohji Yamamoto had presented several years earlier. The deconstructionist designer believed in showing precisely what he was doing, with hemlines unfinished, stitches visible and even the tailor's markings retained. Fashion, he believed, was not an art—it was a craft, 'a technical know-how' for the wearer to explore and enjoy.

Drawing inspiration from flea markets or street style, Margiela would turn sometimes ordinary clothes into fashion by mixing and changing the shapes and fabrics. In the process, he challenged conventional ideas of what fashion could be, showing new ways of wearing familiar items. He also took little notice of the pressures of the modern fashion system to come up with new ideas every six months, preferring to refine and develop concepts over several seasons, revisiting garments again and again. His autumn 1993 collection displayed the breadth of his influences and his willingness to acknowledge his sources, including a dress made from four black flea market dresses sewn together and a nineteenth-century priest's coat that the designer liked so much he did not tamper with the original design. In 2001 cultural studies academic Rebecca Arnold argued that Margiela's approach 'undermined the notion of designer as unique, individual creator, by conceding that each design is the product of fashion's history.' She saw Margiela sharing the same spirit as Japanese designer Rei Kawakubo, recognising imperfection as 'a route to authenticity . . . in contrast to fashion's traditional role as the purveyor of ephemeral, perfect fantasies.'

By the early 1990s, the designer had already achieved an exceptional status, paradoxically fuelled by his reluctance to meet the fashion media, let alone give interviews. Innate shyness was certainly one reason for this. However, he also preferred people to look at his clothes rather than him. A statement from Maison Margiela said: 'The withdrawal of a designer's profile creates a space that the garments may fill.' Back in March 1993 he briefly relented and invited a handful of journalists (including Roger Tredre) to his atelier on the boulevard Saint-Denis. Wearing his trademark navy blue peaked cap with black jeans and a black T-shirt, he explained why he was so media shy: 'I wanted to express myself through the clothes, and consolidate in that way.' The veil of secrecy was reimposed shortly afterwards, with interviews conducted by fax or email with the team rather than with Margiela the individual. The first Margiela label, a scrap of muslin inscribed with no name, no words, was in itself a statement questioning the modern designer system. From 1997, Margiela introduced a series of labels differentiated only by numbers.

Margiela has often preferred to present his clothes on real people rather than models. In an interview with *The Independent* newspaper in 1999, he and his team commented: 'It remains . . . important for us that someone finds their way of dressing as opposed to a way of dressing as prescribed by anyone else or an overriding trend.' All of the house's collections are identified with a number system, from 0 to 22. At the top of the scale of numbers in price terms is number 4, a line of classic Margiela pieces. Number 1 is the fashion show collection, which is shown in Paris. Margiela's arrival at Hermès in 1998 shocked both insiders and outsiders at the venerable French house. Hermès boss Jean-Louis Dumas had become aware of Margiela's work through his daughter, an actress, who had modelled for the designer. Dumas invited him to lunch at his home in early 1997 and considered him 'a good rider for a good horse,' using equine terminology in keeping with the house's tradition. His first show was a low-key kind of triumph, the Margiela iconoclasm tempered by his new role. The versatility of the clothing was a key note, including a coat that could be turned into a cape and seamless sweaters that could be worn inside out.

Writer Rebecca Mead, in a profile for *The New Yorker,* called them 'quietly subversive. Stripped of all ostentation, they were to be valued from the inside, even if the wearer risked drabness.' In 2003 Margiela was succeeded at Hermès by his one-time mentor, Jean Paul Gaultier.

Margiela's long-time uncompromising approach did not translate into overnight business success. Development was slow and often difficult. His first store did not open until the year 2000, in Tokyo. Most of his stores were in hard-to-find locations with fascia that were only intelligible to the insider. Financial pressures recurred, hindering the development of the house. By 2002, the company found a sympathetic investor and kindred spirit in Renzo Rosso, owner of Diesel, Italy's innovative denim brand. Rosso became a majority shareholder and replaced Jenny Meirens as president, helping to bankroll retail openings in key fashion cities, including London and New York. But Margiela and Meirens continued to run the business and make the creative decisions. 'I love this man,' Rosso said, promising a hands-off approach. 'This is not an acquisition. I'm not buying a fashion company like other groups have done. I'm investing in Margiela so two friends can work together to grow a very special brand.'

The deal was a pivotal moment for Margiela's business. After a low-key start to the new relationship, a period marked by heavy investment in shops and production, sales shot up in 2007 by 50 per cent to 60 million euros, driven by the designer's popularity in Japan. Margiela moved into new territory, launching both a fragrance and jewellery. A shop was opened on Via Spiga, Milan's celebrated fashion street. A new wave of professionalism swept through the company. That the business changed dramatically in character is not in doubt. Some voices suggested that Margiela was 'selling out', a charge rejected by Giovanni Pungetti, Margiela's chief executive, in an interview in 2008. 'The brand is exactly the same. It's very, very close to what we bought six years ago.'

In fact, Margiela has become part of a larger experiment by Renzo Rosso to create an alternative kind of luxury fashion group for the twenty-first century. Margiela, together with designers Viktor & Rolf, who are also part of Rosso's Only The Brave group, represents a wave that is unashamedly conceptual and serious minded. Rosso has said: 'My dream is to represent a fresh, modern group for the future—I don't look for establishment designers but someone with important creativity.' In 2008, Margiela's twentieth year in business, rumours circulated that the partnership was in trouble and that Margiela himself was considering retiring. But it was anniversary nonsense, put in its place by an exhibition held in Antwerp, titled simply Maison Martin Margiela, and by the energy of his spring/summer 2009 show, which featured models with their faces shrouded with stocking masks and tumbling hair. By early 2009, the house was exploring new opportunities in home decoration and hotel design.

As for the elusive Margiela himself, his lasting influence as a designer can be observed everywhere, including the denim sector, where the recycling and deconstruction of styles are well-established. A new generation of young designers, led most notably by Nicolas Ghesquière, has also drawn inspiration from his work. In the twenty-first century, when environmental issues of sustainability lend extra fuel to the vintage boom, Margiela may come to be seen as a true pioneer of a new way forward for fashion.

Further reading: Academic Rebecca Arnold makes interesting observations in *Fashion, Desire and Anxiety* (2001). Margiela was well profiled in 'The Crazy Professor' (1998) by Rebecca Mead for *The New Yorker*. *WWD* has reported his career thoroughly, not least through the writing of Paris editor Miles Socha. 'Art versus Commerce: Can Margiela Expand Without Selling Out?' (2 May 2008) explores the challenges for Margiela in recent years.

47 MARC JACOBS (1963–)

If you want to feel the pulse of modern fashion, then Marc Jacobs is invariably the best designer to turn to. Although his career has had its fair number of fashion missteps, no other designer has so consistently influenced the broader clothing market in the modern era, a period when fashion moves with oft bewildering speed from one extreme to another. To his critics, the American designer's collections are dominated by too many pastiches of previous periods, particularly the 1970s, a decade to which he has returned time and time again. To his fans, including most fashion editors and many fashion industry professionals, he is the endlessly inventive New Yorker who has injected a fresh street-inspired spirit into designer fashion. Anna Wintour, editor of American *Vogue* and a long-time admirer, highlights his knack for 'making the conservative seem cool . . . and making the cool seem conservative.'

In a fashion world more competitive than ever before, Marc Jacobs is one of a very small group of designers to have survived the buffetings of building a label from scratch. He has established a status likely to ensure his longevity—with the potential to match American names such as Calvin Klein and Ralph Lauren. For that, the patronage of Bernard Arnault, chairman of LVMH, the world's largest luxury conglomerate, has been critical. Although his celebrated grunge collection of 1993 established him as a designer with a street touch, the primary note of most of his work in the first decade of the twenty-first century has been a simple sense of elegance. Consider his collection of autumn/winter 2007, an homage to the Yves Saint Laurent of the 1970s, thoroughly grown-up and (like all of his clothes) eminently wearable. Marc Jacobs may not have created any striking new design innovations or silhouettes, but he has enthusiastically responded to the fast turnover of trends in the modern period and is the designer of his generation most copied by the international chain stores. Although considered by many of his supporters to be the ultimate downtown designer, in truth Marc Jacobs is uptown by origin, growing up in his grandmother's apartment on the Upper West Side of Manhattan. Perhaps it is the fusion of uptown sophistication mixed with downtown youthful energy and street vibe that best explains his attraction to a wide cross-section of customers.

The full story of Jacobs's childhood is shrouded in some mystery, but the bare facts are that his father, who worked at the William Morris talent agency, died when he was only seven; his mother remarried several times and spent time in various hospitals. The young Jacobs was brought up by his grandmother rather than his mother. Materially, he was comfortably off, although one can only guess at the psychological impact of losing a parent so young. His grandmother took him to New York department store Bergdorf Goodman and encouraged him in his interest in fashion. 'One big thing she taught me was that quality was more important than quantity,' Jacobs recalled many years later. Jacobs grew up fast, realising at an early age that he was gay, checking out copies of *Playgirl* magazine, but has spoken of his insecurity as a young man. At the age of just fifteen, his uncle, who was president of the same agency where Jacobs's father had worked, arranged work experience for him in the company's mail room. One of the agents, covering music, secured him guest-list entry to gigs: 'I loved anything garagey rough—the Speedies, the Screams or Gang of Four,' he recalled decades later in an interview with *Rolling Stone*. 'I would get turned on by a band's look first, and once I did, I found I actually liked the music.' This love of music has remained a constant through his career.

He enrolled in the High School of Art and Design and worked at the fashionable New York boutique Charivari, encouraged by buyer Barbara Weiser who took him (aged just twenty) with her on a tour to Japan. The story goes that the designer Perry Ellis walked into Charivari one day, whereupon Jacobs asked him for career advice. Go to Parsons, said Ellis, referring to New York's Parsons School of Design, the preeminent fashion design college in America. At Parsons, Jacobs made an exceptional impact, creating a student collection in 1984 of sweaters handmade by his grandmother and inspired by the British artist, Bridget Riley. They won him two prestigious Gold Thimble Awards. Among the guests at the awards event was Robert Duffy, a young and ambitious businessman, who swiftly became Jacobs's long-term business partner, sticking with him and guiding him through a decade of see-saw swings in fortune. Duffy, who worked for Reuben Thomas, a Seventh Avenue dress company, persuaded his boss to launch a new collection, named Sketchbook, designed by Jacobs. The first collection, for spring 1985, included spectacularly large hand-knitted sweaters with bright pink smiley faces. From the very beginning, Jacobs has been a designer who believes in an upbeat smiley message for a young generation.

Jacobs's career trajectory in the late 1980s went through a series of twists and turns. Dropped by Reuben Thomas, he worked briefly with Canadian clothing magnate Jack Atkins, followed by a company called Epoch-3 and then Kashiyama-USA. His breakthrough came in 1988 when he was appointed vice-president of design at Perry Ellis (the designer had died in 1986), with his business partner Robert Duffy as president. This was a remarkable achievement for a designer who was only twenty-five, sparking a storm of media interest and gossip on Seventh Avenue. For five years, Jacobs's creative progress at Perry Ellis was scrutinised, analysed and discussed in merciless detail. Already, the Jacobs's signature—youthful, playful,

ironic, accessible—was apparent. His steady creative evolution reached a peak with his spring 1993 collection, the so-called grunge collection, inspired by the street and music scene in Seattle, Washington, and the music of Sonic Youth. Ironically, that scene was defiantly anti-fashion, favouring vintage store clothes and combining styles and influences in a deliberately haphazard manner. Jacobs's catwalk take on this Seattle style caused a maelstrom of media excitement, not all of it complimentary. It was an important moment for high fashion, prompting a reassessment of what designer fashion could mean. Although many designers before Jacobs, most notably Jean Paul Gaultier, had plundered the energy of the street and music scene, few did so with the assurance of Jacobs. Looking back more than a decade later, he said: 'It was my vision and interpretation of street clothes, with the imperfection that I've always loved. It was also a reflection of the attitude of young people towards fashion.'

However, the response from the designer's bosses at Perry Ellis, who had shown courage in approving his appointment in the first place, was unremittingly negative. They considered the grunge collection a step too far, believing it trampled on the Perry Ellis signature and would spell commercial disaster. Jacobs and Duffy were summarily fired. It was a shock, but Jacobs bounced back within three seasons, showing on a shoestring budget in a downtown loft, with star models lending support and the entire New York industry begging for a ticket. Jacobs moved on to another plane in 1997, when Bernard Arnault, chairman of LVMH, signed him as creative director to develop ready-to-wear for Louis Vuitton, the jewel in the crown of his luxury group. The challenge for Jacobs was to develop a signature style for Vuitton, which was known almost exclusively as a luxury luggage and accessories brand. 'My designs are more eclectic, romantic and quite small-scale,' he acknowledged to *WWD*. 'Louis Vuitton is an international name . . . It has to be simple, clean and luxurious. I think it should look contemporary, but not trendy. It's kind of overwhelming to be in a position where nothing has been done, so you start to set your own rules.'

The early collections received a mixed response (some menswear collections in particular were considered woefully misjudged), but Jacobs found his mark through a series of hugely successful collaborations with artists, beginning with Stephen Sprouse. 'I asked Stephen to come and deface the monogram and he obliged,' said Jacobs. The gold insignia became bold graffiti, and Louis Vuitton would never be the same again. A collaboration with Japanese artist Takashi Murakami, launched for spring 2003, was equally popular, particularly the handbags decorated with cherries. An obsession with designer handbags, at ever-spiralling prices, became a phenomenon of the mid-noughties, driven principally by Louis Vuitton. For spring 2007, Jacobs's own label collection included a $22,500 crocodile patchwork bag.

During the 1990s and the noughties, Marc Jacobs was at the centre of a remarkable creative circle, focused on New York but international in outlook, ranging from designers and models to artists and film directors. Key names included Sofia Coppola, actress, muse and ultimately film director, and Juergen Teller, the photographer, who shot Coppola for his first campaign for Marc Jacobs in 2000. In this world, Jacobs partied as hard as he worked, and allegations of his excessive drug-taking circulated through the fashion industry for years, culminating in the designer spending time in a rehab centre in the spring of 1999. The pressures on Marc Jacobs at this time were immense. He was flying between New York and Paris, designing for Louis Vuitton and his own label (also backed by LVMH, which had a third stake). To this workload, he added Marc by Marc Jacobs, a lower-priced collection, in 2000.

Rehab worked for Jacobs, prompting a new spate of creativity and, simultaneously, a greater appreciation of the attractions of a quieter social scene in Paris. In creative terms, Jacobs was energised by the combination of European sophistication and American verve, a reflection again of the uptown/downtown mix that had served him well in New York. Jacobs's rejection of drugs and drink after his period in rehab may well have saved his relationship with LVMH, which was not always easy. In 2004, after lengthy negotiations, Jacobs signed a new long-term deal with LVMH that ensured him creative and financial stability for a 10-year period. By 2008, Jacobs's ability for reinvention had

extended to himself, rejecting an understated look for a flashier image of designer-as-celebrity. He worked out seven days a week, changed his diet to cope with bouts of ulcerative colitis and acquired more than thirty tattoos. Jacobs once commented that he had attention deficit disorder, an insight that might explain his swings in style and design focus. Writer Vanessa Grigoriadis has highlighted his 'polar tastes for high fashion and low celebrity, which helped popularise the current enthusiasm for perversity and art, overt cuteness combined with classic cool.'

For his autumn/winter show in 2008, Jacobs sparked a row with the fashion editors by starting the show two hours late. For spring/summer 2009, he was on time with a collection that received rave reviews, representing a swing through many of the classics of American sportswear style seen through the prism of Paris. Jacobs, said style.com, saw American fashion with an ex-pat's eye. By autumn/winter 2009 he was paying homage to the wilder excesses of 1980s fashion, referencing Stephen Spouse once again. In a talk at Central Saint Martin's College in 2008, he was reluctant to pontificate on his vast range of influences. 'Who cares what inspired it? Ideas are just catalysts for becoming something else. If a girl wants to wear it, that's all that matters.' Doubtless Jacobs will continue to excite and wind up the fashion world for many years to come. As a designer, his willingness to take risks and strike out in new directions has endeared him to an industry where the temptation is often to play safe. American *Vogue* editor Anna Wintour sums him up thus: 'No other American designer has so successfully fused the street style of New York with a reverence for making beautiful fashion.'

Further reading: Brigid Foley's short monograph, *Marc Jacobs* (2004), provides a useful introduction. *Louis Vuitton: The Birth of Modern Luxury* (2005), by Paul-Gerard Pasols, covers his contribution to Louis Vuitton. An outstanding profile by Vanessa Grigoriadis, 'The Deep Shallowness of Marc Jacobs' (December 2008), was published by *Rolling Stone.* 'Jacobs' Ladder' (22 September 1997), written for *The New Yorker* by Zoë Heller, is an in-depth report on the problems Jacobs faced in his early days at Louis Vuitton.

48 TOM FORD (1962–)

American designer Tom Ford was a dynamic force in fashion in the 1990s, responsible for a spectacular makeover of the historic Italian fashion house of Gucci. More than that, he was, in the words of John Demsey, president of Estée Lauder, 'the combustion that drove the entire Nineties'. While Karl Lagerfeld had dominated the 1980s, Ford was the star of the 1990s, becoming as much of a celebrity as the many famous names he dressed. A natural inheritor of the mantle of Halston, Ford had an immaculate personal sense of style, combined with an ability to articulate his vision in interviews that made him a hot favourite with fashion editors. He is also preternaturally handsome. As Graydon Carter, editor-in-chief of *Vanity Fair,* put it: 'Virtually all women who meet him want to have sex with him.' And a good number of men, too.

Ford had an all-embracing vision of fashion, reflecting a decade during which fashion became an ever more influential form of popular culture. 'For me fashion doesn't stop at clothes,' said Ford. 'Fashion is everything. Art, music, furniture design, hair, makeup . . . all those things go together to make a moment in time.' Ford also smashed down any lingering hang-ups about sexuality and sex in the modern world. Anna Wintour, editor of American *Vogue,* noted his work was 'always charged with some kind of erotic frisson.' He was open about his homosexuality, living with the fashion writer Richard Buckley. He explored sexuality fully in his work for Gucci and expropriated imagery from the world of pornography for some controversial advertising campaigns: he always claimed people looked best naked rather than clothed. 'Sex,' he said, with all the confidence in the world, 'is something that I think about all the time.'

Despite his influence and status, there was a view that Ford himself had limited design talents and played more the role of impresario or stylist for his hard-working design studio. It was a charge he deeply resented. 'It just drives me crazy,' he said in an interview for the book *Tom Ford,* published after he left Gucci. 'I don't pose around in a white lab coat with bolts of fabric on the floor like Yves did. But I've been working in this business for 20 years. I know how to cut a dress; I can climb on the table and cut it with scissors and pin it down.' He was proud to be a commercial designer, saying he never wanted to be anything else. His job, he said, was to make women beautiful. 'I feel fashion more than I think it,' he said. 'My first instinct is gut.'

He also had an obsessive, perfectionist eye. No detail of the Gucci brand renaissance escaped his eye. Nothing was too mundane for his attention. *Vogue*'s Anna Wintour dubbed him the 'Flaubert of fashion', after the detail-obsessed French novelist of the nineteenth century. Ford created the 1990s template for a young designer to be catapulted in to revive an old brand. Karl Lagerfeld had led the way at Chanel in the 1980s, but Ford perfected the concept, setting a trend that led to Marc Jacobs at Louis Vuitton, John Galliano at Dior, and many more. However, in retrospect, it is clear that he overreached himself in his later years at Gucci. As the Gucci empire expanded, he took on the ultimate challenge in 1999 after the Gucci Group's acquisition of Yves Saint Laurent by appointing himself creative director of YSL. He drew a wave of criticism in France for his irreverent approach to the YSL legacy. In 2001, he sent out models in a menswear YSL show wearing YSL horn-rimmed glasses. 'They were a nod to Saint Laurent, but I did not want to be too literal,' Ford said. Saint Laurent snubbed the show and made his displeasure even clearer by attending the Dior menswear show on the following day. After leaving Gucci Group, Ford acknowledged that YSL was unfinished business. 'It just hasn't hit its stride yet . . . I wanted to conquer Saint Laurent.' Ford's last collection for YSL, for autumn/winter 2004/2005, with its focus on the Opium and Orientalist phase of Saint Laurent's career, hinted at the direction in which he wanted to head.

Tom Ford was born in San Marcos, Texas, in 1962, and grew up in Santa Fe, New Mexico. His grandmother was a flamboyant influence on his early years, teaching Ford the importance of good dress sense. By the age of twelve, he had his first pair of Gucci loafers. Already, his perfectionist temperament had emerged: he developed an exceptional visual eye, rearranging the furniture at home and eager to dress his family and friends to meet his own exacting standards. But fashion was not his initial calling. At eighteen Ford arrived in New York to study art history at New York University. It was the back end of the 1970s, a decade that was a major inspiration for Ford at Gucci. Nightclub Studio 54 was a favourite haunt for the young man, who got to know Andy Warhol and his entourage. With his dazzling good looks, Ford made money as a leading male model and built an impressive circle of contacts in the fashion world. He dropped out of New York University to switch to Parsons School of Art, enrolling on the environmental design course. He transferred to the Paris branch of Parsons at the age of twenty, a move that had a profound impact. 'I cried the first time I walked around in Paris. Everything was so beautiful I just couldn't believe it . . . I felt instantly comfortable.'

His first job in fashion design was at Cathy Hardwick, who hired Ford because he was attractive rather than for any apparent brilliance in his portfolio. His natural flair for fashion rapidly developed, for he was poached in 1988 by Marc Jacobs and then moved to Perry Ellis as design director, a remarkable role for a man who was still only twenty-six. In 1989, Gucci, an historic but ailing label, hired Dawn Mello, an American retail executive who had transformed the fortunes of New York department store Bergdorf Goodman, to run the business. Although Mello stayed at Gucci little more than a year, it was she who made the key appointment of Ford to design womenswear, recommended by his boyfriend, Richard Buckley. When Mello returned to New York and Bergdorf Goodman, Ford's role at Gucci became more prominent. By 1992, he was design director, but he clashed with Maurizio Gucci, who thought Ford was rather too fashion focused for a label with a history of classic style. Domenico De Sole, then director of Gucci's American operation, stepped in to save Ford. In the early 1990s, the company had to design a team approach, and Maurizio Gucci was usually involved to Fords's intense irritation. There were times when Ford was ready to return to America and start up his own label, but he hung on. 'I had this incredible drive,' he reflected later. 'I was going to be a successful fashion designer if it killed me.'

In 1994, Gucci was bought by Investcorp, an investment firm, and Ford was finally made creative director. A year later, the fashion world was shocked by the murder of Maurizio Gucci, gunned down in a contract killing organised by his ex-wife. Ironically, the year in which Maurizio Gucci died was also the year the brand exploded back into life. With Ford at the creative helm and Domenico De Sole established as chief executive, a partnership was created that turned Gucci into the most successful fashion label of the decade. No expense was spared in creating the Ford vision. Photographer Mario Testino and stylist Carine Roitfeld, later editor of French *Vogue,* were collaborators with Ford in creating the slick, sexy, modern Gucci style. His autumn/winter 1995 collection, shown in the spring of 1995, was a high-octane tribute to the late 1970s, with blue velvet hipsters and satin shirts. It was judged a tour de force. Ford's moment had come.

By the autumn/winter 1996 collection, Ford's vision for Gucci was complete, with its revival of late 1970s glamour combined with touches of history from the Gucci archive and an overriding dose of Italian modernism. The elements included pinstripe tailoring for women, red velvet tuxedos, white jersey gowns with peepholes and gold fastenings, dark eyes and a look of androgyny that recalled the work of photographer Helmut Newton. Sleek, sexy, modern, as Ford put it, claiming he had brought back 'a certain sexual glamour which we probably hadn't seen since the late 70s, because of the way that Aids altered fashion.' Separately, Ford was intensely involved in the business development of Gucci, and ailing licenses around the world were bought back or closed. Gucci stores were designed in collaboration with Bill Sofield, who created an alluring mix of clean lines and rich materials that summed up the new Gucci image. The Asian financial crisis of 1998 was only a blip in the label's forward momentum. Ford took creative risks, including a collection for spring 1999 inspired by the singer and actress Cher, but press and buyers alike lapped it up. Under Ford and De Sole, Gucci became a business worth in excess of $4 billion and boasted a stable of names that included Yves Saint Laurent as well as young British designers Stella McCartney and Alexander McQueen.

Gucci led the way in the true globalisation of luxury and pioneered the broadening of its customer base. As rising income levels around the world brought designer style within the reach of millions more people, designer labels were booming. They were now mass luxury brands, even if many of their customers reserved their spending for the fragrances and accessories rather than the clothes. Even the 9/11 terrorist attack on New York in 2001 appeared to have little effect on business: on the day of the attacks, the New York store of YSL received forty-two calls from women wanting the peasant blouse, Ford meticulously noted. The growth of the luxury sector led to a period of consolidation as leading luxury businesses sought to buy up brands with global potential. As part of this process, Gucci was itself the object of a titanic struggle for control between Bernard Arnault's LVMH and François-Pinault's Pinault-Printemps-Redoute (PPR), ending in the law courts in Amsterdam. PPR won out in 2000, to Ford's approval. Four years later, however, PPR's efforts to exert greater managerial control over Gucci Group led to Ford's downfall.

The departure of both Ford and De Sole in 2004 was abrupt. Although the full details of the fallout are still unclear to this day, PPR executives clearly thought the spotlight of attention was too firmly focused on the personality of Ford himself. The designer was devastated by the outcome. 'I was depressed. I wallowed in self-pity,' he admitted in an interview. Ford expressed interest in developing a career in Hollywood, but this has not so far got off the ground. After more than a year of trying to determine what was best for the future, he launched his own label in 2007, initially focusing on menswear and sold only through a single Tom Ford store at 845 Madison Avenue in New York.

In 2008, the concept was rolled out worldwide through link-ups with leading designer retailers, such as Lane Crawford in Hong Kong. Ford believes there is a genuine gap in luxury menswear. 'Giorgio Armani and Ralph [Lauren] have both dominated but they are both 74 years old,' he said. 'and who is behind them?'

For charisma alone, Ford could arguably claim a place among the world's great designers. 'This job is a total ego thing in a way,' he acknowledged, reviving the concept of designer as style dictator. 'To be a designer and say, "This is the way people should dress, this is the way their homes should look, this is the way the world should be."'

Further reading: Tom Ford produced an outstanding summary of his own career in a collaboration with writer Brigid Foley: *Tom Ford* (2004) features an extended interview with the designer and strong visual coverage of the highlights of his years at Gucci.

49 ALEXANDER MCQUEEN (1969–)

British fashion has produced countless young designers full of loudmouthed attitude and shock-tactics clothes. Many of them have sparkled briefly, like fireworks, only to fall swiftly to earth. However, Alexander McQueen, who could always out-swear his contemporaries and enjoyed creating a furore on the catwalk, has proved a designer with staying power. He is an enduring talent who looks certain to be a major influence in fashion for many years to come. This did not seem so likely back in 1996 when the young designer upset the Parisian fashion establishment after landing the job of head designer at Givenchy. McQueen swiftly alienated the French by making no attempt to speak French, deriding the still-revered Hubert de Givenchy as 'irrelevant', and producing a shockingly ill-judged first collection that even he admitted was 'crap'. In retrospect, the Givenchy experience, which lasted for four years, represented a huge learning curve for the designer.

By late 2000—shortly before leaving Givenchy to the relief of both parties—McQueen appeared to have secured his long-term future by selling 51 per cent of his own label to Gucci Group. In creative terms, the designer was also reinvigorated, producing inspired collections season after season presented through some of the most memorable fashion shows of modern times. At the heart of his collections is superbly constructed tailoring, cut with confidence and elan, skills which are applied to playing with the shape of the body. His best work has a certain toughness about it—he has described his clothes as 'armour'—worn by women who want to look powerful. As he has put it: 'It kind of fends people off. You have to have a lot of balls to talk to a woman wearing my clothes.'

McQueen's work is also shot through with autobiographical influences, a characteristic acknowledged by the designer many times. To take just one specific event from his own life: as an eight-year-old he witnessed one of his sisters being beaten up by her husband, a traumatic event that he says had a profound impact on his attitude to women and to his design. He has joked that he is the fashion industry's therapist. Certainly, fashion shows with a disturbing undercurrent have been a feature of his career, ranging from collections based on Hitchcock heroines, the cult film *Picnic at Hanging Rock,* the William Golding novel *Lord of the Flies* and asylums. 'My own living nightmares,' is how he has described his presentations. Death and decay are McQueen preoccupations, summed up by a dress made from decaying flowers that featured in his autumn 2007 collection. 'I just use things that people want to hide in their head,' he said in 2002. 'Things about war, religion, sex, things that we all think about but don't bring to the forefront. But I do, and force them to watch it.'

But while darkness is often dominant, romance is an equally integral feature of the McQueen vision of the world, as his long-term stylist and friend Katy England has noted. 'We all carry both the dark and the light with us,' he said in 2008. 'I don't see why it shouldn't be reflected in my work.' He often sees beauty in the apparently ugly, with an aesthetic sense that chimes with contemporary British artists such as Jake and Dinos Chapman or Damien Hirst. 'I find beauty in the grotesque, like most artists,' he said in 2007. 'I have to force people to look at things.'

Lee Alexander McQueen, born in 1969, was the youngest of the six children of an East London cab driver, an unlikely background that media reports turned into the fairy tale story of an East End rough lad made good. The designer, who rightly grew to hate the stereotyping, did not serve his own cause well by joking that he was 'a big-mouth East London yob'. The real story of McQueen's rise was more prosaic, founded on a childhood obsession with drawing fashion (he claims to have begun as early as three) and a capacity for working hard. His mother, a genealogist, encouraged him to apply for work in Savile Row in 1986 after he had left school with just two qualifications, both in art. Savile Row was no longer the force it had once been in men's tailoring, but McQueen was fortunate to land his first job at Anderson & Sheppard, perhaps the most demanding and perfectionist of the remaining tailors on the Row. After two years learning how to cut and make trousers, he moved to Gieves & Hawkes, where he focused on jackets. It was an extraordinary learning experience that gave him a technical expertise well beyond any of his contemporaries—and all before he had turned twenty.

After Savile Row, McQueen worked briefly at Bermans & Nathans, the theatrical costumiers, and for the designer Koji Tatsuno. He then landed a job with Romeo Gigli by buying a one-way plane ticket to Milan and presenting his portfolio. A year on, when Gigli's business was under pressure, McQueen returned to London and undertook a postgraduate fashion degree at Central Saint Martins College of Art & Design. His degree collection was bought by the eccentric talent-spotter Isabella Blow (1958–2007), then a fashion editor at *Vogue,* who promptly made it her mission to bring the name Alexander McQueen (Lee had been dropped) to the attention of the wider world. McQueen's early collections drew mixed reviews, including accusations of misogyny, which the designer fiercely rejected, blaming fashion editors' misinterpretations. An early collection, titled Highland Rape (from 1995, reprised and developed in his autumn/winter 2006 collection), was not intended as a tasteless reference to the act of rape, but was a reference to the English slaughter of the Scottish clans in the eighteenth century. The models wore ripped and shredded clothes mostly pieced together by McQueen himself from fabric shop remnants. A later show

for Givenchy using fibreglass mannequins was not a rejection of real women but an exploration of a blank canvas as a more objective means of viewing a new collection. McQueen's early creation of bumsters (trousers cut so low that the cleft of the buttocks was revealed) also did not endear him to some of his female critics, although it was intended as an experiment in lengthening the torso—and was a harbinger of a low-rise jeans trend in the broader fashion market.

Working and living out of a studio in Hoxton, East London, McQueen built his label steadily although finances were always tight, as they were (and still are) for most young British designers. In 1996, the opportunity to take the helm at Givenchy, despite having designed no more than eight collections under his own name, was too good to be missed. Givenchy, owned by the LVMH conglomerate, chose McQueen as a second young British designer in succession, following in the steps of John Galliano, provoking the suggestion among the Parisian fashion set that the venerable house of Givenchy had been turned into a nursery for new talent. Speaking in 2000, McQueen commented: 'Maybe I was too young to take on Givenchy. But nobody in my position would have done any different. I had to accept it.' Years later, he was philosophical about the experience, acknowledging that he learned a lot from the atelier. His mistake, he said, was to try to be someone he isn't. 'When I was in Paris I tried to mould in with this concept of couture and this hierarchy, but it's just not me. I can't play that game. I think it looks stupid when designers play these bourgeois characters. At the end of the day, I'm left with the real me. What you see is what you get.'

The acquisition of a majority stake in his own label by Gucci Group in 2000 did not mean the end of the pressure for McQueen. In 2004, when Gucci Group creative director Tom Ford and chief executive Domenico De Sole left the business they had dominated, McQueen found himself answering to a new chief executive, Robert Polet, who declared that all the smaller labels in the Gucci Group should break even within three years or expect to be sold. McQueen, who had sensibly nurtured his own label all through the Givenchy years (displaying an impressive business acumen, unusual for a British designer), tripled sales within three years and achieved the Polet target by 2007 through a variety of new projects, including the McQ secondary line, menswear, accessories and footwear. A skull-print scarf was a particular hit, selling phenomenally and prompting a flood of street fashion copies. In 2009, McQueen also created a capsule collection for Target, a mainstream American retailer.

McQueen had also found a new personal equilibrium, becoming a Buddhist and marrying his long-term partner George Forsyth in 2000 (although that relationship has since ended). The designer appeared to have mellowed. In 2005, he commented: 'For a long time I was looking for my perfect equilibrium, my mojo. And now I think I'm getting there: I've found my customer, my silhouette, my cut.' A year later, still aged only thirty-seven, he commented: 'The more I mature, the less confrontational I become. I've softened a bit in my old age.' The death by suicide of his long-time supporter Isabella Blow in 2007 also spurred him on. 'I found a new love for [designing] because she loved it and she found me because of what I was good at . . . It was a wake-up call.' McQueen subsequently went on a pilgrimage to India and the results fed into his next collection.

His fashion shows are artistic events, sharpened through McQueen's interest in historical references, shot through with spectacle, mystery, violence, tenderness and beauty. For his memorable spring 1999 collection, the model Shalom Harlow played the role of a dying swan while being spray-painted by robots. His spring/summer 2001 collection, titled Voss, was staged in a large mirrored box, on which audience and models could watch their own reflections. The provocative show ended with the naked appearance of fetish writer Michelle Olley wearing a fetishist's mask and covered in moths. Fashion historian Caroline Evans wrote: 'In the staging of this show, McQueen oscillated between beauty and horror, turning conventional ideas of beauty upside down.'

Working with leading London stylist Katy England and film and special effects teams, McQueen has produced spellbinding fashion shows that tend to blow through his budgets but leave even veteran show attendees speechless. For his autumn/winter 2006 collection, staged in March 2006, he concluded with an apparently glass pyramid at the heart of which appeared a curl of white smoke that unfurled to reveal the shape of the model Kate Moss in a white ruffled dress. The vision, created through a hologram, danced and blurred and vanished—a moment of magic. His spring/summer 2009 show featured a video of a spiralling Earth and a runway surreally adorned with stuffed animals. McQueen explained he had been exploring the thoughts of Charles Darwin and the effects of industrialisation on nature.

In recent years, McQueen has increasingly retreated from the fashion circuit, rarely staying long at parties, preferring his own company or that of a close-knit circle of friends. In an interview with British *Harper's Bazaar* in 2007, he acknowledged his preference for outsider status. 'I came to terms with not fitting in a long time ago. I never really fitted in. I don't want to fit in. And now people are buying into that.' He remains an obsessive about his work, determined to make an enduring mark: 'I'm interested in designing for posterity . . . There are only a handful of designers that influence other designers, and I have to keep one step ahead of the game. As a designer, you've always got to push yourself forward; you've always got to keep up with the trends or make your own trends. That's what I do.'

Further reading: Alexander McQueen still awaits a biographer, but there have been plenty of perceptive interviews, particularly in the British press, where writers have followed his career from the early days. McQueen features in Susannah Frankel's *Visionaries* (2001) and has been interviewed by Frankel on several occasions. Other interviews include 'The New Kingdom of Alexander McQueen' by Nick Compton for *iD* (August 2002) and 'Killer McQueen' by Harriet Quick for *Vogue* (UK, October 2002). *Fashion at the Edge: Spectacle, Modernity and Deathliness* (2003), by Caroline Evans, makes many interesting observations about his work.

50 NICOLAS GHESQUIÈRE (1971–)

The youngest designer in this book, Nicolas Ghesquière was barely noticed when he first arrived at the ailing house of Balenciaga in 1997. Perhaps more by luck than by design, the owners of Balenciaga had discovered a designer with a genuine admiration for the late couturier and sharing his same exacting standards. Ghesquière was also a child of the 1980s, looking resolutely forwards. Over several seasons, he developed a confident signature of his own that referenced the glorious past of Balenciaga but also hurtled it forward into a new century as one of the most influential labels in fashion. Commenting on his autumn/winter 2008 collection, Suzy Menkes, fashion editor of *The International Herald Tribune,* wrote: 'The makeover of Balenciaga is exceptional because of the seamless flow of past and present, often uniting in a single outfit.'

Ghesquière is every bit the modern designer: full of inspired creative ideas but seeing no inconsistency with the concept of building a brand and driving forward a business. The fusion between creativity and commerce, noted by fashion historian Nancy Troy in her study of early twentieth century couturiers such as Paul Poiret, is complete. Applauding his spring 2007 collection, fashion editor Cathy Horyn of *The New York Times* wrote: 'If he isn't the most important designer of his generation, it's hard to think who would be. Certainly, Mr Ghesquière is one of a handful of young visionaries trying to look at the future of fashion in a believable way.' Balenciaga under Ghesquière produces ready-to-wear rather than couture, but the young designer saw a new middle way for high fashion, merging craft and couture touches with high-tech materials and street inspiration. For ready-to-wear, he works with

Lesage for embroideries and Lemarie for feathered work, both specialist names associated with couture. 'I don't think couture fits our world,' he said in 2007. '[But] anyway I have the luxury of using the couture techniques in my ready-to-wear.'

Unlike Balenciaga, who draped fabric directly, Ghesquière prefers to sketch. 'I have my ideas in drawing form on a board, along with the fabric, and then I try to find the shape and silhouette, and work through each idea to build the show collection.' His team then brings the ideas to life. In common with Balenciaga, he has an obsession with precise cut and with perfecting every piece. 'There is no compromise," he told *Women's Wear Daily.* 'If we have to try 20 times [to perfect] a dress, I try it 20 times.' Discipline and a perfectionist sensibility drive him forward. The process of editing is also important, he has said. 'Fashion is about selection, editing. You have to be very severe in your selection, so you keep something to yourself—even in the way you present yourself.' This sense of severity was also tempered with a dose of mischief-making: for his spring/summer 2004 collection, he chose to show no trousers on the runway, puzzling fashion editors by excluding the garment for which he was then most admired.

His influence on the broader fashion market is immense. Ghesquière has a futuristic touch, creating a kind of sci-fi fashion that excites his customers. He is also gloriously unpredictable, making the shows at the crowded Balenciaga showroom in Paris among every season's hot tickets. When he revived floral prints for his spring/summer 2008 collection, buyers and press alike decreed florals as one of the key trends for that summer. His signature looks of slim-line trousers, shrunken jackets and soft handbags have been widely admired and copied. His trousers made young women drool in the early noughties. James Aguiar of Bergdorf Goodman told *Vogue* in 2001: 'What Ghesquière has done is to give a young girl the thing she wants most: to look cool and hip. And he cuts the sexiest trousers for women.'

Ghesquière is the son of a Belgian golf-course owner and a French mother. Born in Comines in the north of France in 1971, he spent most of his childhood in the provincial French village of Loudun in western France. The young Ghesquière was an enthusiast for sports, including riding, fencing and swimming—he still swims regularly in the Ritz swimming pool in Paris. At the tender age of twelve he said he wanted to be a fashion designer, sketching dresses in his school books and creating dresses from curtains. Internships as a schoolboy at Agnès B and Corinne Cobson gave him a taste of the fashion industry. School over, he assisted at Jean Paul Gaultier for two years, an important period during which Ghesquière said he learned 'an aesthetic of mixing'. He then moved to design knitwear at Pôles, followed by a series of freelance design jobs, including Callaghan in Italy. At Balenciaga, he began by working for the Asian licensee, designing the unpromising categories of uniforms and funeral clothes. By the mid-1990s, the house of Balenciaga was a shadow of its former self: the great perfectionist couturier had closed the business in 1968 and its revival as a serious fashion house was considered unlikely.

Ghesquière was appointed head of design at Balenciaga in 1997 at the age of twenty-five, replacing Josephus Thimister, a move that barely raised a ripple of interest in the media. Balenciaga owners Groupe Jacques Bogart had recognised the young man's talent when he produced a promising small collection for a Japanese licensee. 'When I arrived at Balenciaga, it was full of ghosts—good ghosts and bad ghosts,' Ghesquière has recalled. 'Some people didn't speak to me . . . Maybe they thought I would just do something disrespectful, or try to re-do things right away. And, of course, that was not my intention.' His first few collections attracted little buzz in Paris and Ghesquière was hampered

by the fact that he had no access to the Balenciaga archives, relying instead on books and Irving Penn's photographs. Even so, by 2001 the word was beginning to circulate that Ghesquière was someone special, and the designer was profiled at length in American *Vogue*. His interest in vintage and in the 'unbeautiful' was noted by *Vogue* writer Sally Singer. From the beginning, Ghesquière had also been exploring new volumes, reacting to years of slim silhouettes. Blousons of linked circles and apron tunics that spiralled in strips around the body were highlights of his first collection. Then came fleece batwing tops with tight cuffs, followed by leggings, referring back to the 1980s. For spring 2001, he decorated jersey cocktail dresses with touches of lace, ruffles and pearls.

Inez van Lamsweerde, the Dutch photographer, pointed out that the designer's starting points 'are things that come from a collective memory. There are certain elements you remember from your childhood—something you saw, something you wore—and these can trigger a string of associations. The way a jacket is closed, for instance, can make you recall music. Nicolas takes a cue like that and then strips it down and rebuilds it in a modern way.' Steadily, the fashion world began to acknowledge that here was a young man who was not only reviving a celebrated fashion house but was a major force in his own right. His flatteringly cut trousers became must-haves for fashion editors, while his ability to mix couture style with a contemporary dress-down sensibility drew the attention of the high street copyists.

Tom Ford's enthusiasm for Ghesquière led to PPR-owned Gucci Group buying Balenciaga in 2001 and, with it, access to the archives. But when Ford and chief executive Domenico De Sole walked out in 2004 and a new chief executive, Robert Polet, was brought in, the omens did not look good for Ghesquière. Balenciaga, despite its heritage, was lumped in with emerging brands such as Alexander McQueen and Stella McCartney. The pressure was on to turn the business into profit. Ghesquière's insistence on maintaining a high-cost atelier in Paris (the clothes were manufactured in Italy) was considered an expensive luxury by the new management team. On top of this, the young designer had a reputation for being uncompromising and troublesome.

It was a sign of insecurity, the designer said later. 'I used to be more defensive and less comfortable because I was feeling threatened.'

With the Lariat handbag, Ghesquière created a money-spinner that pleased his new boss. Celebrities and wealthy customers worldwide fell over themselves to place orders for the multi-zipped bag with a braided handle and dangling pulls. In 2003, Ghesquière launched a collection titled Balenciaga Edition, recreating ten or fifteen couture pieces from the archives. His autumn/winter collection for 2006 was a highly praised homage to the great couturier, timed to coincide with a major Balenciaga retrospective at the Musée de la Mode et du Textile in Paris. From the boxy suits to the windowpane checks, the spirit of Balenciaga ran through every piece, but always reworked to make them fresh for a twenty-first century audience. While Ghesquière's collections had tended to reflect Balenciaga's own preference for round shapes, for spring 2007 the designer opted for a straight silhouette, with pinched, padded and highlighted sleeves. Cathy Horyn of *The New York Times* called it 'an ideological break with the retro futurism of Balenciaga. What we are now seeing is the contemporary future of Nicolas Ghesquière.'

By then his status was ensured. Ghesquière was featured in *Time*'s 100 Most Influential People of 2005. He was made a Chevalier des arts et lettres, an award of merit bestowed by the French government which highlights contributions to French culture. Through all this, he has kept a low personal profile, but all that is likely to change when he launches his own signature label, which seems inevitable as his reputation continues to flourish. He believes his own line could be developed in tandem with continuing to work at Balenciaga. 'Balenciaga is part of my identity,' he said in 2005. 'If I want to start my own line, I have to find a very specific and special concept.' Ghesquière is cautious about overstating the role of fashion as commentary on the world. 'You have to look at the world and then forget it,' he said in 2007. 'Of course I live in my time and I'm really curious. But, at the same time, I don't think it has a direct impact on my worth.'

Although designer fashion in the early twenty-first century has become big global business, Ghesquière believes there is still the freedom to experiment. 'What is really interesting about being a designer today is that you can occupy those two positions: being a forward thinker and at the same time someone who sells clothes.' Unlike any other designer in this book, Ghesquière's best work may be yet to come. In the great economic slowdown of 2009, the fashion world looked to Ghesquière to suggest a new way forward for design. The austerity of his autumn 2008 collection seemed to presage the onset of hard times. His spring/summer 2009 collection featured innovative cocoon shapes and fabric that appeared to melt around the body, prompting further eulogies, even from those who found his designs hard to pin down. As Julie Gilhart, a veteran buyer for Barneys New York, put it: 'He has a knack for showing us things that are not quite in our vernacular yet.'

Further reading: Nicolas Ghesquière has yet to be the subject of a monograph, although its arrival can only be a matter of time. He was exhaustively interviewed in the early years of the twenty-first century.

ILLUSTRATIONS

1: Madame Worth wearing a gown by Charles Frederick Worth, 1860.
Photo: Getty Images.   8

2: Marie-Louise Herrouett wears a *robe du soir* by Callot Soeurs. Image:
Time & Life Pictures/Getty Images.   12

3: Evening gown and mink-trimmed jacket, 1934. Photo: Getty Images.   16

4: Poiret at work, 1925. Photo: Getty Images.   20

5: Fortuny gown, c.1912. Photo: The Granger Collection/TopFoto.   24

6: Dress by Jeanne Lanvin, 1926. Photo: Getty Images.   34

7: Chanel in Paris, 1929. Photo: Getty *I*mages.   38

8: Coat and dress by Jean Patou, 1926. Photo: Getty Images.   42

9: Model in Vionnet dress, 1935. Photo: Roger Viollet/Getty Images.   46

10: Butterfly dress by Elsa Schiaparelli, 1937. Photo: Roger Viollett/Getty Images.   50

11: Evening dress and fur-trimmed cape by Mainbocher, 1935.
Photo: Getty Images.   54

12: Joan Crawford in *Letty Lynton,* dressed by Adrian. Photo: Getty Images.   58

13: Salvatore Ferragamo slips on a shoe, 1950. Photo: Time & Life Pictures/
Getty Images.   62

14: Madame Alix Grès dress, 1952. Photo: Getty Images.   66

15: Balenciaga dress, 1953. Photo: Getty Images.   76

16: Dior in his Paris studio, 1952. Photo: Getty Images.   82

17: A Charles James fashion show with the designer in the background, 1950.
Photo: Time & Life Pictures/Getty Images.   86

18: Claire McCardell adjusts a child's dress for a fashion show.
Photo: Time & Life Pictures/Getty Images.   90

19: Hubert de Givenchy designs, 1952. Photo: Time & Life Pictures/Getty Images.   94

20: Pierre Cardin show, 1970s. Photo: Chris Moore.   98

21: Mary Quant and models at a fashion show in Milan, 1967.
Photo: Getty Images.   102

22: Rudi Gernreich at work, 1968. Photo: Getty Images.   106

23: Mrs. Charles McGaha wears a Norman Norell culotte suit, 1960.
Photo: Time & Life Pictures/Getty Images.   114

24: Yves Saint Laurent, spring/summer 2002 couture. Photo: Chris Moore.   118

25: André Courrèges dress. Photo: Chris Moore.   122

26: Valentino, autumn/winter 2004. Photo: Chris Moore.   128

27: Chanel, designed by Karl Lagerfeld, spring/summer 2009. Photo: Chris Moore.   132

28: Halston with model, 1968. Photo: Getty Images.   136

29: Kenzo, spring/summer 1988. Photo: Chris Moore.   140

30: Ralph Lauren, autumn/winter 2001. Photo: Chris Moore.   144

31: Issey Miyake, autumn/winter 1989. Photo: Chris Moore.   150

32: Geoffrey Beene, autumn/winter 2000. Photo: Chris Moore.   154

33: Calvin Klein, autumn/winter 1990. Photo: Chris Moore.   160

34: Giorgio Armani, autumn/winter 2002. Photo: Chris Moore.   166

35: Comme des Garçons, designed by Rei Kawakuo, spring/summer 2009.
Photo: Chris Moore.   174

36: Yohji Yamamoto, spring/summer 1985. Photo: Chris Moore.   178

37: Vivienne Westwood, autumn/winter 1993. Photo: Chris Moore.   182

38: Paul Smith, spring/summer 2004. Photo: Chris Moore.   186

39: Azzedine Alaia, autumn/winter 2001. Photo: Chris Moore.   190

40: Gianni Versace, autumn/winter 1994. Photo: Chris Moore.   194

41: Jean Paul Gaultier, autumn/winter 1990. Photo: Chris Moore.   200

42: Dolce & Gabbana, autumn/winter 1992. Photo: Chris Moore.   204

43: John Galliano, spring/summer 2008. Photo: Chris Moore.   210

44: Donna Karan, spring/summer 1995. Photo: Chris Moore.   214

45: Prada, autumn/winter 1996. Photo: Chris Moore.   224

46: Martin Margiela, spring/summer 2009. Photo: Chris Moore.   228

47: Marc Jacobs, spring/summer 2009. Photo: Chris Moore.   234

48: Gucci by Tom Ford, autumn/winter 1995. Photo: Chris Moore.   238

49: Alexander McQueen, spring/summer 2005. Photo: Chris Moore.   242

50: Balenciaga, designed by Nicolas Ghesquière, spring/summer 2007.
Photo: Chris Moore.   246

BIBLIOGRAPHY

Arnold, R. (2001), *Fashion, Desire and Anxiety,* London: I.B.Tauris.

Ash, J., and Wilson, E. (eds.) (1992), *Chic Thrills: A Fashion Reader,* London: Pandora.

Baines, B.B. (1981) *Fashion Revivals: From the Elizabethan Age to the Present Day,* London: Batsford.

Ballard, B. (1960), *In My Fashion,* New York: David McKay.

Barber, L. (1998), 'The Frock Prince', *The Observer,* November 29.

Barille, E. (1997), *Lanvin,* Paris: Editions Assouline.

Barnes, R. (1994), *Mods!* London: Plexus.

Beaton, C. (1989), *The Glass of Fashion,* London: Cassell.

Beene, G., Wolcott, J., Luther, M. and Parmal, P.A. (2005) *Beene by Beene,* New York: Vendome Press.

Benaim, L. (1997), *Issey Miyake,* London: Thames & Hudson.

Bender, M. (1967) *The Beautiful People,* New York: Coward-McCann.

Bergé, P. (1997), *Yves Saint Laurent,* Fashion Memoir series, London: Thames & Hudson.

Bergé, P., Muller, F. and Bowles, H. (2008), *Yves Saint Laurent Style,* New York: Abrams.

Bertin, C. (1956), *Paris A La Mode,* tr. M. Deans, London: Victor Gollancz.

Blasberg, D. (2005), Gaultier interview, *Ten,* Winter.

Bluttal, S., and Mears, P. (2001), *Halston,* London: Phaidon.

Bond, D. (1992), *Glamour in Fashion,* London: Guinness Publishing.

Boudot, F. (1996), *Alaia,* Fashion Memoir series, London: Thames & Hudson.

Boucher, F. (1996), *A History of Costume in the West,* London: Thames & Hudson.

Boudot, F. (1997), *Yohji Yamamoto,* Fashion Memoir series, London: Thames & Hudson.

Boudot, F. (1999), *Fashion: The Twentieth Century,* London: Thames & Hudson.

Breward, C. (1994), *The Culture of Fashion: A New History of Fashionable Dress.* Manchester: Manchester University Press.

Breward, C. (2003), *Fashion,* Oxford: Oxford University Press.

Breward, C., Becky C., and Cox, C., (eds.) (2002) *The Englishness of English Dress,* Oxford: Berg.

Breward, C., Ehrman, E., and Evans, C. (2004), *The London Look: Fashion from Street to Catwalk,* London: Yale University Press.

Breward, C., Gilbert, G., and Lister, J. (2006), *Swinging Sixties Fashion in London and Beyond 1955–1970,* London: V&A Publications.

Brubach, H. (1992), 'The Religion of Woman', *The New Yorker,* July 6.

Brubach, H. (1999), *A Dedicated Follower of Fashion,* London: Phaidon Press.

Buxbaum, G. (ed.) (2005), *Icons of Fashion: The 20th Century,* Munich: Prestel.

Carter, E. (1977) *The Changing World of Fashion,* New York: Putnam's.

Carter, E. (1980), *Magic Names of Fashion,* London: Weidenfeld and Nicolson.

Cartner-Morley, J. (2000), 'Drama Kings', *The Guardian,* September.

Cawthorne, N. (1996), *The New Look: The Dior Revolution,* London: Hamlyn.

Celant, G. (ed.) (1994), *The Italian Metamorphosis 1943–1968,* New York: Guggenheim Museum Publications.

Celant, G., Sischy I., et al. (2001), *Armani,* New York: Guggenheim Museum Publications.

Charles-Roux, E. (1976), *Chanel,* London: Jonathan Cape.

Charles-Roux, E. (1981), *Chanel and Her World,* London: Weidenfeld and Nicolson.

Chase, E.W., and Chase I. (1954), *Always in Vogue,* London: Victor Gollancz.

Chenoune, F. (1993), *A History of Men's Fashion,* Paris: Flammarion.

Chenoune, F. (1996), *Jean Paul Gaultier,* Paris: Editions Assouline.

Chenoune, F. (2007), *Dior: 60 Years of Style,* London: Thames & Hudson.

Clarke, L. (ed.) Polan, B. (2007), *The Measure, Vivienne Westwood in Conversation,* London: University of the Arts London.

Colegrave, S. and Sullivan, C. (eds.) (2001), *Punk: A Life Apart,* London: Cassell.

Coleman, E.A. (1989), *The Opulent Era: Fashions of Worth, Doucet, Pingat,* London: Thames & Hudson.

Coleridge, N. (1988), *The Fashion Conspiracy,* London: Heinemann.

Collins, A. F. (1994), 'Haute Coco', *Vanity Fair,* June.

Compton, N. (2002), 'The New Kingdom of Alexander McQueen', *iD,* August.

Cosgrave, B. (2007), *Made For Each Other: Fashion and the Academy Awards,* London: Bloomsbury.

Cox, C. (2004), *Stiletto,* London: Mitchell Beazley.

Craik, J. (2005), *Uniforms Exposed: From Conformity to Transgression,* Oxford: Berg.

Cullerton, B (1995), *Geoffrey Beene,* New York: Harry N. Abrams.

Cunningham, P.A. (2003), *Reforming Women's Fashion, 1850–1920,* Kent State University Press.

Daria, I. (1990), *The Fashion Cycle,* New York: Simon & Schuster.

De Combray, R. (1982), *Armani,* Milan: Franco Maria Ricci Editore.

De la Haye, A. (1996), *The Cutting Edge: 50 Years of British Fashion,* London: V&A Publications.

De la Haye, A., and Dingwall, C. (eds.) (1996), *Surfers, Soulies, Skinheads and Skaters: Subcultural Style from the Forties to the Nineties,* London: Victoria and Albert Museum.

De la Haye, A., and Tobin S. (1994), *Chanel: The Couturiere at Work,* London: V&A Publications.

De La Haye, A., and Wilson, E. (eds.) (1999), *Defining Dress: Dress as Object, Meaning and Identity,* Manchester: Manchester University Press.

De Marly, D. (1980), *Worth, Father of Haute Couture,* New York: Homes Meier.

De Marly, D. (1990), *History of Haute Couture, 1850–1950,* London: B.T. Batsford.

De Osma, G. (1984), *Fortuny,* London: Aurum Press.

De Réthy, E., and Perreau, J-L. (1999), *Christian Dior: The Early Years 1947–1957,* London: Thames & Hudson.

Dermonex, J. (1991), *Madeleine Vionnet*, tr. A. Audubert, London: Thames & Hudson.

Derrick, R. (2003), *People in Vogue: A Century of Portraits,* London: Little, Brown.

Descott, A-M. (1978), 'Seeking Your Fortuny', *Sunday Times Magazine,* July 23.

Deslandres, Y. (1987), *Poiret,* London: Thames & Hudson.

Dior, C. (1954) *Christian Dior's Little Dictionary of Fashion: A Guide to Dress Sense for Every Woman,* London: Cassell.

Dior, C., Donnedieu de Varbres, R., Arnault, B., Dufresne, J-L. (2005), *Christian Dior: Man of the Century,* Granville: Musée Christian Dior.

Dolce, D., and Gabbana, S. (1996), *10 Years of Dolce & Gabbana*, New York: Abbeville Press.

D'Orazio, S. (2007), *Gianni and Donatella,* Hamburg: teNeues.

Drake, A. (2006), *The Beautiful Fall: Fashion, Genius and Glorious Excess in 1970s Paris,* London: Bloomsbury.

Dufresne, J-L. (2006), *Christian Dior et Le Monde,* Granville: Musée Christian Dior.

Dufresne, J-L. (2007), *Dior: 60 Annees Hautes en Couleurs,* Granville: Musée Christian Dior.

Duras, M. (1988), *Yves Saint Laurent: Images of Design 1958–1988,* New York: Alfred A. Knopf.

Eastoe, J., and Gristwood, S. (2008), *Fabulous Frocks,* London: Pavillion.

Edelman, A.H. (1997), *The Little Black Dress,* London: Aurum.

Elting, L. (1999), 'Revealing the Accomplishments of Madame Paquin, the Very Queen of Dressmakers,' MA thesis, Courtauld Institute of Art, London.

English, B. (2007), *A Cultural History of Fashion in the 20th Century: From the Catwalk to the Sidewalk,* Oxford: Berg.

Esquevin, C. (2008), *Adrian: Silver Screen to Custom Label,* New York: Monacelli Press.

Etherington-Smith, M. (1983), *Patou,* London: Hutchinson.

Evans, C. (2003), *Fashion at the Edge: Spectacle, Modernity, and Deathliness,* New Haven: Yale University Press.

Evans, C. (2008), 'Jean Patou's American Mannequins: Early Fashion Shows and Modernism', *Modernism/modernity*, 15/2, April.

Evans, C., and Thornton M. (1989), *Women and Fashion: A New Look,* London: Quartet Books.

Ewing, E., and Mackrell, A. (1992), *History of 20th Century Fashion,* London: Batsford.

Fairchild, J. (1965), *The Fashionable Savages,* New York: Doubleday.

Fairchild, J. (1989), *Chic Savages,* New York: Simon & Schuster.

Ferragamo, S. (1957), *Shoemaker of Dreams,* London: Harrap.

Flanner, J. (1940), 'Pioneer', *The New Yorker,* January 13.

Foley, B. (2001), 'Who's Number One?', *WWD special edition,* July.

Foley, B. (2004), *Marc Jacobs,* New York: Editions Assouline.

Ford, T. (2004), *Tom Ford*, London: Thames & Hudson.

Frankel, S. (2001), *Visionaries,* London: V&A Publications.

Frankel, S. (2004), 'The Feeling Is Miuccia', *The Independent,* February 21.

Fraser, K. (1981), 'Feminine Fashions', *The New Yorker,* July 13.

Fraser, K. (1984), *The Fashionable Mind: Reflections on Fashion 1970–1982,* New York: Random House.

Friedman, V. (2008), 'Prada', *Ten,* Autumn.

Gaines, S. (1991), *Halston,: The Untold Story,* New York: Putnam.

Gaines, S., and Churcher, S. (1994), *Obsession: the Lives & Times of Calvin Klein,* New York: Birch Lane Press.

Gale, C., and Kaur, J. (2004), *Fashion and Textiles: An Overview,* Oxford: Berg.

Galloni, A. (2007), 'The Designer Defends Prada', *The Wall Street Journal*, January 25.

Gaultier, J.P. (1990), *A nous deux la Mode,* Paris: Editions Flammarion.

Golbin, P. (ed.) (2006), *Balenciaga Paris,* London: Thames & Hudson.

Golbin, P. (2008), *Valentino: Themes and Variations,* New York: Rizzoli.

Gorman, P. (2001), *The Look: Adventures in Pop and Rock Fashion,* foreword by Malcolm Mclaren, London: Sanctuary.

Green, J. (1998), *All Dressed Up: The Sixties and the Counterculture,* London: Pimlico.

Grigoriadis, V. (2008), 'The Deep Shallowness of Marc Jacobs', *Rolling Stone,* December.

Gross, E., and Rottman, F. (1999), *Halston: An American Original,* London: Harper Collins.

Gross, M. (1995), *Model: The Ugly Business of Beautiful Women,* New York: William Morrow.

Gross, M. (2003), *Genuine Authentic: The Real Life of Ralph Lauren,* New York: HarperCollins.

Guillaume, V. (1998), *Courrèges,* Fashion Memoir series, London: Thames & Hudson.

Hall, S., and Jefferson, T. (eds.) (1996), *Resistance Through Rituals, Youth Sub-Cultures in Post-War Britain,* London: Routledge.

Hastreiter, K. (2008), *Geoffrey Beene: Fashion Rebel,* Paris: Assouline.

Hawes, E. (1938), *Fashion Is Spinach,* New York: Random House.

Heathcote, P. (1960), `The House of Dior', *The Guardian,* August 1.

Hebdige, D. (1993), *Subculture: The Meaning of Style,* London: Routledge.

Heller, Z. (1997), 'Jacobs' Ladder', *The New Yorker,* September 22.

Holborn, M. (1995), *Issey Miyake,* Koln: Taschen

Hollander, A. (1978), *Seeing Through Clothes,* Berkeley: University of California Press.

Hollander, A. (1994), *Sex and Suits,* New York: Alfred Knopf.

Hopkins, H. (1963), *The New Look: A Social History of the Forties and Fifties in Britain,* London: Secker & Warburg.

Horyn, C. (1998), 'Naked Ambition', *Vanity Fair,* May.

Horyn, C. (2007), 'Q&A: Nicolas Ghesquière', *The New York Times,* June 29.

Howell, G. (1990), *Sultans of Style,* London: Ebury Press.

Howell, G. (1991), *In Vogue,* London: Random Century.

Howell, G. (1998), *Diana: Her Life in Fashion,* London: Pavilion.

Jacobs, L. (1999), *Beauty and the Beene: A Modern Legend,* New York: Harry. N. Abrams.

Janbon, C. (1999), 'Callot Soeurs,' MA thesis, Courtauld Institute of Art, London.

Join-Dieterle, C.. Train, S., and Lepicard, M-J. (1991), *Givenchy: 40 Years of Creation,* Paris: Paris Musées/Palais Galliera.

Jones, T. (ed.) (2001), *Smile I-D: Fashion and Style. The Best from 20 Years of I-D.* Cologne: Taschen.

Karimzadeh, M. (2006), 'Can You Handle It?', *WWD The Magazine,* Fall.

Kawamura, Y. (2004), *The Japanese Revolution in Paris Fashion,* Oxford: Berg.

Keogh, P.C. (1999), *Audrey Style,* New York, HarperCollins Publishers.

Kirke, B. (1998), *Madeleine Vionnet,* San Francisco: Chronicle Books.

Koda, H. (1987), *Three Women: Madeleine Vionnet, Claire McCardell, Rei Kawakubo,* New York: Fashion Institute of Technology.

Koda, H. (2001), *Extreme Beauty: The Body Transformed,* New York: Metropolitan Museum of Art Publications.

Koda, H. (2003), *Goddess: The Classical Mode,* New York: Metropolitan Museum of Art Publications.

Koda H., and Bolton A. (2005), *Chanel,* New York: Metropolitan Museum of Art Publications.

Koda H., and Bolton A. (2007), *Poiret,* New York: Metropolitan Museum of Art Publications.

Koren, L. (1984), *New Fashion Japan,* Tokyo: Kodansha International.

Krell, G. (1997), *Vivienne Westwood,* Fashion Memoir series, London: Thames & Hudson.

Langle, E. (2005), *Pierre Cardin: Fifty Years of Fashion and Design,* New York: Vendome Press.

Laver, J. (1969), *A Concise History of Costume*, London: Thames & Hudson

Lee, S.T. (ed.) (1975), *American Fashion: The Life and Lines of Adrian, Mainbocher, McCardell, Norell, and Trigére,* New York: Fashion Institute of Technology.

Lobenthal, J. (1990), *Radical Rags: Fashions of the Sixties,* New York: Abbeville Press.

Lonsdale, S. (2000), *Japanese Style,* London: Carlton Books.

Loyaute, B. (2006), *Pierre Cardin Evolution,* Paris: Flammarion.

Mackrell, A. (1990), *Paul Poiret,* London: B.T. Batsford.

Mackrell, A. (1992), *Coco Chanel,* London: B.T. Batsford.

Madsen, A. (1990), *Coco Chanel,* London: Bloomsbury.

Marsh, L. (2003), *The House of Klein: Fashion, Controversy and a Business Obsession,* New York: Wiley.

Martin R. (1987), *Fashion and Surrealism,* New York: Rizzoli.

Martin, R. (1998), *American Ingenuity: Sportswear 1930s–1970s,* New York: Metropolitan Museum of Art Publications.

Martin, R. (1997), *Gianni Versace,* New York: Metropolitan Museum of Art/Abrams.

Martin, R. (1997), *Versace,* Fashion Memoir series, London: Thames & Hudson.

Martin, R. (1998), *Charles James*, Fashion Memoir series, London: Thames & Hudson.

Martin, R., and Koda, H. (1989), *The Historical Mode: Fashion and Art in the 1980s,* New York: Rizzoli.

Martin, R., and Koda, H. (1990), *Giorgio Armani: Images of Man,* New York: Rizzoli.

Martin, R., and Koda, H. (1994), *Orientalism: Visions of the East in Western Dress,* New York: Metropolitan Museum of Art Publications.

Martin R., and Koda H. (1996), *Haute Couture,* New York: Metropolitan Museum of Art Publications.

Massey A. (2000), *Hollywood Beyond the Screen,* Oxford: Berg.

Mead, R. (1998), 'The Crazy Professor', *The New Yorker,* March 30.

McCardell, C. (1956), *What Shall I Wear?* New York: Simon & Schuster.

McConathy, D. (1975), 'Mainbocher', in S.T. Lee (ed.), *American Fashion*: *The Life and Lines of Adrian, Mainbocher, McCardell, Norell, and Trigere*, New York: Fashion Institute of Technology.

McDermott, C. (1987), *Streetstyle: British Design in the Eighties,* London: Design Council.

McDermott, C. (1999) *Vivienne Westwood,* London: Carlton Books.

McDowell, C. (1987), *McDowell's Directory of Twentieth Century Fashion,* 2nd ed., London: Frederick Muller.

McDowell, C. (1989), *Shoes: Fashion and Fantasy,* London: Thames & Hudson.

McDowell, C. (1997), *Forties Fashion and the New Look,* London: Bloomsbury.

McDowell, C. (1997), *John Galliano,* London: Weidenfeld & Nicolson.

McDowell, C. (1997), *The Man of Fashion: Peacock Males and Perfect Gentlemen,* London: Thames & Hudson.

McDowell, C. (2000), *Jean Paul Gaultier,* London: Cassell & Co.

McDowell, C. (2002), *Ralph Lauren: The Man, the Vision, the Style,* New York: Rizzoli

McDowell, C. (2003), *Fashion Today,* London: Phaidon

McRobbie, A. (ed.) (1989), *Zootsuits & Second-Hand Dresses, An Anthology of Fashion & Music,* London: Macmillan.

McRobbie, A. (1994), *Postmodernism and Popular Culture,* London: Routledge.

Mears, P. (2007), *Madame Grès: Sphinx of Fashion,* New York: Fashion Institute of Technology.

Mellor, D.A., and Gervereau, L. (eds.) (1997), *The Sixties: Britain and France,1960–1973 The Utopian Years,* London: Philip Wilson.

Mendes, V. (1990), *Pierre Cardin: Past, Present, Future,* London: 3Nishen Publishing.

Menkes, S. (2006), 'The Mistress of Us All', *The International Herald Tribune*, February 27.

Menkes, S. (2008), 'Balenciaga—Austerity Chic', *The International Herald Tribune*, February 26.

Merceron, D.L. (2007), *Lanvin,* New York: Rizzoli.

Miglietti. F.A. (2006), *Fashion Statements: Interviews with Fashion Designers,* Milan: Skira.

Milbank, C.R. (1985), *Couture: The Great Fashion Designers,* London: Thames & Hudson.

Milbank, C.R. (1989), *New York Fashion: The Evolution of American Style,* New York: Harry N. Abrams.

Milinaire, C., and Troy, C. (1978), *Cheap Chic*, New York: Crown Publishers.

Miller, A., Tarr, P., and Dalva, N. (2005), *Geoffrey Beene: A Design Tribute,* New York: 2wice Arts Foundation.

Miller, L. E. (1993), *Balenciaga,* London: Batsford.

Miller, L. E. (2007), *Balenciaga,* London: V&A Publications.

Mitchell, L., English, B., and Fukai, A. (2005), *The Cutting Edge: Fashion from Japan,* Sydney: Powerhouse Publishing.

Moffit, P., and Claxton, W. (1991), *The Rudi Gernreich Book*, New York: Rizzoli.

Mohrt, F. (1998), *The Givenchy Style,* Paris: Assouline.

Molho, R., and Shugaar, A. (2007), *Being Armani: A Biography,* Milan: Baldini Castoldi Dalai.

Molloy, J.T. (1980), *Women: Dress For Success*, New York: Foulsham.

Morais, R. (1991), *Pierre Cardin: The Man Who Became a Label,* London: Bantam Press.

Morand, P., (2008), *The Allure of Chanel,* tr. E. Cameron, London: Pushkin Press.

Morris, B., (1978), 'Halston's special way with Tradition', *New York Times*, December 20.

Morton, C. (2008), 'John Galliano's Year of Magic', *Harper's Bazaar* (UK), April.

Mower, S. (2005), *20 Years Dolce & Gabbana,* Milan: Dolce & Gabbana S.r.l.

Mulvagh, J. (1988), *Vogue: History of Twentieth Century Fashion,* London: Viking.

Mulvagh, J. (1998), *Vivienne Westwood: An Unfashionable Life,* London: HarperCollins.

Nava, M. (1992), *Changing Cultures, Feminism, Youth and Consumerism,* London: Sage.

Norman, P. (1990), *The Age of Parody: Dispatches from the Eighties,* London: Hamish Hamilton.

Pasi, M. (1987), *Versace Teatro,* tr. W. Weaver, Milan: Franco Maria Ricci.

Pasols, P-G, (2005), *Louis Vuitton, The Birth of Modern Luxury*, tr. L. Ammon, New York: Harry N. Abrams.

Penn, I., Kitamura, M., and Holborn, M. (introduction) (1998), *Irving Penn Regards the Work of Issey Miyake,* London: Jonathan Cape.

Piacenti, K.A., Ricci, S., and Vergani, G. (1985), *Salvatore Ferragamo,* Florence: Palazzo Strozzi.

Piaggi, A. (1980), *Lagerfeld's Sketchbook,* New York: Weidenfeld & Nicolson.

Piaggi, A. (1982), *Armani,* Milan: Franco Maria Ricci.

Pochna, M-F., and Galliano, J. (2008), *Christian Dior: The Biography,* New York: Duckworth.

Poiret, P. (1931), *My First Fifty Years,* tr. S.H. Guest, London: Victor Gollancz.

Polan, B. (1979), 'A New Look from the Man Behind the Mini', *The Guardian,* August 15.

Polan, B. (1982), 'Mary Comes Back into Fashion', *The Guardian*, March 4.

Polan, B. (ed.) (1983) *The Fashion Year 1983,* London: Zomba.

Polan, B. (ed.) (1984), *Fashion 84,* New York: St Martins Press.

Polan, B (2000), 'Armani,' *How To Spend It Magazine*, *The Financial Times* (London).

Polhemus, T. (1994), *Street Style: From Sidewalk to Catwalk,* London: Thames & Hudson.

Probert, C. (1981), *Shoes in Vogue Since 1910,* London: Thames & Hudson.

Quant, M. (1965), *Quant by Quant,* London: Cassell.

Quick, H. (2002), 'Killer McQueen', *Vogue* (UK), October.

Quick, H. (2006), 'Saint Nicolas', *Vogue* (UK), August.

Rawsthorn, A. (1998), *Yves Saint Laurent,* London: Harper Collins.

Ricci, S. (2006), *Walking Dreams: Salvatore Ferragamo 1890–1960,* Mexico City: Editorial RM.

Ricci, S. (ed.) (2008), *Salvatore Ferragamo: Evolving Legend 1928–2008,* Milan: Skira.

Richards, M. (2000), *Chanel Key Collections,* London: Hamlyn.

Riello, G., and McNeil, P. (eds.) (2006), *Shoes: A History from Sandals to Sneakers,* Oxford: Berg.

Riley, R. (1975), 'Adrian', in S.T. Lee (ed.), *American Fashion: The Life and Lines of Adrian, Mainbocher, McCardell, Norell, and Trigere,* New York: Fashion Institute of Technology.

Rossi, W.A. (1977), *The Sex Life of the Foot and Shoe,* London: Routledge & Kegan Paul.

Rowbotham, S. (2001), *Promise of a Dream: Remembering the Sixties,* London: Verso.

Sainderichin, G. (1998). *Kenzo,* Fashion Memoir series, London: Thames & Hudson.

Saint Laurent, Y., Vreeland, D, et al. (1983), *Yves Saint Laurent,* New York: Metropolitan Museum of Art Publications.

Sato, K. (1998), *Issey Miyake: Making Things,* Paris: Fondation Cartier/Scalo.

Savage, J. (1991), *England's Dreaming: Sex Pistols and Punk Rock,* London: Faber and Faber.

Schiaparelli, E. (1954), *Shocking Life,* New York, E.P. Dutton.

Schoumann, H. (2002), *Chloé,* New York: Editions Assouline.

Singer S. (2001), 'Bonjour Jeunesse', *Vogue* (U.S.), March.

Sirop, D. (1989), *Paquin,* Paris: Editions Adam Biro.

Sischy, I. (1998), *Donna Karan New York,* New York: Vendome Universe of Fashion.

Sischy, I. (2004), *The Journey of a Woman: 20 Years of Donna Karan,* New York: Assouline.

Smith, P. (2001), *You Can Find Inspiration in Everything (And If You Can't, Look Again),* London: Violette Editions.

Socha, Miles (2008), 'Art versus Commerce: Can Margiela Expand Without Selling Out?', *WWD,* May 2.

Sozzani, F. (1999), *Dolce & Gabbana,* London: Thames & Hudson.

Sparke, P. (1987), *Japanese Design,* London: Swallow Publishing.

Steele, V. (1991), *Women of Fashion,* New York: Rizzoli International Publications.

Steele, V. (1996), *Fetish: Fashion, Sex and Power,* Oxford: Oxford University Press.

Steele, V. (1997), *Fifty Years of Fashion: New Look to Now,* New Haven: Yale University Press.

Steele, V. (1998), *Shoes: A Lexicon of Style,* London: Scriptum Editions.

Steele, V., and Park, J. (2008), *Gothic: Dark Glamour,* New Haven: Yale University Press.

Stegemeyer, A. (1996), *Who's Who in Fashion,* New York: Fairchild Publications.

Stevens, J. (1987), 'Introduction' in N. Coleridge and S. Quinn (eds.), *The Sixties in Queen,* London: Ebury Press.

Stewart, M.L. (2005), 'Copying and Copyrighting Haute Couture: Democratizing Fashion, 1900–1930s', *French Historical Studies,* 28/1, winter.

Sudjic, D. (1990), *Rei Kawakubo and Comme des Garçons,* New York: Rizzoli International Publications.

Teboul, D. (2002), *Yves Saint Laurent, 5 Avenue Marceau, 75116 Paris France,* New York: Abrams.

Thomas, D. (2007), *Deluxe: How Luxury Lost Its Lustre,* London: Allen Lane.

Trasko, M. (1989), *Heavenly Soles: Extraordinary Twentieth Century Shoes,* New York: Abbeville Press.

Tredre, R. (1990), 'The Grind Behind the Glamour', *The Independent,* October 18.

Tredre, R. (1990), 'A One-man Revolt Against the Cliche', *The Independent,* August 2.

Tredre, R. (1990), 'Who Is that Guy Everyone's Talking About?', *The Independent.*

Tredre, R. (1990), 'The World According to Paul Smith', *He Lines.*

Tredre, R. (1992), 'Galliano Meets His Maker', *The Independent,* August 13.

Tredre, R. (1994), 'Kaiser Karl', *The Observer,* August 7.

Tredre, R. (1995), 'King of Couture', *The Observer,* July 23.

Tredre, R. (2001), 'YSL Menswear', *WGSN.com,* February 1.

Troy, N.J. (2003), *Couture Culture: A Study in Modern Art and Culture,* Boston: MIT Press.

Tsurimoto, S. (ed.) (1983), *Issey Miyake: Bodyworks,* Tokyo: Shogakukan.

Vergani, G. (1992), *La Sala Bianca: the Birth of Italian Fashion,* Milan: Electra.

Vermorel, F. (1996), *Fashion and Perversity: A Life of Vivienne Westwood and the Sixties Laid Bare,* London: Bloomsbury.

Vinken, B. (2005), *Fashion Zeitgeist,* tr. M. Hewson, Oxford, New York: Berg.

Vreeland, D. (1997), *D.V.,* New York: Da Capo.

Vreeland, D., and Isozaki, A. (1978), *Issey Miyake: East Meets West,* Tokyo: Heibonsha.

Walford, J. (2007), *The Seductive Shoe: Four Centuries of Fashion Footwear,* London: Thames & Hudson.

Walker, M. (2006), *Balenciaga and His Legacy,* New Haven: Yale University Press.

Wallach J. (1998), *Chanel: Her Style and Her Life,* New York: Doubleday.

Watson, L. (1999), *Vogue: Twentieth Century Fashion,* London: Carlton.

Welters, L., and Lillethun, A. (2007), *The Fashion Reader,* Oxford: Berg.

White, N. (2000), *Reconstructing Italian Fashion.* Oxford: Berg.

White, P. (1973), *Poiret,* London: Studio Vista.

White, P. (1986), *Elsa Schiaparelli: Empress of Paris Fashion,* London: Aurum Press.

Wilcox, C. (ed.) (2001), *Radical Fashion,* London: V&A Publications.

Wilcox, C. (2003), *Vivienne Westwood,* London: V&A Publications.

Wilcox, C. (ed.) (2007), *The Golden Age of Couture: Paris and London 1947–57,* London: V&A Publications.

Wilcox, C., Mendes, V., and Buss, C. (2002), *The Art and Craft of Gianni Versace,* London: V&A Publications.

Williams, B. (1945), *Fashion Is Our Business,* Philadelphia: J.B. Lippincott,

Wilson, E. (1985), *Adorned in Dreams,* London: Virago.

Wood, G. (2007), *The Surreal Body,* London: V&A Publications.

Yamamoto, Y., and Sozzani, C. (2002), *Talking to Myself,* Milan: Carla Sozzani Editore/ Tokyo: Yohji Yamamoto Inc.

Yohannan, K., and Nolf, N. (1998), *Claire McCardell: Redefining Modernism,* New York: Harry N. Abrams.

Zahm, O. (2008), 'Nicholas Ghesquière', *Purple Fashion Magazine,* spring/summer.